Communal Reformation

STUDIES IN GERMAN HISTORIES
Series Editors: Roger Chickering and Thomas A. Brady, Jr.

PUBLISHED

Communal Reformation
Peter Blickle

German Encounters with Modernity
Katherine Roper

FORTHCOMING

Karl Lamprecht
Roger Chickering

Communal Reformation

The Quest for Salvation in Sixteenth-Century Germany

Peter Blickle

Translated by Thomas Dunlap

Humanities Press
New Jersey ▼ London

Originally published as *Gemeindereformation. Die Menschen des 16. Jahrhunderts auf dem Weg zum Heil,*
©1985 R. Oldenbourg Verlag GmbH (Munich)

First published in English 1992 by Humanities Press International, Inc., Atlantic Highlands, New Jersey 07716, and 3 Henrietta Street, Covent Garden, London WC2E 8LU.

©English Translation by Humanities Press International, Inc., 1992

Library of Congress Cataloging-in-Publication Data

Blickle, Peter.
 [Gemeindereformation. English]
 Communal reformation : the quest for salvation in sixteenth-century Germany / Peter Blickle ; translated by Thomas Dunlap.
  p. cm. — (Studies in German histories)
 Translation of: Gemeindereformation.
 Includes bibliographical references and index.
 ISBN 0-391-03730-7
 1. Reformation. I. Title. II. Series.

BR305.2.B5313 1992
274.3'06—dc20   91-33112
          CIP

A catalog record for this book is available from the British Library.

Maps 1, 2, and 3 were originally published in *Turning Swiss: Cities & Empire, 1450–1550* by Thomas A. Brady, Jr. (Cambridge: Cambridge University Press, 1985).

Printed in Mexico

To Ursula Schatz

For her challenging company
over the past ten years

Contents

List of Illustrations   ix

Editors' Note   x

Preface to the English Translation   xi

From the Preface to the German Edition   xiii

1. Introduction: Storm Years of the Reformation?   1
2. Reformation and Society   11
3. The Burghers' Reformation   63
4. Communal Reformation—The Peasants' and Burghers' Reformations as a Unified Historical Phenomenon   98
5. Church and Gospel in the Reformers' Theology   111
6. The Communal Reformation in the Tradition of Late Medieval Political Culture   153
7. Conclusion: The Reformation of the Princes versus the Communal Reformation   193

Bibliography   205

Index   213

List of Illustrations

Maps

1. South Germany About 1519   xv
2. South German Free Cities About 1500   xvi
3. The Swiss Confederacy in 1519   xvii
4. Geographical Distribution of Demands for Election of
   Pastors in Central Europe   xviii
5. Peasant Revolts in the Late Medieval Holy Roman
   Empire   xix

Figures

1. Stages of Peasant Reformation in Upper Swabia   25
2. Evangelical Movement in the Cities   106
3. Internal Organization and Values of Communalism   180
4. Ideology and Reality in the Communal Reformation   185

Editors' Note

Peter Blickle's *Communal Reformation* builds on his well-known interpretation of the Peasants' War, *The Revolution of 1525* (English ed., 1981). It extends to the religious reformation of the sixteenth century his argument about the active and deliberate action of the common people in reshaping feudal society to their own needs and values. His boldly revisionist approach unites political, social, and religious history from a locally determined perspective.

Communal Reformation is the second volume in the series, "Studies in German Histories," which aims to present original works and translations on the histories of the German-speaking and closely related peoples of Central Europe between the Middle Ages and the present. The series brings forward new and neglected perspectives on important subjects and issues in the histories of these peoples. The volume has been prepared with the generous and able editorial assistance of Katherine G. Brady.

ROGER CHICKERING AND THOMAS A. BRADY, JR.

Preface to the
English Translation

The original edition of this book met with an enthusiastic response, particularly in England and the United States. I am therefore delighted that it is now available in an English translation. It would not have come about without the interest of my colleague, Thomas A. Brady, Jr., and the conscientious work of the translator, Thomas Dunlap. My thanks to both for their contribution to this book. I would also like to thank my assistant, Sabine Kraut, for giving the English version a careful reading.

From the Preface to the German Edition

For some time now I have been thinking about the problem of the commune or community (*Gemeinde*), the subject proper of this book. No matter how I approached the past—whether by way of regional, constitutional, or agrarian history—the community always proved to be an institution with considerable historical importance of its own. It is surprising that it enjoys little esteem in Germany and Austria, at least in historiographical scholarship. How else can we explain that it has not been used as a means of characterizing or marking off the boundaries of historical periods, even though the community represents, next to the family, undoubtedly the most important form of social organization for the common people far into modern times? This problem acquired added fascination for me when I moved to Switzerland, for it is worth reflecting on why the political culture in Switzerland draws so heavily on the communal tradition, while in Germany it does not. It is not without interest to point out that Adolf Gasser's attempt to construct a history of Europe from the perspective of the community was placed on the index of forbidden exports in Nazi Germany. Theodor Heuss's dictum that "communities are more important than states" still awaits in Germany empirical historical verification.

Interest and methodology are connected. The fact that the compass of historical scholarship today points no longer to sociology but to anthropology is hardly accidental. This change in orientation arises no doubt from the experience that social history, as the dominant subfield of the past two decades, has reached the boundaries of its inherent explanatory possibilities. There are various ways of arriving at comprehensive insights and explanations. One such way is surely to relate social history to intellectual history, especially since the potential of such a cross-disciplinary dialogue has certainly not been exhausted. As evidence for this one might point to the flood of scholarly publications in 1983, the anniversary of Luther's birth. The frequent call for "more intellectual history in social history," and its echo of "more social history in intellectual history," are certainly justified, especially when the subject under investigation lies at a point where both fields intersect. In dealing with the community in Central Europe, which reached its height and importance primarily in the late Middle Ages and the early modern period, a penetrating inquiry reveals that its history and fate cannot be explained within the confines of social history alone. Answers to our questions lie in the approach to the reformation as the history of ideas.

This backdrop explains the present work, which seeks to be a history of the reformation in Germany, Switzerland, and Austria in so far as the center of gravity for the reformation was in the community, both socially and theologically. I shall argue that the original, undistorted, unadulterated character of the reformation is its manifestation as a communal reformation. In view of the fact that the reformation quickly turned into an affair of the authorities, one might regard the communal reformation as little more than an early phase. But it will not be possible to take this view if we can show, with some degree of plausibility, that the reformation within the community and arising from the community is the hinge between the medieval and the modern world in Central Europe.

When I speak about the community with confidence and conviction it is primarily in regard to rural society. Fortunately my work has been helped and supplemented by a field of scholarship which arose in Germany at the same time and which examines the connection between the reformation and the cities. The stimulating dialogue with these studies, which both confirmed and questioned my own positions, added a breadth and depth to my reflections which they would otherwise have lacked. Beyond that, I sincerely hope that his book will reveal just how much I am indebted to Tübingen and its supporters abroad.

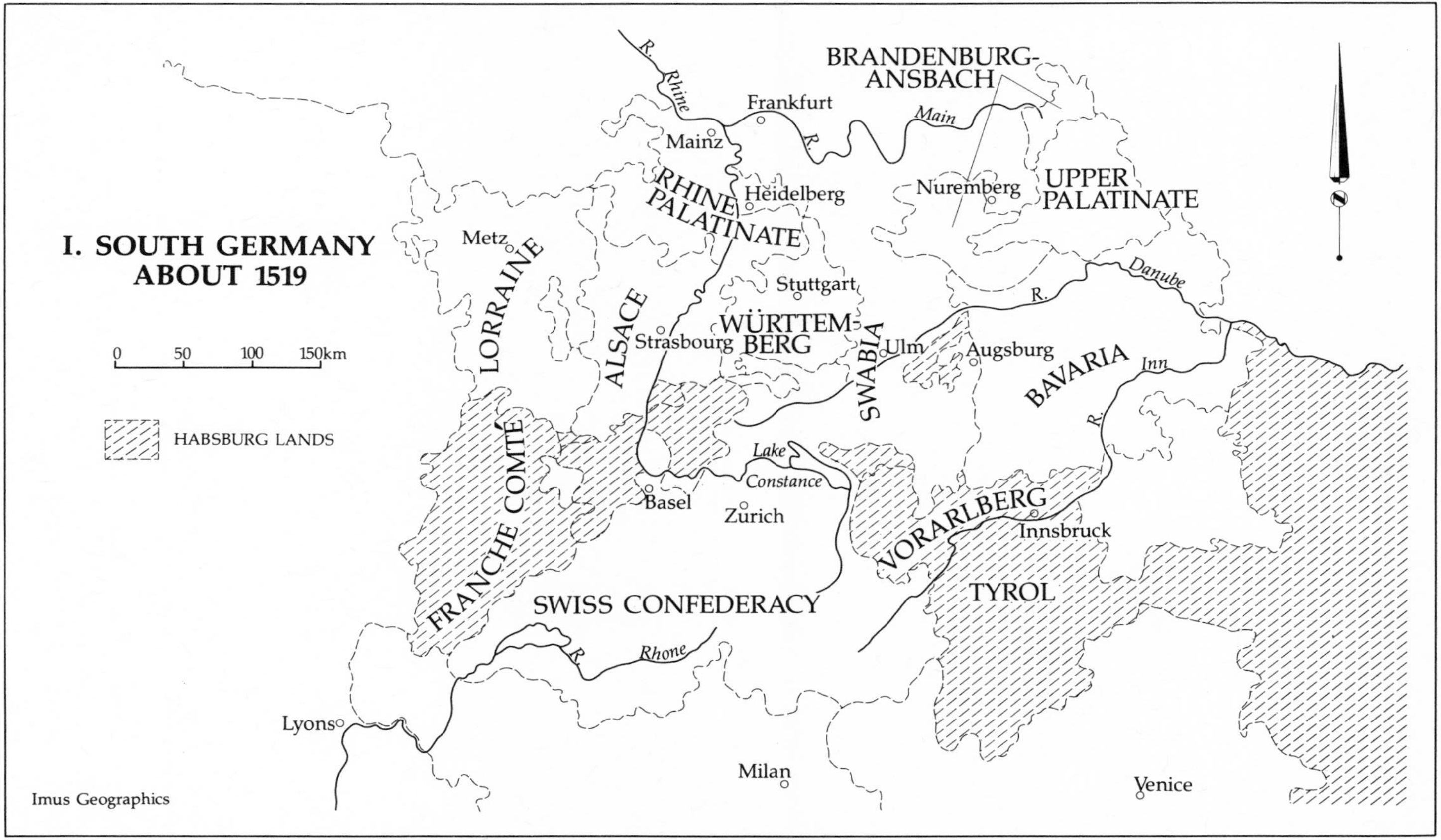

I. SOUTH GERMANY
ABOUT 1519

HABSBURG LANDS

0   50   100   150km

MAP 1

BRANDENBURG-
ANSBACH

UPPER
PALATINATE

Nuremberg

Main

Frankfurt

R.

Mainz

Rhine

R.

Heidelberg

RHINE
PALATINATE

Stuttgart

WÜRTEM-
BERG

Strasbourg

ALSACE

Metz

LORRAINE

Danube

R.

Augsburg

BAVARIA

Inn

R.

Ulm

SWABIA

Lake Constance

Zurich

Basel

SWISS CONFEDERACY

FRANCHE COMTÉ

Rhone

R.

Lyons

VORARLBERG

Innsbruck

TYROL

Venice

Milan

Imus Geographics

xv

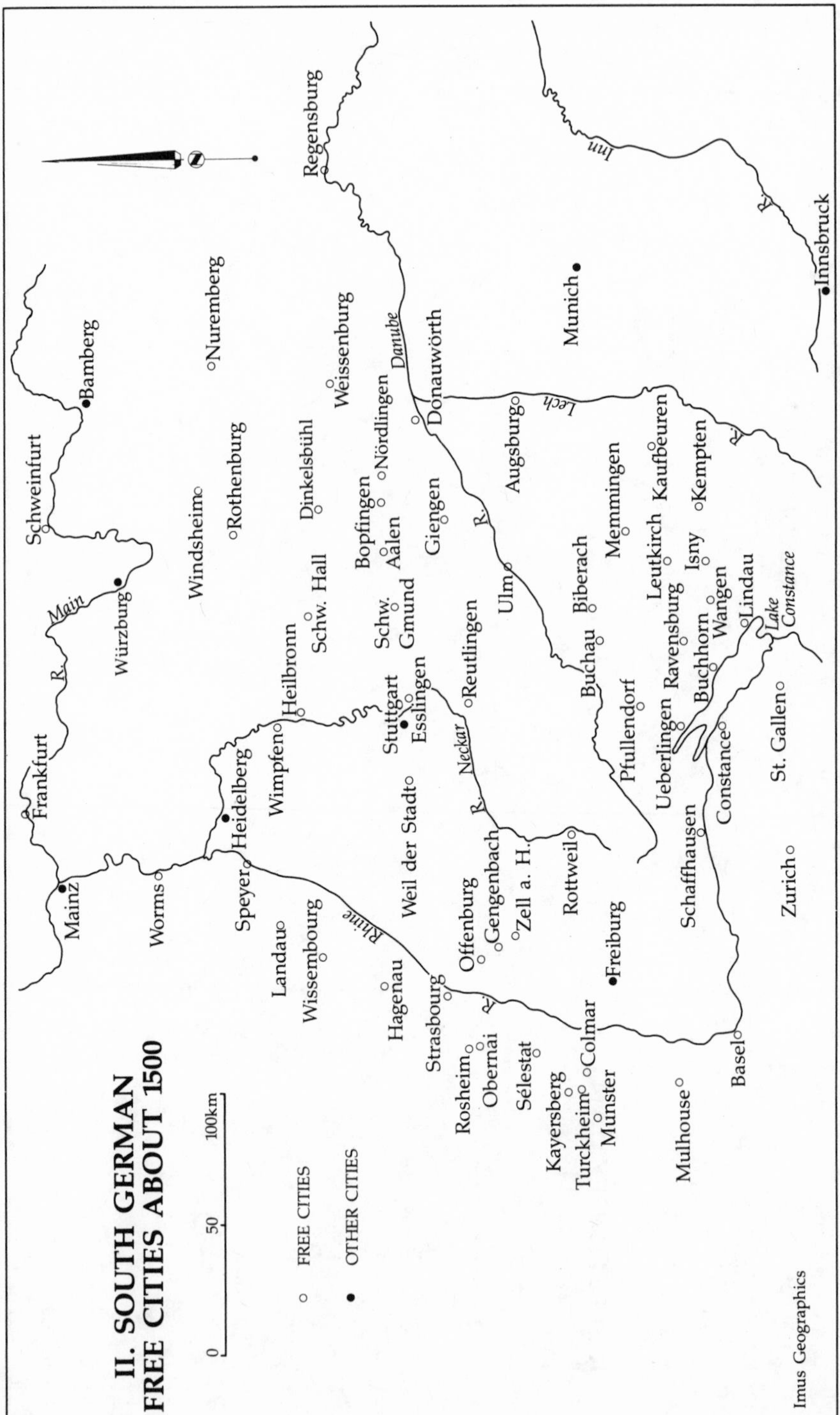

II. SOUTH GERMAN
FREE CITIES ABOUT 1500

○   FREE CITIES

●   OTHER CITIES

0   50   100km

MAP 2

Imus Geographics

Regensburg

Inn

Innsbruck

Bamberg

Schweinfurt

Nuremberg

Munich

Weissenburg

Danube

Donauwörth

Lech

Mainz

Frankfurt

Main

R.

Würzburg

Windsheim

Rothenburg

Dinkelsbühl

Bopfingen

Nördlingen

Aalen

Schw. Gmund

Giengen

Augsburg

Memmingen

Leutkirch Kaufbeuren

Isny   Kempten

Worms

Speyer

Heidelberg

Wimpfen Heilbronn

Schw. Hall

Stuttgart

Esslingen

Neckar

R.

Reutlingen

Ulm

R.

Buchau

Biberach

Ravensburg

Ueberlingen Buchhorn

Wangen

Lindau

Lake
Constance

Landau

Wissembourg

Weil der Stadt

Offenburg

Gengenbach

Zell a. H.

Rottweil

Pfullendorf

Constance

St. Gallen

Rhine

Hagenau

Strasbourg

Freiburg

Schaffhausen

Rosheim

Obernai

Sélestat

Kayersberg

Turckheim Colmar

Münster

Basel

Mulhouse

Zurich

xvi

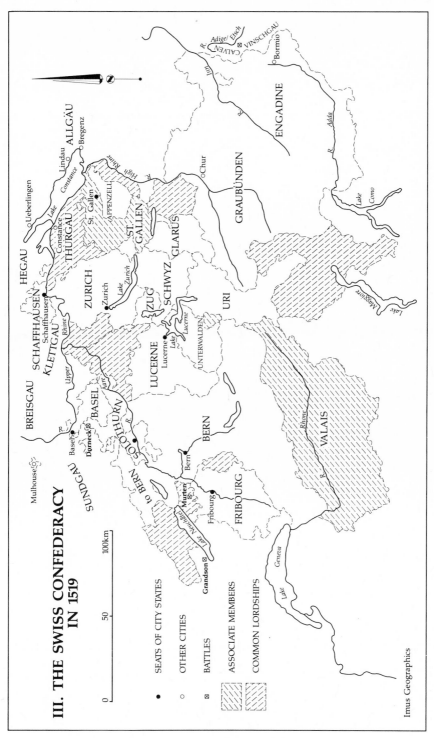

III. THE SWISS CONFEDERACY
IN 1519

Imus Geographics

MAP 3

SEATS OF CITY STATES
OTHER CITIES
BATTLES
ASSOCIATE MEMBERS
COMMON LORDSHIPS

0   50   100km

xvii

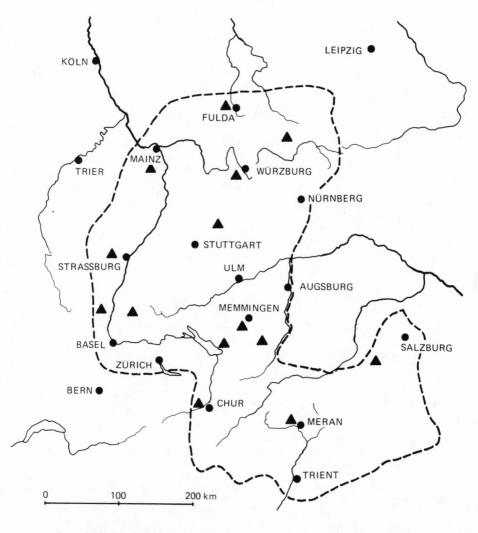

LEIPZIG ●

KÖLN ●

FULDA

TRIER ●

MAINZ

WÜRZBURG

NÜRNBERG ●

STUTTGART ●

STRASSBURG

ULM

AUGSBURG ●

MEMMINGEN ●

BASEL ●

SALZBURG ●

ZÜRICH ●

BERN ●

CHUR ●

MERAN ●

TRIENT ●

0   100   200 km

▲ regional articles (includes election of pastors)
--- limits of demands for election of pastors
● reference points

MAP 4   GEOGRAPHICAL DISTRIBUTION OF DEMANDS FOR ELECTION OF
PASTORS IN CENTRAL EUROPE

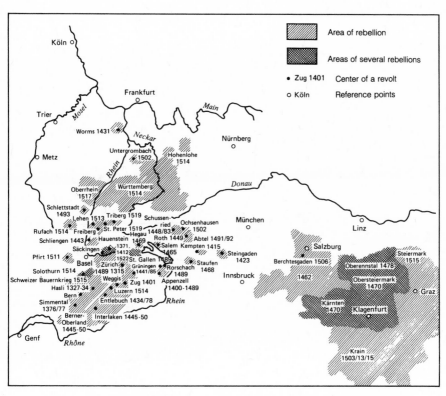

MAP 5   PEASANT REVOLTS IN THE LATE MEDIEVAL HOLY ROMAN
EMPIRE

1

Introduction: Storm Years of the Reformation?

The theological thinking of the Protestant reformers led them to seek the salvation of humankind; the practical thinking of the common people led them to seek the salvation of the world. Were the reformers and the other theologians and intellectuals deeply separated from the common people, the artisans, the peasants, by a different way of thinking and mutually exclusive cultures? Did Emperor Maximilian I (r. 1493–1519) in his court chapel in Innsbruck not venerate the same saints, and with the same deep fervor, as the manorial tenants of the suburban monastery of Wilten? Did the patricians in Bern and the peasants in the Bern countryside not watch the play of "The Last Judgment" with the same emotional involvement? Did the noblemen, townsmen, and peasants of the Tyrol not deliberate the same political issues as the council of Archduke Sigmund? These rhetorical questions aim to call our attention to the bonds that still tied together the different social strata in the later Middle Ages. The theologian was also interested in the salvation of the world, and the common man in the salvation of mankind—though naturally to varying degrees.

The convergence of the interests of the theologians and the interests of the common people infused the reformation with its importance and world-historical significance. The desire to redefine the paths that lead both humankind and the world to salvation was a frontal assault on traditional ecclesiastical, social, and political structures. Scholars speak of the "storm years" (*Sturmjahre*)[1] and of the "wild growth" (*Wildwuchs*) of the reformation[2] to describe the initial character of the movement as something threatening, violent, unstable, and still unformed. Both terms have their clear chronological end points, for the "storm years" of the reformation gave way to the calm years of an orderly reformation carried out by the territorial rulers, and the "wild growth" came to an end when the reform theologies that deviated from Luther split off. The reformation thus found its historical fulfillment in the Lutheran territorial churches, that is to say, in a reforming impulse narrowed down to Luther and a church organization centered on the territorial rulers. Such metaphorical language arouses vivid images, but it hardly satisfies the need for an intellectually

1

sound understanding of a historical event. Recent reformation scholarship also reveals that this familiar terminology leaves something to be desired. There have been attempts, for example, to replace the "storm years" of the reformation with the "reformation movement"[3] and the "wild growth" with the "revolt against the priests."[4]

It would seem that reformation scholarship has difficulty in finding a suitable label for a period widely interpreted as a distinct phase of the reformation. Scholars agree on both its chronological starting point as well as the character of the period that followed. The storm years, riotous growth, reforming movement, and revolt against the priests came to an end around 1525; thereafter began the reformation of the territorial rulers, of the authorities, of the state, in short, the "princes' reformation."[5] The aim of this book is to find a label for the reform movement in the years up to 1525.

The creation of broad historical concepts and terms depends heavily on the groundwork laid by studies that examine narrowly defined questions. Historical concepts are built from the ground up in a careful process of abstraction. Their validity and usefulness depend on the extent to which they are broadly and firmly rooted in historical reality. New scholarship and new insights demand new terms of abstraction. The process of creating such concepts and terms for reformation history has surely not been completed.[6] On the contrary, new terms and new ways of labeling chronological periods are constantly being tested.[7] Behind these efforts lie new studies, especially of social history, which deal primarily with the phenomena clustered around the phrase, "reformation in the cities." More than ten years ago, Arthur G. Dickens identified two phases, an "urban" reformation followed by a "princely" reformation,[8] and his terms have by now come to be accepted as "alternatives of an ideal type."[9] There is, in any case, hardly an argument now about whether the "princely" reformation was preceded by an "urban" reformation.[10] To realize what this has meant for our understanding of the reformation, we must recall the state of scholarship in the 1960s. Broadly speaking, the reformation had been assigned a place between the history of ideas and political history, between Luther's theology and its implementation by the territorial rulers. With the "reformation of the cities," a third dimension of the reforming movement was revealed, namely, the social history of the reformation. Since then we have established a chronological sequence composed of theological appeal, social reception, and political reaction, although the contours of these phases, which overlap both chronologically and in subject matter, are by no means clearly discernible. Only recently have studies of northern German examples revealed the highly complex interrelationship between the reformation of the cities and that of the territorial princes.[11] Studies focusing on the imperial cities of southern Germany have shown that the reception of reforming ideas among the townsmen was a very complicated process, and urban historians agree that without the interest "from below," the reformation would have remained the kind of esoteric-intellectual affair it had been at the outset. Bernd Moeller is convinced that without cities, "the reformation would not have taken place."[12]

These reflections lead us to the question that the social historian Hans Rosenberg once put to Heiko A. Oberman: Why did he, Oberman, and with him reformation scholarship in general, distinguish merely a "city reformation" and a "princes' reformation" as ideal types, considering that we must not overlook the so-called people's reformation à la M. M. Smirin?[13] What had Smirin meant by "people's reformation"?

M. M. Smirin first introduced the term into the scholarly debate with his book *The People's Reformation of Thomas Müntzer and the Great Peasants' War*.[14] The book's very title also defined its essential argument: there was an offshoot of the reforming movement, embodied in Thomas Müntzer, which should be defined more precisely as a people's reformation, and which was causally linked to the Peasants' War of 1525. As Smirin interpreted the teachings of Müntzer, the true "understanding of God" demanded the "establishment of the foundations of human morality and human reason." This could be realized by the "conscious translation into daily life of the ethical idea of the subordination of private interests to the whole and the community," if need be "through revolutionary actions of the people." Müntzer's theology of the "lordship of Christ in this world" found concrete expression in an idea of popular *translatio imperii*, that is, the transfer of governance to the common people. The important thing about Müntzer's theology, in Smirin's interpretation, is that it shaped "the notions of the people" into a coherent theory that was a useful agitating tool. The ideas of the people in turn found their abstract expression in the "ideal of equality," an idea that functioned as a kind of focal point for the "concrete demands of the peasants."[15] Smirin's concept of the people's reformation centered on the interdependence and interaction of theory and practice, and geographically it was strictly limited to Thuringia.

Josef Macek attempted to claim the concept of the people's reformation for Michael Gaismair in the Tyrol,[16] and Max Steinmetz considered whether the "leading men of the people's reformation" should not also include a number of Anabaptists and peasant military leaders.[17] These moves, however, rob the notion of the "people's reformation" of its usefulness as a historical concept, since the line separating it from the "Peasants' War" becomes indistinct.[18]

The concept of the people's reformation can nonetheless lead to further reflections. First of all, it has been said that Müntzer's concept embodied a theory of equality, morality, and reason, but there is no convincing reason why the theological thought of Huldrych Zwingli, Balthasar Hubmaier, or Martin Bucer, to name only a few examples, should not also meet the same criteria. To put it differently, on empirical grounds it is not possible to refute the claim that the revolutionary forces that arose in rural society could have also sprung from the theology of Zwingli, Hubmaier, and Bucer. Second, the concept of the people's reformation is based on the assumption that the people themselves were incapable of thinking through their fears, sufferings, needs, hopes, and yearnings on a theoretical level and shaping them into an ideologically usable form. In this interpretation we search in vain for any reforming ideas among the people. But does it even make sense to speak of a people's reformation, if the people had no idea of reform?

These questions about the potency and usefulness of the concept of the people's reformation also reflect a certain respect for its heuristic function. The people, in Smirin's sense, are for the most part the peasants, and the "reformation of the cities" is thus joined by a "peasants' reformation." There is good reason to think that the "reformation of the cities" and the "people's reformation" might be connected in some way, even though scholarship on the reformation in the cities pays no serious attention to the peasants, while scholarship on the people's reformation is equally negligent of the city. There exists a scholarly tradition in Germany which has repeatedly emphasized the "many points of contact and the interrelationships between city and village," although this has not found the desired echo in scholarship on the reformation.[19] Yet, during the past ten years scholars studying the historical development of terms and concepts have worked out convincing structural similarities between city and village. I refer to the concept of the "common man," the wide-ranging discussion of which has clarified differences in interpretation. It has also revealed where the concept itself lacks clarity, although this does not render it useless, since all concepts of political language invariably have a certain vagueness.[20] What is nonetheless clear is that "common man" is a general term for townsmen and villagers. It describes, in the first place, something "common," general, widespread, as is expressed in the analogous uses in "common Christendom" and "common weal." The language of that age posed "self-interest" as the opposite of common weal. The common man also had his "opposite" or counterpart in the estates of the nobility and the clergy, or, to put it more broadly, in the manifestations of personalized authority, which separated the common man from his superiors in the social hierarchy. There is also a line of demarcation against those below the common man, which must be drawn differently from one region and locality to the next, depending on the criteria of residency, communal law, obligations to allegiance, fitness for military service, etc.[21] In general, though, the category of the common man definitely did not include male and female servants, mercenaries, beggars, and vagrants.[22] To put it another way, above the common man were the lords, lay and clerical, and below him were the lower social classes and those groups entirely outside the hierarchy of social estates. Contemporary usage thus strongly emphasized the fact that rural and urban societies formed one single entity. This was especially true in the reformation era, but already in the second half of the sixteenth century, the concept of the common man underwent a profound change in meaning, and soon it could be used interchangeably with both "peasant" and "subject."[23]

It is paradoxical that the success that the concept of the common man also enjoyed in related disciplines, such as ethnology, German philology, and legal history—and even in the media—greatly compromised its usefulness to historians. It offered a convenient replacement for the problematic and unwieldy notion of the "people."[24] But this conceptual assimilation has robbed the common man of his uniqueness. What made him distinct and attractive has become diluted to a colorless uniformity, for the common man is precisely not "the people" (das Volk) as such.

These reflections and comments on the reformation of the cities, the people's reformation, and the common man are intended to help define the subject of the present study more precisely, which is the reformation as a social movement. The belief that city and countryside were closely connected, and that the term "common man" was a contemporary expression of this fact, is confirmed by the recent work on popular religion. A Swiss expert on sixteenth century Germany and the Anglo-American debate about "popular culture" and "popular religion" has translated these terms into German as "culture and religion of the common man" (Kultur und Religion des gemeinen Mannes).[25] This choice of words is important, because it is based on the claim that, for Europe as a whole, we cannot speak of separate urban and rural cultures in the period preceding the separation of these two cultures in the modern era.[26] Judging from the more recent verdict of the reformation historian Bernd Moeller, the situation in Germany was very different. In the cities, he tells us, even Luther's doctrine on redemption was "by no means inaccessible, hard to understand, and complicated—as one reads again and again—rather, instead precisely its essence was easy to understand and highly topical."[27] In contrast, it would seem that "the peasants . . . , in the face of the reformation, persisted in their ahistorical life bound by their natural and local parameters, as though they had never heard of the new doctrines—after all, they were barely educated."[28]

Today, not even all theologians share this view of the peasants.[29] And if students of popular religion took note of such verdicts, it would be to point out that they merely "perpetuate the myth of the nature-bound, ahistorical peasant" or to gently ridicule such prescientific judgments.[30] At least for Germany, work in the late medieval and early modern periods has shown that the peasantry as such had certainly reached the point where it became an actor in political processes and a factor in the making of history.[31] Anyone who denies this reveals an unsatisfactory grasp, if not a deliberate ignorance, of the literature and the sources.

This tour of the various historical disciplines and their contributions to the history of the reformation should not close without a glance at the more recent work on popular culture and religion, especially since its practitioners claim, as James Obelkevich has put it, to be investigating the real-life context (Sitz im Leben) of the religious practices of the common people.[32] Unfortunately, such investigations have concerned primarily the post-reformation period.[33] When scholars have dealt with the late Middle Ages and the reformation era, the emphasis, in part owing to the extant sources, has been heavily on the study of the cults of the saints.[34] Despite the fact that these studies have been limited in scope, methodologically they can teach us that cultural channels didn't run only "in a single direction, from the top down. On the contrary, the flow was multidirectional, and often the lines are so deeply intertwined as to suggest that the structure of religiousness was not purely hierarchical."[35] The study of the veneration of saints in Europe, in particular, has demonstrated that these cults and other religious practices spread from the bottom to the top and were eventually recognized by the institutional church.[36] Such insights are a warning not to assume too large a gap between the religious experiences and theological understandings of the common people and those of the educated people, between the theologians, preachers, and pamphleteers, on the one hand, and the merchants, artisans, and peasants, on the other.[37]

There is another finding that is of great methodological significance for the study of the reformation. Scholars of popular religion argue that the various forms of piety and magical practices were highly developed all over Europe without notable variations by region or language area.[38] If we accept this, then popular piety is not a meaningful way of approaching the question of why the reformation became in Central Europe a social movement that was broadly rooted among townsmen and peasants, whereas in England and France it did not, even though the call for a reformation was also heard in those countries.[39] The present study does not explain the reformation as a social movement on the basis of popular forms of piety and religious practices, but on the basis of the concrete and real conditions of the lives of peasants and townsmen.

It is now possible to indicate this study's main line of argument in terms of three questions. First, what did "reformation" mean to the peasants and the townsmen, and to what extent can we detect a common understanding of the reformation? Second, what did peasant society appropriate from the reformers, and what were its original contributions? Or, to put it differently: Is there a distinct reformation of the common people? And third, what was the process by which reformation ideas were received within society? I have previously suggested that the history of the reformation might have something to do with the community (*Gemeinde*),[40] and this idea shall serve as our heuristic guide.

Notes

1. Walther Peter Fuchs, "Das Zeitalter der Reformation," in Bruno Gebhardt, *Handbuch der deutschen Geschichte*, 9th ed., vol. 2 (Stuttgart, 1971); Ernst Walter Zeeden, "Deutschland von der Mitte des 15. Jahrhunderts bis zum Westfälischen Frieden (1648)," in Theodor Schieder, ed., *Handbuch der europäischen Geschichte*, vol. 3 (Stuttgart, 1971); Stephan Skalweit, *Reich und Reformation* (Berlin, 1967).
2. Franz Lau, "Reformationsgeschichte bis 1532," in Franz Lau and Ernst Bizer, eds., *Reformationsgeschichte Deutschlands bis 1555*, Die Kirche in ihrer Geschichte, vol. III K (Göttingen, 1964), 17f.; Bernd Moeller, "Luther und die Städte," in Bernd Moeller, *Aus der Lutherforschung. Drei Vorträge*, edited by the Gemeinsame Kommission der Rheinisch-Westfälischen Akademie der Wissenschaften and the Gerda-Henkel-Stiftung (Cologne and Opladen, 1983), 20f.

3. Rainer Wohlfeil, "Das Schicksal der Reformation vor und nach dem Augsburger Reichstag," in Bernhard Lohse and Otto Hermann Pesch, eds., *Das "Augsburger Bekenntnis" von 1530 damals und heute* (Munich and Mainz, 1980), p. 83.

4. Hans-Jürgen Goertz, "Aufstand gegen den Priester. Antiklerikalismus und reformatorische Bewegungen," in Peter Blickle, ed., *Bauer, Reich und Reformation. Festschrift für Günther Franz zum 80. Geburtstag* (Stuttgart, 1982), esp. 182ff.

5. This phrase has been elaborated upon by Marxist historiography, but it is also used by western church historians, for example, Heiko A. Oberman.

6. Characteristic is Rainer Wohlfeil, *Einführung in die Geschichte der deutschen Reformation* (Munich, 1982).

7. Most recently Heiko A. Oberman, "Die Reformation als theologische Revolution," in Peter Blickle, Andreas Lindt, and Alfred Schindler, eds., *Zwingli und Europa. Referate und Protokoll des Internationalen Kongresses aus Anlaß des 500. Geburtstages von Huldrych Zwingli vom 26. bis 30. März 1984* (Zurich, 1985), and the minutes of the discussion.

8. Arthur G. Dickens, *The German Nation and Martin Luther* (New York, 1974), esp. 182, 196.

9. On this discussion see "Stadtreformation und Fürstenreformation als idealtypische Alternativen," in Lewis W. Spitz, ed., *Humanismus und Reformation als Kulturelle Kräfte in der deutschen Geschichte*, Veröffentlichungen der Historischen Kommission zu Berlin, vol. 51 (Berlin, 1981), 174–187.

10. For a kind of interim summary see Heiko A. Oberman, *Werden und Wertung der Reformation. Vom Wegestreit zum Glaubenskampf* (Tübingen, 1977), 352–357.

11. Compare Heinz Schilling, *Konfessionskonflikt und Staatsbildung. Eine Fallstudie über das Verhältnis von religiösem und sozialem Wandel in der Frühneuzeit am Beispiel der Grafschaft Lippe*, Quellen und Forschungen zur Reformationsgeschichte, vol. 48 (Gütersloh, 1982); Olaf Mörke, *Rat und Bürger in der Reformation. Soziale Gruppen und kirchlicher Wandel in den welfischen Hansestädten Lüneburg, Braunschweig und Göttingen*, Veröffentlichungen des Instituts für historische Landesforschung der Universität Göttingen, vol. 19 (Hildesheim, 1983).

12. Moeller, "Luther und die Städte," 16.

13. Hans Rosenberg in Spitz, *Humanismus und Reformation*, 174.

14. M. M. Smirin, *Die Volksreformation des Thomas Münzer und der große Bauernkrieg* (Berlin, 1952; 2d ed., 1956; original Russian ed., 1947). Subsequent references are to the 2d German ed.

15. Ibid., 97, 96, 164, 96, 294, 653, 600 (in the sequence in which they appear in the text).

16. Josef Macek, *Der Tiroler Bauernkrieg und Michael Gaismair*, trans. R. F. Schmiedt (Berlin, 1965), 88, 109, 111, 127, 245, 370, for his imprecise, slogan-like use of the term; Max Steinmetz, "Über den Charakter der Reformation und des Bauernkriegs in Deutschland," in Rainer Wohlfeil, ed., *Reformation oder frühbürgerliche Revolution* (Munich, 1972), 144–162, here at 154.

17. Max Steinmetz, "Der geschichtliche Platz des deutschen Bauernkriegs," in Gerhard Brendler and Adolf Laube, eds., *Der deutsche Bauernkrieg 1524/25. Geschichte, Traditionen, Lehren*, Akademie der Wissenschaften der DDR. Schriften des Zentralinstituts für Geschichte, vol. 57 (Berlin, 1977), 15–33, here at 31. It remains somewhat unclear whether Steinmetz would include the peasant leaders he mentions by name in the people's reformation. But he clearly does extend the concept beyond Müntzer and Gaismair.

18. Compare the cautious use of the term "people's reformation" by Günter Vogler, *Nürnberg 1524/25. Studien zur Geschichte der reformatorischen und sozialen Bewegung in der Reichstadt* (Berlin, 1982), 312, 314, 316.

19. Most recently emphasized by Karl Siegfried Bader, *Das Dorf als Friedens- und*

Rechtsbereich (Cologne/Graz, 1957), 230. Bader's verdict is all the more important, because he is also an expert on the cities. See also Bader, "Reichsadel und Reichsstädte in Schwaben am Ende des alten Reiches," in *Aus Verfassungs- und Landesgeschichte. Festschrift zum 70. Geburtstag von Theodor Mayer*, vol. 1 (Constance, 1954), 247–263; Bader, "Die Reichstädte des schwäbischen Kreises am Ende des alten Reiches," *Ulm und Oberschwaben* 32 (1951): 47–70. For an attempt to situate the cities within the forms of political authority, see Bader, *Der deutsche Südwesten in seiner territorialstaatlichen Entwicklung*, 2d. ed. (Sigmaringen, 1978), esp. 149–160.

20. Although the use of the phrase "the common man" was already common in the nineteenth century, it received its first reflective treatment in Peter Blickle, *Die Revolution von 1525*, 1st ed. (Munich, 1975), 177ff. The theme was next picked up by Heinz Schilling, "Aufstandsbewegungen in der Stadtbürgerlichen Gesellschaft des Alten Reiches," in Hans-Ulrich Wehler, ed., *Der Deutsche Bauernkrieg, 1524–1526*, Geschichte und Gesellschaft, Sonderheft 1 (Göttingen, 1975), 193–238, esp. 237f. (Nachtrag: Bemerkungen zu Peter Blickles Interpretation des Bauernkrieges als Revolution des "gemeinen Mannes" in Stadt und Land). The theme was subsequently taken up more broadly in 1976 by Rainer Wohlfeil, "Der 'gemeine Mann' im Bauernkrieg," in Fridolin Dörrer, ed., *Die Bauernkriege und Michael Gaismair*, Veröffentlichungen des Tiroler Landesarchivs, vol. 2 (Innsbruck, 1982), 283–288. There are useful discussions in Winfried Schulze, "Theoretische Probleme bei der Untersuchung vorrevolutionärer Gesellschaften," in Jürgen Kocka, ed., *Theorien in der Praxis des Historikers*, Geschichte und Gesellschaft, Sonderheft 3 (Göttingen, 1977), 55–85, esp. 69f., 83f.; and from a Marxist perspective, Adolf Laube, "Bemerkungen zur These von der 'Revolution des gemeinen Mannes,'" *Zeitschrift für Geschichtswissenschaft* 26 (1978): 607–614 (attempt to defend the concept of "Volk"). There is an interim survey in Rainer Wohlfeil, "Vorbemerkungen zum Begriff des 'Gemeinen Mannes,'" in Hans Mommsen and Winfried Schulze, eds., *Vom Elend der Handarbeit. Probleme historischer Unterschichtenforschung*, Geschichte und Gesellschaft. Bochumer Historische Studien, vol. 24 (Munich, 1981), 139ff. For new perspectives, especially for the cities, see Heinrich R. Schmidt, *Reichsstädte, Reich und Reformation. Korporative Religionspolitik 1521–1529/30*, Veröffentlichungen des Instituts für europäische Geschichte Mainz, vol. 122 (Wiesbaden, 1986).

21. This is the central question of Robert H. Lutz, *Wer war der gemeine Mann? Der dritte Stand in der Krise des Spätmittelalters* (Munich, 1979), the most extensive study of the history of this term.

22. Or, apparently, women of any status. See Lyndal Roper, "'The common man,' 'the common good,' 'common women': Gender and Meaning in the German Reformation Commune," *Social History* 12 (1987): 1–22 (Editors' note).

23. On the subsequent history of the term see Peter Blickle, "Untertanen in der Frühneuzeit. Zur Rekonstruktion der politischen Kultur und sozialen Wirklichkeit Deutschlands im 17. Jahrhundert," *Vierteljahrschrift für Sozial- und Wirtschaftsgeschichte* 70 (1983): 493–497.

24. The term "the people" (*das Volk*) is problematic, because of its use by militant nationalist and racialist groups in modern Germany (Editors' note).

25. Kaspar von Greyerz, "Religion und Gesellschaft in der frühen Neuzeit (Einführung in Methoden und Ergebnisse der sozialgeschichtlichen Religionsforschung)," *Schweizerische Gesellschaft für Wirtschafts- und Sozialgeschichte* 3 (1984): 14, 20, 26, 31.

26. For Spain, see William A. Christian, Jr., *Local Religion in Sixteenth-Century Spain* (Princeton, 1981), esp. 8; Robert Scribner, *For the Sake of Simple Folk. Popular Propaganda for the German Reformation*, Cambridge Studies in Oral and Literature Culture, vol. 2 (Cambridge, 1981); Donald Weinstein and Rudolph M. Bell, *Saints and Society. The Two Worlds of Western Christendom, 1000–1700* (Chicago and London,

1982); Peter Burke, *Popular Culture in Early Modern Europe* (New York, 1978).
27. Moeller, "Luther und die Städte," 23. Compare my earlier formulation in *Reformation*, 111:

> It cannot be said that the peasants did not understand what the Reformers were preaching . . . This statement will not seem particularly daring if one bears in mind that the Reformation doctrine of justification—reduced to its essential core—could be understood by anybody. The process of tracing religion back to a few basic categories and deriving its justification from them made religion accessible to all of society.

28. Bernd Moeller, *Reichsstadt und Reformation*, Schriften des Vereins für Reformationsgeschichte, no. 180 (Gütersloh, 1962), 91.
29. Marc Lienhard, *Martin Luther. Un temps, une vie, un message* (Paris and Geneva, 1983), 132, at least raises the question of why scholars speak of a city reformation and a princes' reformation but not of a "réforme paysanne."
30. Greyerz, "Religion und Gesellschaft," 25; Natalie Zemon Davis, "Some Tasks and Themes in the Study of Popular Religion," in Charles Trinkhaus and Heiko A. Oberman, eds., *The Pursuit of Holiness in Late Medieval and Renaissance Religion. Papers from the University of Michigan Conference*, Studies in Medieval and Reformation Thought, vol. 10 (Leiden, 1974), 309. Compare Weinstein and Bell, *Saints and Society*, 12; Martin Scharfe, "Subversive Frömmigkeit," in Jutta Held, ed., *Kultur zwischen Bürgertum und Volk*, Argument-Sonderband, no. 103 (Berlin, 1983), 117–135, esp. 130.
31. The contributions by Winfried Schulze and by me to Gunter Birtsch, ed., *Grund- und Freiheitsrechte im Wandel von Gesellschaft und Geschichte* (Göttingen, 1981). For a broader empirical underpinning see, in addition to my older study *Landschaften*, especially Winfried Schulze, *Bäuerlicher Widerstand und feudale Herrschaft in der frühen Neuzeit*, Neuzeit im Aufbau, vol. 6 (Stuttgart-Bad Canstatt, 1980). For a regional differentiation see the various contributions in Schulze, *Aufstände*, and the volume edited by myself, *Aufruhr und Empörung? Studien zum bäuerlichen Widerstand im Alten Reich* (Munich, 1980). The most comprehensive critical assessment of this scholarly approach is in Werner Troßbach, "Bauernbewegungen im Wetterau-Vogelsberg-Gebiet 1648–1806: Soziale Bewegung und politische Erfahrung," Ph.D. dissertation (Bochum, 1983), 1–40.
32. James Obelkevich, "Introduction," in his edited volume, *Religion and the People, 800–1700* (Chapel Hill, NC, 1979), 4. See also Davis, "Some Tasks," 312. Surveys of the scholarship by Robert W. Scribner, "Interpreting Religion in Early Modern Europe," *European Studies Review* 13 (1983), 89–105; Greyerz, "Religion und Gesellschaft"; and Gunther Lottes, "Popular Culture in England (16.–19. Jahrhundert)," *Francia* 12 (1984): 614–641, esp. 637ff.
33. The study of popular religion is indebted for important impulses to the work of Keith Thomas, *Religion and the Decline of Magic* (New York, 1971), whose emphasis is on the Stuart and Tudor periods.
34. I should point out especially the work of Weinstein and Bell, *Saints and Society*, and Christian, *Local Religion* and *Apparitions*. For Germany compare the interpretations of Lionel Rothkrug, which seem rather muddled, judging from the southern German material. See his *Religious Practices and Collective Perceptions: Hidden Homologies in the Renaissance and Reformation*, Historical Reflections, vol. 7, no. 1 (Montreal, 1980); Rothkrug, "Popular Religion and Holy Shrines. Their Influence on the Origins of the German Reformation and Their Role in German Cultural Development," in Obelkevich, *Religion and the People*, 20–86.

35. Weinstein and Bell, *Saints and Society*, 12; and it is emphasized by Christian, *Local Religion*.
36. Weinstein and Bell, *Saints and Society*.
37. Miriam U. Chrisman, however, argues for a sharp separation between the culture of the intellectuals and the culture of the common people. Miriam U. Chrisman, *Lay Culture, Learned Culture. Books and Social Change in Strasbourg, 1480–1599* (New Haven, CT, and London, England, 1982), esp. xxff., 281ff.
38. Thomas, *Religion and the Decline of Magic*, x; Burke, *Popular Culture*, 12; Will-Erich Peuckert, *Deutscher Volksglaube des Spätmittelalters* (Stuttgart, 1942; reprinted, Hildesheim and New York, 1978), esp. 7–12.
39. See on this the case studies by Emanuel Le Roy Ladurie, *Les paysans de Languedoc*, vol. 1 (Paris, 1966), 333–414; and Margaret Bowker, *The Henrician Reformation. The Diocese of Lincoln under John Longland 1521–1547* (Cambridge, 1981), 17–64.
40. I approached this topic step by step in my earlier studies: *Die Revolution von 1525* (Munich, 1975), 274–278; *Deutsche Untertanen. Ein Widerspruch* (Munich, 1981), 124ff.; *Die Reformation im Reich*, Uni-Taschenbücher, vol. 1181 (Stuttgart, 1982), 122–133.

2

Reformation and Society

One of the noteworthy products of reformation scholarship during the past ten to fifteen years has been the insight that the reformation as a "political" event was preceded by the reformation as a "social" event. In other words, an urban phase of the reformation preceded the reformation of the territorial princes. Historians who study how reformation ideas were spread and received in society have consequently come to assign the townsmen a favored place among the other social groups. By contrast, the nobility and the peasantry, the two other lay estates, have been largely ignored. So far as the nobility is concerned, this attitude is understandable, since it is hard to discern within this group a broad interest in the reformation during the period of the reformation in the cities. Franz von Sickingen's spectacular feud against the archbishop of Trier is best viewed as a movement that was socially and geographically limited to a segment of the lower nobility in the western part of the empire. It is remarkable, however, that the urban focus has not also sharpened scholarly awareness of the village, or at least aroused an interest in rural society. How do we explain this? If we leave aside the argument that one generation of scholars can accomplish only so much—which is always true and therefore doesn't explain much—reasons for this disregard of the peasantry are easy to find, even though it cannot be methodologically justified. Where the reformation is seen as an essentially intellectual movement—summed up in the phrase, "without books no reformation"—the peasant, an illiterate member of society, remains excluded from the circle of potential recipients of reformation ideas.

If this assumption is rejected, then, given the present state of scholarship, the most sensible approach begins by investigating the reformation within peasant society, the largest segment of the population in Central Europe. We can then proceed, secondly, to compare this reformation with the better known "reformation of the cities." And, finally, we will assess the common elements as well as differences between the peasants' and the burghers' reformations.

THE PEASANTS' REFORMATION

The basic sources for a study of the peasants' understanding of the reformation are the petitions, grievances, and articles that were drawn up by individual communities or entire regions. They fall in the years 1523 to 1525, with a particularly dense cluster in 1525, the year of the "revolution of the common man," more commonly called the Peasants' War. The thousands of documents that were drafted in the course of this uprising offer, among other things, insight into "peasant theology." The fact that among the peasants the reformation movement was closely linked to a revolutionary movement has kept scholars to this day from dealing with the religious beliefs of the peasants, let alone treating them as a worthwhile subject and one which might advance the scholarly discussion about the reformation. After Martin Luther had denounced the peasants' uprising as the work of the Devil, his verdict on the peasants' understanding of the new doctrine—that they were merely trying to redress their economic and social grievances under the pretext of the gospel—has been echoed unchallenged from the sixteenth century down to our own day.[1] This charge stifled any analytical investigation of the peasants' understanding of the reformation. It also improperly narrowed down the entire study of how reformation ideas were received within society, as we can see from the recent demonstration that a genuine "peasant theology" existed in Alsace.[2]

Any attempt at reconstructing the peasants' understanding of the reformation must start from the normal methodological premise that historical documents must first of all be accepted at face value. Only the second stage of a critical analysis can then proceed to examine to what extent the statements of a source may have been "falsified" through the intrusion of hidden interests, outside influences, or other forces. These methodological considerations might seem too obvious to need mentioning, but they are important in that they determine the course of our inquiry. The first step must be to define the peasants' understanding of the reformation on the basis of the available sources. This requires that we isolate and draw out the theological and religious statements in the texts. Any analysis of the reconstructed notion of reform must follow this step, not precede it.

In order to avoid misunderstandings, I should emphasize that I do not intend to examine the Peasants' War as such or to add anything to its explanation, but rather to provide a kind of historical framework for our discussion. This will make it easier to follow the analysis of the peasants' understanding of the reformation, with its frequent and unavoidable references to the conceptual world that is characteristic of the Peasants' War.

The revolt of the German peasants can be summarily characterized as the most important mass uprising in premodern Europe. After initial disturbances in the region of the upper Rhine in 1524,[3] Upper Swabia moved into the center of events during the first months of 1525. Thousands, even tens of thousands of peasants massed between Ulm and Biberach, in the Allgäu and around Lake Constance. Where negotiations with the lords—the princes, counts, knights, bishops, prelates, and imperial cities—were already begun, village and regional grievance lists were quickly, even hastily, drafted. Soon these lists were combined on a regional level. One of the most famous of these manifestos is the

Twelve Articles of the peasants of Upper Swabia. They represent a summation and abstract primarily of the village articles from northern Upper Swabia. Compiled and edited with the help of Sebastian Lotzer, a furrier journeyman, and Christoph Schappeler, a preacher from Memmingen, they were printed and widely circulated. At about the same time the peasants between Ulm and Biberach, at Lake Constance and in the Allgäu, combined into a "Christian Union" and created a rough, preliminary constitution for themselves in the form of a Federal Ordinance (*Bundesordnung*). With the help of the printing press this document also found a wider circulation in the empire.

These propaganda activities of the Upper Swabian peasants were not unimportant for the spread and subsequent course of the movement, as the frequent references to the Twelve Articles in other regions document. Larger peasant unions were formed at the end of March around Rothenburg ob der Tauber, in the Odenwald, as well as in the archbishopric of Würzburg; eventually they spread over all of Franconia. The bands of Franconian peasants scored some spectacular successes. Near Weinsberg they forced an aristocratic garrison to capitulate and, in accordance with the law of war, made them run the gauntlet. The archbishopric of Mainz was forced to declare allegiance to the "Twelve Articles," which the Franconians had adopted from the Upper Swabians with minor modifications. Riding the crest of these victories, two burgher partisans of the Franconian peasants started to think of ways of how the archbishoprics of Cologne and Trier, and the electorates of Brandenburg and Saxony, which so far had not been touched by the uprisings, might be integrated into a comprehensive peasant alliance.

In mid-April the revolt also erupted in the Klettgau, the Black Forest, and Alsace. In Lower Alsace, Erasmus Gerber gathered peasants who were subjects of many different lords into a tight organization. The peasants along the upper Rhine used persuasion, threats, and military force to compel the cities to join them. Their final victory was the capitulation of Freiburg im Breisgau. Before Freiburg had fallen to the rebels, the peasants in Tyrol rose up, for part of the time, at least, under the ideological leadership of Michael Gaismair. The miners, mining entrepreneurs (*Gewerken*), and peasants in the neighboring archbishopric of Salzburg followed their example, and in distant Thuringia Thomas Müntzer became the leader of rebellious peasants and miners. From the upper Rhine the uprising swept into the Palatinate and into the Swiss Confederation (Basel, Solothurn, Zurich). From Upper Swabia it spread to St. Gall, the Habsburg portion of the Rhine valley, and Graubünden. From Franconia it reached the Duchy of Württemberg. The sacking of monasteries and assaults on castles were familiar sights in all areas of the uprising; monasteries were plundered to provision the peasant bands, often 10,000 strong, and castles were stormed to preempt possible military countermeasures.

At first the lords seemed to respond hesitantly, but eventually they mounted a determined counterattack in the short span of just over three weeks. In mid-April the general of the Swabian League, Georg Truchsess of

Waldburg, succeeded in neutralizing the peasants from Upper Swabia with a peace treaty. Soon after, the Württemberg peasants were defeated at Böblingen (May 12th), the Thuringians at Frankenhausen (May 15th), the Alsatians at Zabern (May 16th), and the Franconians at Königshofen (first week of June). The duke of Lorraine, the landgrave of Hesse, and the prince electors of Saxony, Brandenburg, the Palatinate, Mainz, and Trier and their troops crushed the peasant armies.

Between the time the peasants began banding together and the time they were suppressed by military force, a great many lists of grievances and demands—mostly in the form of so-called articles—were drawn up in villages and on the local, regional, and territorial levels. In fact, hardly any other period in premodern Europe has such an abundance of these documents. As the peasant movement spread it also became better organized. The peasants everywhere formed "bands," military or paramilitary organizations, which frequently joined together into larger Christian Unions. Since the feudal power structure had collapsed, these groups inevitably took on the character of political associations. Both the peasant bands as well as the Christian Unions have left behind Military and Federal Ordinances.

Hardly a single one of the local articles, and certainly none of the regional grievances or Military and Federal Ordinances, neglected to address the question of the reformation. They therefore allow us to reconstruct the peasants' understanding of the reformation, both the essential common characteristics as well as the regional differences. Of course the necessary focus on the year 1525 must not obscure the fact that peasant interest in the reformation actually began earlier, on a larger scale from 1524 onward in Alsace[4] and in Franconia,[5] and in the region around Zurich after 1523.

EXAMPLES, CENTERS OF ACTIVITY, REPERCUSSIONS

During Easter week of 1523, the abbot of Wettingen complained to the mayor and council of Zurich that the community of Kloten was demanding that he, as the holder of the patronage, provide them with a priest who would preach the gospel after the celebration of the Eucharist. If he acceded to this demand it would diminish his rights as a prelate of the church. Zurich's council took the position that the monastery's legal privileges should not be impaired in any way, but it did give the community permission to hire a priest and support him from community resources.[6]

About two weeks later the community of Kloten took its own complaints to Zurich. The priest (Leutpriester) and his assistant did not satisfy their religious wishes; the abbot of Wettingen should use part of the tithe income from the village to hire a priest who would preach to them "the gospel and the godly scripture."[7] Apparently the community was not only determined to be provided with religious services it deemed proper. It also demanded that the revenues of its ecclesiastical patron, the tithes, be used for this purpose. At a court day two weeks later Zurich gave its decision in the presence of the priest and delegates from the community and the monastery: the lay priest Ulrich Kern was to hire an assistant "who would preach the gospel with the mandate from the community" and who would be supported by the abbot of Wettingen.[8] Under the protection of Zurich, Kloten had thus been able to achieve two things: to adjust the pastoral care to the religious needs of the peasants—the community had outlined the duties of the lay priest's assistant in the form of a mandate—and to shift the burden of supporting the assistant onto their patron lord.[9]

What the content of such a mandate may have looked like can be seen from a glance at the Franconian village of Wendelstein, a long way from Zurich. In the fall of 1524, the patron lord, Margrave Casimir of Brandenburg, assigned a priest to the parish. The village mayor and the community soon let the priest know "what it is we desire and request, which henceforth you must follow."[10] In a concisely, if not to say sharply, worded statement the community informed their priest of his position and duties:

> Thus we shall not recognize you as a lord, but simply as a servant of the parish. You do not command us, but we command you. And we order you henceforth faithfully to preach to us the gospel and the Word of God, pure and honest in accordance with the truth (untarnished and unobscured by human doctrine).

This introductory article, with its move of subjecting the priest to communal authority and obligating him to proclaim the "pure doctrine," established the basic framework for the community's subsequent demands:[11] the priest should be an example to the rest "in the parish, and in church you must follow the gospel in deeds as a faithful servant of Jesus Christ"; the sacraments should be administered in accordance with the scriptures, "as the Lord has taught and commanded us"; in the future the community would refuse the hitherto customary requests of the clergy, "that is to say alms, bequests for the welfare of one's soul (*Seelgerecht*), remunerations, and other invented things, which have cost us dearly," but it would not refuse to provide a proper livelihood from the communal church income (*Pfarrwiddum*); finally, the priest would have to take any claims against members of the parish to the local or margravial court, not to the ecclesiastical court in Eichstätt.

The newly appointed priest pledged to adhere to this village mandate without raising a word of objection: "And the priest of Wendelstein has taken on the post of the parish with this Christian intent, and he has also agreed to obey the parish as a faithful servant of the Christian community, so help him God."[12]

Three or four years earlier, around 1520, the abbot of Wettingen would never have allowed the community of Kloten to chose its own preacher, nor would the priest of Wendelstein have agreed to place himself under the peasants' authority in this way, since parishioners were considered the "priest's subjects," and the community was the "universitas subditorum parochiae."[13] But now the village community insisted on determining the content of the religious teachings and obliging the priest to adhere to it in his preaching. In an explanation that preceded the description of the priest's duties, the community of Wendelstein justified this in the following terms to the margravial officials:

The holy scripture indicates that it is proper for a Christian community to ask the Lord our God to send workers to his harvest, and the community thus also has the power to choose for the community a reputable and upright man who will preach the word of God to them in accordance with the truth, as a faithful servant of Jesus Christ, and who will give a good example. The same community also has the authority to dismiss him from his post and to appoint someone else in his place.[14]

Are these examples, which are geographically far apart, isolated incidents, or are they indicative of a more general phenomenon?

THE ZURICH REGION

The territory of the imperial city of Zurich—the Zurich Landschaft—was among those areas where the peasants very early took an interest in the reformation doctrine and agitated on its behalf. First indications emerge from the letter of the notary Johannes Widmer, dated June 1523, to Heinrich Göldli in Rome. Göldli was planning to come to Zurich with a cantor, but Widmer did not think that was a good idea, "for the situation here is such that we priests don't really know how safe we are in the city, not to say anything about when we go out hunting and ride through the peasants' enclosures [hâg]."[15] The common man despised the Mass as "an idolatry and corrupter of souls," and in the pulpits it was declared to be "an open cheat and a fraud." The people, Widmer continues, were blaming the priest for leading mankind astray for 1,400 years. Only now in the "time of Luther and Zwingli" was the gospel reemerging. What was nowadays being done to the Scripture "is agreeable to the common man, who is led to hope by their screaming and preaching . . . [that] the benefices will be divided up among the common folk." But since neither pope, nor cardinals, nor bishops were coming to the aid of the beleaguered clergy, the priests had the option "of abandoning their faith and all religious service in all haste or being killed by the common man."

The three charges that Widmer leveled against the common man—that he threatened the life of the clergy, that he was eager to enrich himself by laying hands on the wealth of the church under the pretext of the gospel, and that he despised the rituals of the church—can serve as the point of entry for the discussion of reformation activities and ideas in the Zurich countryside.

What kind of awareness did the peasants have about religious and theological issues in 1523? There are a number of useful sources that allow us to see the reformation ideas of both individuals and entire communities.[16] On Corpus Christi Day in 1523, Dr. Lorenz, parish priest at the Großmünster in Zurich, became involved in a revealing argument in the village of Zollikon.[17] After Lorenz's sermon, an old, bearded fellow approached him and proclaimed "with stinging, harsh, and intolerable words" that he, Lorenz, "has preached them lies and not the truth." In the course of the dispute the "peasant" revealed that he did not agree with Lorenz's view of the Eucharist. Finally, he brusquely declared that he would only continue going to the Lord's meal if it were offered "to him . . . in both forms of body and blood." On his way home to Zurich, Lorenz was stopped a second time, once again because of his sermon in Zollikon, which, understandably enough on Corpus Christi Day, had dealt with the sacrament of the Eucharist. This time he was approached by one Jakob Hottinger, who reproached him for having preached "how the sacrament of the altar in the form of the bread embodies the true God, his humanity, blood and flesh." Hottinger continued: "This is not true, and you should no longer tell lies from the pulpit." Lorenz defended himself and tried to prove through Scripture "that the true God exists in the form of the bread, both flesh and blood." Hottinger, however, insisted on receiving "the sacrament . . . in both forms"; Lorenz's proof was "derived from philosophy," whereas his "came from the gospel . . . for Christ took the bread, gave it to his disciples and spoke: take, this is my body; afterwards he took the cup and spoke: take, this is my blood."

The events I have described, which are based on the eyewitness testimony of Dr. Lorenz and Nikolaus Billiter, the "early mass priest" (*Frühmesser*) of Zollikon, convey a sense of how strongly the common people were affected by the Protestant preaching that undoubtedly came from the cathedral in Zurich in the sermons of Huldrych Zwingli. But they also indicate the theological interest of the common people, which, judging at least from this early evidence, was neither expressed as militant anticlericalism nor aimed at personal enrichment by secularizing and confiscating church property. Additional evidence exists to substantiate this predominantly theologically oriented reformation attitude of the peasants in 1523.

In the spring of 1523, the community of Witikon had gotten into a dispute with the provost and chapter of the cathedral in Zurich. Witikon belonged to the larger Zurich parish and owed a tithe to the cathedral, but it had hired its own pastor, undoubtedly with the hope that the tithe could be used to support him.[18] In the summer of the same year, Witikon, together with Zollikon, Fällanden, Unterstrass, and two other communities, made another attempt to dissolve the tithe obligations to the cathedral in Zurich. It was now argued that the people "have been informed and taught by the holy gospel" that the tithes are alms, although the canons were using them "for useless and frivolous things." It was simply not acceptable that the faithful had to pay "for the ringing of the bells, for baptism, tombstones, and funerals," while the canons were squandering the tithes.[19] Compared to the spring, the language was now more direct and forceful, which probably had something to do with the growing polarization of the old believers and the adherents of the new doctrine. This polarization led to the exchange of insults: in the 1520s, the Zurich council almost daily had to examine, punish, and forbid "invective and insults."[20] The pulpit served both camps as the platform for proclaiming their views. The record of the examination of a witness tells us what the Witikon priest Wilhelm Röubli—a follower of Zwingli, of course—was preaching.[21] He played the "pious peasant" off against the "stinking burgomaster," the "stinking bailiff," and the "murdering, heretic, and thieving priest." Nuns were told that it would be better for you to come out and take a husband than to stay in the convents. As you are grown up and independent and would like to have a man or desire to be in the company of men, and as you are not able to fulfill your desires with your lovers, you take your fingers and scratch your bone and your thing until the desire passes.

It does not take a great deal of imagination to envision the impact of this kind of preaching.

Given the heated and irritated atmosphere, the Zurich council may have thought it politically wise to allow the community of Witikon at the end of 1523 to appoint a pastor. However, the community itself had to support him, unless it managed to reach an amicable agreement with the cathedral in Zurich concerning the tithe.[22]

Witikon is not an isolated case. Elsewhere communities were also pushing to obtain reformist preachers, even if it meant accepting a financial burden.[23] We can get an insight into the motivations behind the demand of the communities to appoint their own pastors by looking at what Marthalen, Truttikon, and Benken, three communities near Schaffhausen, demanded in the summer of 1524.[24] Although in each case the peasants insisted more or less clearly on pure preaching and did not wish to hear any "fables," the primary concern was the availability of proper pastoral care within one's own community. The community of Marthalen considered it burdensome to keep visiting their parish church in Rheinau. It was a long way to Mass, it was often impossible to get hold of the priest when the dying had to be looked after or children needed to be baptized, and the monks of Rheinau refused to take over these pastoral duties. For all these reasons the village had taken on a pastor, although it also expected the abbot of Rheinau, who collected their tithe, to pay the expense to support him. In any case the community imposed a temporary halt to tithe payments to the monastery. The communities of Truttikon and Benken said similar things. After protracted negotiations,[25] during which Zurich was called in, permission was given to Marthalen and Benken at the end of 1525 to hire their own preachers, and the abbot of Rheinau was placed under obligation to contribute to the expenses for supporting them.[26]

Around the middle of 1524, demands for the appointment of pastors by the community had already ceased, and in view of the size of the Zurich region they were not all that numerous even for 1523 and 1524. Undoubtedly this had something to do with the fact that the reformation in Zurich was progressing quickly under the urging of Zwingli. Zurich's reformation also shows a unique feature. Unlike what happened in the imperial cities of southern Germany, in Zurich each level of change achieved by the reforming movement was immediately declared by decree to be the binding, enforceable standard for the entire territory. In October of 1523, the council passed a ruling "concerning the Mass and idols," in which it prohibited the destruction of images, ordered that the Mass be maintained "until further notice and the appearance of a soon-to-be released explanation," and directed all priests and preachers in the city and the countryside to preach "the holy gospel clearly and faithfully in accordance with the spirit of God."[27] Judging from the length of the text, the emphasis of the decree was on this last provision: printed instructions explaining what was meant by the gospel in accordance with the spirit of God would soon be sent out to the parish priests, and "a number of learned priests" were to be dispatched into the countryside to proclaim the Word of God as understood in Zwingli's doctrine.[28] This confirmed a decree which the council had already published in January following the Zurich Disputation but which seems to have had little if any effect up to that time. The earlier decree had declared that the clergy "should not undertake or preach anything except that which can be verified by the holy gospel or by other proper godly Scriptures."[29] The preaching provisions of the decree preempted an independent unfolding of the peasants' reformation, which in most cases was grounded in the concern for the pure preaching of the gospel. When it came to the crucial theological issues—preaching, the Mass, the Eucharist—neither the Zurich council nor the Zurich theologians had any intention of allowing the communities a larger sphere of action.[30] Communal autonomy in questions of religion was limited to deciding whether the "idols" should remain in the churches or should be removed;[31] violent incidents, which were the work of individuals, had already occurred earlier in the countryside.[32] The disciplined introduction of the reformation under the guidance of the authorities was in line with the policy which the Zurich council followed toward the reformist demands of the communities, a prudent policy dictated by political considerations. The council prohibited religious confrontations in the street— the sort that had occurred in Zollikon—declaring that one should "let the preachers straighten things out."[33] It protected the cathedral's rights to the tithe against the claims of Witikon and other communities;[34] initially it also did the same for the monastery of Rheinau in its quarrel with the communities of Marthalen, Benken, and Truttikon,[35] although not without expressing its sympathy for the demands of the peasants.

The extent of the consensus created in this way between the reformation in the city and the reformation in the countryside can be gauged from the "plebiscite" of November 1524. The council of Zurich approached the guilds in the city and the communities in the countryside in order to enlist broad support for its foreign policy toward France and its religious policy toward the Catholic communities of Switzerland—both issues were a severe strain on the Confederation.[36] Of the surviving replies from 36 communities, 15 declared themselves explicitly in support of the prevailing religious policies of Zurich, and the remainder did so more or less implicitly. Occasionally there were also more fervent responses. The peasants of Neuamt, for example, wanted "to place their life and property in service to the Word of God, to their lords and superiors, and to the city of Zurich."[37] In vain do we look for independent positions on the reformation, which could have been articulated on this occasion. All we get are scattered requests to Zurich for a better preacher, here and there the desire "that some agreement be reached regarding the Mass, the Word of God, and the images, so that one person doesn't go this way and another that way."[38]

It required an outside impetus to reignite the reform movement in the countryside, although this time with an unmistakable emphasis on primarily worldly demands. Clearly inspired by the Twelve Articles of the Upper Swabian peasants, the better part of the Zurich countryside—the lordships and districts (Ämter) of Greifensee, Kyburg, Eglisau, Andelfingen, Neuamt, Rümlang, and Grüningen—demanded at the end of April and the beginning of May 1525 the right of the communities to appoint their own pastors.[39] Following a proven procedure, the peasant demands were deliberated upon by commissions,[40] whose vote the council eventually adopted.[41] It was decided to give a careful hearing to the complaints of the communities and, if necessary, to provide them with decent preachers; thus the initiative could come from the communities, but the final decision remained with the council.[42]

In the initial phase of the reformation movement in 1523, when the city fathers had not yet channeled the reformation stirrings in the countryside with the help of decrees, the communities insisted on the appointment of reformation-minded pastors. They were also willing to support them, even though the demand that their livelihood should be paid from the tithe was present, first as a latent undercurrent and then openly expressed. The theological substance of the peasants' understanding of the reformation should not be underrated, even though it cannot be empirically substantiated as much as we would like. At least the events in Zollikon reveal that the common people had some grasp of the controversial points regarding the Eucharist. In the wake of the city-directed reformation in the countryside the beginnings of an independent peasant theology faded away. As a result no impulses for social and political change arose from the countryside. The concerns which Johannes Widmer conveyed to his correspondent in Rome turned out to be unfounded—the common man in the Zurich countryside had no intention of enriching himself at the expense of the traditional church, and he was not seeking violent revenge against its clergy.

"AN ENTIRE COMMUNITY BY ITSELF SHALL CHOOSE A PASTOR" —THE CASE OF UPPER SWABIA

On 6 and 7 March 1525, peasant delegations from all of Upper Swabia met in the imperial city of Memmingen to deliberate.[43] They had been sent by three peasant bands that had formed in January and February in the Allgäu, at Baltringen, and near Lake Constance. They thereby established the "Christian Union" in Upper Swabia, a peasant league very similar in purpose to a territorial peace. As its programmatic name declares plainly enough, it was created "for the praise and honor of the almighty and eternal God, for the exaltation of the holy gospel and the Word of God, and in support of justice and godly law."[44] Among the "legislative" measures of the Union was an ordinance on preaching, which was intended to place the clergy of Upper Swabia under obligation "to read, teach and preach solely the Word of God, and to explain its proper meaning." Should a pastor adhere to the "old ways and customs . . . a parish congregation may forthwith dismiss him and appoint someone else in his place, who might seem competent and agreeable to them."[45]

The demand of the community to appoint its own pastor was set by the Upper Swabian peasants within a larger explanatory context in the so-called Twelve Articles. Drafted at about the same time as the preaching ordinance, the Twelve Articles went through 25 printings in two months and had a remarkably powerful resonance throughout the empire.[46] It would therefore be wise to begin by reconstructing the peasants' understanding of the reformation on the basis of the Twelve Articles. The peasants began their list of grievances and demands as follows:

> First of all, we humbly ask and beg, and we all agree on this, that henceforth we ought to have the authority and power for the whole community to elect and appoint its own pastor. We also want authority to depose a pastor who behaves improperly.[47]

The pastor was placed under obligation to teach in accordance with the Scriptures; he should "preach the holy gospel purely and clearly, without any human additions, doctrines, or precepts."

The pastor "who clearly preaches the Word of God" should be supported from the grain tithe, which "from now on . . . our church wardens, appointed by the community, shall collect and receive." It was the task of the wardens to use the tithe "to provide our elected pastor with a decent and adequate living for himself with the consent of the whole community." What was left from the tithe was to be distributed to the poor "according to need and with the community's consent," all this "as the Bible commands."

What the Upper Swabian peasants demanded in this document, and propagated all over the empire in tens of thousands of pamphlets, was the reestablishment of the church on the basis of the village community. The noble and ecclesiastical patron lords, who had hitherto selected the candidates for the post of parish priest, were shut out. The bishops, who had hitherto confirmed the candidates of the patron lords, were passed over. The tithe holders—princes, counts, knights, bishoprics, monasteries, and hospitals—were either dispossessed or compensated for the loss of income. The community took over the rights and privileges of all these people and institutions—the community was "communalizing" the church.

The Twelve Articles—trenchantly argued, succinctly worded, and supported only with brief biblical references—were the end result of a lengthy and difficult process that gave rise to a peasant concept of the reformation. Starting out as a rude anticlericalism expressed only in negative terms, the peasant's understanding eventually developed into a refined and positive conception of communal Christianity.

From the Allgäu comes an eyewitness account, written by the nobleman Georg von Werdenstein. Owing to Werdenstein's personal involvement and realistic description of the events, his testimony can claim a high degree of authenticity.[48] We are told that Werdenstein's family was planning to celebrate the feast of St. Valentine with a festive mass in the castle's chapel. But as the day began, some unexpected trouble cast a cloud over the atmosphere. A group of peasants suddenly appeared in the courtyard of the castle. Their designated spokesman, Schmid by name, declared, as Werdenstein reports, "that they would no longer pay me interest or taxes, nor would they be obedient or subject to me in any way." Werdenstein asked, "My dear fellows, of what do you accuse me, or what have I done to you?" To which Schmid responded that Werdenstein

> had not done anything that other lords don't also do; but they did not wish to have a lord any longer, and Schmid continued to say that they also wanted the priest to preach as was done at Kempten, and especially like the preacher on the hill (who has been hanged) and in Sankt Martins Zell (who has fled)

—a reference to places of early reformation preaching in the Allgäu. "The priest is right here," Werdenstein replied to Schmid, "I cannot tell him how to preach," and the priest explained: "Dear fellows, until now I have told you the truth and reason, and I don't know how to preach any other way, to that I will pledge you my soul." Werdenstein reported, "At this the same Schmid replied and said to the priest: 'I shit on your soul, you cannot pledge your soul for us. . . .'" With their anger possibly dissipated by this dramatic confrontation, the peasants left. The priest and Werdenstein went "up to the castle; we took the morning meal together and were both not very happy, as everyone can probably well imagine."

The anticlericalism expressed by these peasants did not go very far, and even such as it is, it is not substantiated by contemporary peasant sources. One day after these events at the castle, Tigen Rettenberg, an Allgäu lordship belonging to the prince-bishop of Augsburg, formulated its grievances, which allow us to describe more clearly the goals of peasant anticlericalism.[49] Here the demand was raised that the pastor know theology, that he reside in the community, and that he not enrich himself through the sacraments. Those "who do not adhere to the regulations concerning the pastors should be relieved of their offices and incomes." The clergy was not to exercise any high justice, and it was to be subject to the secular court in worldly matters, pay dues to the secular authorities for its landed property, contribute to the taxes, and stay out of secular professions.

A few days later the Allgäu peasants joined together, among them subjects of Werdenberg and Augsburg. A preamble to the public announcement of the formation of the "Allgäu Band" gave a brief justification for this step: "Thus we wish to stand by one another and by the holy gospel and the Word of God and the godly law, and to help each other attain justice. To achieve this we pledge our bodies and our possessions and everything God has given us."[50] Consistent with this expressed purpose, the list of subsequent articles is headed by the concrete request that the pastor within the community "preach the holy gospel, the Epistles, the Old and New Testament, and whatever is equal to these scriptures, and not human inventions and precepts." The preaching of the "pure gospel" is a fundamental requirement, as the following provision underscores: "and whoever does not wish to do this and refuses to be instructed shall be dismissed and gotten rid of."   .

Of course one must be careful not to push the interpretation of this limited evidence too far. At least the following generalization, however, can be drawn from the sources: the basic and fundamental demand for the preaching of the gospel, a demand not open to debate, necessarily required that pastors who refused to fall into line had to be dismissed.

There are no surviving village demands for the Allgäu, but we have such demands for the region that was under the influence of the Baltringen Band, which took its name from its camp at Baltringen south of Ulm. These demands confirm the developments in the Allgäu, which went from the plea for the preaching of the "pure doctrine" to the right of dismissing "nonevangelical" pastors. But they also show how the general demand for the communalization of the church emerged from village grievances and gradually took shape.

The articles of the villages attached to the Baltringen Band were drafted in mid-February, and a majority of them—in so far as they addressed religio-ecclesiastical issues at all, which is true for at most 10 percent[51]—demanded merely the preaching of reformation doctrine. The peasants of Achstetten requested "that we be provided with a pastor who will bring us the pure and plain word of God,"[52] while the tenants of the Biberach hospital demanded "that the word of God be preached to us as well as that which is contained in the gospel."[53] The villages of Erolzheim, Waltershofen, and Binnenrot, however, went further. They introduced their list of articles with the demand

> that we may ourselves appoint preachers who shall preach to us the holy Word of God purely and clearly without any human addition; their preaching shall be based solely on the Bible and the holy Scripture. We ourselves shall provide these same preachers with the necessities of life.[54]

In this instance the appointment of a pastor is justified through the concern for the true preaching of the Word of God, and the community is willing to shoulder the expense. A few weeks later the community of Weicht, in a letter to their patron lord, the monastery of Steingaden, more or less reversed the argument:

> The peasants no longer wish to pay the pastor the small tithe, offerings [opfer], and gifts for the salvation of one's soul [seelgerett]; and if the pastor does not do what he owes them, they will not refuse the tithe, but will collect it them-selves and use it to support a pastor who is agreeable to them.[55]

In insisting that a pastor fulfill his duties, which would be enforced, if all else failed, by the choice of a new pastor, the community of Weicht adopted elements from the arguments used by Tigen Rettenberg.

The peasants from Lake Constance expressed their understanding of the reformation more clearly and forcefully than either the Allgäu or Baltringen peasants. Their delegates to Memmingen came with a set of instructions, the Three Articles, which developed ideas of a communal Christianity that seem closely related to the Christian Union and the Twelve Articles:

> First of all we desire and demand that the holy gospel and the Word of God, unobscured and unadulterated by human doctrine and judgment, along with its fruits, be preached and taught to us clearly and purely by men learned in the Holy Scriptures and suitable for the task. Furthermore, these same men shall furnish and provide us with all the Christian rites and needs free and not for money, as has been the case until now. Item, secondly, that we wish to furnish these men and theirs with an adequate livelihood, just as St. Paul has told us to. Item, thirdly, that we and our communities shall have the authority to select, appoint, and dismiss all those who are our pastors and instructors in the Word of God, and whom we support, as was said above.[56]

If we carefully classify the data from the Upper Swabian sources, we can gain some general insights into the gradual nature of the process that gave rise to a peasant understanding of the reformation. Of course the applicability of these general observations must for now remain strictly limited to Upper Swabia. It would appear that two starting positions are conceivable (see Fig. 1).

Once the two original requests became nonnegotiable demands, this raised the question of what the consequences would be if the pastor refused to preach the new doctrine or failed to reform his pastoral conduct. Both circumstances gave rise to the demand by the peasants that under these circumstances the pastor be dismissed. Of course it was not to be expected that the patron lord or the bishop would take this step, and so it would have to be done by the parishioners, that is, by the community. This had additional ramifications. For example, how was a deposed pastor to be replaced, or how could a new cleric, an adherent of the new doctrine, be appointed alongside the existing pastor? The answer was: appointment of the pastor by the community. But this immediately raised the question of how to support the pastor, to which the peasants gave two answers. Some were willing to shoulder the expense themselves. Others demanded that the cost be defrayed by the tithe, which in their eyes had originally been a church tax; now, under communal control, it should serve to support the clergy.

What I have given is a reconstruction of the stages in the peasants' thinking about religious preaching and its implications, based on the chronology of local and regional articles and ordinances. It is not unimportant for the future course of our inquiry that the period in which the evidence can be placed is very short: four to six weeks in the months of February and March of 1525. We have no evidence earlier than this.

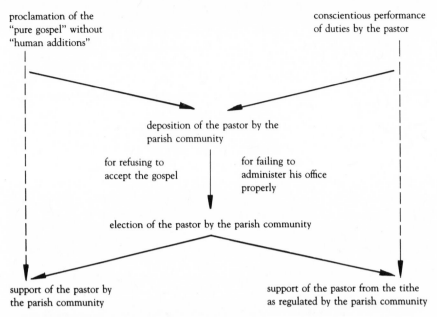

proclamation of the
"pure gospel" without
"human additions"

conscientious performance
of duties by the pastor

deposition of the pastor by the
parish community

for refusing to
accept the gospel

for failing to
administer his office
properly

election of the pastor by the parish community

support of the pastor by
the parish community

support of the pastor from the tithe
as regulated by the parish community

FIGURE 1   STAGES OF PEASANT REFORMATION IN UPPER SWABIA

A comparison of the sources in their chronological sequence reveals the
slowly emerging notion that the church, so badly in need of reform, could only
be a church established on and rooted in the community. The appointment of
the pastor by the community, maintenance of the pastor by the community or
with the help of the tithe, over which the community was to regain control, and
the distribution of the tithe revenue by the community—all this demonstrates
repeatedly that the peasants focused the organizational framework of the reformation movement closely on the village. At the same time there can be no
doubt about the religious seriousness, the deep piety, and the yearning for
salvation expressed by the peasants. The Upper Swabian peasants demanded in
their Twelve Articles "to hear the gospel and to live accordingly";[57] the Allgäu
peasants were willing "to lose our lives for the gospel, for we are brothers in
Christ";[58] the peasants at Lake Constance wanted the gospel "preached solely
for the salvation of our souls";[59] and the peasants of the Hospital of Biberach
demanded pure preaching, because Christ "has left his eternal word to
strengthen us, with which and through which we are supposed to live and
govern, and to follow him."[60] The practical consequences which the peasants
derived from such an understanding of Christianity underscore the seriousness of
their desires; they were willing to shoulder the financial burden of their convictions by supporting at their own expense a priest who preached in accordance
with the gospel.

The line of reasoning used by the majority of the peasants progressed as follows: pure preaching; dismissal of the pastor; appointment of the pastor by the community; and, finally, support of the pastor by the community itself. These guiding ideas also inform the Federal Ordinance adopted by the Christian Union of the Upper Swabian peasants on 7 March 1525:

> Item, wherever there is a pastor or a vicar, they shall be kindly asked and requested to preach the holy gospel. Those who are willing to do so shall receive a proper livelihood from their parish. But those who refuse to do this shall be dismissed, and the parish shall be provided with someone else.[61]

Repeated printings of the Federal Ordinance spread this three-tiered regulation—pure gospel, appointment of the pastor by the community, support of the pastor by the community—far beyond Upper Swabia.[62] The Twelve Articles, whose radius of influence was even wider, differ from this regulation in one point: support for the pastor would come from the tithe. The regional differences which thus emerge within Upper Swabia need to be more closely defined, although for this we need more comparative material from other areas. It would appear that the idea of regaining communal control of the tithe, from which the pastor's salary would come, was introduced into the Twelve Articles by the Baltringen peasants. Close to 50 percent of all local articles of the Baltringen Band demand the abolition of the small tithe and the abolition or conversion of the large tithe; in the Allgäu and at Lake Constance such demands are weakly attested or not at all.[63] In view of these findings our investigation must take regional differentiations into consideration. It is not possible to simply speak of a uniform concept of reformation among the peasants.

"ALL GODLESS PEOPLE MUST BE EXTERMINATED"
—THE TYROL AND SALZBURG

In his territorial constitution (*Landesordnung*) of 1526, Michael Gaismair told the Tyrolean peasants "to exterminate and put away all godless people who persecute the eternal Word of God, oppress the common man, and obstruct the common good," and he called upon them "to set about and erect a wholly Christian order which is based in all things on the holy and eternal Word of God, and live by it completely."[64] Gaismair was a tireless propagandist for a complete and thorough Christianization of government and society, and he campaigned for the implementation of his goals with Zwingli and in Zurich, in Venice and among the Salzburg peasants.[65] With his radically egalitarian, biblical–Old Testament program he drew up a constitution whose specific demands reveal that it was firmly rooted in the regional grievances of the Tyrol peasants. We have four regional grievance lists from Tyrol, two from northern and two from southern Tyrol, each of which can claim to be representative of several villages and hamlets: the articles of the rural districts (*Landgerichte*) of Thauer-Rettenberg and Sonnenburg and those of the "peasants at the Etsch river" (probably the communities south of Meran) and of the subjects of the prince-bishopric of Brixen/Bressanone.[66] The dates at which the articles were put into writing do not allow us to rule out entirely influences from outside (for example, from Upper Swabia and the Allgäu), but they clearly rule out the possibility that these texts influenced each other, since they were composed in quick succession on May 14, 15, and 16.

The peasant understanding of the reformation in the Tyrol can be basically summarized in four points (compare the synopsis of the regional grievances in the Tyrol on pp. 27–30):

1. The peasants demanded the freedom to preach the pure gospel. This explains the appeal to the territorial prince, Archduke Ferdinand of Austria, to release the imprisoned preachers. This demand is understandable in the area of the lower Inn valley (Thauer-Rettenberg and Sonnenburg), since the nearby mining regions with the smelting houses (*Pfannen*) and foundries around Schwaz, Hall, and along the lower Inn, had been centers of reformation preaching from 1520 on. The Innsbruck authorities time and again suppressed these activities, although apparently with little success.[67]

2. In order to guarantee preaching of the pure gospel, the peasants demanded the right for a community to appoint its pastor.

3. As elsewhere, the tithe was to be used to support the pastor, although with the remarkable stipulation that the entire tithe revenue (Sonnenburg) or half of it (Brixen) should go to the territorial prince, on the grounds that it was he who protected the land.

4. All four regional grievance lists uniformly demanded a thorough reform of the regular and chapter clergy. At the very least the peasants demanded that the monasteries and prince-bishoprics (*Hochstifte*) be stripped of their secular jurisdictions, although some went further and called for their expropriation (peasants at the Etsch) or secularization (Brixen peasants). We cannot fail to note that the anticlerical sentiment is noticeably stronger in southern Tyrol. The explanation for this undoubtedly lies in the fact that the political and economic importance of the church—as represented by the prince-bishoprics of Brixen/Bressanone and Trent—was much more visible and pronounced here than in northern Tyrol, which had only a few monasteries with modest jurisdictions.

SYNOPSIS OF THE REGIONAL GRIEVANCES IN THE TYROL

The articles dispense with more extensive justifications. The sole exceptions are the articles of Thauer-Rettenberg, whose preamble conveys a more detailed picture of the peasants' understanding of the reformation.[68] Man does not live by bread alone, but by every word that comes from the mouth of God—with these words the rural districts of Thauer-Rettenberg began their articles to the territorial prince. But since the Word of God "has until now been so greatly obscured with human doctrine that our future salvation has been seriously endangered," the Word of God must once again come to light "pure, clear, and unadulterated." This is all the more imperative as the end result of differing and contradictory theologies is that "a simple person does not know which one to adhere to and follow, and is thereby driven to conspiracy and rebellion against his will (since he doesn't know what to do and what not)." Only the preaching of the pure gospel can guarantee the restoration of "peace and quiet." The salvation of the soul of the individual person and the political peace within the community are the guiding principles to which the individual demands are subordinated—and both seem guaranteed only if the pure Word of God is preached.

The individual articles of the regional grievances were picked up and developed further by the Meran Articles that were drafted two weeks later; on 22 June they were presented to the territorial prince at the diet of Innsbruck as the binding program of the peasants and burghers of Tyrol.[69] Fundamental to the program were still the repeatedly expressed demands for the preaching of "the Word of God without any self-serving additions" or "unjustified additions," and the desire "that each city and district [gericht] shall have the authority to elect, appoint and dismiss its own pastor," and that the pastor be supported through the tithe.[70] The regulations concerning the regular and chapter clergy were formulated more extensively and justified at greater length. The monasteries in the region (Land) were to be reduced to a maximum of three, the bishoprics dissolved, convents abolished, and the mendicant orders outlawed. In so far as monasteries remained in existence or were newly established, they had no claim to secular jurisdiction of any kind, their material circumstances were to be limited to a modest subsistence, the number of monks or nuns was to be restricted, and admission into the monastic house was to be dependent upon a theological qualification in accordance with reformation doctrine.[71] The peasants justified their demands by arguing that especially the clergy had to live up to the maxims of the Christian teachings: they "should no longer lead such an elevated lifestyle as has been the case until now," be content with "adequate food, drink, and clothing," and "behave decently and not hang around in the taverns."[72]

The same criteria were applied to the secular clergy. The pastor would be properly supported with a benefice, but pluralism and the levying of "servile death taxes, fees for services for the dead [selgrat], confessional fees, preaching fees [verkündtgelt]," as well as fees for "blessing new mothers and newlyweds" were resolutely opposed.[73] To the believer the church had to be not only free of charge, it also had to be present and available, hence the pastor was obligated to reside in the community. By paying the pastor a modest but adequate and decent income, and by secularizing church income, the community would free up revenues that had previously been wasted. In keeping with the Christian commandment of charity, these revenues could be spent on the poor. Hospitals were to be established not only in every city, but in every district (Landgericht), "in which each district could provide for and help its poor, not only the lame and the cripples, but also the 'home-poor' (*hausarme*), provided they behaved faithfully, piously, and decently."[74] A solution thus seemed at hand for the problem of begging and poverty throughout the land.

The Meran Articles elaborated a vision of the reformation which had the potential of reaching deeply into the social and political spheres of life. The gospel-inspired reform of the church—with its demand that the clergy preach the Christian message and live adequately and modestly in keeping with its teachings—found its counterpart in the gospel-inspired reform of the world to promote greater altruism and the common welfare. This opened a broad range of new possibilities, allowing the common man in Tyrol to demand reforms in the economic, social, and political spheres. It is important to note that the 96 Articles are variations upon the basic theme of the "pure Word of God." The comprehensive nature of the peasants' vision of reform was thus outlined with corresponding clarity in the preamble:

> Therefore, in order that the glory and Word of God be preached without any self-interested addition, that brotherly love be kept and the common welfare promoted, we request that Your Princely Highness establish the following articles for the benefit of Your Princely Highness and the common welfare, and create a new territorial constitution.[75]

The final goal was a new territorial order, which was to be guided by the principles of the Word of God, brotherly love, and the *bonum commune*.

The peasants and miners in Salzburg were also aiming for a new territorial order based on the principles of the reformation. The "Twenty-four Articles of the Common Assembly of Salzburg" called upon

> each and every lover of evangelical truth and godly law to take counsel, with the consent of all the authorities, on how to take measures and steps to preserve the glory of God and the Christian order; and in so far as these have been perverted by the enemies of God, how to reform them again and return them to their proper order and nature.[76]

The enemies of God, the "anti-Christian villains, destroyers of souls, and seducers" have "led the multitude of the common people far from the path of evangelical truth and to the devil with very seductive means, and in the process have devoured the common welfare."[77] The articles portrayed the loss of the salvation of souls and the chaos in the world as a result of the suppression of evangelical truth, which had to form the basis of a reformation of the ecclesiastical and secular order. The proposals put forth by the Salzburg peasants were nothing new, but they do reveal the profound pent-up hatred for the Roman church that was released by the reformation movement. In the first place, they demand that the pure Word of God must be "preached without any human nonsense or precept or embellishment." This demand is justified with reference to simony, fraud, the raging against evangelical truth, and the false councils and decrees, which have "cast a veil over the eyes of true Scripture."[78] Second, the articles assert that the community shall have the authority to appoint and dismiss its pastor. This demand is justified with reference to Rome's practice of appointing courtiers to the parishes, who never carried out their duties, "never preached," appointed incompetent vicars to take their place, and left "their mistresses and children" to the charity of the community. No longer should considerations of any kind be shown to clerics of this sort, "instead one must tear open the bag-string and pour out the filth and see such simony and villainy and robbery in the light of day."[79] Third, the articles declare that the pastor will be supported through the tithe, which henceforth would be collected by the church wardens and serve to supply the pastor with housing, clothing, and food, in accordance with the judgment of the community. An end should be put to the abuses related to the tithe. These abuses had been driven by greed and fraud and had merely contributed to the "gluttony of the rich and the strengthening of their arrogance." But if the tithe was meant as an offering to God, which it now wasn't, it belonged to the poor; consequently whatever was not needed to support the pastor would go to the poor.[80]

This powerful denunciation of the clergy probably came from the pen of a preacher,[81] but the grievances from Gastein attest that this mood and these kinds of demands were widespread throughout the region.[82] This is also confirmed by the way the community of Gastein dealt with its pastor in June of 1525, who under threat of violence was forced to return the parish's assets, which he had taken to safety outside the valley.[83]

THE MESSAGE SPREADS

The Zurich countryside, Upper Swabia, and Tyrol were centers of peasants' reformation. Impulses radiated from here into the neighboring territories and promoted the vision of a new kind of church. Upper Swabia, however, was particularly prominent, because the repeated reprinting of the Twelve Articles that were drafted here ensured them a particularly wide radius of influence.

The peasants of distant Ichtershausen, near Gotha, informed Duke Johann of Saxony at the end of April "that we want to choose, as we see fit, a pastor who shall proclaim to us the Word of God clearly and unadulterated with human doctrine; to supply the same pastor with a suitable income, and, if he acts improperly, to dismiss him."[84] The historical context makes it quite clear that this demand was inspired by the Twelve Articles.[85] At the same time the peasants around Fulda demanded the following: "since there is need to save the souls of mankind, the gospel shall be preached pure and clear without any human additions, and we are to be provided with evangelical priests and curates." And they referred implicity to the source of their demands by saying that "the Twelve Articles, as they have now emanated from the peasants of the Black Band, shall remain in force."[86]

A line of continuity connects the grievance list from the Rheingau with the customary of 1324 from the same region.[87] The following demand, however, seems to reflect outside inspiration: "henceforth an entire community shall have the authority to choose its own pastor, who will proclaim the truth; where this is not done, the same community shall have the authority to dismiss its pastor and choose another one."[88] A few weeks earlier, the peasants in the county of Hanau-Lichtenberg, on the western border of the empire, had sent a paraphrased and shortened version of the Twelve Articles to the imperial city of Strasbourg along with a note "to establish the gospel in this manner."[89] In the territory of the city of Basel, the following threefold demands appeared at the beginning of May: election of the pastor, support of the pastor through the large tithe, and abolition of the small tithe. At the end of August, finally, these same demands were faintly echoed in the Bern countryside.[90]

It is likely that influences radiating from Zurich and Upper Swabia crossed paths in Basel and Bern, although wherever they spread, they always underwent an independent development. Franconia is a test case that allows us to illustrate this general observation in greater detail. The Amorbach Articles adhered very closely to their Upper Swabian model, down to the choice of words.[91] The demand for the right to appoint the pastor played a particularly important role among the Twelve Articles, as might be inferred from the oath which Franconian nobles had to swear when they joined the peasant federation, either voluntarily or under compulsion. Apart from a general obligation to uphold the Twelve Articles, the formula of the oath placed special emphasis on the following provision:

wherever there is a hamlet or district belonging to a nobleman, in which the pastor is unlearned and bad at preaching the Word of God, that pastor shall be dismissed and the community shall choose someone who is more capable and agreeable to them.[92]

In fact, it can be shown that more regionally limited peasant articles, as for example those from the villages of Rothenburg's territory from the end of March, did not yet contain an article concerning the election of the pastor.[93] However, one should not derive from this the general conclusion that the peasants in Franconia did not develop similar conceptions of the reformation; in fact, the example of the community of Wendelstein which I cited earlier seems to suggest exactly the opposite. Further confirmation comes with the events of the summer of 1524, when pro-reformation movements led to widespread refusals to pay the tithe in and around Forchheim and in the Nuremberg region.[94]

All this leads us to believe—even in the almost complete absence of local grievances—that the Twelve Articles touched a latent predisposition for a communal reformation among the peasants. From Franconia also arose the efforts to ensure such a vision of the reformation would receive general recognition within the empire. The following provision was inserted into Friedrich Weygandt's reform program for the empire: "let every community strive for good shepherds who will pasture their flock solely on the Word of God as grounded in the Scripture; it shall appoint and dismiss them";[95] this in turn imposed upon the community the obligation of supporting their pastor. In principle Weygandt always maintained that a "Reformacion" of the empire would need the help of the theologians; after all, the widespread demand in Franconia for a "Reformacion" involved a thorough Christianization of society as an extension and continuation of reformation doctrine. But the right of appointing pastors was hardly among the issues that were still considered open for discussion. Prior to the planned meetings between the peasants and the authorities, the spiritual and secular princes, the electorates of Cologne and Trier, Brandenburg, Bavaria, the nobility, and the imperial cities were to promise on oath to accept the Twelve Articles. If it were necessary the peasants would force them to do so, following the example of the Franconian peasants, who had compelled the archbishopric of Mainz in May of 1525 to accept the Twelve Articles.[96] By binding the imperial estates to the Twelve Articles on oath, Weygandt wrote to Wendel Hipler, "that other undertaking [he means the "Reformacion"] would gain an instrument with its own inherent means of enforcement. For if any prince or lord does not keep his word and breaks his seal and oath, there is no doubt that his own subjects will kill him."[97] What emerges in these words is a political dimension of the peasants' reformation that was very threatening to the princes. It would be premature, however, to discuss it at this time. It is sufficient to point out that Weygandt's ideas were rooted in the Franconian reformation movement. In Amorbach he had joined the "bright shining band" of peasants, and as a fiscal official (*Rentamtmann*) in the town of Miltenberg, in the territory of the electorate of Mainz, he had actively campaigned for a reformation-minded preacher.[98]

Our analysis has shown that, despite local variations in details, the peasants' conception of reformation was centered on the appointment of the pastor by the community. Secondary were the implications which flowed from this central concern, and which were elaborated to varying degrees from one region to the next. The southern boundary of the demand for the election of the pastor ran from Solothurn across the Zurich countryside to St. Gall, and from there via Rhaetia to the Trentino and finally into the Salzburg area.[99]

In the north the line ran from Erfurt via Fulda and Mainz to the western border of the empire.[100] Lorraine and Burgundy marked the boundary in the west. Bavaria became a barrier to the further spread eastward and prevented a direct link-up of Franconia and Salzburg.

PRECONDITIONS AND CONSEQUENCES OF THE PEASANT IDEA OF REFORMATION

Wherever peasants stood up for the reformation movement, they insisted on the appointment of the pastor by the community. The community for its part would assume the responsibility of supporting the pastor, either at its own expense or by placing the tithe under communal control. This was the essence of the peasant conception of the reformation, which we encounter in the most diverse regions of Central Europe.

To place this finding in the proper perspective, we must first examine whether the scattered references about the extent of this peasant conception can be made generally valid. In the case of Upper Swabia it is enough to point out that its Federal Ordinance adopted the article on the appointment of pastors, and this covers the area between the Lech River and the Black Forest, between the Danube and Lake Constance. One may estimate that perhaps 30,000 peasants stood behind the program of the Upper Swabians.[101] The communal reformation had equally broad support in the duchy of Württemberg and Franconia.[102] The area adjacent to Upper Swabia and Württemberg, the Upper Rhine region—the Black Forest, Breisgau, Sundgau—decreed the following in its Federal Ordinance:

> Item, wherever there are pastors (vicars we totally reject), they shall be kindly asked from now on to proclaim the gospel and to recognize and put an end to their error. Those who wish to do so shall receive from their parish an adequate livelihood suitable to their office. But those who do not wish to do this shall be dismissed and the parish shall be given to someone else elected by the parishioners.[103]

About 10,000 peasants—not counting the Sundgau, for which we have no figures—must have supported this demand.[104] The Meran Articles, representing at first only the peasants of southern Tyrol, were presented at the diet in Innsbruck and thus became the binding program for all districts and towns of the Tyrol. The same goes for the Twenty-four Articles of the Common Assembly of Salzburg, which the cities, hamlets, and rural districts took as the basis for their negotiations with Archbishop Matthäus Land in the provincial assembly.[105] The so-called Second Ilanz Manifesto (Artikelbrief) of 1526 laid down for the three Rhaetian leagues that "each community shall have the authority to elect and dismiss its pastor at any time, as it sees fit."[106]

This sketch of the peasants' ideas regarding religion and the church covers the area from Alsace to Salzburg and from Graubünden to Franconia, thus emphasizing the extremely broad appeal of reformation stirrings in rural society. What were the conditions in rural society that allowed the reformation movement to spread so widely?

RURAL PREDISPOSITION TOWARD
COMMUNALIZATION OF THE CHURCH

A particularly good example for studying the background to the communalization of the church is the canton of Graubünden. There are two reasons for this: first, in Graubünden the right of the community to elect its pastor was not inseparably linked to reformation doctrine, a fact which allows us to isolate the areas of conflict between peasant society and the old church; second, the problems that were seen to affect the church and the faith were very broadly conceived, and this allows us to define more precisely the question we are examining.

Our analysis will be based on two constitutional documents, the two so-called Ilanz Manifestos (*Artikelbriefe*) from 1524 and 1526.[107] They were issued by the "district judges [*lanndrichter*] and the community of the Three Unions [*drü pünth*] . . . for us and all those who reside in and live in our Three Unions."[108] The Three Unions referred to were the League of God's House (*Gotteshausbund*), the League of the Ten Jurisdictions (*Zehngerichtebund*), and the Gray League (*Grauer Bund*), all of which had emerged during the late Middle Ages. Characteristic of all Unions was a strong representation of the peasant-communal element,[109] although the leagues varied in the vigor of this representation. The League of the Ten Jurisdictions was an exclusively peasant association, while the League of God's House was more or less a corporation of territorial estates with the bishop of Chur as its territorial lord. The older local historians summed up the historical development of Graubünden with the phrase "from feudalism to democracy."[110] Although this terminology is not without its problems, it does indicate a real trend, namely the growing influence of rural communes. The shift of political weight within the estates is revealed by the fact that the bishop of Chur no longer placed his seal on the first comprehensive Federal Charter of the Three Unions, in which we can see the outlines of a communal polity of "Graubünden."[111] The sources we are about to examine are therefore texts which clearly bear the imprint of peasant communes.[112] Since they applied to all of Graubünden, we may assume that the problems and solutions they outline are very broadly representative.

The first of the Ilanz Articles of 1525 decreed:

> in order that the word and teaching of Christ will be more faithfully proclaimed to the common man and he will not be lead astray, henceforth no one—be he pastor, chaplain, monk, courtier, or of whatever estate or title—shall be accepted as an absentee holder of the benefices in our Unions nor shall we give out such absentee appointments. Instead, every pastor shall reside in and personally look after his parish or benefice, assuming he has one and has been appointed to it.[113]

If a clergyman had good reasons for why he could not meet the residence requirement, and if the pastoral duties were to be entrusted to a different clergyman, this had to be done "with the goodwill and consent of community or parishioners in which the benefice is located." Anyone who made clandestine arrangements behind the community's back "has forfeited his benefice, and the parishioners shall appoint someone else who seems suitable and competent." The same sentiment informs the stipulation that in filling a vacant post, the "feudal lord" of the church—a common Swiss term for what in southern Germany is more frequently known as the "patron lord"—must act in concert with the "parishioners." The community wants its pastor in the village, and it wants to have a say in deciding who that pastor will be. The peasants were primarily concerned about reliable pastoral care; consequently, "each pastor shall remain with his subjects in times of mortal danger, he shall faithfully look after and comfort them as best he can, on pain of losing his benefice." But a

second concern was that pastors set a good example of Christian living, "so that the common man may learn and follow their good example."
Two years later the demand for better pastoral care read:

It is our belief that from now on each and every pastor shall be given a decent and proper livelihood as he deserves, from whatever property [*guott*] a community deems appropriate, as is just and proper, and each and every community shall also have the authority at any time to appoint and dismiss its pastor, as it sees fit.[114]

The pastor thus became totally dependent on the parish community, in regard to both his income and his job security. This radicalization was the logical extension of a movement that was no longer willing to accept the validity of traditional Christian norms or put up with the growing abuses within the church. The radicalization of the church ordinances that were issued for Graubünden no doubt owed something to the reformation movement, which experienced a certain high point in 1525, as the Religious Disputation of Ilanz attests. Under the direction of the delegates of the Three Unions, a dispute was held in Ilanz in January of 1526, but it eventually ended without having produced any concrete results.[115] No theological agreement was reached, although the anticlerical sentiment seems to have intensified considerably. We see this reflected in the Second Ilanz Manifesto, and the explanation may be the Religious Disputation itself, which failed to bring about the breakthrough of the reformation doctrine, apparently because of the canons of Chur, whose influence still seems to have been considerable.

If we return to a comparison of the two manifestos, the growing aggression toward the Roman church manifested itself also in restrictive legislation aimed at the ecclesiastical court of the bishop of Chur. In 1524, the peasants decreed by "statute" that "masses and other Christian services shall be conducted" even if the commune and the land have been placed under interdict,[116] since the interdict was being irresponsibly and improperly used. Moreover, the court's alleged illegal expansion of its jurisdiction was strongly cut back in favor of the commune:

This we have decreed and decided to staunchly uphold: from now on a cleric cannot cite a layman before the ecclesiastical court, or a layman a cleric, or a layman another layman, nor in any way place him under ban on account of money owed, insults, felonies [*fräffel*], or any other quarrels,[117]

with the exception of marital disputes and demands for the payment of rents to the church or benefice; the disputes now fell within the jurisdiction of the communal court of the defendant. The ecclesiastical court in Chur was further prohibited from charging inflated court fees and was ordered to conduct the proceedings in the German language.[118] The Second Ilanz Manifesto of 1526 replaced these elaborate stipulations with the terse statement that the bishop should be stripped of every kind of jurisdiction.[119]

In 1524, the peasants contemplated several measures concerned with an "inexpensive" church; the pastors were to behave "in a priestly manner, as is becoming to their position."[120] Because "the poor, honest common people had been burdened with great expenses for consecrations [wichen], be they of churches, chapels, altars, liturgical vestments, or other things," the leaders of the Unions reduced the customary special revenues for the suffragans to food and a suitable gift. In 1526 the "inexpensive" church was no longer a problem; the secular jurisdiction of the bishop was abolished and the monasteries were placed on the road to eventual secularization. These measures provided the communes with sufficient income to give their pastors a suitable livelihood.

Graubünden is an interesting test case, because the reformation movement here did not boast of any particularly distinguished exponents of theological matters. Moreover, communications between the city of Chur, which was favorably inclined toward the reformation, and the outlying districts was enormously difficult because the latter were in isolated locations and could be reached only via mountain passes that were often impassable for months at a time. All this strengthens the argument that outside influences, carried either by peasants from other areas or prominent theologians, remained relatively negligible. Thus the Bündner sources touch upon three areas of conflict: pastoral care for the community, the "inexpensive" church, and the ecclesiastical court.

First among the demands repeatedly raised by the peasants were the residency requirement for the pastor and the elimination of vicars as preconditions for obtaining proper pastoral care for the community. As we learn from the Federal Ordinances of the upper Rhine and Upper Swabia as well as from the Articles of Tyrol and Salzburg, opposition to the vicariate was not directed against the institution itself but against its abuse.[121] Because of incorporation, absenteeism, or pluralism, parishes were not adequately staffed and the pastoral duties were left to vicars who were not even paid enough. In 1525 the community of Gossau, in the jurisdiction of the prince-abbey St. Gall, complained to the communities under the monastery's overlordship "that parishes and their revenue are no longer bestowed upon proper pastors who reside in the benefices; instead parishes are looked after by vicars who are given a salary while the remainder is collected by the monastery."[122] The case of Gossau sheds some light on the reasons behind the rejection of vicars, which often seems puzzling because it is not explained. Gossau complained to the monastery that its previous abbot, Franz Gaisberg, had, "with papal authority," brought the parish "into the hands and power of the monastery, seizing for itself the rents, tithe, revenues, and landed property belonging to the parish."[123] The parish had been granted to the deacon of the monastery, who for his part used the revenues to pay for a vicar. The chronicler of the imperial city of St. Gall, a credible witness and one who was familiar with local conditions, reported that in 1516 the abbot of the monastery

had [obtained] a papal bull that he might lease all his incorporated benefices to the members of the convent. The latter may then provide the parishes with lay priests who have to be changed as they see fit, and thus the lords are in the convent and the priests do the work.[124]

This passage may contain the real motive for the peasants' rejection of the vicars: a proper parish was entitled to a proper pastor. And a proper pastor was entitled to draw from his benefice and the church revenues—for example, the tithe—a proper income appropriate to his standing and office. The mayor (*Schultheiß*) and council of Liestal demanded from their tithe holder, the cathedral chapter of Basel,

> that you sincerely provide our churches and us with the word of God from the three parts of the tithe, which we pay and in return for which you do nothing for us, so that we shall not suffer any shortcoming or injury, and especially that you compensate our current priest, whom we like, so that he can remain and will not be taken from us.[125]

Appointing candidates to benefices that were still occupied, absenteeism, incorporation, and pluralism—all these practices alienated a church from its village. In the prince-abbey of St. Gall the papal Curia obtained the right to appoint future candidates to numerous parishes, of course only to those which yielded a very substantial income. What this could lead to can be seen in the case of Henau. Its pastor, a certain Schindelin, who had held the post since 1502, had to vacate the parish in 1506 on orders from the abbot of St. Gall to make room for the courtier Jakob Stäbiner; and since Schindelin initially refused to leave, he was excommunicated in addition to being dismissed.[126] The various diocesan bishops granted the right to be an absentee holder of a benefice in return for a fee; how widespread absenteeism was is difficult to gauge.[127] Absenteeism could severely affect the quality of pastoral care and be seen as an insult by the community, as we learn from the case of Gantersheim, whose pastor Gebhard had purchased from the court the right of nonresidence between 1479 and 1482.[128]

More important still were, undoubtedly, the practice of incorporation and the entire system of benefices. Through incorporation a parish church along with its income was absorbed by an ecclesiastical institution—a monastery, a prince-bishopric, or a hospital. The revenues of the benefice that originally went to the pastor—church revenues, a portion of the tithe or specific kinds of tithes, endowments—would now flow into the coffers of the incorporating institution, and the pastoral duties would thereafter be in the hands of chaplains, vicars, or possibly monks. But in every case the pastoral care for the community suffered. Vicars and chaplains commonly drew a very meager salary, which explains why they tried to better their income by charging fees for some of their services. As members of monastic orders, monks were naturally not required to reside within the parishes. Frequently they only celebrated Sunday Mass and were not available to the faithful for emergency sacramental services, such as Extreme Unction. In Augsburg, 57 percent of the 1,000 parishes were incorporated on the eve of the reformation; in the dioceses of Worms, Constance, and Strasbourg the percentage may have been even higher; in Württemberg the ratio of pastors to vicars has been estimated at 1:5.[129]

Pluralism had the same deleterious effects. If a single cleric held numerous appointments, he was not able to meet the pastoral duties in each benefice but had to entrust them to a vicar or curate. Naturally the latter were paid less than the benefice yielded—that, after all, was the logic of the system. The extent of pluralism is almost impossible to recover from the sources. However, we must imagine a broad range, from the three benefices of Wattwil, Henau, and Jonschwil held by Dr. Anton Thalmann of Toggenburg[130] (territory of St. Gall), to a Dutch cardinal's 100 benefices all over Europe.[131]

All this explains the peasants' demand that the pastor must reside in the village and be properly supported. The purpose of these changes was to reestablish what was believed to have been the original, purer form of pastoral care, the "inexpensive" church. "And since we have been informed by the gospel" that divine services "are given free of charge by God and not sold for money,"[132] the peasants in Wendelstein (Franconia) refused to pay for any of the pastor's services. The pastor of the Upper Swabian community of Langenerringen, who had "no house of his own" and received so little of the grain tithe that "he can barely feed his chickens," was to receive a "proper livelihood" from the large tithe. To that end the community threatened to stop paying the tithe unless their tithe lord supported the pastor properly.[133] The Salzburg peasants complained that the clergy had "urged simple people in confession to give money . . . when someone was taken ill, the confessors urged the sick person and got a florin for the confessor." Finally, they had "sold the holy ground dearly for a lot of money, as they demanded from a dead body 4, 5, 6, or even 8 or 10 fl."[134] At Hochheim near Mainz, it was customary that when "a poor man or servant wishes to get married, he must give the pastor a fee of 6 albus and 1 wax candle."[135] The villages of the city of Schaffhausen on the upper Rhine demanded that the tithe be used exclusively for communal needs. It was to be used primarily

> to support the one who serves the community, preaches the Word of God, administers the sacraments to the people and also looks after them in life and death, so that from now on we shall be free from other burdens, such as services for the dead, ban fines [bannschätz], for penance fees, court fees [Richtgeld], baptismal fees, offerings, and all the other hardships.

Outside the parish village, in hamlets and isolated places, "in times when heavy storms . . . water or snow" make it impossible for the people to come to church, "a mass shall be celebrated there at no expense to the poor people and for no special fee."[136]

Where the authorities supported and promoted the reformation movement, as for example in the city of Zurich, such grievances were redressed and thereby acknowledged to be legitimate. Similarly the imperial city of Basel promised the districts in its territory that it would take steps so that "the secular priests . . . will be [provided for] by the large tithe, in order that they will have an adequate livelihood and must no longer search for an income by burdening their subjects, as has hitherto been the case."[137] Indeed, even the nobility and the cities on the upper Rhine apparently could not evade the legitimate demands of the peasants. In an agreement they conceded

that the pastors shall have a decent, suitable, and adequate support from these tithes, such that a pastor—as it should be—will not press for additional exactions in church, be they offerings, confessional fees, or other dues; rather, he shall be at the service of each and every parishioner without any special compensation.[138]

The demand for a resident pastor and a "cost-free" church were complementary, as the examples have amply demonstrated. A pastor who drew a proper living from the revenues of his church had no need to burden his subjects with special fees for pastoral care and to sell his services like so much merchandise. Of course, communal control seemed the best guarantee that this demand would in fact be met. The communal principle which emerged here also formed part of the basis for the enormously strong opposition to the ecclesiastical court.

The effectiveness of the ecclesiastical courts must have varied considerably from region to region. We know of very few complaints from Upper Swabia and the Tyrol, while in Alsace, in the Rhine valley in Vorarlberg and Graubünden, and in Salzburg they seem to have been widespread and were directed against the ecclesiastical courts of the bishops of Strasbourg, Chur, and Salzburg.[139] The Salzburg peasants complained to the clerics that they were being sued in the ecclesiastical court "for debts, worldly goods, injuries, insults, fights, blows, sexual misconduct [Unzucht], and material or worldly matters," even though "these things did not concern matters of the faith or the gospel." The peasants now demanded that such cases be heard before a secular court.[140] The same thing was demanded by the city of Forchheim and its surrounding villages: the clerics were to sue for rent and debt in regular secular courts.[141] The Rheingau peasants declared that henceforth they "would not accept . . . any summons, inhibition, edict, and the like in worldly cases, such as concerned secular goods, debts, and like matters."[142]

The peasants' opposition to ecclesiastical courts had two aspects. First, they refused to tolerate any longer the special status of clerics, their separate jurisdiction, their aloofness from society—a sentiment which goes very well with the noticeable trend toward a communalization of the church. Second, they refused to accept any longer ecclesiastical punishments for secular transgression, meaning punishment through the exclusion or temporary exclusion from the church.

The ecclesiastical courts in the empire competed with their secular counterparts. They held jurisdiction over clerics and in issues relevant to canon law, such as adultery, oath-breaking, and the tithe. Whenever the church was involved in legal transactions—whether through its representatives in person or through monasteries, cathedral chapters, or hospitals as rent collectors—adjudication could go to the ecclesiastical courts, with possibilities of appeal first to the relevant episcopal court and eventually all the way to Rome. A trip to the ecclesiastical court was long and costly for a peasant, and the whole procedure could be rather meaningless because the proceedings were not infrequently conducted in Latin. Karl Stenzel, who has done one of the few detailed studies on ecclesiastical courts, has described the working of the court of the bishop of Strasbourg:

> . . . with no regard for the prescribed or proper timetables, people are dragged right from the field in the midst of their work for every trivial matter, to answer before the court as defendant or witness. Harsh sentences are swiftly passed, imprisonment [Fröhnungen] is ordered even if there is no reason to fear that the defendant might abscond and in the absence of any other danger. Notwithstanding the strict prohibitions in the statutes, the ban, expulsion, suspension of the Mass, and the interdict are placed upon the insolvent debtor and the entire community in the most trivial matters, and the former is driven from his house and home into misery without any pity or mercy.[143]

Apparently such extreme abuses were not found everywhere. I have earlier noted the absence of complaints in the Tyrol against the ecclesiastical courts. The reason for this was probably that the territorial constitution of 1404, republished in 1486, had severely restricted the jurisdiction of the ecclesiastical courts to matters involving the tithe, services for the dead, and marital issues. I should mention, though, that the preamble to the constitution speaks of earlier complaints as one of the reasons for its redaction.[144]

THEOLOGICAL JUSTIFICATION AND EVANGELICAL LOGIC OF THE COMMUNAL REFORMATION

The neglect of pastoral care, the commercialization of sacramental services, the abuse of ecclesiastical courts—from the perspective of the peasants these were corruptions and aberrations within the church which had to be corrected. Naturally enough a peasants' reformation of the church, given its view of things and its needs, had to start from the very foundation of the church hierarchy, the parish community. It was within the community that the conditions of the church had to be set right again. This could be most readily accomplished if the community itself obtained greater say in the appointment of the pastor and regained control over how its contributions to the church—tithe, Widdum, and endowments—would be administered. Concern for the welfare of souls was certainly the decisive impulse behind these efforts. It is also well known that already in the Middle Ages, and increasingly so in the late Middle Ages, rural people strove to obtain better pastoral care by means of a denser network of parishes. Moreover, the evidence of the few existing visitation records from the end of the fifteenth century shows that rural communities in general took a strong interest in the Mass and religious instruction.[145] These fundamentally religious needs also explain why the demand for the election of the pastor could prevail only if it was based on a predominantly theological justification. The demand for the pure preaching of the gospel "without human additions"—a contemporary slogan for the rejection of traditional Roman church doctrine—was the only justification invoked, and its inherent logic invariably led to the demand for communal appointment of pastors and the idea of communal Christendom. To back this up again with references to the sources would simply be a repetition of my regional analyses. I will only briefly recapitulate the argument: the categorical demand of a "pure gospel" placed the pastor under obligation to behave accordingly, and it obliged the patrons and feudal lords to provide their parishes with evangelical preachers. Where that was not done, the community, for the welfare of its soul, had to take matters into its own hands, even if that meant violating existing legal rights. Of course this was always the final step; as far as we can tell, there is no known case where the peasants did not initially try to obtain an evangelical pastor by petitioning their patron lord and the authorities.

The abuses within the church made the peasants generally predisposed for a reform of the church on a communal basis; only the theology of the "pure gospel" gave rise to the concrete demand to elect the pastor and to the comprehensive and total communalization of the church.

We can reexamine and empirically verify this argument by looking at the controversies involving the tithe. The reassertion of communal control over the tithe and the right to appoint the pastor were in a sense reciprocally linked; each was the precondition and consequence of the other. Correspondingly, the "pure gospel" was of equal importance as a justification in both cases. The tithe was among those rights of lordship most strongly denounced by the peasants.[146] The primary reason for this was probably not the fact that the tithe, in the form of the large tithe of grain, loomed largest among all the charges exacted from the peasants, normally far exceeding the rent to the lord, not to mention the taxes to the territorial ruler.[147] Rather, what needs to be emphasized is the fact that the tithe was constantly expanding—usually under the name of "small tithe." The peasants of Hochheim near Mainz had to pay the small tithe on lambs, pigs, chickens, geese, apples, pears, and nuts, the Salzburg peasants on all livestock, the peasants on the upper Rhine on all livestock and fruit, as well as on wood, flax, beets, and onions.[148] It appeared that there was no limit to what could be tithed. The peasants of Truttikon in Switzerland saw no logic in this system; it was unreasonable that they had to tithe pigs and chickens, since they had already paid the tithe on the feed for the animals. At Christmas time the abbot of Rheinau sent a servant who collected from every resident [*Hausgenosse*] a penny as tithe on each calf and each herb garden.[149] All this explains the strong emotional opposition to the tithe in general, and it invariably grew even more intense wherever the idea gained ground "that the tithe was nothing other than a charitable offering"[150] that belonged to the poor, or that the tithe had to be repaid with a return service, namely pastoral care. These ideas probably never completely disappeared from rural society, for without them it would be difficult to explain why even before the "pure gospel" dictated the amount and use of the tithe, the Upper Swabian peasants demanded in 44 percent of their grievance lists the abolition of the small tithe, and in 41 percent the conversion of the large tithe or its rededication to a different use.[151]

It is quite clear that the fundamental attack on the tithe was launched from the basis of the "pure gospel." Peasants in Alsace denied that they had to pay more than the grain tithe: "in this we base ourselves on scripture."[152] Peasants in the Swabian-Franconian border region declared that "according to the gospel we are not obligated to pay" the small tithe.[153] The villages of the imperial cities of Memmingen and Solothurn rejected all legal claims to every kind of tithe, "because," as the Memmingen peasants put it, "the New Testament does not impose this duty on us"; they declared their willingness, however, to support the pastor.[154] To the Salzburg peasants the tithe became the veritable work of the devil, because it "has no foundation in Scripture."[155]

What eventually prevailed were relatively uniform ideas regarding the obligation of paying the tithe and the use to which it should be put, ideas that were probably strongly influenced by the Twelve Articles, although we cannot be certain of that.[156] The small tithe was in principle no longer paid. The large tithe was withdrawn (with or without compensation) from those who collected it (cathedral chapters, monasteries, hospitals, nobles) and redirected to new uses: to support the pastors, to help the village poor, and, if necessary, to pay for taxes. Control passed into the hands of the community, which collected the tithe and determined how much would be distributed to the pastor and the poor.

The appointment of pastors and the communal control of the tithe greatly expanded the community's sphere of jurisdiction, but this growth in autonomy was grounded solely in the peasants' interpretation of the "pure gospel."

It appears that the practical application of the theoretical principle of the pure gospel quickly led to uncertainties and difficulties for the peasants. What was to be done if a pastor claimed to be preaching in accordance with the gospel, while the community believed he was not? Who would decide which view of the Eucharist was truly evangelical, that of the Roman church, Luther's, or Zwingli's? Which cleric was interpreting the message of the New Testament correctly? Interpretation could clearly not boil down to mere biblical philology—the Sermon on the Mount, if taken literally, could expose mankind to starvation. The linking of the two principles "pure gospel" and "appointment of the pastor by the community" in the end had to place the decision on correct doctrine into the hands of the community—a conclusion which the peasants drew only hesitantly, unwillingly, driven by circumstances rather than conviction. Correspondingly rare were statements demanding the authority over doctrine in the same uncompromising way that they demanded the right to elect the pastor. What we read in the Federal Ordinances of the upper Rhine and Upper Swabia seems comparatively forceful. In cases of doctrinal disputes between adherents of the old faith and the new faith,

> the pastors of the same region or villages [Flecken] shall be called together with their Bibles, and they shall decide and settle the matter in accordance with the content of Holy Scripture and not in accordance with human discretion, in the presence of the common parishioners of the same localities.[157]

In doubtful cases a religious debate was thus to be held, apparently based on the premise that the Bible was its own interpreter, and—here our interpretation runs into uncertainties—that the faithful, the parishioners, were able to distinguish true from false doctrine. The Tyrolean peasants seem to have believed that such issues could be settled through the constitutional powers and institutions of the land, the territorial ruler and the diet; that, in any case, is how one could interpret their presentation of demands to Archduke Ferdinand.[158] The only religious debate that was in fact organized by peasants was the Ilanz Disputation,[159] although we must seriously ask whether the Three Unions did not arrange this event in their capacity as a governing body. The Franconian peasants, by comparison, were inclined to let "those learned in the holy, godly, true Scripture" decide "what is established by the holy gospel."[160]

Despite such uncertainties the reformation demand for the "pure gospel" set free a powerful social dynamic within the evangelical movement, whose manifestations deserve close examination. What prompted the peasants to transfer the pure gospel into the secular realm was the intent—in the language of the Twelve Articles—"to hear the gospel and to live accordingly."[161] The gospel should not only be preached, but one "should follow it and live in accord with it," as the Württemberg peasants said.[162] As the peasants of the district of Thauer-Rettenberg in Tyrol saw it, the gospel gave rise to the command "henceforth to live in its godly spirit in accordance with its statutes and commandments."[163] Thus the gospel became the guiding principle for the life of the world—the evangelical logic of the communal reformation was beginning to unfold. The social and political orders were measured with the yardstick of the gospel. The villages of the imperial city of Rothenburg wrote to the city council that on the basis of the "eternal Word of God we find . . . that we are sorely oppressed in many ways," and this was the justification for presenting their demands.[164] And the peasants of the Klettgau demanded from the city of Zurich, the arbiter in their dispute with the counts of Sulz, a judgment "in accordance with the only true guideline (that is, the Word of God)."[165]

This practice of legitimizing the demands to the authorities by deriving them from the gospel was widespread.[166] Because of the many copies in which the Twelve Articles were circulated, its wording became the classic model. All demands by the lords were justified to the extent that they could be grounded in Scripture, and all grievances of the peasants were justified to the extent that they could be verified with biblical passages.[167] As far as we can tell, the formulation in the Twelve Articles was a more precisely thought out and more carefully worded successor to a version that is attested earlier on the upper Rhine. The latter had intended to take measures "for the peace of the land and the quiet of the poor," to the extent that the measures "conformed to Scripture," and it renounced all demands "that are seen to be incompatible with or even contrary to Scripture."[168] The chancery of the Baltringen peasants in a sense anticipated the wording of the Twelve Articles when it wrote: "Whatever that same Word of God takes and gives, we shall gladly accept it and take what good and bad it brings us."[169] The gospel no longer pointed the way only to the salvation of the soul; in equal measures it outlined the secular order.

Understandably enough, the real problem for the peasants was formulating consistent guidelines for an evangelical life based on Scripture. The initial helplessness of the peasants is well described in the account of Johann Kessler of St. Gall concerning the events in the camp of the Baltringen peasants in February 1525; in view of Kessler's close personal ties to Upper Swabia, his report is considered highly authentic. When a delegation of the lords appeared in the camp for negotiations, the leader of the Baltringen Band, Huldrich Schmid, asked "for forgiveness," but there was no need for a court session (*Rechtstag*) since "there was no complaint here." The lords, however, insisted on a judicial settlement of the peasants' demands and suggested that the Imperial Cameral Court (*Reichskammergericht*) be used as the authoritative tribunal. Asked by the lords which law the peasants intended to invoke,

Huldrich answered: godly law, which tells every estate what it should and should not do. The lords responded with mocking words: Dear Huldrich, you are asking for godly law. Tell us, who will render such law? God will hardly come down from heaven and hold a court day for us.

Huldrich Schmid did not hesitate with his reply. He would urge all priests to pray to God "that he might indicate and appoint for us learned, pious men who know how to judge and settle this dispute in accord with pure godly Scripture."[170]

The distinction between the gospel and godly law was admittedly slight.[171] Godly law nevertheless joined the gospel as a rallying cry, and we cannot really grasp the peasants' idea of reformation without examining it. The line dividing the gospel and godly law ran between heaven and earth, between the hereafter and life on earth, between the church and the world, although the idea that the two concepts were interlinked, even closely intertwined, was never abandoned. In other words, mankind needed the gospel for the salvation of the soul and godly law for life on this earth. The Upper Swabian Federal Ordinance declared that "whatever we are obliged to render to ecclesiastical or secular authority owing to godly law" shall be duly rendered.[172] The Klettgau peasants considered all services to their lords as questionable "without instruction from godly law."[173] In a brief letter to Archduke Ferdinand of Austria (a mere forty lines), the Allgäu peasants used the phrase "godly law" no less than nine times.[174] Here, too, it was employed as a yardstick to measure to what degree the obligations they owed their lords were admissible. The peasants called upon Ferdinand to be "the protector of godly laws, . . . to graciously protect, shield, and rule [hanthaben] us under the godly laws, and not to let us be oppressed." The appeal was directed not to the archduke as the territorial prince but to Ferdinand "as governor and deputy of the Roman imperial majesty"[175]; the emperor was thereby placed under obligation to be the protector of the law,[176] something the peasants did not expect of any territorial prince.[177]

What had the peasants gained by invoking godly law?[178] First of all it gave them a concept to oppose to "venerable law," to "venerable tradition," to the historically evolved law which circumscribed the rights and obligations of peasants and lords. For the peasants to have played off godly law against venerable law makes sense only if they believed that the old law had lost its ethical function, that it was no longer considered useful in solving actual problems and responding to concrete needs. One thing the peasants had clearly learned in the years leading up to the reformation: subjective legal claims could no longer be pushed through on the basis of the old law. We know of sixty peasant revolts in the fifteenth and sixteenth centuries, in each of which the rebels justified their actions with the claim to be restoring the old law.[179] For the most part they achieved no notable success, and reasons for this failure are easy to find. The difficult economic conditions during the late Middle Ages, which affected peasants and lords alike, fueled the struggle over the distribution of agricultural resources. As the peasant revolts show, this struggle eventually turned violent. To prevent the peasants from leaving the land, the lords reactivated older legal titles of serfdom; to take maximum advantage of the high price of timber they used their jurisdiction over the forests to monopolize the woods; to raise rents they undermined the peasants' claims to the land by invoking old land registers (*Urbare*); to raise taxes they dressed up their patronage and protective rights as territorial sovereignty. Old law could now hold its own only if it was "codified" old law. Its ethical substance was weakened as individual self-interest became increasingly dominant, with the result that the legal norms were defined by the powerful. The making of law by the lords increasingly displaced the legal principles of the peasants,[180] chartered law acquired greater force than witness testimony,[181] and forged charters were played off against the traditional rights of the peasants.[182] The hopeless impotence of the old law explains why the peasants sought refuge in godly law.

We can illustrate these developments I have sketched out in the abstract with some examples. Around 1490, the peasants of St. Gall expressed their helpless frustration toward their lords with the following battle song: "We're going to catch the abbot's councilors, they are well versed in legal matters . . . they help him make false documents, make them look old and hang them into the smoke, and many other a ruse they think up."[183] The complaint that the monastery's lawyers were forging documents by smoking new pages of parchment drew only a half-hearted denial from the abbot. More important for our purposes is the obvious helplessness and frustration which the song expresses. This explains why the peasants of St. Gall also had recourse to godly law. "Since it has now come about by God's grace and help and through the Word of God," the peasants of the community of Steinach declared in 1525, "that they and others may present their grievances, they believe they should be allowed once again to cut building timber and firewood, as it used to be of old."[184] The liberating power of the gospel becomes strikingly apparent here. Even the use of wood could no longer be regulated within the system of the old tradition. It was only the invocation of the newly discovered gospel which made it possible to formulate grievances in the first place. All the problems which the previous generations had been unable to solve now came to the fore. Death taxes were "against the doctrine and the Word of God, and against Christian brotherly love," the confiscation of the estates of illegitimate children was "against godly law, against the holy Scripture, and no longer acceptable." The demand for freedom to hunt and fish was justified "because all animals on earth and the fish in the water were created by God the Almighty for the common use and sustenance of all mankind." Such concrete issues eventually gave rise to the general demand by the subjects of St. Gall that they should be allowed to live with "the holy Word of God, the gospel, the holy Scripture, and godly truth."[185]

Winfried Becker has labeled godly law as "characteristically empty of content and arbitrary in nature."[186] This may be so, but it hardly diminishes the godly law in comparison with the old law, for the latter was certainly no less arbitrary. Unlike the old law's indeterminacy or arbitrariness, which was based on privileges, the godly law presents us with a more self-critical arbitrariness, for the peasants themselves pleaded with the theologians to provide it with substance or content.

Of course godly law was not merely a negation of the old law. By pointing to the gospel as the source of all norms in human life, it introduced into the hardened mental categories of this pre-Enlightenment society new possibilities of thinking about the nature of man. With godly law as the foundation of all human legal order, natural law was reintroduced to the social discourse, from which the social doctrine of scholasticism had eliminated it by "merging godly law and positive, 'old' law" in the concept of relative natural law.[187] What godly law intended was to "define the content of the central values that are binding in a Christian society, thus holding all legislative action to a predetermined goal."[188] Since many theologians persisted in rejecting the request for clarification, the peasants had no choice; unless they were willing to abandon their reformation they were forced to define godly law through the formulation of ethical principles. The fact that they did this, and the manner in which they did it, had consequences more far-reaching than anyone could have imagined.

POLITICAL CONSEQUENCES: THE GOSPEL'S LOGIC AND THE GODLY LAW

The desire and need to give the gospel and godly law an imminent presence in this world compelled the peasants to create biblically based ethical principles for the social and political orders. By establishing the church in the community, the community as a political institution was given new dignity and legitimacy, which served to elevate the community to a new level of importance as a foundation for political order in the consciousness of rural society.

ETHICAL PRINCIPLES FOR THE
SOCIAL AND POLITICAL ORDER

In the mind of the peasants the gospel and godly law presupposed each other. In so far as the peasants had the firm conviction that godly law could be expounded through the gospel, they frequently used the gospel and godly law as synonymous or mutually interconnected concepts. Once again I should point out that a clean distinction of the gospel and godly law was undoubtedly beyond the peasants' mental powers of abstraction. Nevertheless, we can detect the rudiments of different approaches in deducing ethical norms. Broad ethical guidelines were justified more frequently through the gospel and thus through the New Testament, while individual ethical principles were more likely justified through godly law.

To praise and honor God, to reveal the gospel, and to promote godly law—these were the aims invoked by the Christian Union in Upper Swabia to justify the alliance, which the peasants entered into "especially to increase brotherly love."[189] Kunz Diebold, the leader of the Stephansfeld Band in Alsace, justified the actions of the peasants to the city of Strasbourg by declaring that they wished to promote "the honor of god and the brotherly love of one's fellow man."[190] The peasants in the Black Forest in southwest Germany wanted to serve "the common weal,"[191] and the rural folk in Brixen intended to prohibit usury, "which is after all un-Christian and completely against the common weal."[192]

It is thus not surprising that brotherly love and the common weal were given a prominent place at the very beginning of the regional manifestos and ordinances as guiding principles. The manifesto of the Black Forest peasants tried to get cities and villages to join the Christian Union "in order that the common Christian weal and brotherly love be established, raised up, and increased," and it presented this as the will of God.[193] At the Innsbruck diet of 1525, the representatives of the cities and districts demanded a new territorial constitution, so that "brotherly love will be kept and the common weal promoted," a program that was indirectly justified with reference to the will of God.[194] Even where these two concepts were not explicitly used to describe the aims of the peasants, they were implicit or they followed from the intent of individual demands.

Godly law was held up as justification for demanding the release of hunting, fishing, and the commons from the control of the lords. And occasionally the "Word of God" was invoked with reference to Genesis, as for example in the articles of the villages of Memmingen, which point out that when God created man, "he gave him power over the fish in the seas, the birds in the sky, and over all animals on earth."[195] An interesting argument from natural law appears here, and it soon gained wide popularity. It claims that the use of uncultivated land was open to everyone, a position which found some support even from a historical perspective. Land not under cultivation, whether forests or meadows, rivers or lakes, had always been used by the peasants: the forest for building timber and firewood, the rivers for fishing and for irrigating the meadows. In the fifteenth century this relatively open system was gradually restricted by prohibitions and rules imposed by the lords. The high price of wood, the result of rising demand in the growing cities, led to the exclusion of the peasant from the forest. To satisfy their insatiable hunting passion, the nobility and the clergy preserved too much wild game, and this led to frequent devastation of the fields by deer and wild boars. The lucrative business of raising sheep gave rise to exclusive jurisdictions over the commons by seigneurial and territorial lords.[196]

We cannot begin to estimate the damage to the peasant economy from these restrictions. Judging from the sources from Upper Swabia, the commons, fishing, and hunting were initially not among the primary grievances;[197] apparently it was only the notion of godly law which allowed them to come to the fore. Owing to "godly and common written laws . . . all running waters [shall] be free and open to everyone for fishing and any other uses. . . . on account of godly and righteous laws" everyone shall be allowed "to hunt, shoot, and catch game, both large and small, free of punishment."[198] In the end hardly any of the transregional grievances or programs lacked the demand for the freeing of forest, water, and commons. The explanation for this may be that the concept of godly law or the interpretation of God's intention as expressed in Genesis reactivated old ideas of natural law.[199]

A much clearer connection existed between traditional, general ideas of liberty based on natural law and the demand for the abolition of serfdom, which is found in all articles and programs, and for the most part at the top of the list. The peasants of the upper Rhine fought against serfdom with the argument that "by law every person is originally born free," while the Salzburg peasants rejected it with the comment "that we all are by nature and by God's liberty free and not in bondage."[200] Serfdom was certainly a considerable, sometimes oppressive burden, especially in southwestern Germany and Switzerland. Restrictions on marriage, no freedom of mobility (Freizügigkeitsverbot), frequently high death taxes that could amount to the confiscation of half the inheritance—all this impinged upon the peasants' life in very tangible and direct ways.[201] The titles of the seigneurial lords (Leibherren) were based on the historical law of older servitude.[202] In Central Europe natural law always remained subordinated to historically evolved law until the old feudal order dissolved. Only during the reformation period was the now commonplace concept of fundamental personal liberty successfully justified on theoretical grounds. If God is Lord, the peasants concluded, there can be no lords (Leibherren) over people. "No one but God, our creator, father, and Lord, shall have bondsmen," the villages of Schaffhausen demanded, and many manifestos picked up this direct and concrete justification.[203] In addition, serfdom was also challenged through godly law, and in this way the link to natural law was reestablished, as for example among the peasants at Lake Constance, who felt forced into bondage "against all justice and godly laws."[204]

The gospel and godly law furnished ample arguments to attack various elements of the social and political order and to challenge its very legitimacy. The concept of "brotherly love," derived from the New Testament and applied to the secular order, invariably favored egalitarian tendencies. The "common weal," employed as a concept to counter the "self-interest" of the powerful and the lords, could not but subject the entire system of feudal rents and dues to a critical examination. The reassertion of communal control over the tithe made deep inroads into the system of ownership in the early sixteenth century and could be a serious threat to the economic foundation of feudal lordship; not infrequently the tithe accounted for half of a lord's entire revenues.[205] The demand for the release of forests, waters, and commons threatened not only a status symbol by attacking the feudal monopoly on hunting; given the rapidly rising price for wood, it also endangered economically lucrative privileges. In large parts of upper Germany the rejection of serfdom could essentially uproot noble and ecclesiastical lordship, because lordship as such was not infrequently based on the power over people. It is no coincidence that the manifestos again and again assured the lords that the demand for liberty should not be read as the abolition of every kind of lordship.[206] But it was clear that the nature of authority was to be reexamined, especially since the peasants put a great variety of demands before their lords and the authorities, guided by the goal expressed in the preamble of all manifestos: "to open the gospel," "to support the word of God," and "to protect godly justice." The logic of peasant theology was given an exemplary formulation in the articles of the community of Embrach to the council of Zurich. It is here that serfdom was first challenged with the help of the gospel. The gospel was the source and foundation of "the freedoms," and these freedoms the peasants interpreted in concrete terms to mean "that from now on no one shall be subject to such bondage in body or property."[207] This argument attacked two of the three fundamental, mutually supportive pillars of feudal lordship: serfdom and lordship over the land. Only legal jurisdiction remained unchallenged, and consequently Zurich's lordship was now reduced to the exercise of legal protection. The gospel had thus made the entire political order suspect and had cast its very legitimacy into doubt. Since the lords could not submit to the gospel or to the ethical principles derived from it without abolishing their own positions, the peasants had to redefine the political system themselves. And nothing was more natural for rural society than to approach the problem of the social and political order from the basis of the community.

THE COMMUNITY AS THE BASIS OF THE POLITICAL ORDER

The "pure gospel" had made it possible to communalize the church and had thus strengthened the autonomy of the community. The belief that the community should judge what was true doctrine and was capable of doing so—a belief that was only slowly accepted and then not everywhere—gave the community a completely new and vastly more important place in the broader structure of political groups. The community had arisen in the late Middle Ages from wild roots, as it were, and it had no real place in the political structure of estates or their theoretical underpinnings. Now for the first time this institution was given a theological justification, and in an age virtually obsessed with piety and religiosity—who would dispute that the "reformation century" was such an age?—such justification invariably represented the highest form of legitimacy.

With a church scaled down to the communal level the Roman church became superfluous, and with it the clergy as the leading estate of the existing political order. This loosening of the hierarchical structures could turn into their dissolution under the impact of the ideas of freedom derived from holy Scripture and godly law. The individualism of a personal freedom grounded in God's order of creation could be played off against the traditional feudal ties that bound the peasants.

This background explains the vitality which the community displayed in the reformation period. The peasants' plans for a new political order always took the community as their starting point.[208] In the small territories of the empire, in Upper Swabia, along the upper Rhine, and in Alsace, the communities came together to form so-called bands, which in turn grouped together into the federative structures of the Christian Unions. In this way Upper Swabia, the area of the upper Rhine centered around the Black Forest, and Lower Alsace became political entities, which they had not previously been. Where the peasants encountered political structures based on the estates, they adopted the institutional framework but gave it a totally different character. It was no longer the "estates" that were represented in the diets, but communities—villages and rural communes (Landgemeinden), urban communes and mining communities. Since the institutional Roman church had now been reduced to insignificance, deprived of its political rights and stripped of its economic privileges, the only question that needed to be solved concerned the role of the nobility within the political system. On the whole the peasants were inclined—although it was not always so clearly expressed—to accept the nobility, provided it was willing to submit to the communal associations, the bands, or the Christian Unions.

Irrespective of the regions' differing constitutional structures, as the basic unit of the state the community advanced the principle that elections should determine how political offices were assigned. The communities chose their deputies to the peasant bands or to the territorial diets. The bands elected their representatives in the Christian Unions, and the diets determined through election the provincial government. These political associations, based on completely new principles, were given a constitutional basis in the so-called territorial constitutions (Landesordnungen). In the Tyrol, Salzburg, Württemberg, Alsace, on the upper Rhine, and in Upper Swabia, territorial and federal constitutions were to be drafted, guided by the principle that they should embody principles of the gospel and of godly law and thus lead to a Christianization of society. A still predominantly peasant society thus seemed to have found a form of political organization that was suited to its needs and its disposition. As Ivan Vargas has put it, "the transcendentalization of political protest is the only path toward politicization of the transcendent."[209]

THE SWISS AND GERMAN REFORMATIONS
GO THEIR SEPARATE WAYS

With the theoretical concept of a communally based political order, which was realized in 1525 in Alsace, on the upper Rhine, in Upper Swabia, and in rudimentary forms also in Franconia, the region of southern Germany between the duchy of Lorraine and the duchy of Austria approached the constitutional structures of the Swiss Confederation. In doing so it posed a serious threat to the continued existence of the empire. In the Zurich countryside itself the communal reformation did not produce any far-reaching political ideas—unless one interprets the later Anabaptist movement as such. The explanation for this lies no doubt in the fact that the community held a secure place within the structure of the state. Zurich headed off the peasants' reformation when the council itself vigorously promoted the spread of the reformation in the countryside, unless political considerations dictated otherwise. It did this not only in an authoritarian fashion, but also by wooing and winning the active consensus of the communities in the countryside. Swiss historiography tends to characterize the "plebiscites" of 1524 rather as a formality while emphasizing the authoritarian nature of the evangelical movement.[210] This is not incorrect, but it needs to be qualified once we examine the issue comparatively by bringing in the region of southern Germany that belonged to the empire. In the latter no effort was made anywhere to coordinate the choice for or against the evangelical movement with the communities. Even imperial cities such as Strasbourg, Nuremberg, and Memmingen showed relatively little interest in the mood in the countryside as long as there was no serious threat to the political peace. In Zurich, on the other hand, a broad consensus existed between the urban and rural communities in regard to the position to be taken in confessional matters. At the basis of this were constitutionally established ideas about consensus and participation, which were applicable beyond Zurich, as the example of Bern can attest.

The first pro-reformation sentiments were voiced in Bern in 1523 with the preaching mandate, although they did not come to fruition until after the Bern Disputation of 1528, when the city and its territory joined the reformation.[211] This decision came at the end of a gradual, five-year maturation process, during which time there was constant contact and communication with the Bern countryside. In preparation for the assembly (*Tagsatzung*) of the confederates, scheduled for Lucerne in 1524, and whose agenda included also the question of faith, the council sought a broad basis for its vote by conducting a "consultation of the districts" (*Ämterbefragung*) to find out whether the "new doctrine should be extinguished" or whether "the holy gospel and the godly Scripture, as well as the New and Old Testaments, should be secured and implemented."[212] The districts voted overwhelmingly in favor of retaining the old faith or they left it to the council as the "protector" to make the necessary decisions.[213] As a result the council continued in the tracks of the established church when it came to questions of religious policy in its territory and within the Confederation, although not without pushing for reforms on this basis.[214] When the religious issue became heated between Zurich and the Catholic Forest Cantons in 1526, and there was growing unrest on the eve of the planned pan-confederate religious disputation, Bern turned to its subjects in February and May and got back the answer that they wished to remain in the old faith.[215] And when in 1527 a clear majority in favor of the reformation emerged and carried the day in

Bern, there was yet another consultation of the districts.[216] It is true that on this occasion Bern made it quite clear where it stood and what it expected, but it was also just as interested in the freely rendered decisions of the communities.[217] After the majority of the communities had voted in favor of the new doctrine, the official reformation mandate for the city and territory of Bern was issued in February of 1528, after the Bern Disputation.[218] The mandate was once again presented to the communities for confirmation, and in case there was no clear support for it, it was left up to the parish communities to decide by majority vote whether or not "the mass and images [should be] eliminated."[219]

We do not have to decide to what extent Bern's "coaching" influenced the voting during the consultation of the districts. Important for our purposes is solely the fact that the city was clearly interested in obtaining an active consensus in its territory. This concern is also reflected in the fact that the rural communes of Bern had more extensive rights than their counterparts in Zurich, where the communities could decide only about "images," but not about the Mass.

Wherever the evangelical movement in Switzerland was headed off or appropriated by the urban councils or unfolded under their careful leadership, the peasants' communal reformation could not become politically dangerous. The better part of Switzerland—after all, Bern and Zurich controlled the largest territories in the Confederation—thus presents a picture of the peasants' reformation that is very different from what we find in the southern German lands of the empire. There the communal reformation could only realize itself by becoming the vehicle of a fundamental antifeudalism. The strength of the feudal structures thus became a crucially important factor in shaping the course of the reformation. This is confirmed by those areas of modern Switzerland that were ruled by ecclesiastical territorial lords. In the territory of St. Gall political unrest broke out both in the "old lands"[220] (Alte Landschaft) of the abbey's traditional core and in the county of Toggenburg, which had been in the monastery's jurisdiction since the fifteenth century. Compared to the ancient lands, Toggenburg possessed much broader political rights through its own Territorial Council and independent ties to the outside world in the form of alliances with Schwyz and Glarus. After 1524, the prince-abbot of St. Gall continually complained that the communities were appointing pro-reformation pastors on their own initiative.[221] In the following years the reformation movement resulted in the de facto—if temporary—separation of Toggenburg from St. Gall, after the Territorial Council had taken it upon itself to decide on the true doctrine and had called a synod in 1529 which brought the land over to the reformation.[222] Much the same goes for Graubünden, where the bishop and the cathedral chapter of Chur felt the political expansion of the reformation movement in the form of massive attacks on their rights of lordship.

In the empire the peasants' reformation provoked a fundamental crisis of the political order, since the recourse to the "pure gospel" and its concrete application to the structure of social and political life meant that lordship was no longer accepted as God-given unless it could show itself to be Christian lordship. And it was "Christian" in the eyes of the peasants only if it subordinated its actions to scriptural norms and principles of godly law, or at least if it claimed to be doing so. Zurich and Bern did this and thus provided the peasants' concept of reformation no political point of attack. As a result the peasants' communal reformation remained a side branch of the broader movement of urban reformation and could hardly develop its own identity and character. The princes and lords in the empire, on the other hand, were concerned to recapture the legitimacy which the evangelical movement had undermined. This they could accomplish only through a military confrontation and by crushing the peasants. Once that had happened the peasants' reformation had no chance to take root, let alone flourish.

The reformation in rural society is best characterized as a communal reformation. Beginning in 1523 in the Zurich countryside, it quickly spread northward to the upper Rhine and in 1515 seized the entire region of southern Germany. By 1530 it had run its course, crushed by the princes or incorporated by the cities. Characteristically enough it prevailed only in those areas where feudal lordship was so weak that it did not survive politically the fury of the reformation, as in Graubünden, or where the political structures were based on the communities, as in Swiss Glarus.[223] In this way eastern Switzerland moved closer to Zurich and Bern, both in regard to its confessional choice and the internal structure of the church. The gap between Switzerland and the empire widened. "Pig-Swabians" and "Cow-Swiss," to use epithets of the time, were henceforth separated not only by different political identities but also by different confessional identities.[224]

Notes

1. Selected references in Peter Blickle, *Die Revolution von 1525*, 2d ed. (Munich and Vienna, 1981), 244 note 11.
2. Franziska Conrad, *Reformation in der bäuerlichen Gesellschaft. Zur Rezeption reformatorischer Theologie im Elsaß*, Veröffentlichungen des Instituts für Europäische Geschichte Mainz, vol. 116 (Stuttgart, 1984). Among Luther scholars, Marc Lienhard has recently challenged the attitude that reduces the life and concerns of the common people to the socio-economic level. Marc Lienhard, *Martin Luther. Un temps, une vie, un message* (Paris and Geneva, 1983), 134.
3. Basic for the course of events is Günther Franz, *Der deutsche Bauernkrieg*, 11th ed. (Darmstadt, 1977).
4. Conrad, *Reformation in der bäuerlichen Gesellschaft*, 86–92.
5. Günther Vogler, *Nürnberg 1524/25. Studien zur Geschichte der reformatorischen und sozialen Bewegung in der Reichstadt* (Berlin, 1982), 83–95.
6. Emil Egli, *Aktensammlung zur Geschichte der Zürcher Reformation in den Jahren 1519–1533* (Zurich, 1879; reprint, Aalen, 1973), 128, no. 354 (11 April 1523).
7. Ibid., 129, no. 359.
8. Ibid., 129, no. 360 (9 March 1523).

9. The meaning of the passages, in the form in which they are given by Egli, is not entirely clear; but the context reveals that the patron was to pay a part of the salary or all of it.

10. Günther Franz, ed., *Quellen zur Geschichte des Bauernkrieges*, Ausgewählte Quellen zur deutschen Geschichte der Neuzeit. Freiherr vom Stein-Gedächtnisausgabe, vol. 2 (Darmstadt, 1963), 315f., no. 97.

11. I list here only the more important points; the so-called request itself is more detailed.

12. This quote and all previous ones in Franz, *Quellen*, 315.

13. Gerhard Pfeiffer, "Das Verhältnis von politischer und kirchlicher Gemeinde in den deutschen Reichsstädten," in Walther Peter Fuchs, ed., *Staat und Kirche im Wandel der Jahrhunderte* (Stuttgart, 1966), 79. There is a broader discussion by Karl Siegfried Bader, "Universitas subditorum parochiae—des pfarrers untertanen. Zur Auffassung und Bezeichnung der spätmittelalterlichen Pfarrgemeinde," in his *Schriften zur Rechtsgeschichte* (Sigmaringen, 1984), 240–254.

14. *Dorffmayster vnnd / Gemaind zu wendelstains fürhal- / ten / den Amptleüten zu Schwa- / bach und jrem new angeend- / dem Pfarrherrn gethan* (1524).

15. Egli, *Aktensammlung*, 134ff., no. 372 (28 June 1523). When Egli gave the complete texts of the sources, he frequently provided additions in brackets in order to make them more readily readable, but these additions often changed the texts grammatically and in meaning. In principle I have omitted these additions.

16. The edited documentary material that is available for Switzerland (see the bibliography of sources and secondary literature) far exceeds in extent and depth comparable editions for Germany and Austria, at least concerning the issues I am addressing.

17. Egli, *Aktensammlung*, 133f., 369 (23 June 1523).

18. Ibid., 125, no. 351 (19 March 1523).

19. Ibid., 132f., no. 368 (22 June 1523).

20. References in Egli, *Aktensammlung*, passim.

21. Ibid., 137, no. 378.

22. Ibid., 179f., no. 450.

23. Ibid., 128, no. 354; 140f., no. 383; 178, no. 444.

24. J. Strickler, *Eidgenössische Abschiede*, vol. 4,1a: 450f.

25. Egli, *Aktensammlung*, 246f., nos. 568, 569.

26. Johannes Strickler, *Actensammlung zur Schweizerischen Reformationsgeschichte in den Jahren 1521–1532 im Anschluss an die gleichzeitigen eidgenössischen Abschiede*, vol. 1: *1521–1528* (Zurich, 1878), 291, no. 839. The Allowances of wine and grain are indicated.

27. Egli, *Aktensammlung*, 173f., no. 436 (27 October 1523).

28. On the background to the decree see Leonhard von Muralt, "Renaissance und Reformation," in *Handbuch der Schweizer Geschichte*, vol. 1 (Zurich, 1972), 450f.

29. Egli, *Aktensammlung*, 114f., no. 327. Already in 1522 the Zurich *Landkapitel* had accepted the scriptural principle, for which see Oskar Vasella, "Bauernkrieg und Reformation in Graubünden 1525–1526," *Zeitschrift für Schweizerische Geschichte* 20 (1940): 43.

30. Compare, for example, Egli, *Aktensammlung*, 234ff., no. 543.

31. Ibid., 237, no. 546.

32. Ibid., 177f., no. 440; 214, no. 491.

33. Ibid., 134, no. 369.

34. Ibid., 132f., no. 368.

35. Ibid., 246, no. 568.

36. Ibid., 254–264, no. 589.

37. Ibid., 258.
38. Ibid., 261.
39. Ibid., 323–326, no. 710 (7 May 1525); 319ff., no. 703 (2 May 1525); 318f., no. 702 (25 April 1525).
40. Ibid., 332–336, no. 725. On the article concerning the election of pastors there are two different votes by commission members (both of which were adopted by the council); in the final analysis they both preserved the council's right to make appointments, although the right of appeal by a community was not ruled out.
41. Ibid., 336–339, no. 726. On the article concerning the appointment of pastors see Egli, *Aktensammlung*, 338.
42. Kurt Maeder, "Die Bedeutung der Landschaft für den Verlauf des reformatorischen Prozesses in Zürich (1522–1532)," in: Bernd Moeller, ed., *Stadt und Kirche im 16. Jahrhundert*, Schriften des Vereins für Reformationsgeschichte, no. 190 (Gütersloh, 1978), 91–98, emphasizes the importance of 1525; other than that he gives a rather cursory overview.
43. For the historical background see Franz, *Quellen*, 127–130.
44. Ibid., 196, no. 51.
45. Preaching ordinance of the Christian Union of May 1512, printed in Franz, *Quellen*, 198, no. 53.
46. Helmut Claus, *Der deutsche Bauernkrieg im Druckschaffen der Jahre 1524–1526. Verzeichnis der Flugschriften und Dichtungen*, Veröffentlichungen der Forschungsbibliothek Gotha, vol. 16 (Gotha, 1975), 24–29.
47. Faithful textual reproduction in Alfred Götze, ed., "Die zwölf Artikel der Bauern 1525," in *Historische Vierteljahrschrift* 5 (1902): 9–15. There is a more readable, modernized text in Franz, *Quellen*, 175–179, no. 43; my references are to this edition.
48. The account is in Franz, *Quellen*, 136f., no. 29. He is describing events that occurred on 14 February 1525.
49. Ibid., 163f., no. 35. We are dealing here with a kind of summary version of the peasants' statements (originally probably expounded more fully) incorporated into a city chronicle.
50. The so-called Allgäu Articles are printed in Franz, *Quellen*, 166f., no. 38.
51. Compare the synopsis of the grievances in Blickle, *Revolution*, 296–301.
52. Günther Franz, ed., *Der deutsche Bauernkrieg. Aktenband*, 2d ed. (Darmstadt, 1968), 147 note 26a.
53. Ibid., 150, no. 26d.
54. Ibid., 154, no. 26 note.
55. Ibid., 165, no. 31.
56. Franz, *Quellen*, 190, no. 47.
57. Ibid., 175, no. 43.
58. Ibid., 166, no. 38.
59. Ibid., 190, no. 47.
60. Franz, *Bauernkrieg Aktenband*, 150, no. 26d.
61. Franz, *Quellen*, 197, no. 51.
62. Claus, *Der deutsche Bauernkrieg*, 29ff., lists eight editions.
63. The statistical analysis is difficult because we cannot determine in every case whether a village belonged to the Baltringen Band. Of all the available grievance lists, 44 percent demand the abolition of the small tithe, 41 percent the abolition or conversion of the large tithe. See Blickle, *Revolution*, 38, plus the synopsis of the grievances in 296–301.
64. Jürgen Bücking, *Michael Gaismair: Reformer-Sozialrebell-Revolutionär. Seine Rolle im Tiroler "Bauernkrieg" (1525/32)*, Spätmittelalter und Frühe Neuzeit. Tübinger

Beiträge zur Geschichtsforschung, vol. 5 (Stuttgart, 1978), 154.

65. Ibid., 96–105.

66. Hermann Wopfner, ed., *Quellen zur Geschichte des Bauernkrieges in Deutschtirol 1525*, Acta Tirolensia, vol. 3 (Innsbruck, 1908; reprint: Aalen, 1973), 70–78, no. 18; 78–82, no. 19; 68f., no. 17; Bücking, *Michael Gaismair*, 149–152. Bücking attributes the grievance list from Brixen to Michael Gaismair and labels it his "first" territorial constitution; consequently the only Gaismair constitution hitherto known, from the spring of 1526, is called the second constitution. There is no doubt that a broader consensus existed among the peasants, though there is no compelling reason for attributing the individual parts to Gaismair. See Bücking, *Michael Gaismair*, 63, 149.

67. Adolf Laube, "Der Aufstand der Schwazer Bergarbeiter 1525 und ihre Haltung im Tiroler Bauernkrieg," in Fridolin Dörrer, ed., *Die Bauernkriege und Michael Gaismair*, Veröffentlichungen des Tiroler Landesarchivs, vol. 2 (Innsbruck, 1982), 171–184, esp. 175.

68. Wopfner, *Quellen*, 70f.

69. Ibid., 35–47, no. 15a; 50–67, no. 16. Largely identical with the Meran Articles, expanded by the so-called Innsbruck Additions to a total of 96 articles.

70. Ibid., 35, 37, 44.

71. Ibid., 36f., with minor variations, 51f.

72. Ibid., 36.

73. Ibid.

74. Ibid. *Hausarme* were respectable people who had been reduced to poverty through no fault of their own and did not wish to be publicly supported as beggars or alms receivers.

75. Ibid., 35; analogously, 50f.

76. Franz, *Quellen*, 297, no. 94. For evidence of the important role the articles played in the debates at the subsequent diets in the archbishopric of Salzburg, see Blickle, *Revolution*, 268f. On the background to the (provisional) territorial constitution drafted in 1526 (along with the text) see now Franz Viktor Spechtler and Rudolf Uminsky, *Die Salzburger Landesordnung von 1526*, Göppinger Arbeiten zur Germanistik, vol. 305 (Göppingen, 1981).

77. Franz, *Quellen*, 295f.

78. Ibid., 297, 299.

79. Ibid., 298f.

80. Ibid., 300f.

81. Friedrich Leist, ed., *Quellen-Beiträge zur Geschichte des Bauern-Aufruhrs in Salzburg 1525 und 1526* (Salzburg, 1888), 6–10, no. 1.

82. I quote here the article concerning the appointment of the pastor (Leist, *Quellen-Beiträge*, 6f.):

> . . . in these our grievances we consider this the first point and most necessary article: that we have properly God-fearing pastors who know and preach the Word of God, in the manner described above, without any fear and human threats; we also earnestly desire that when we elect or appoint such a pastor among us, no ecclesiastical or secular authorities of any kind shall dismiss him without a compelling reason or good cause; instead, a satisfactory investigation shall first be undertaken whether this pastor behaved decently or not.

83. Leist, *Quellen-Beiträge*, 19f., no. 13.

84. Franz, *Quellen*, 540, no. 170.

85. Franz, *Bauernkrieg*, 244.

86. Franz, *Quellen*, 466f., no. 155.

87. A *Weistum* is a record of customary law in the form of a collection of judicial sentences which serve as precedent. On the placement of the article concerning the election of the pastor, see Adolf Waas, *Die Bauern im Kampf um Gerichtigkeit 1300–1525*, 2d. ed. (Munich, 1976), 155f.
88. Franz, *Quellen*, 447, no. 147.
89. Ibid., 238f., no. 71.
90. Emil Dürr and Paul Roth, eds., *Aktensammlung zur Basler Reformation in den Jahren 1519 bis Anfang 1534*, 6 vols. (Basel, 1921–1950), vol. 1: 246; Franz, *Bauernkrieg Aktenband*, 323, no. 153.
91. Printed in Franz, *Quellen*, 342f., no. 107.
92. Ibid., 370, no. 121.
93. Ibid., 328f., no. 101.
94. Günther Vogler, "Ein Vorspiel des deutschen Bauernkrieges im Nürnberger Landgebiet 1524," in Gerhard Heitz et al., eds., *Der Bauer im Klassenkampf. Studien zur Geschichte des deutschen Bauernkrieges und der bäuerlichen Klassenkämpfe im Spätfeudalismus* (Berlin, 1975), 49–66.
95. See the recent critical edition in Klaus Arnold, "Damit der am man vnnd gemainer nutz iren furgang haben . . . Zum deutschen 'Bauernkrieg' als politischer Bewegung: Wendel Hiplers und Friedrich Weygandts Pläne einer 'Reformation' des Reiches," *Zeitschrift für Historische Forschung* 9 (1982): 297.
96. See Franz, *Bauernkrieg*, 195.
97. Arnold, "Hiplers und Weygandts Pläne," 309.
98. On Weygandt's life most recently see ibid., 278f.
99. For the Zurich territory, see Egli, *Aktensammlung*, 318f., no. 702; 319f., no. 703; 323ff., no. 710 (Zurich). For St. Gall, see the grievances of Gossau in Johannes Strickler, *Amtliche Sammlung der älteren eidgenössische Abschiede*, vol. 4,1a (Lucerne, 1876): 716f., no. 289. This document in all likelihood presupposes a knowledge of the Twelve Articles; see Peter Blickle, "Bäuerliche Rebellionen im Fürststift St. Gallen," in Peter Blickle., ed., *Aufruhr und Empörung? Studien zum bäuerlichen Widerstand im Alten Reich* (Munich, 1980), 279f. For Rhaetia, see Constanz Jecklin, ed., *Urkunden zur Verfassungsgeschichte Graubündens*, Beilage zu Jahresberichte der historisch-antiquarischen Gesellschaft von Graubünden, 3 parts (Chur, 1883–1886), 97. For the Trentino, see U. Corsini, "La guerra rustica nel Trentino e Michael Gaismair," *Studi Trentini di scienze storiche* 59 (1980): 164, plus the Italian version of the Meran Articles in Wopfner, *Quellen*, 48, no. 15b. For the Salzburg area, see Leist, *Quellen-Beiträge*, 7.
100. See the relevant references in Otto Merx and Günther Franz, eds., *Akten zur Geschichte des Bauernkriegs in Mitteldeutschland* (Leipzig, 1923–1924; reprint, Aalen, 1964), 122f., 341, 406; and in W. P. Fuchs and Günter Franz, eds., *Akten zur Geschichte des Bauernkrieg in Mitteldeutschland*, 2 vols. (Jena, 1942; reprint, Aalen, 1964), 34, 71f., 101f., 110, 113, 115f., 118–120, 127, 144, 168, 250, 265, 315f.
101. The numbers are estimated after Franz, *Bauernkrieg*, 118, 133, and Hans-Martin Maurer, "Der Bauernkrieg als Massenerhebung. Dynamik einer revolutionären Bewegung," in *Bausteine zur geschichtlichen Landeskunde von Baden-Württemberg* (Stuttgart, 1979), 256.
102. Günther Franz, "Aus der Kanzlei der württembergischen Bauern in Bauernkrieg," *Württembergische Vierteljahresheft für Landesgeschichte* 41 (1935): 304f., no. 90; *Quellen*, 369f., no. 121.
103. Peter Blickle, "Nochmals zur Entstehung der Zwölf Artikel," in Peter Blickle, ed., *Bauer, Reich und Reformation. Festschrift für Günther Franz zum 80. Geburtstag* (Stuttgart, 1982), 288; on the reconstruction of the previously unknown Federal Ordinance from the upper Rhine see Blickle, "Nochmals zur Entstehung," 288–300.

104. Maurer, "Massenerhebung," 255f. It should be noted especially that Maurer was able to confirm the reliability of the contemporary estimate with the help of "objective" sources.
105. On the reconstruction of the broader context see Peter Blickle, *Landschaften im Alten Reich. Die staatliche Funktion des gemeinen Mannes in Oberdeutschland* (Munich, 1973), 526–532.
106. Jecklin, *Urkunden Graubünden*, 93.
107. Ibid., 78–83, no. 37 (4 April 1524); 89–98, no. 38 (25 June 1526).
108. The quote is based on the protocol of the First Ilanz Manifesto, ibid., 78; similar wording in the Second Manifesto, ibid., 89.
109. On the constitution of the individual Unions and the position of the communities see Vasella, "Bündnerische Bauernartikel," 66ff.
110. Peter Liver, *Vom Feudalismus zur Demokratie in den graubündnerischen Hinterrheintälern*, dissertation, Zurich (1929).
111. I am referring to the Federal Charter (*Bundesbrief*) from 23 September 1524. Printed in Jecklin, *Urkunden Graubünden*, 83–89, no. 38.
112. On the details of the obscure process of redaction, see Oskar Vasella, "Die Entstehung der bündnerischen Bauernartikel vom 25. June 1526," *Zeitschrift für Schweizerische Geschichte* 21 (1941): 68ff.
113. Jecklin, *Urkunden Graubünden*, 79. The subsequent quotes are also from 79.
114. Ibid., 93.
115. See the contemporary, though partisan, account of the participant Hofmeister. It appeared as a pamphlet and was published in 1904 by the Religiös-freisinnige Vereinigung des Kantons Graubünden und der Stadt Chur under the title *Sebastian Hofmeisters Akten zum Religionsgespräch in Ilanz*. See also Vasella, "Reformation," 42f.
116. Jecklin, *Urkunden Graubünden*, 79f.
117. Ibid., 80.
118. Ibid., 81.
119. Item 17. "Thus we believe that no community or district within the parish shall bring an appeal to the bishop of Chur or his lawyers"; instead, other impartial tribunals were to serve as courts of appeal. Although this article was undoubtedly concerned primarily with the bishop's secular jurisdiction, we cannot completely eliminate the possibility that his ecclesiastical jurisdiction was also meant to be included. This is suggested by the anti-episcopal tenor of the entire document, and by the fact that the ecclesiastical court is mentioned at no other time in 1526.
120. Jecklin, *Urkunden Graubünden*, 81.
121. Blickle, "Nochmals Zwölf Artikel," 298; Franz, *Quellen*, 197, 271; Wopfner, *Quellen*, 69.
122. Walter Müller, ed., *Die Rechtsquellen des Kantons St. Gallen*, part 1: Die Rechtsquellen der Abtei St. Gallen, 2d series, vol. 1: *Die allgemeinen Rechtsquellen der alten Landschaft*, Sammlung Schweizerischer Rechtsquellen, vol. 14 (Aarau, 1974), 189.
123. Ibid.
124. Joachim von Watt [Vadian], *Chronik der Äbte des Klosters St. Gallen*, second part (1875), 398. For the larger context also Strickler, *Eidgenössische Abschiede*, vol. 4, 1a: 716f., no. 289.
125. Dürr and Roth, *Aktensammlung*, vol. 1: 215, no. 367.
126. Gottfried Egli, Die Reformation im Toggenburg, Ph.D. dissertation, Zurich, 1955, 70f.
127. No figures are available for the specific region under discussion. In the region of Osnabrück we know from the early phase of the Reformation (1517–1534) that 43 of 100 rural parishes were looked after by vice-curates for longer than a year (23 for

more than ten years, 16 for five to seven years); Heide Stratenwerth, *Die Reformation in der Stadt Osnabrück*, Veröffentlichungen des Instituts für europäische Geschichte Mainz, vol. 61 (Wiesbaden, 1971), 22. It has been shown that numerous
absentee holdings existed in the bishopric of Eichstätt, although the parishes
generally seem to have been properly looked after. See Peter Thaddäus Lang,
"Würfel, Wein und Wettersegen—Klerus und Gläubige im Bistum Eichstätt am
Vorabend der Reformation," in Volker Press and Dieter Stievermann, eds., *Martin
Luther. Probleme seiner Zeit* (Stuttgart, 1985), 219–243.

128. Egli, Toggenburg, 74.
129. Rudolf Hohl, Die Inkorporationen im Bistum Augsburg während des Mittelalters,
dissertation, Freiburg, 1960, 81–98; Henry J. Cohn, "Anticlericalism in the German Peasants' War 1525," *Past and Present* 83 (May 1979): 21; Willy Andreas,
Deutschland vor der Reformation. Eine Zeitwende, 6th ed. (1959), 91.
130. Egli, Toggenburg, 70f.
131. Bernd Moeller, *Reformation*, 40.
132. Franz, *Quellen*, 316, no. 97.
133. Ibid., 201f., no. 56.
134. Ibid., 299f., no. 94.
135. Wolf-Heino Struck, ed., *Der Bauernkrieg am Mittelrhein und in Hessen. Darstellung
und Quellen*, Veröffentlichungen der Historischen Kommission für Nassau, vol. 21
(Wiesbaden, 1975), 177.
136. Franz, *Quellen*, 263f., no. 87.
137. Strickler, *Eidgenössische Abschiede*, vol. 4,1a: 641.
138. Franz, *Quellen*, 565.
139. Alfred Rosenkranz, *Der Bundschuh. Die Erhebungen des südwestdeutschen Bauernstandes in den Jahren 1493–1517*, vol. 1: *Darstellung* (Heidelberg, 1927) (numerous
references); Vasella, "Reformation," 9ff.
140. Franz, *Quellen*, 299f.
141. Ibid., 325, no. 96.
142. Ibid., 448, no. 147.
143. Karl Stenzel, "Die geistlichen Gerichte zur Straßburg im 15. Jahrhundert," *Zeitschrift für die Geschichte des Oberrheins*, new ser. 29 (1914): 404. See also the source
which formed the basis of Stenzel's study, now edited by P.-J. Schuler, "'Reformation des geistlichen Gerichts zu Straßburg.' Eine Reformschrift aus der Mitte des 15.
Jahrhunderts," *Francia* 9 (1981): 177–214.
144. Hermann Wopfner, *Beiträge zur Geschichte der freien bäuerlichen Erbleihe Deutschtirols
im Mittelalter*, Untersuchungen zur Deutschen Staats- und Rechtsgeschichte,
vol. 67 (Breslau, 1903), 203–209.
145. See Dietrich Kurze, *Pfarrerwahlen im Mittelalter. Ein Beitrag zur Geschichte der
Gemeinde und des Niederkirchenwesens*, Forschungen zur kirchlichen Rechtsgeschichte, vol. 6 (Cologne and Graz, 1966); and Lang, "Klerus im Bistum Eichstätt,"
23f. Using the visitation records for Eichstätt, Lang has also been able to prove
(ibid., 19) that rural people at the end of the fifteenth century regularly attended
Sunday Mass and went to the yearly confession and communion at Easter.
146. See the indices in the relevant source collections, for example Franz, *Quellen*,
653f.; Franz, *Bauernkrieg Aktenband*, 443; Wopfner, *Quellen*, 213.
147. Documented in the case of southwestern Germany by Wolfgang von Hippel, *Die
Bauernbefreiung im Königreich Württemberg*, vol. 1, Forschungen zur deutschen
Sozialgeschichte, vol. I,1 (Boppard am Rhein, 1977), esp. 209f., 292.
148. Struck, *Bauernkrieg am Mittelrhein*, 175; Franz, *Quellen*, 293, 564. As yet there
is not a monograph on the tithe in the late Middle Ages. For now see Gunter
Zimmermann, *Die Antwort der Reformatoren auf die Zehntenfrage. Eine Analyse des*

Zusammenhanges von Reformation und Bauernkrieg, Europäische Hochschulschriften, ser. III, vol. 164 (Frankfurt a. M. and Bern, 1982), 20–30.

149. Strickler, *Eidgenössische Abschiede,* vol. 4,1a: 451.
150. Egli, *Aktensammlung,* 132. See the arguments of the villages of Rothenburg, in Franz, *Quellen,* 329.
151. Blickle, *Revolution,* 38. In this context we should note the mention of individuals who refused to pay the tithe, contained in the visitation records of the bishopric of Eichstätt. See Lang, "Klerus im Bistum Eichstätt," 25.
152. Franz, *Quellen,* 239.
153. Ibid., 410.
154. Ibid., 265f., 169.
155. Ibid., 300.
156. Article 2 of the Twelve Articles. Ibid., 176.
157. Text according to Franz, *Quellen,* 194; corrected version ("Kriegsgenossen" to "Kirchgenossen") on the basis of archival sources in Blickle, "Nochmals zur Entstehung," 290.
158. Wopfner, *Quellen,* 50–67, no. 16.
159. Vasella, "Reformation," 42f.
160. Franz, *Quellen,* 368.
161. Ibid., 175, no. 43.
162. Ibid., 420, no. 137.
163. Wopfner, *Quellen,* 70.
164. Franz, *Quellen,* 328, no. 101.
165. Ibid., 226.
166. Egli, *Aktensammlung,* 319, 324; Franz, *Quellen,* 168.
167. Franz, *Quellen,* 178f.
168. Text in Blickle, "Nochmals zur Entstehung," 297.
169. Vogt, "Correspondenz Artzt," no. 883.
170. Emil Egli and Rudolf Schoch, eds., *Johannes Kesslers Sabbata mit kleineren Schriften und Briefen* (St. Gall, 1902), 175.
171. Thus we can show in many sources that the gospel and godly law were interchangeable. See, for example, G. Franz, *Quellen,* 153f., 167f.; *Bauernkrieg Aktenband,* 148; Wilhelm Vogt, "Die Correspondenz des schwäbischen Bundeshauptmannes Ulrich Artzt von Augsburg aus den Jahren 1524–1527. Ein Beitrag zur Geschichte des Schwäbischen Bundes und des Bauernkrieges," *Zeitschrift des Historischen Vereins für Schwaben und Neuburg* 6 (1879): 281–404; 7 (1880): 233–380; 9 (1882): 1–62; 10 (1883): 1–298, here at nos. 883, 893.
172. Franz, *Quellen,* 196. Similar formulations of the Upper Swabians appear in the sworn articles and in their correspondence. Ibid., 191, 197f.
173. Ibid., 231, no. 66.
174. Ibid., 191f., no. 49.
175. I think it should be emphatically pointed out that when Ferdinand was to be bound to godly law, he was addressed merely as the emperor's deputy.
176. I would like to point to an interesting reference, although it does not come directly from the pen of the peasants. On 13 December 1524, the city of Villingen wrote to the estates of nearer Austria that the peasants had informed them in a letter "they would not deny the house of Austria anything of what belonged to it by godly and imperial law." Karl Hartfelder, "Urkundliche Beiträge zur Geschichte des Bauernkrieges im Breisgau," *Zeitschrift für die Geschichte des Oberrheins* 34 (1882): 406.
177. See, for example, the writing of the Buchlo Band to Duke Wilhelm of Bavaria, in Franz, *Quellen,* 209, no. 60.
178. See on this Blickle, *Revolution,* 140–149.

179. See Peter Blickle, "Bäuerliche Erhebungen im spätmittelalterlichen deutschen Reich," *Zeitschrift für Agrargeschichte und Agrarsoziologie* 27 (1979): 208–231, esp. 220–224.

180. Karl Heinz Burmeister, "Genossenschaftliche Rechtsfindung und herrschaftliche Rechtssetzung," in: Peter Blickle, ed., *Revolte und Revolution in Europa*, Historische Zeitschrift, Beihefte new ser. 4 (Munich, 1975), 171–185.

181. Peter Blickle, "Auf dem Weg zu einem Modell der bäuerlichen Rebellion," in: Peter Blickle, ed., *Aufruhr und Empörung? Studien zum bäuerlichen Widerstand im Alten Reich* (1980), 304.

182. Everything indicates that the fifteenth century saw the monasteries once again engaged in forgery on a vast scale. Massive forgeries (for the purpose of pushing through alleged rights over the peasants) are attested, for example, in Kempten (Franz, *Bauernkrieg*, 11) and St. Gall (Johannes Häne, "Der Klosterbruch zu Rorschach und der St. Galler Krieg 1489–1490," *Mitteilungen zur vaterländischen Geschichte*, hg. vom Historischen Verein des Kantons St. Gallen 26 [1895]: 81). We may assume they existed also in other regions. See Peter-Johannes Schuler, "Die 'armen lüt' und das Gericht. Eine Straßburger Schrift über die Reform des geistlichen Gerichts," in: Peter Classen, ed., *Recht und Schrift im Mittelalter*, Vorträge und Forschungen, vol. 23 (Sigmaringen, 1977), 229.

183. Rochus Freiherr von Liliencron, ed., *Die historischen Volkslieder der Deutschen vom 13. bis 16. Jahrhundert*, vol. 2 (Leipzig, 1866; reprint, Hildesheim, 1966), 284.

184. Müller, *Rechtsquellen*, 201.

185. Ibid., 164f., 174, 175, 160 (references in the sequence in which they are quoted).

186. Winfried Becker, "'Göttliches Wort,' 'göttliches Recht,' 'gottliche Gerechtigkeit.' Die Politisierung theologischer Begriffe?" in: Peter Blickle, ed., *Revolte und Revolution in Europa*, Historische Zeitschrift, Beiheft new ser. 4 (Munich, 1975), 232–263, here at 261.

187. Peter Bierbrauer, "Das Göttliche Recht und die naturrechtliche Tradition," in Peter Blickle, ed., *Bauer, Reich und Reformation. Festschrift für Günther Franz zum 80. Geburtstag* (Stuttgart, 1982), 221.

188. Ibid., 234.

189. Franz, *Quellen*, 196.

190. Hans Virck, ed., *Politische Correspondenz der Stadt Straßburg im Zeitalter der Reformation*, vol. 1 (Strasbourg, 1882): 123, no. 216.

191. Franz, *Quellen*, 504, no. 169.

192. Bücking, *Michael Gaismair*, 152.

193. Franz, *Quellen*, 235.

194. Wopfner, *Quellen*, 50f.

195. Franz, *Quellen*, 170.

196. See H. W. Eckardt, *Herrschaftliche Jagd, bäuerliche Not und bürgerliche Kritik. Zur Geschichte der fürstlichen und adligen Jagdprivilegien vornehmlich im südwestdeutschen Raum*, Veröffentlichungen des Max-Planck-Instituts für Geschichte, vol. 48 (Göttingen, 1976). And see Blickle, *Revolution*, 58–65, 116–122, where the historical background is described in greater detail.

197. Blickle, *Revolution*, 62, 296–301.

198. Ibid., 122, 117.

199. See on this the conjecture of Bierbrauer, "Das Göttliche Recht," 228.

200. Ibid., 121, 302.

201. In recent years scholarship has broadened its range considerably, and as a result the problem of serfdom has been more closely examined than any other right of lordship in the late Middle Ages. The basic study is that of Claudia Ulbrich, *Leibherrschaft am Oberrhein im Spätmittelalter*, Veröffentlichungen des Max-Planck-Instituts für

Geschichte, vol. 58 (Göttingen, 1979). The connection to the demands for freedom in the reformation period has been brought out especially by Walter Müller, "Wurzeln und Bedeutung des grundsätzlichen Widerstandes gegen die Leibeigenschaft im Bauernkrieg 1525," *Schriften des Vereins für Geschichte des Bodensees und seiner Umgebung* 93 (1975): 1–41; and Blickle, *Revolution*, 40–50, 105–111.

202. Müller, "Widerstand gegen die Leibeigenschaft," 2–6.

203. See Franz, *Quellen*, 263 (Schaffhausen), 164 (Schussenried); Egli, *Aktensammlung*, 318 (Grüningen), 319 (Kyburg); Franz, *Bauernkrieg Aktenband*, 148 (Äpfingen).

204. Vogt, "Correspondenz Artzt," nos. 881–895.

205. Broad comparative material is lacking, but the studies to date seem to point in this direction. See Hippel, *Bauernbefreiung*, 209; Blickle, *Revolution*, 27f.

206. This was formulated with particular emphasis in the third of the Twelve Articles (Franz, *Quellen*, 176f.), and from here it was spread further.

207. Egli, *Aktensammlung*, 213f.

208. Instead of supplying extensive references, I refer the reader to the treatment of this topic in Blickle, *Revolution*, 196–223.

209. Ivan Vargas, "The politicisation of the transcendent: a quasi-sociological postscript," in: Janos M. Bak and Gerhard Benecke, eds., *Religion and Rural Protest. Papers presented to the Fourth Interdisciplinary workshop on Peasant Studies, University of British Columbia* (London, 1982), 481.

210. See, for example, Muralt, "Renaissance und Reformation," where the reformation in the Zurich countryside is hardly mentioned, and G. W. Locher, *Zwinglische Reformation*, 271–281. The assessment is vague in Oskar Vasella, "Bauerntum und Reformation in der Eidgenossenschaft," *Historisches Jahrbuch* 76 (1957): 47–63.

211. The essential study, with a critical examination of the older literature, is now that of Ernst Walder, "Reformation und moderner Staat," *Archiv des Historischen Vereins des Kantons Bern* 64/65 (1980/81): 445–583.

212. Rudolf Steck and Gustrav Tobler, eds., *Aktensammlung zur Geschichte der Berner Reformation 1521–1532*, vol. 1 (Bern, 1923), 98f., no. 382.

213. Ibid., 101–112, no. 384.

214. Walder, "Reformation und moderner Staat," 506.

215. The responses of the communities in Steck and Tobler, *Aktensammlung*, 312ff., no. 891. On their placement see Walder, "Reformation und moderner Staat," 511.

216. Steck and Tobler, *Aktensammlung*, 397–400, nos. 1195, 1196.

217. Walder, "Reformation und moderner Staat," 519.

218. The responses in Steck and Tobler, *Aktensammlung*, 403–427, no. 1205; 629–634, no. 1513.

219. Ibid., 644f., no., 1534; 645. See Walder, "Reformation und moderner Staat," 522f.

220. The most important sources are in Müller, *Rechtsquellen*, 153–252.

221. Strickler, *Actensammlung*, vol. 1: 313f., no. 912; *Eidgenössische Abschiede*, vol. 4,1a: 1021f., no. 411.

222. K. Wegelin, *Geschichte der Landschaft Toggenburg*, Part 2 (1833), 42–49.

223. Muralt, "Renaissance und Reformation," 487; M. R. Wick, "Der 'Glarnerhandel.' Strukturgeschichtliche und konfliktsoziologische Hypothesen zum Glarner Konfessionsgesetz," *Jahrbuch des Historischen Vereins Glarus* 69 (1982), esp. 114.

224. See the delightful comments of Hans-Martin Maurer, *Schweizer und Schwaben. Ihre Begegnung und ihr Auseinanderleben am Bodensee im Spätmittelalter*, Konstanzer Universitätsreden 136 (Sigmaringen, 1983).

3

The Burghers' Reformation

During the past decade, the early phase of the reformation—the period between Luther's first public stance on behalf of the evangelical movement, and the public support of the imperial princes for Luther's cause—has been increasingly labeled, following A. G. Dickens' phrase, as an "urban event," an affair of the cities.[1] The massive scholarly output in recent years on the topic "city and reformation," including monographs on Augsburg, Frankfurt, Kitzingen, Lemgo, Nördlingen, and Strasbourg,[2] plus a flood of articles,[3] confirms this verdict through its sheer volume alone. There can thus be no doubt that the scholarship on the "burghers' reformation" far surpasses the work that has been done on the "peasants' reformation," which justifies treating the reformation in the cities more briefly in the context of the problem I am examining.[4]

It would be wrong to think that the abundance of scholarly studies signifies scholarly consensus. Today, a narrow focus on individual cities clearly prevails over a systematic, comparative approach. Comparisons are thus rendered impossible, because the methodologies used vary greatly, as do the interpretations. The student who reads the most recent work on the urban reformation will therefore come away rather confused. It is not surprising, then, that the interpretations scholars regard as secure and largely undisputed are few and are based mostly on the three comprehensive monographs on the urban reformation written in this century: Alfred Schultze's *Stadtgemeinde und Reformation* (1918), Bernd Moeller's *Reichsstadt und Reformation* (1962), and Steven Ozment's *Reformation in the Cities* (1975). Some points are widely accepted.[5] First, the cities functioned as "pacemakers" in the early phase of the reformation. Second, while special emphasis is laid on the religious needs of urban society, an important role is assigned to factors that were not primarily theological: for example, the constitutional and social structures, the role of the council and/or rising urban elites, the cultural background (e.g., the level of humanistic learning in a city), and the external political bonds (e.g., the need to accommodate the wishes of the emperor). Third, the process of the reformation movement in the cities occurred in phases and often extended over more than a decade, as can be shown for Nuremberg, Osnabrück, Constance, Rostock, and other cities.[6] Finally, councils and communities cooperated.

63

It can hardly be said that this brief list imparts enough content to the phrase "urban reformation" to turn it into a useful *terminus technicus* for reformation historiography. This has the advantage, of course, that the heuristic approach I have developed in examining the peasants' reformation can be legitimately widened to include the cities as well. But this approach requires that we refer back once again to the specialized literature.

BURGHERS AND REFORMATION—THREE EXAMPLES

The background I have sketched above allows me to examine the reformation in the cities from a particular and narrow point of view: who in urban burgher society promoted the evangelical movement, under what conditions, with what aims and consequences? This raises some methodological problems, since the sources available for rural society, the grievances and manifestos, have no counterpart in the cities. There is good reason why scholars try to reconstruct the intentions of the burghers by analyzing pamphlets[7] or official documents, such as a city's correspondence and council minutes.[8] In some cases this leads to problems of interpretation—with council minutes, for example, the question arises whether the vote is in fact that of the council, or whether the community is dictating the council's vote. These problems deserve a lot of critical attention, and in all likelihood they prevent us from knowing fully the attitude of the burghers.

"AND FURTHERMORE, ALL MASSES ARE BEING STOPPED"— THE CASE OF ERFURT

At the end of May 1525, at the height of the reformist anticlerical movement in Erfurt, the clerics of the city wrote to the archbishop of Mainz that 25 churches in the jurisdiction of the Erfurt's Church of Our Lady had been consolidated into ten parishes staffed with supporters of Luther; "and furthermore . . . all masses have been stopped."[9] What had preceded these events was a gradual, slow process of implementing reformist intentions since 1521.

At the beginning of the reformation century, Erfurt's character was shaped by its famous university and its elitist circle of humanists, its fading renown as a trading city, growing social tensions, and its isolated political position as a region in the jurisdiction of the electorate of Mainz surrounded by land ruled by the duke of Saxony.[10] Erfurt was among the cities in Germany in which the evangelical movement began earliest. Two months after Luther had stopped and preached in Erfurt on his way to Worms, the city experienced the infamous "assault on the clergy" (*Pfaffensturm*) with the destruction of the canons' houses.[11] The participants included students and artisans, whose motive—in addition to an anticlericalism which we cannot define more precisely—was probably the tax-exempt status of the cathedral and chapter clergy.[12] This seems to find some confirmation in the reaction of the council, which promised a certain protection to the clergy if they in return renounced their privileges and submitted themselves to civic obligations.[13] Thus we can note that the civic incorporation of the clergy became the first goal of the reformation movement in Erfurt.

Closely linked to this goal was the call for the preaching of the pure gospel, which we can infer from the fact that four parishes procured pro-Lutheran clergy as preachers through election by the parishioners.[14] It is true that students took a leading role in pushing through these aims, but one must point out that all social strata in the city supported these efforts.[15]

The next high point of the anticlerical pro-reformation movement was not reached until 1525 in connection with the Peasants' War. In the interim, however, the evangelical movement had made measurable progress, as nuns and monks abandoned their cloisters in growing numbers, pro-reformation currents were stirred in the city's territory, communion was administered to the laity under both kinds, and the clergy began to marry.[16] All along the clergy's exemption from secular jurisdiction was repeatedly emphasized as one motivating grievance behind the constant innovations, which were accompanied time and again by anticlerical excesses.[17]

The council watched these developments with an aloof sympathy, since they did further its own ambitions of loosening its ties to the territorial lord, the prince elector of Mainz. Nevertheless, the policy of the magistrates in religious questions was guided by the premise that the peace within the city had to be maintained at all cost. When a polemical and slanderous quarrel erupted in 1522 between the Augustinian monk Arnoldi of Usingen and the preacher Johann Culsaner, the council summoned the two men to a hearing and admonished them to preach only what they could justify on the basis of Scripture.[18] And when the authorities drew up an inventory of church and monastic property, this may also have been a precautionary move dictated by a concern for internal peace, although it could also be seen as a prelude to the secularization of these institutions.

These were the conditions within the city when the Peasants' War erupted. On 28 April 1525, the council opened the city gates to the peasants under the condition that they carefully refrain from injuring citizens or their property, thereby freely exposing ecclesiastical possessions to be plundered by the peasants.[19] Therewith the last remaining holdouts of the old church collapsed. The Mainzer Hof was looted and then turned into the peasants' headquarters. The council's hopes of controlling the nearly 11,000 peasants encamped in Erfurt in its own interest proved illusory.[20] The old council was replaced by an "eternal council," and its political activities were controlled through committees of the communities in the city hall and through the peasants on the Petersberg.[21] Grievances of the burghers and peasants were jointly deliberated and were eventually drawn up in a final version of 28 articles.[22] The council accepted them on 9 May and was placed under oath to implement them.[23]

Two points are of interest in the events surrounding 9 May and should be emphasized for a broader interpretation:

[1]. It would appear that the opposition to the council within the city had used the demonstration of power by the peasants to push through its demands.[24] The twenty-eight Erfurt Articles represent a primarily urban grievance list. In addition to relief from dues, they demanded in particular a stronger control of the council through the "city districts and artisans of the community" (Articles 6 and 7), and a relaxation, if not outright abolition, of the constraints imposed by the guilds. The opening article, however, clearly indicates the importance of the evangelical movement by giving it a prominent place. The parishes would be newly regulated, "according to circumstances," which probably means depending on concrete, current needs, with the additional stipulation that

the community of each parish shall appoint and dismiss its own pastor. And through the same appointed pastors the pure Word of God shall be proclaimed without any additions, without any human injunctions, statutes, and doctrines[25]

—a demand that was soon met. On the other hand, the close connection between urban artisans (the "community," as they called themselves) and the peasants (the "countryside," as they were repeatedly called in the sources) was preserved. In the articles is disclosed, for example, the stipulation that tax increases required the consent of the urban community and the peasant communities (Article 21). In day-to-day political activities it was reflected in the fact that even after the peasants had withdrawn from the city on 6 May,[26] urban and peasant communities continued to cooperate closely.[27] This is revealed particularly in the "new oath" of the council, which "the delegates [verordnete] of city quarters, artisans, and the entire community together with the delegates of the entire countryside of the city of Erfurt . . . [have] resolved upon."[28]

With the crushing of the Peasants' War in Thuringia, Erfurt's position obviously became very precarious, and the Catholic-episcopal party gradually and unmistakably recovered ground. In 1526 the Mass was reintroduced on a limited basis. In 1528 a "religious coexistence" was established. Four parish churches each were assigned to the Lutherans and the Catholics; the cathedral church and the two monastic churches would be open to both confessions, and the remaining eleven parish churches as well as three monastic churches were closed.[29]

Our analysis of the events in Erfurt shows that the reformation was implemented from the bottom up. Carried by a broad stratum of urban groups which did not participate in city government, the influence of the pre-reformation party was successively expanded, from the control over four parish churches in 1521 to the final imposition of the reformation in all parish and monastic churches in 1525. At all times the efforts were bound up with the aim of the preaching of the pure gospel, which was to be guaranteed by giving the communities the power to appoint their pastors. We should further note that the final triumph of the reformation as the sole norm of religious and church life in the city was achieved only with the help of the peasants in 1525. The predisposition of the urban community toward the evangelical movement is something we cannot grasp very clearly; apparently there was a strong desire to place the many clerics in Erfurt on a equal footing with the other townsmen in terms of rights and obligations, to eliminate their special jurisdiction, and to abolish the regular clergy. Whatever got in the way of the evangelical movement, even the authority of bishops and civic magistrates, was soon forced to yield. Political structures had to guarantee the doctrine of the pure gospel in order to be considered legitimate.

THE CITY OF THE BLINDED—THE CASE OF KITZINGEN

On 7 June 1525, Margrave Casimir of Brandenburg-Ansbach, engaged in a campaign of revenge against the Franconian peasants, entered Kitzingen with 2,000 men. His investigations identified 134 alleged leaders and instigators. Sixty of these were apprehended, and on 9 June their eyes were gouged out by the margrave's executioner, on the grounds that they had refused to look upon the margrave as their lord.[30] Together with the other guilty townsmen, those who survived this ordeal—twelve died as a result of the blinding—were banished from the city along with their families. Contemporaries, too, considered these events utterly outrageous, as we learn from the letters which the clergy and the council of Kitzingen wrote to Casimir, pleading with him to mitigate the punishment.[31] All they accomplished, however, was to arouse the margrave's anger. Is there a link between these events and the reforming movement in Kitzingen?

The first reforming efforts in Kitzingen are attested for the year 1522.[32] In a letter to the city's lord, Margrave Casimir, the council requested that the priest either reside in the city or give up part of his income so that the vicar of the parish could be properly supported.[33] The benefice was held by the dean of the cathedral of Eichstätt, who drew from the post, after subtracting the expenses for the administrator he appointed, a yearly income of about 60 to 100 fl. This led the parish administrator to use his preaching to defend and justify fees for his services, and the result was that "a community is being starved of the preaching of God's word, and that the preaching was not true and pure." As we can see, the council was concerned, to use its own words from a different occasion, with the "proclamation of the evangelical doctrine and the Word of God," a demand that was not really open for negotiation. Unless the situation changed very quickly, the city would claim the right "to invoke evangelical freedom and choose pastors and chaplains it considered virtuous and suitable, and to control the parish revenues."

This document very clearly expresses the idea that the pastor, in return for his regular income, should provide the congregation with pastoral care without any additional impositions, which could only be guaranteed if the pastor resided in the community, and should preach the "pure gospel." Should the authorities fail to meet these conditions, the city itself would elect a pastor and would administer for him the revenues originally intended for the church.

In 1523 the city was able to hire a parish administrator who was sympathetic to the new doctrine. Evangelical preaching thus became the most prominent element in the divine services, the communion was soon given in two kinds, and alms and endowments for the poor were administered by the city through a communal chest.[34] All these pro-reformation measures were taken in close consultation between the council and the territorial prince.

There is some evidence for the broad resonance which the reformation movement had in Kitzingen. When Diepold Peringer, the so-called peasant of Wöhrd who had been a popular lay preacher in the Nuremberg countryside before his expulsion from Nuremberg, preached in Kitzingen on several occasions in 1524, he drew a crowd of 8,000 listeners. The preaching by Peringer was arranged at the initiative of the burghers. The council merely tolerated it but in the end was compelled to put an end to it when the margrave lodged a protest.[35] What was obviously a socially broad-based reform movement was confronted in 1525 with the events of the Peasants' War in Franconia. Kitzingen joined the radical Tauber Valley Band,[36] a step that was backed by the full social spectrum of the city, even though the majority (75 percent) of those who supported the Peasants' War came from the lower classes and the lower middle class.[37] What remains to be answered is whether the move to join the peasants' side can be linked to the reform movement in the city.

Anyone who joined the Tauber Valley Band must have necessarily identified with its goals. The Tauber Valley peasants summed them up in the slogan: "Whatever raises up the gospel shall be raised up, whatever lays it low shall be brought down."[38] This formula was meant as the guiding principle for the socio-political order, and it had its theological counterpart in the opening article of the military ordinance of the Tauber Valley Band: "First: by means of this brotherly, Christian Union we wish that the Word of God, which is nourishment to the soul, . . . be preached to the people purely and clearly."[39] In keeping with this vision, the government of the city, now composed of the council and a committee of 24 chosen from the community, was likewise placed under oath to follow the gospel in all its decisions.[40]

Kitzingen reveals a growing radicalization of the evangelical movement from its inception in 1522 to its high point in 1525. The course of the movement is not unlike what we saw in Erfurt, even though the correspondence of the city council does not allow us to separate with sufficient clarity the interests of the council from those of the community. The community became more prominent as the motor of the reform movement only from 1524 on, and it brought about the alliance with the peasant movement, a step that seems reasonable enough for a city that was very definitely only a small farming town.[41] It was for this that the 60 burghers lost their eyes. That the new faith still managed to survive in Kitzingen was entirely due to the fact that Casimir of Brandenburg placed his territory as a whole on the side of Luther, which also meant, of course, that "the city reformation was integrated into the territorial reformation"[42] and was deprived of its independent identity. The reformation in the cities was absorbed by the "princes' reformation."[43] After this time it is no longer possible to speak of a communal movement.

If we compare Kitzingen to Erfurt, we find both common and divergent features, which help us to define more precisely the picture of the urban reformation and thus focus our perspectives for later, systematic questions on specific points. Common to both cities was that the evangelical movement initially demanded the preaching of the "pure gospel" solely out of concern for the salvation of the soul. Only in the atmosphere of growing radicalization brought on by the Peasants' War was the gospel then also invoked for far-reaching social and political demands. In both cities this radicalization found concrete expression in the fact that a committee of burghers was set up to keep watch over the council.

In contrast to Erfurt, the desire of the urban community for a resident pastor and a "cost-free" church was more pronounced in Kitzingen. On the other hand, the pressure "from below" in pushing through the reformation cannot be proved with the same clarity in Kitzingen. Still, "what happened in Kitzingen was not a 'magistrates' reformation,'"[44] since the measures that were taken carried the support of the community, which made itself heard more clearly after 1525 and eventually imposed a more comprehensive notion of the gospel, one which included also the social and political spheres. To deny "that a movement among the burghers of Kitzingen had an active and initiating role in the reformation"[45] is possible only if one argues that the social and political consequences that could be derived from the demand for the pure gospel had nothing to do with the reformation.

"THE HONOR OF GOD AND THE PEACE OF AN ENTIRE CITY"— THE CASE OF BASEL

It was the guilds of Basel which, in December of 1528, forcefully demanded that the council promote "the honor of God" (which meant outlawing the old church).[46] Behind this demand stood a majority of the citizenry of Basel, who, like the Catholic minority, had assembled at various locations around the city dressed in military gear.[47] A civil war seemed unavoidable if the council did not fall into line with the majority. When the council gave in to this pressure, the reformation movement in Basel reached its culmination; it had taken a decade to finally triumph.

At the beginning of the reformation Basel was a city in political, economic, and cultural transition. In 1501 the council was able to strengthen its links to Switzerland, from being an associated member (*zugewandter Ort*) it became a full member of the Swiss Confederation, which would eventually embrace thirteen cantons. In 1521 the city broke away from the bishop's lordship. Artisans and craftsmen gained political ground by pushing back the merchant guilds as economic and political factors in the city. An interested citizenry open to new ideas gathered around the center of the new humanistic studies at the university, with its internationally famous leader Erasmus of Rotterdam. Twelve editions of

Luther's New Testament alone were sold in the bookshops of Basel and the rest of Switzerland between 1522 and 1525.

The unfolding of an evangelical movement in Basel can be broken down into three phases, which are centered, respectively, on the years 1523, 1525, and 1529. Already in the first phase we note that the parishes of Basel strongly promoted the reforming movement by expressing a clear preference for preachers and pastors who were, by the standards of the day, progressive. In 1519 the parish of St. Theodore appointed Max Bertschi, while the parish of St. Alban installed Wilhelm Reublin.[48] Both men were considered early supporters of Luther.[49] The bishop and the cathedral chapter soon created problems for Reublin and planned to have him dismissed in 1522. The parish, however, which had no intention of letting anyone take away their pastor, blocked these attempts, and a parish assembly was dissolved only after the council had promised to use its influence on Reublin's behalf.[50] When the Franciscan superior, the provincial, apparently under pressure from the cathedral chapter and the university, tried to remove Conrad Pellican from the city, he ran into the determined resistence of the citizenry. This in turn led the council to react with remarkable severity; if Pellican were removed from Basel, the council would have the entire convent dissolved, for Pellican had done nothing wrong. Quite the contrary, he was, as the council declared, "agreeable to us and to the common people of our city of Basel," and he "has well and truly taught and preached the true Word of God, the holy gospel."[51] The community's involvement is also evident in the appointment of Johannes Oecolampadius as vicar of St. Martin, since well-informed circles tell us that the council acted in response to demands from the community. In the same year the council even assigned him a professorship over the opposition of the university.[52]

The council's policies in 1522–1523 cast more light on the new movement. As early as 1522 the council felt compelled to prohibit public discussion about enforcing the Lenten fast and the gospel.[53] Following the Corpus Christi procession in 1522, the council did expel Reublin, whom it had earlier protected. They gave as their reason the fact that during the procession Reublin had not carried relics but the Bible, declaring that "this is the true sacred object, the rest are dead bones."[54] The continuous disturbances between followers of the new faith and adherents of the old eventually led to the proclamation of the first preaching mandate in May or June of 1523.[55] It obliged both regular and secular clergy to preach nothing "except only the holy gospel and the teachings of God," in so far as they could justify them "through the true Scripture, namely the four evangelists, St. Paul, the prophets, and the Bible, in sum, through the Old and New Testament." Sermons with references to other teachings—be they of the Church Fathers, "be they of Luther"—would henceforth not be tolerated.[56] As in earlier instances, the council was motivated by concern for the peace within the city. The preaching mandate was promulgated because "there may be cause to fear tumult and uprisings in our community," but also because ambiguous preaching "was misleading the common, poor people, who are eager to live as Christians in accordance with the teachings of God."[57]

The preaching mandate marks a first turning point. The parish communities of the city were driving the reform movement forward, backed up by the demand to appoint their own pastors. The council was trying to keep the peace, not without revealing a restrained and guarded sympathy for the reform movement. At this very moment the humanists in Basel broke away from the reform movement.[58] Henceforth the fate of the movement would be decided in the dialogue between the community and the council.

Through the weavers' guild of Basel the reforming movement entered its second phase, which coincided with the revolt of the peasants in the Basel countryside.[59] From this time on the guilds became crucial propagandists for the reformation. The events are chronologically centered around 1 May, which the guilds of Basel always celebrated with special festiveness.[60] A large crowd gathered, tumultuous scenes occurred, including the arrest of thirty weavers, and abusive words were hurled against the clergy and the authorities. The weavers' guild had already caused a stir some time before, when it had simply removed a lamp it was maintaining in the church of St. Martin.[61] On that occasion the weavers were summoned before the council to explain their action, and their answer allows an insight into the common man's idea of the reformation. God himself, they declared, was "the true and eternal light . . . , which needs no other light or fire than the light and heat of the true, passionate love of our hearts and our longing for Him and from Him."[62] They had "been no longer willing to light [the altar]," because God, "with the staff of his godly and true Word," had guided them "from the prickly thistles of human inventions to the delicious, most sweet pasture of his most holy gospel, from darkness to the bright, clear light of his godly Word."[63] The gospel had to be grasped "not only with the spirit, but also with the hands." Scripture demanded no "ceremonies, knickknacks, external splendour, and material ornaments before the eyes of God." Rather, it asked that "we look out for the need of our fellow man from love and the true faith." And for that very reason the expenses for the lamp, which we must not picture as a modest affair, would henceforth be given to a guild brother or to a "poor man who in the winter lacks wood, candles [liechter] or other necessaries."[64] We do not know whether any preachers supplied the theological arguments for this justification of the weavers. If we take the words as reflecting the weavers' beliefs, it would mean that they had understood and absorbed much of the reformation preaching, especially the principle of biblicism, faith as a source of good works, and the irrelevance of external ceremonies. But we must also emphasize how practical their idea of the reformation was. They wanted to live in accordance with the gospel, and in this way an element of the justice of good works flowed back into their arguments. The redirection of funds for the lamps at the altar of St. Martin to the use of the poor was justified with the claim that God "rewards only the works of compassion."[65]

The interest in concrete changes based on the new doctrine was also the driving force behind the tumultuous events around 1 May. As far as we can reconstruct the demands of the weavers, they insisted that the gospel be fully implemented in the city, that the regular and secular clergy be called upon for guard duty and taxes, that the monasteries be secularized, and that the council membership be changed.[66] On the same day, and following some earlier unrest, the first large gathering of peasants occurred in neighboring Liestal, a village in the city's jurisdiction.[67] A distance of ten to fifteen kilometers separated the rebels in the city from those in the countryside. Both sides sought contact, but our sources do not reveal to what extent they may have influenced each other. But the anticlerical, pro-reformation impulse that came from the weavers' guild was certainly taken even further by the demands of the rebels in the countryside: the large tithe should be used to pay for the lay priest and should thus fall under communal administration, the small tithe should be done away with, the appointment of pastors should be in the hands of the communities, and the ecclesiastical court should be abolished.[68]

Although the council managed to calm the weavers and to prevent a closer link-up between the city and the countryside, the events in May did result in resolute progress on the path toward reform. Already on 2 May the cathedral and chapter canons of the cathedral and of St. Peter were given full citizenship and thereby made liable for all civic obligations, such as guard duty, military service, taxes, and the excise tax (*Ungeld*).[69] The next day all guilds were informed of the council's intention of extending this measure to all the clergy in the city.[70] This was eventually carried out in the following year, more or less simultaneously with the efforts to restrict the jurisdiction of the ecclesiastical court to "marriage matters and matters that are truly clerical [*geistlich*],"[71] thus fulfilling the demands from the countryside.

The Peasants' War in neighboring Sundgau, the Black Forest, and the Breisgau, and in the territory of the Swiss Confederation in the districts of Solothurn, Bern, and Zurich, nourished the belief in the empire and in the Confederation that the gospel was a tool of unrest and revolt. As a result there were setbacks for the reform movement on a broad front. Basel, too, was not immune from this restorative pressure, and so the council hesitated to advance any further down the path it had chosen.[72] Apart from the measures begun in 1525, the council did not take up basic questions relating to the faith until the summer of 1527, in response to urgings from the reformation party in the city. At that time it called upon all the clergy in the city to justify their views on the Mass from Scripture. To be sure, the elaborate and long-winded statements did not provoke the council into making a final decision.[73] The mandate concerning the Mass that was published in September had the sole purpose of preserving peace within the city, and so it decreed that no one should "be forced to hold Mass and no one should be forced to hear it or kept by force from hearing it."[74] This was a most ineffective way of safeguarding the confessional peace in the long run, as would soon become clear.

Two days before Christmas in 1528, all the guilds submitted a petition to the council.[75] They demanded the exclusive "proclamation of the pure and true gospel" in the city and the abolition of the Mass in order to secure the "peace of the entire city." Lengthy negotiations between the council and the appointed committee of the guilds found points of agreement only with considerable difficulty. Among them we must single out as particularly important the council's willingness to set up a disputation concerning the Mass and to make the final decision dependent upon the majority vote of the guilds.[76] The council thus adopted from those guild members who supported the new doctrine the view that the community should decide on the correct teaching. The planned disputation never took place. On 8 February 1529, the city hall was surrounded by 800 armed burghers, the city gates were locked, the arsenal was guarded, and all cannons were confiscated; the rebels wanted a final and definitive decision.[77] Frantic negotiations brought no results, especially since the community was now loudly demanding the expulsion of twelve Catholic magistrates from the council. On the following morning, the tired, edgy, and disappointed crowd, which had spent the entire night in front of the city hall, stormed the cathedral and the other churches in the city and smashed the religious images and altars.[78] The council gave in: twelve councilors were removed from office, new elections were planned, and on 1 April the Reformation Decree (*Reformationsordnung*) was published.[79]

THE CONTENT AND THE EXTERNAL CONDITIONS OF THE BURGHERS' CONCEPT OF REFORMATION

Erfurt, Kitzingen, Basel—three examples of the reformation in the cities which are hardly comparable in their backgrounds and external conditions. What does the "free" imperial city of Basel, allied with the "free" Swiss Confederacy, have in common with Erfurt, an enclave of Mainz surrounded by the two Saxonies? What did Basel and Erfurt have in common with Kitzingen, a territorial city whose ability to act was severely restricted by the bailiff? The lack of comparability in political matters can be extended to other areas: the bases of their economies differed, as did their types of social stratification. Where lay the common focus for Erfurt, the internationally renowned trading city, and Kitzingen, a local community of wine growers and farmers? Perhaps it is all the more remarkable that the cities were strikingly similar in regard to the reformation movement. The reformation was apparently a movement that struck deep down to the roots, exposing the very foundations on which the urban communes were built and rendering the surface differences unimportant. If we recapitulate what reformation meant in the three cities by summarizing the common elements, we can formulate some leading questions for the following systematic outline of the problem of the "burghers' reformation."

The central concept in the urban reformation was gospel. "Gospel" became the shortest possible abbreviation for "pure gospel," itself short for "gospel without human additions." This verbal contraction made sense only if the resultant loss in specificity was made up for by the heightened symbolic meaning and power of the abbreviated phrase. "Gospel" became the universally understood slogan for the prevailing sentiments and trends in the 1520s. It is probable that no other word was used more often in the pulpits, discussed more frequently in the pamphlets, or heard more often in the taverns. The reformation movement in Central Europe in the 1520s, an evolutionary or revolutionary movement, depending on one's point of view, found its symbolic center and the core of its arguments in the gospel. Inherent in the concept of the gospel were deep religious convictions and a grave concern for salvation. But the "gospel" also became a catch phrase for progress as such. Whoever was for the gospel was on the side of progress, whoever was against it was a die-hard reactionary. To put on the mantle of the gospel also had its revolutionary chic. This explains at least in part the high and growing number of urban uprisings that were caused or furthered by the reformation: 16 in 1525, 52 in 1522, 44 in 1523, 40 in 1524, and 51 in the year of the Peasants' War.[80] It was hard to reject the aggressively fashionable force of the reformation without suffering in consequence some kind of social degradation. This is perhaps what the Catholics of Sélestat understood when they claimed that the gospel was "black leather of the sort that is used to make the *Bundschuh* [peasant boot]."[81] If we overlook that in this sense the mantle of the gospel could be worn in two different ways, we limit its possible functions and compromise our understanding.

The appeal to "the gospel" had at least four distinct functions in the burghers' reformation. First, the "pure gospel" gave rise to certain consequences, namely, demands for the abolition of the Mass, the removal of "idols" from the churches, the dissolution of the monasteries, and the elimination of the caste-like separation of the clergy from the urban commune. The slogan "gospel and church" thus describes a first issue which we must examine systematically. Second, the massive attack on the institution of the church in Erfurt, Kitzingen, and Basel raised the question about the nature of the relationship between city and church in the pre-reformation period and about the lines of continuity that extended from the late Middle Ages into the reformation era. Third, in all three cities the community—represented in Erfurt, Kitzingen, and Basel by ad hoc burgher committees—sought to push through its ideas of reformation, and this poses the broader question about the social strata that carried the evangelical movement. Fourth and finally, the communal ideas of reform gave rise to questions about the political consequences of the movement in the cities.

GOSPEL AND CHURCH—
THE IDEA OF REFORMATION IN THE CITIES

The demand for the "gospel" was first of all an appeal for preaching in accordance with the Scripture. The mayor and council of Mulhouse in Alsace decreed the following in their preaching ordinance of 1523:

> . . . our secular priests [*lütpriester*], as well as all other priests and members of the regular clergy, those who preach in our parish churches, monasteries,

and chapels here in Mulhouse, whoever they may be, shall freely, publicly, and openly preach and proclaim nothing but the holy gospel and the teachings of Christ, and whatever they can defend and support through the true holy Scripture, that is the Old and New Testaments; and they shall in no way accept or adopt any other doctrines, arguments, or lies [*tandmeren*] that are not in keeping with the true godly Scripture.[82]

In response to complaints from the city of Stolberg, far from Mulhouse, Count Botho of Stolberg assured the city that in the future "the gospel would be preached . . . pure and clear without any human additions or teachings."[83] When Ulm hired Konrad Sam as a preacher in 1524, his charge stated that he was to proclaim "the pure Word of God, grounded in Biblical and evangelical Scripture, in a pure manner without any additions of human doctrine, yet peacefully and without any quarrel."[84] In imperial cities, such as Frankfurt, Mühlhausen in Thuringia, Kaufbeuren, Colmar, Strasbourg, or Reutlingen; in episcopal cities like Salzburg, Bamberg, Würzburg, Osnabrück, or Mainz; and in many territorial cities, such as Stralsund, demands were raised for evangelical preaching and the setting aside of the doctrines of the Roman church.[85] At the urban diets (*Städtetage*) in 1524, the majority of the imperial cities insisted on scriptural preaching in their communities.[86] Indeed, it can be generally said that in both southern and northern Germany the reform movement was always and primarily a movement to implement the pure gospel.[87] To guarantee the preaching of the pure gospel in the cities, it was necessary to find a way of making sure that only reformist clergy would be allowed to preach and undertake pastoral duties. In many cases the reform movement linked the demand for the preaching of the pure gospel to the demand for the election of pastors by the community. In Erfurt and Basel, as well as in other cities—including Frankfurt, Würzburg, Meran, and Salzburg—the demand was raised very assertively that the parishioners choose their own pastors.[88] In addition to communal appoint-ment, we find many other forms of ensuring evangelical preaching. In Mainz— and similarly in many other cities[89]—the clergy was to be "chosen, appointed, and dismissed by the church wardens [*Kirchengeschworne*]."[90] Since the latter were often members of the city's governing elite and sat on the council,[91] this indicates that it was not entirely clear whether the appointment of the clergy was not also the task of the council. When Johannes Wanner, a preacher at the cathedral in Constance, was dismissed in 1524 under pressure from Archduke Ferdinand, the council, at the request of the community, had to appoint him to St. Stephan's.[92] In Reutlingen we have the case of the preacher Alber, a vigorous supporter of the reformation. After 1523 he celebrated the Mass in German, and in 1524 he replaced it with the Eucharist and abolished confes-sion. At the urging of the Habsburgs he was summoned before the diocesan bishop of Constance, but the community blocked this move by gathering in arms in the market square and putting the council under obligation "to stick to the gospel."[93] These two examples (and many more could be added) show that the measures needed to safeguard the preaching of the pure doctrine were secondary to the demand for the preaching itself. It seemed open, indeed irrelevant, whether the community or the council assigned the ecclesiastical offices in the city. This is confirmed not only by events in individual cities, but also by the position papers drawn up by the imperial cities to guide the decision-making at the urban diets. The declaration that was requested from Constance for the diet planned for the end of 1524 provided for an election of the clergy by the community or the council. It left open "the possibility for the rudiments of communal self-government at an intermediate level between the council and the citizenry."[94] In the cities the "pure gospel" was not inseparably linked to the election of pastors by the communities. At first glance this is a striking difference to the peasants' reformation, where this link was fundamental and essential. This naturally raises the question about the social strata that carried the reformation in the cities. Since this question provides in a sense the key to the city reformation and presents itself as a very complex problem, I shall postpone it for a moment and inquire first into the consequences of the "pure doctrine" for the cities.

Unlike in the countryside, the evangelical movement in the cities was a lengthy process that went on over several years. In Nuremberg it stretched from 1520 to 1533, in Osnabrück from 1521 to 1542, in Constance from 1520 to 1531, and in Rostock from 1525 to 1534.[95] One can question the validity of such dates; depending on the criteria used, there are often very different ideas about the importance of these dates and which ones should be emphasized. Scholars debate whether the reformation was introduced in Zurich in 1523 or 1525 and in Constance in 1523 or 1531.[96] My concern here is not a more precise chronology but a definition of what lies behind these uncertainties. One can be of divided opinion whether a mere preaching decree promulgated by the council, which lays down scriptural preaching, allows us to label a city as "reformed"; whether a better criterion for dating the reformation might not be the abolition of the Mass, the very core of sacramental piety in the old church; or whether it is necessary that the new doctrine along with congenial forms of the Mass be established as the exclusive faith within the walls before we can speak of a reformed city. These remarks reveal that the implementation of the "pure doctrine" in preaching was at most the first step on the road toward the reformation in a city. Its further implications included those we might summarily describe as the implementation of confessional unity in the cities on the basis of their understanding of the gospel. This included undoubtedly the abolition of the Mass and its replacement by new forms of divine service in the evangelical spirit. Here and there it included the removal of "idols" from the churches. In central Germany this was only a local phenomenon, in southern Germany a regional one, and in the Swiss Confederation a very common one.[97] Finally, it included—from the theological perspective rather a formal consequence—the integration of the clergy into burgher society.

The secular and regular clergy in the cities were set apart like a caste from burgher society through their privileged legal status and their exemption from the communal obligations (taxation, guard duty, military service). This situation changed wherever the evangelical movement triumphed. Indeed, we can really only speak of a successful reformation when and where the reformers succeeded in subjecting the clergy to citizenship status; perhaps it would be more appropriate to say that they subjected them to the obligations of a citizen. By looking at the examples of Strasbourg and Nuremberg we can show the individual steps of this process of the "civic incorporation" of the clergy. The wider importance of these two case studies lies in their general applicability to other cities.[98]

In 1523 Strasbourg offered the clergy of the city the chance "to form themselves into a guild like the other citizens . . . to take on all the civic burdens; but they are free in their persons to travel and shall pay money for the night watch."[99] In concrete terms this meant that the clergy was called upon for civic taxes and for guard duty, the latter in the form of a payment. Forty-five clerics responded to the invitation. But since they represented only part of the clergy of Strasbourg, the council, after lengthy negotiations in 1524, promulgated a decree in January of 1525. It compelled all clergy, with the exception of the members of the cathedral chapter, to accept citizenship within a prescribed period of time. By the middle of February another 114 clerics had entered their names into the citizenship list. The assimilation of the status of the clergy and the citizenry had thus been largely accomplished.

In regard to its policy of incorporating the clergy into the citizenry, Strasbourg is considered a model for other cities,[100] possibly including Nuremberg. In May of 1525, the council of Nuremberg, after it had earlier published a position paper, promulgated a decree which took the clergy "into the civic obligations," thus calling upon them for the "civic tax, property tax, excise tax, and other things" in return for the protection offered by the city.[101] The justification put forth by the Nuremberg council for these measures sheds some light on the political motives behind its decision that "among the common citizens a good deal of slanderous talk" is heard about the clergy, "this idle people, who live solely off the sweat and blood of others and do nothing at all in return." The decree would diffuse "the loathing, hatred, and annoyance . . . among the citizenry and . . . in the community."

The civic incorporation of the clergy had a theological side and a social side. Among the implications of the "pure doctrine" was the abolition of the Mass and with it the elimination of the sacramental character of the church; as a consequence the status of the priest was desacralized. The special caste-like position of the clergy ceased to be anything other "than a mere social fact and thus a social injustice."[102] The nontheological justification of the measures and the timing of their implementation point to a "socio-critical and socio-revolutionary motive." The pressure came not only from within the city, but was intensified by the peasant movement of 1525, which had numerous links to the cities. The peasants' militant anticlericalism also spilled into the cities, and thus we are justified in counting the civic incorporation of the regular and secular clergy "among the effects of the Peasants' War in the cities."[103]

CITY AND CHURCH—THE PRECONDITIONS
FOR THE REFORMATION IN THE CITIES

It is clear that the demand in the cities for the "gospel" owed its main impulses to the reformers' theology and its propagation through preaching and pamphlets. But the broad resonance of the reformation's appeal would be unthinkable, had there not already existed in the late medieval city a widespread desire to improve the quality and organizational framework of pastoral care.

The anticlericalism of the reformation period, which in the cities eventually led to the abolition of the clergy's exclusive status, would hardly have erupted if it could not have built on older traditions.

The civic governance of the church, which was established wherever the city fully embraced the reformation, would hardly have been so successful if there had not been earlier tendencies in that direction. An insight into the preconditions within the cities for the reception of reformationist ideas is an indispensable prerequisite if we wish to understand the role reformation theology played in the city reformation, and to what extent urban society may have developed even further the ideas it received.

Making pastoral care more responsive to the needs of the parishioners demanded institutionally established forms of communal participation, which in the late Middle Ages would have been possible only through the right of patronage. In the late medieval cities, especially the imperial cities, it is quite apparent that the councils strove to gain control of patronage, which was often in the hands of an outside monastery or a cathedral chapter.[104] On the whole their efforts had little success. Nuremberg and Sélestat, which were successful, are exceptions. As a rule the city had no influence on the appointments to parish posts. In Upper Swabia only Ulm succeeded in acquiring the right of patronage by building the cathedral.[105] All this is confirmed when we survey the empire as a whole; communal rights in the appointment of pastors can be attested in only eighty-two of the empire's 3,000 cities.[106] The possibility for the city to gain larger influence in the appointment of its pastors could come through endowments, which sometimes supplemented and sometimes competed with the pastoral care by the parish and monastic churches. Where altars, chaplaincies, or preacherships were endowed by the burghers, the principles of the proprietary church system provided at least the theoretical possibility that the donor could reserve for himself the right of appointment, which he often transferred to the council.[107] In this way the council of Nördlingen had, by the end of the fifteenth century, secured the right to nominate candidates for eight of the city's thirteen benefices.[108] Appointment to altar posts, chaplaincies, or parish posts by the city had the advantage that it could guarantee that the burghers' wishes concerning the residence and personal qualifications of the candidates would be taken into account. One type of endowment very popular in the cities was the preachership. It was intended to "satisfy the hunger for preaching," an element of pastoral care which the Roman church, with its emphasis on the sacramental Mass, rather neglected.[109] The endowment of preacherships was oriented toward the burghers' need for the preaching of the Word, and it is no coincidence that the preacherships became the bridgehead of the reformation movement. Except for Esslingen and Schwäbisch Gmünd, all the Upper Swabian imperial cities had endowed preaching posts. With their academic qualifications, which were often demanded by the endowment charters, the men who held these preacherships not infrequently stood out against the pastors of the city churches and the monks in the monasteries.[110]

This broader trend toward involving the church more deeply in civic life was continued on the level of the parishes. While the official church was inclined to look upon the parishioners as "subjects,"[111] we notice here and there clear signs that the parishes in the fifteenth century desired a greater say in parish life, even when that involved seemingly marginal issues, such as the administration of the cemeteries or participation in school affairs. Here we must emphasize the historical fact that "the community already existed in rudimentary form at the end of the fifteenth century, and was not created only during the Reformation."[112]

The interest of the citizens in the church should rule out an interpretation of the measures taken by the cities as indicating an anti-church sentiment. The demands for an "inexpensive church," for model behavior of the clergy and their presence in the city, must also be seen as arising from a genuine concern about salvation. Only occasionally do we find in late medieval cities demands that the sacraments be administered free of charge, that the pastors reside in the communities, do their duties conscientiously, and show personal integrity; the latter concern was often articulated in biting comments about *Pfaffenweiber*, a contemptuous reference to the priests' women.[113] Still, all these examples do not add up to much if we compare them to the complaints raised by the peasants, and they reveal that the level of pastoral care for the faithful in the cities was considerably better than in the countryside. Of course, this comes as no surprise, given the fact that there was an overabundance of clerics and monasteries in the cities.

If the demands for the preaching of the Word and the sacraments free of charge reflect religious needs, the cities' endeavors to integrate the clergy socially and politically were driven more by economic motives. In 1179 the Lateran Council (canon 19) had enshrined the immunity of the clergy in canon law. In the life of the city it meant that the clergy did not bear the civic obligations of the urban community—taxes, guard duties, military service. Worse still, through the monastic economy, which was tax-exempt, the clergy competed with the city's crafts and trade. Moreover, they were not subject to the city's jurisdiction; in all legal disputes involving a cleric or church revenues, the clergy went to the outside ecclesiastical court.[114] It is not surprising that the status of the secular clergy, the exemption of the monasteries and cathedral chapters, and the privileged jurisdiction of the secular and regular clergy gave rise to many quarrels and directed the efforts of the cities toward cutting back the church's privileges wherever possible. Although in the late Middle Ages the impregnable defenses of the cities provided the best possible protection for the extensive urban properties of the church, the clergy did not feel any legal or moral obligation to help support the enormous costs of maintaining a city's fortifications.[115] Only by applying consistent pressure were the magistrates in some cities able to keep property purchased "mortmain" liable for city taxes, to collect milling fees from the clergy, or to levy the excise tax.[116] All these efforts could have succeeded only if the authorities had managed to impose citizenship—or better, civic obligations—on the clergy. But in the end, all efforts in that direction had only modest results. We can see this in the case of Strasbourg, where fewer than two clergymen per year assumed full citizenship, and Strasbourg's policy of civic incorporation of the clergy is considered to have been very successful compared to those of other cities.[117] This policy of incorporating the clergy entered its final stage at the earliest after 1525, when the cities were able to exploit the weakness of the established church. In a decree of the imperial city of Nordhausen in 1525, we read the following:

> . . . our lords, the council and the master artisans, have decided with the consent of the community that all members of the clergy . . . who now live here in Nordhausen shall be like burghers in oaths and obligations and shall make themselves equal in status in regard to dues, guard duties, and the common city tax.[118]

Before that it had never been possible to tax the clergy fully and consistently. "It was nowhere seriously questioned that clergy and laity were two separate classes of people."[119]

Of course the efforts at including the clergy in the civic duties were also targeted at the regular clergy. In fact the religious orders posed an even more serious problem, since the monasteries maintained workshops and commercial businesses in their immunities. These were especially hated as competitors to the city's trades and commerce, and they also violated every sense of fairness because the monasteries claimed the privilege of tax exemption for their products. There is good reason why we find the demand to put an end to such abuses in many grievance lists of the communities.[120] However, with the regular clergy, as well, the cities rarely had any great success in their policies. The most that was achieved was to make the monastic products liable for taxation; hardly ever do we hear of subjecting the regular clergy to the civic duties.[121]

The judicial exemption of the clergy could interfere deeply in the life of the city as criminal and civil suits were removed from the city's jurisdiction if clergymen were involved. "It was hard to tolerate and very difficult to understand that there should be a group of inhabitants who in principle sought justice outside the city walls and who could not be held accountable within the city itself."[122] Nevertheless, it seems that the legal exemption of the clergy aroused far less opposition than its tax exemption.[123] In so far as local studies provide us with information, it was more often the ecclesiastical punishments of the episcopal courts—the ban and the interdict—that drew the burghers' anger.[124] In only a few cities did the authorities succeed in expanding the city's jurisdiction to include the clergy, and then only in precisely defined cases, or at least in restricting the ecclesiastical court to its original jurisdiction in cases relating to marriage or church income. Most efforts in these directions no doubt led to no concrete results at all.[125]

On the whole, we must note both the remarkable tenacity of the cities' efforts as well as their frequent failure. The attempts of the cities to incorporate the clergy into the citizenry kept pace with the cities' growing political autonomy.[126] In the end, however, they had only partial success against a church that had the support of the papal Curia with its universal authority and the international backing of religious orders spread all over Europe.

The more a city detached itself from its overlord, the more it had to take on the tasks of public administration. Given the size of the cities and the resultant economic and social problems, these tasks continually expanded. There was good reason why "good administration" (*gute Polizei*) developed earliest in the cities.[127] *Polizei* in this sense soon spread also to the religious sphere. In part this expansion was no doubt also intended to support ecclesiastical measures, but it was soon accompanied by the increasingly clear claim that the authorities should also set the norms for religious life. Civic administration competed with church law by issuing decrees against cursing and swearing, promulgating penal codes for adultery, and publishing regulations concerning baptisms, weddings, and funerals.[128] By taking the hospitals into civic jurisdiction, establishing schools, and organizing public charity, civic administration moved into areas that had previously been reserved for the clergy.[129] The demand to enforce the city's statutory jurisdiction made itself felt toward the preachers of indulgences, whose preaching was tied to certain conditions: for example, the proceeds of their work had to be deposited with the city to ensure that they would actually be used for their true purpose, or part of the take had to be given over to civic institutions.[130] Here, too, I must emphasize that these measures were not motivated by antireligious sentiments. Quite the contrary, for not infrequently a council passed a decree with the conviction that it could thus "ordain" God's blessing for the city. A particularly nice expression of this occurs in Zurich's decree on dancing, which states that "in order that the Lord our God may protect us and send us good weather, seeing that the crops are in the field, nobody shall dance."[131]

The measures taken by the councils to expand the city's influence over the church were never only affairs of the authorities, but often originated from communal initiatives. The sources for the late Middle Ages are not detailed enough to allow us to determine in each instance the share of the council and of the community. But at least we can attest to communal activities at the parish level. Moreover, we can well imagine that the guild of tavern keepers fought against the tax-exempt sale of wine and beer by the monasteries, and that the guild of weavers protested the competition from the Beguine Houses. Which brings us back to the question about the role the community played in the process of implementing the reformation in the cities.

GOSPEL AND COMMUNITY—
PILLARS OF THE BURGHERS' REFORMATION

The reformation in the cities is an indistinct phenomenon, characterized both by tumultuous gatherings by the citizens to push through certain goals of the reformation, as well as by vigorous measures taken by the authorities against clerics and monasteries who remained faithful to the Roman church. This raises the question of what the reformation in the cities actually represents in socio-historical terms: a reformation by the councils or a communal reformation.[132] If we evaluate the many specialized studies from this perspective, we find a clear, although preliminary, verdict: the reformation in the cities was not a magistrates' reformation. Then what was it? The answers that have been put forth cover a very broad spectrum. Kurt Kaser already saw the reformation in the cities as a "popular movement."[133] This is also the interpretation of Bernd Moeller, who noted that in all the southern imperial cities "the evangelical movement begins . . . in the first half of the sixteenth century . . . almost exclusively among the people," and of Steven Ozment, who characterized the reformation in the German and Swiss cities and towns as a "popular movement."[134] Alongside the designation of the reformation in the cities as a movement carried by "the people," behind which we can see the vague outlines of the concept of a "people's reformation," we find in the more recent scholarship, which approaches the problem from the perspective of social history, the concept of a reformation "from below." Thomas A. Brady, Jr., has described the reformation in Strasbourg as "a story of attack and threat from below."[135] His verdict is echoed for northern Germany by Heinz Schilling, who says the reformation in the northwestern German cities was initiated and carried "from below."[136] Another, similar term frequently used for this phenomenon is that of the "citizenry." The citizenry pushed through the reformation in the Swiss and Hanseatic cities; occasionally it figures as the basic vehicle of the reformation movement in the cities.[137]

The lack of a clear terminology arises from the historical phenomenon itself, for it has proved exceedingly difficult to identify precisely the champions of the evangelical movement and their social or political place. Nevertheless, the variant terminology expresses one common idea, that the reformation in the cities was not an affair of the authorities, that it was not begun by the councils and magistrates.[138] Yet it is also clear and incontestable that the councils did not simply let the reformation process take its course. Through their decisions they were involved in many different ways, indeed the final completion of the reformation process usually bears the official stamp of approval in the form of church constitutions (*Kirchenordnungen*). Analyzing in greater detail the place of the council in the reformation process is thus the most important preliminary step if we wish to clarify further what it means to speak of a city reformation carried by "the people," "from below," and by "the citizenry."

A first glance at the councils and their attitude toward the reformation movement "from below" shows that they "picked up the impulses coming from the people and led the reformation . . . to victory."[139] It has been argued that the magistrates were cautiously restrained because, as the rich and powerful class, they were naturally suspicious of innovations, and because it was comparatively easy for them to pay the expenses that were necessary to ensure salvation within the old church.[140] This general argument, which claims to be broadly valid, has been examined in terms of social relations at Strasbourg. For the "ruling class" of noblemen and leading merchants, the rituals and instruments of salvation of the Roman church represented a religious sanctioning of their conservatism and aristocratic rule. The emotional rejection of the Mass and religious images by the reformers threatened the chapels, altars, and Mass which the ruling class had endowed, and this endangered both status symbols and the salvation of the soul. The attacks on the regular and chapter clergy, driven by the eventual goal of secularizing and dissolving the monasteries and prince-bishoprics, threatened important institutions that provided for the future generations of patrician sons. The refusal to pay dues and tithes, which not infrequently went to the patricians themselves, had to strike those entitled to them as a challenge to the entire system of property.[141] Despite its empirical breadth and analytical rigor, this thesis by Thomas A. Brady, Jr., has been criticized because it does not regard the council's eventually positive attitude as arising also from religious conviction.[142] Although devoted to one case, Strasbourg, this analysis provides a possible answer as to why the urban councils initially opposed the evangelical movement. It also explains that they eventually supported it in order to secure the position and power of the urban elites: "the aristocracy and oligarchy of Strasbourg weathered the crisis of the mid-1520s. They had altered as little as possible but as much as necessary and had survived the storms with hegemony intact."[143]

This sharp assessment of the motives of the Strasbourg council, focused on the social and political interests of the political elite, does not necessarily contradict the more common verdict we can derive from the language of the sources: namely that the councils eventually came around to the evangelical movement "from below" primarily in order to secure the peace within the city. The sources for Basel and Erfurt show that the protection of peace was presented as the primary goal of the religious policies of the authorities, and this finding has solid documentary support in most cities.[144] The imperial city of Mulhouse in Alsace promulgated its preaching decree of 1523 "in order that Christian brotherly love and unity among our people may unfold and be implanted." It obliged the clergy to preach in accordance with Scripture, so that "the evangelical truth will be revealed and preached to us Christians more clearly and faithfully than before," and also because the Catholics were calling the innovators "heretics, rogues, knaves, and the like," which "might mislead the common people, and what is more, could cause an uprising of our community."[145] To sixteenth century minds, the maintenance of peace was undoubtedly the central function of authority and the legitimating justification of its existence. If the authorities could no longer fulfill this task they lost their legitimacy and could be replaced. Under these conditions the councils naturally ran the risk of making their decisions dependent on political necessity. Safeguarding the peace in recognition of the will of the majority, at least of the involved and active majority, secured the political and social position of the councils; from the perspective of contemporaries it bestowed upon them the prestige of being modern and progressive, and in the eyes of reformation intelligentsia it charged them with a task of world-historical importance.

If we are justified in singling out the concern for peace as the dominant, if not sole, criterion that explains why the urban authorities were either for or against the reformation, it necessarily follows, and is also substantiated by the sources, that the councils are of little help in defining the reformation movement in the cities. This raises the question of whether we can define more precisely, in political and social terminology, the stratum that carried the reformation, which so far has been rather vaguely circumscribed with the terms "people," "citizenry," and analogous concepts.

Because social stratification in Central European cities was extremely diverse, we can hardly expect to reach a more precise definition of the social stratum that carried the reformation in the cities by focusing on occupational, income, or status groups. A useful term, which integrates both the special place of the councils within the reformation movement as well as the interchangeable terms to designate the social group that carried it ("the people," "from below," "the citizenry"), can be found in the sources themselves: that of the "commune" or "community" (Gemeinde). The cities were structured by "council" and "community." At Mühlhausen in Thuringia the evangelical preachers were to be appointed by "the community with the participation of the honorable council"; at Frankfurt "an honorable council and the community" were henceforth to install the pastors.[146] The examples could be easily multiplied. Of course, the contrast between community and council, which is frequent if not predominant, has not been entirely overlooked by scholars, even though the above-mentioned terms are used far more frequently. The term "community" has only recently been noticed for Bern, Esslingen, and Dortmund, to support attempts to explain more broadly the driving forces of the reformation movement.[147]

The usefulness of the term "community" is confirmed once we take a closer look at the process that led to the success of the reformation movement in the cities. Expanding and modifying a suggestion by Otthein Rammstedt,[148] we can divide this process into three successive phases, which can be described as (1) protest, (2) articulation of protest, and (3) institutionalization of the articulated protest.[149] The protest began in relatively unorganized and amorphous forms on the level of the parish or the guilds, or among parts of the citizenry. The articulation of the protest was usually the work of a "committee," which presented a concrete list of demands and grievances to the council. The institutionalization of the protest, finally, was accomplished by the council with the participation of the community or its committee.

Since the social substratum of the reformation movement is very difficult to grasp, the first phase is of little use in our effort to find a more precise terminological definition of the reformation movement. The second phase, however, allows us to develop very clearly our definition of the movement as a "communal reformation." One characteristic of the reformation in the cities—as the examples of Erfurt, Kitzingen, and Basel have plainly shown—is the fact that the committee became the vehicle for pushing through the evangelical movement wherever the council did not already pick up and implement the reform ideas during the first phase. But since the first reaction of the councils was usually to reject the reformation movement, the committees deserve the credit for pushing through the reformation. This was the case at Braunschweig, Hamburg, Hannover, Lemgo, Lübeck, Magdeburg, Memmingen, Mühlhausen in Thuringia, Stralsund, and Wismar, to give only a few examples.[150] The formation of the committee could occur on the basis of the parish (as in Hamburg and Magdeburg), it could grow out of the guilds (as in Memmingen and Sélestat), or it could arise from the citizenry as a whole (as in Braunschweig and Lübeck). A glance at Basel and Strasbourg shows that in social terms there were often close connections between guilds and parishes. At Basel the weavers' guild, which at times played a leading role in that city's reformation, had its center in the suburb of Steinen and had its parish center at St. Leonhard's.[151] The focus of religious life for the gardeners' guild at Strasbourg, most of whose members also lived close together in one section of the city, was the parish church of St. Aurelia.[152] Parish and guild were therefore often interchangeable.

Where the formation of the committee occurred on the basis of the parish or the guild, this merely reflected older constitutional traditions of the city. At Hamburg the committee could fall back on an older committee of sixty, which had already been set up in 1410 on the basis of the parishes.[153] At Memmingen the city constitution itself was based on the guilds, so that communal activities naturally enough had to emanate from them.[154] The crucial element of all these committees is that they articulated the will of the community to the council. Recent scholarship on urban history has convincingly characterized the use of committees to push through communal demands as "the right of each citizen, grounded in the city's communal principle, to protest against the authority of the council," and thus as a "constitutional" procedure.[155] From the perspective of this tradition, as well, which had deep roots in the late Middle Ages, the use of committees, a practice that was reactivated as needed in times of crisis and hence also during the reformation period, turns out to have been an instrument for asserting communal interests.

The role of communal interests is also reflected in the final phase of implementing the reformation, which took place "in a great many, if not all, cities with the direct participation of the community,"[156] either through formal plebiscites in the guilds, or through communal assemblies, which are attested for Biberach, Esslingen, Goslar, Heilbronn, Constance, Memmingen, Reutlingen, Ulm, and Wissembourg. The council did not introduce the reformation; rather, it established the peace within the city through the majority decision of the community and its representative organs. This is confirmed also in the decisions that were reached through the new method of disputations. At the disputation of Memmingen in 1525, one representative from each guild was summoned in "the name of the community."[157] At the disputation in Sélestat, the council was to be joined by five, six, or ten members of each guild.[158] The Hamburg disputation of 1528 was organized by forty-eight church wardens (Gotteskasten- verwalter) elected from the parishes.[159] At all disputations we can sense very clearly that the appeal of the community either induced or forced the council to hold the religious debate. All these events point back to the Zurich Disputation of 1523, which was "something of an innovation," since before that time disputations outside the university and decisions by the laity about right doctrine had not been customary.[160] The fact that the disputations were usually followed in the cities by government decrees concerning preaching, the Mass, or religious images was occasionally used by older scholarship as justification for calling the movement the "magistrates' reformation." The extensive examination of the Zurich Disputation, along with the demonstration that many cities merely followed the Zurich model, has shown that this verdict is untenable.[161] At Zurich the authorities did not reach their decision in the narrow circle of the Small Council, but in consultation with the Council of Two Hundred, which can be seen as a kind of institutionalized committee; hence we may speak of a decision made by the "lay community."[162] At Zurich and elsewhere, the council claimed the right to keep order (ius pacificandi), which in the situation of continuing conflict was expanded to a right to decide (ius iudicandi).[163] All disputations were concerned with making a "decision," and this pressure turned the disputation into a trial. The court, now expanded—to remain with the image—from the municipal court (Schöffengericht) of the Small Council to the collective assembly of the representatives of the community, was partisan to the extent that it established the gospel as the basis for reaching a decision. The verdict would go to whichever side could produce better scriptural arguments in support of its position. This meant that in the final analysis the community would, after all, decide the outcome of the disputation. Since the communal representatives in the Large Councils and committees were generally not adher- ents of the old faith, there could hardly be any serious doubt about the outcome of the disputations. Who can blame the Catholics for thinking that this entire procedure was a set-up?[164]

CONSEQUENCES OF THE EVANGELICAL MOVEMENT IN THE CITIES

As in the countryside, the evangelical movement in the cities did not remain limited to matters of the church in the narrower sense, but expanded and took on new economic, social, and political dimensions. In the course of the evangelical movement in the cities, which usually extended over several years (sometimes over more than a decade), the demands of the community always spilled over into the secular sphere. At Colmar, demands for the pure gospel, the civic incorporation of the clergy, and the curbing of the jurisdiction of the ecclesiastical court were accompanied by demands for a reduction of labor services, the opening of the commons, and a restructuring of rents and tithes.[165] At Memmingen the introduction of the reformation was accompanied by refusals to pay the tithe and the demand that citizens be imprisoned only in felony cases.[166] The community in Mainz added to its known reformation goals the request for the commutability of rents and dues; the reduction of the excise duty on animals, grain, and salt; a price reduction on the procurement of wood; improvements in the administration of justice; and the election of a committee drawn from the guilds, whose members' full-time occupation should be to represent the interests of the community before the governor and executive council of the electorate of Mainz.[167] In the course of the reformation movement in Stralsund, the community pushed through a number of demands: the committee of forty-eight had to be notified of elections for the council, the city's finances were to be controlled by the committee, and statutes could be drafted and passed only in consultation with the committee.[168] So far there have been no attempts to systematically classify the demands raised in the cities.[169] But an examination of the material, of which I have presented only selections so as to avoid a lengthy discussion, reveals how difficult it is to compare the demands of the urban communities from one overarching perspective embracing all of Central Europe. The ecclesiastical movement could lead to the creation of new constitutional organs without involving economic demands, but it could also press for financial relief for the burghers without touching the existing constitutional arrangements. We learn from this that the consequences which people in the city drew from the gospel were rather amorphous, that they defy rigid classification and are thus noticeably different from the coherent programs that were articulated in the wake of the "peasants' reformation."

Even though many Catholic councilors left their cities as the reformation was implemented, to be replaced, not infrequently, by Protestants, and despite the fact that communities occasionally succeeded in consolidating the right of participation by institutionalizing the committee system, the reformation in the cities did not establish a communally based church. That could have occurred only if, during the initial stages of the evangelical movement, the parishes in the cities had overturned the prevailing principle of patronage, which was traditionally the exclusive privilege of "lordship," and had reclaimed the election and maintenance of pastors as their own exclusive right. This did not happen. Apparently the burghers could simply not conceive of a conceptual separation of church community and urban community. In this respect we can agree with Bernd Moeller's interpretation that the city saw itself as a miniature *corpus christianum*.[170] The community always sought the council's confirmation and sanctioning of its wishes. In extreme cases that could lead to councilors being deposed or put to flight, but such steps were always taken with the hope that one could thereby obtain the council's approval of the reformation. This meant, of course, that the communal reformation lost its original impulse toward a fundamental restructuring of church organization. Once the council had decreed evangelical preaching, had abolished the Mass, and had absorbed the clergy into the citizen body, it seemed only natural to move the decision-making about the city's church life from the streets into the council chamber. In the 1530s and 1540s it is quite clear that the councils only rarely sought the consensus of the community for its decisions, and they did not have to. "Even though the Reformation movement had often started from the individual parishes, in the end it was always the councils who took charge of the new church governance [*Kirchenregiment*]."[171] This broad assessment by Bernd Moeller has been fully confirmed by modern scholarship.[172] Although new theological ideas were implemented, the institutional framework of the church was still the same or very much the same. Differences emerge only between Switzerland and Germany. Whereas in Germany the authoritative character of the church was increasingly consolidated, in the Confederacy the community was granted at least a modest degree of participation in the marriage courts and ecclesiastical courts.[173]

Notes

1. The quote is from Arthur G. Dickens, *The German Nation and Martin Luther* (New York, 1974), 182. See Hans-Christoph Rublack, "Forschungsbericht Stadt und Reformation," in Bernd Moeller, ed., *Stadt und Kirche im 16. Jahrhundert*, Schriften des Vereins für Reformationsgeschichte, no. 190 (Gütersloh, 1978), 24.
2. Rolf Kießling, *Bürgerliche Gesellschaft und Kirche in Augsburg im Spätmittelalter. Ein Beitrag zur Strukturanalyse der oberdeutschen Reichsstadt*, Abhandlungen zur Geschichte der Stadt Augsburg, vol. 19 (Augsburg, 1971); Sigrid Jahns, *Frankfurt, Reformation und Schmalkaldischer Bund. Die Reformations-, Reichs- und Bündnispolitik der Reichsstadt Frankfurt am Main 1525–1536*, Studien zur Frankfurter Geschichte, vol. 9 (Frankfurt am Main, 1976); Hans-Christoph Rublack, "Die Reformation in Kitzingen," in Dieter Demandt and Hans Christoph Rublack, *Stadt und Kirche in Kitzingen. Darstellung und Quellen zu Spätmittelalter und Reformation*, Spätmittelalter und Frühe Neuzeit. Tübinger Beiträge zur Geschichtsforschung, vol. 10 (Stuttgart, 1978), 34–96, 101–321; Heinz Schilling, *Konfessionskonflikt und Staatsbildung. Eine Fallstudie über das Verhältnis von religiösem und sozialem Wandel in der Frühneuzeit am Beispiel der Grafschaft Lippe*, Quellen und Forschungen zur Reformationsgeschichte, 48 (Gütersloh, 1982); Hans-Christoph Rublack, *Eine bürgerliche Reformation: Nördlingen*, Quellen und Forschungen zur Reformationsgeschichte, vol. 51 (Gütersloh, 1982); Thomas A. Brady, Jr., *Ruling Class, Regime and Reformation in Strasbourg, 1520–1555*, Studies in Medieval and Reformation Thought, vol. 22 (Leiden, 1978).
3. Here I cite only the most recent collections: Bernd Moeller, ed., *Stadt und Kirche im 16. Jahrhundert*, Schriften des Vereins für Reformationsgeschichte, no. 190

(Gütersloh, 1978); Wolfgang J. Mommsen, ed., *Stadtbürgertum und Adel in der Reformation*, Veröffentlichungen des Deutschen Historischen Instituts London, vol. 5 (Stuttgart, 1979); Franz Petri, ed., *Kirche und gesellschaftlicher Wandel in deutschen und niederländischen Städten der werdenden Neuzeit*, Städteforschung, vol. A 10 (1980); Ingrid Bátori, ed., *Städtische Gesellschaft und Reformation. Kleine Schriften 2*, Spätmittelalter und Frühe Neuzeit. Tübinger Beiträge zur Geschichtsforschung, vol. 12 (Stuttgart, 1980).

4. The phrase, "burghers' reformation," translates "bürgerliche Reformation," which I borrow from Rublack, *Nördlingen*, who speaks of a "burghers' reformation" in the title of this book, and from Schilling, *Konfessionskonflikt*, 139–144, who speaks of the "city reformation as a burgher movement" ("Stadtreformation als Bürgerbewegung"). The phrase is also suggested already by the earlier definition of a "peasants' reformation."

5. This list follows the five points identified by Rublack, "Forschungsbericht," 24. For obvious reasons, I did not include in this list of "secure" interpretations the question concerning the problem of continuity versus discontinuity, which Rublack says is disputed. For the literature through 1983, see Kaspar von Greyerz, "Stadt und Reformation. Stand und Aufgaben der Forschung," *Archiv für Reformationsgeschichte* 76 (1985): 6–63. Gerhard Müller's study, *Reformation und Stadt. Zur Rezeption der evangelischen Verkündigung*, Akademie der Wissenschaften und der Literatur, Geistes- und sozialwissenschaftliche Klasse, Jg. 1981, no. 11 (1981), deals primarily with Nuremberg.

6. References to the cities mentioned in S. Ozment, *The Reformation in the Cities. The Appeal of Protestantism to Sixteenth-Century Germany and Switzerland* (New Haven and London, 1975), 128ff.

7. Thus Ozment, *Reformation in the Cities*.

8. See, for example, the more recent works of Rublack, *Kitzingen* and *Nördlingen*.

9. Walther Peter Fuchs and Günther Franz, eds., *Akten zur Geschichte des Bauernkrieges in Mitteldeutschland*, 2 vols. (Jena, 1942; reprint, Aalen, 1964), vol. 2: 402.

10. See the broad characterization by Dickens, *Luther*, 169f.; Günther Franz, *Der deutsche Bauernkrieg*, 11th ed. (Darmstadt, 1977), 245ff.

11. See Robert W. Scribner, "Civic Unity and the Reformation in Erfurt," *Past and Present* 66 (1975): esp. 40, a broad account that also examines the historical background. On this see also the eyewitness account in Karl Schottenloher, "Erfurter und Wittenberger Berichte aus den Frühjahren der Reformation nach Tegernseer Überlieferungen," in O. Scheel, ed., *Festschrift für Hans von Schubert* (Tübingen, 1929), 79–85.

12. Thus Dickens, *Luther*, 172.

13. More detailed in Scribner, "Erfurt," 40. Apparently taxes were thereafter levied also on the clergy. See on this the writing of the Erfurt council to the abbot at Pforta in Fuchs and Franz, *Akten*, vol. 2: 41, no. 1131.

14. Dickens, *Luther*, 41.

15. Scribner, "Erfurt," 40.

16. For references see Scribner, "Erfurt," 41ff., and Dickens, *Luther*, 173ff.

17. Thus Scribner, "Erfurt," 41.

18. Ibid., 40, 42.

19. The most vivid account of the events is still that of Franz, *Bauernkrieg*, 246f.

20. Fuchs and Franz, *Akten*, vol. 2: 445–450, no. 1639.

21. A writing to the officials (*Amtleute*) in Erfurt (6 June 1525) said: "We [the council] together with the guardians [*vormunden*] and delegates [*verordneten*] from the city quarters [*vierteln*], artisans, and countryside unanimously regard as good and have decided . . ." Fuchs and Franz, *Akten*, vol. 2: 211, no. 1336.

22. Printed in Fuchs and Franz, *Akten*, 250ff., no. 1390.
23. Ibid., 252f., no. 1390a; 253, no. 1391.
24. However, it may be necessary to correct the widespread, explicitly or implicitly expressed notion that the peasants' interests were suppressed in favor of the city's interests (see Franz, *Bauernkrieg*, 247f.; Scribner, "Erfurt," 45). It is generally overlooked that in the council's acceptance letter of May 9, 1525 (Fuchs and Franz, *Akten*, vol. 2: 252) the articles as such were presented as those of the *vogteien* (bailiwicks), *pflegen* (districts), *dorfschaften* (village communes), and *Landschaften* (country communities) and of the city community. More interesting still are the contents of the articles according to the acceptance letter. We read about "compulsory labor" (*frohne*), "dues" (*dienste*), and a "hunting ban" (*wiltpan*), which are not mentioned at all in the 28 Erfurt Articles, which leads one to think that there may have existed in addition to the 28 Articles separate rural articles that have been lost.
25. Fuchs and Franz, *Akten*, vol. 2: 250.
26. Scribner, "Erfurt," 46.
27. On this see the text in Fuchs and Franz, *Akten*, vol. 2: 252f.
28. Ibid., 153.
29. This arrangement was contractually confirmed in the treaty of Hammelburg in 1530 between the city and the archbishopric of Mainz. Scribner, "Erfurt," 48f.; Dickens, *Luther*, 175.
30. Klaus Arnold, "Die Stadt Kitzingen im Bauernkrieg," *Mainfränkisches Jahrbuch für Geschichte und Kunst* 287 (1975): 30f.
31. Rublack, "Kitzingen," 228–241, no. 52; 235ff., no. 51. On the dating of the writings and the margrave's reaction to them, see Arnold, "Kitzingen," 31.
32. For the general historical background see Rublack, "Kitzingen," 34–90; Rublack's discussion should be supplemented by the account of Arnold, "Kitzingen," 11–50. In parts of the wording I follow my older discussion in *Die Reformation im Reich*, Uni-Taschenbücher, vol. 1181 (Stuttgart, 1982), 87–91.
33. Text printed in Rublack, "Kitzingen," 203ff., no. 203.
34. The pertinent sources in Rublack, "Kitzingen," 216–221, nos. 34–38.
35. Ibid., 224ff., nos. 42, 43. On Peringer, see now Günter Vogler, *Nürnberg 1524/25. Studien zur Geschichte der reformatorischen und sozialen Bewegung in der Reichsstadt* (Berlin, 1982), 135–151.
36. For a detailed account of the events, see Arnold, "Kitzingen," 24ff.
37. Pathbreaking and fundamentally important is the work of Klaus Arnold, "Spätmittelalterliche Sozialstruktur, Bürgeropposition und Bauernkrieg in der Stadt Kitzingen," *Jahrbuch für fränkische Landesforschung* 36 (1976): 173–214, esp. 201ff. Arnold's arguments have been criticized. See Ingrid Bátori, "Ratsherren und Aufrührer. Soziale und ökonomische Verhältnisse in der Stadt Kitzingen zur Zeit des Bauernkriegs und der Reformation," in Mommsen, *Stadtbürgertum*, 149–214. The difficulty of isolating and defining social strata within a city has now also been shown by Ingrid Bátori and Erdmann Weyrauch, *Die bürgerliche Elite der Stadt Kitzingen. Studien zur Sozial- und Wirtschaftsgeschichte einer landesherrlichen Stadt im 16. Jahrhundert*, Spätmittelalter und Frühe Neuzeit. Tübinger Beiträge zur Geschichtsforschung, vol. 11 (Stuttgart, 1982), esp. 64f., 157.
38. Franz, *Bauernkrieg*, 182f.
39. Günther Franz, ed., *Quellen zur Geschichte des Bauernkrieges*, Ausgewählte Quellen zur deutschen Geschichte der Neuzeit. Freiherr vom Stein-Gedächtnisausgabe, vol. 2 (Darmstadt, 1963), 348.
40. Arnold, "Kitzingen," 25f.
41. Thus explicitly and with solid arguments by Bátori and Weyrauch, *Kitzingen*.

42. Rublack, "Kitzingen," 91.
43. H.-C. Rublack, "Gravamina und Reformation," in Bátori, *Städtische Gesellschaft*, 308–311.
44. Rublack, "Kitzingen," 93.
45. Ibid., 92.
46. Emil Dürr and Paul Roth, eds., *Aktensammlung zur Geschichte der Basler Reformation in den Jahren 1519 bis Anfang 1534*, 6 vols. (Basel, 1921–1950), vol. 3: 201 and note 73.
47. See on this Fridolin Ryff's very vivid chronological account, based on solid archival work, in Wilhelm Vischer and Alfred Stern, eds., *Basler Chroniken* (Leipzig, 1872), vol. 1: 66–91.
48. Rudolf Wackernagel, *Geschichte der Stadt Basel*, vol. 3 (Basel, 1924), 325f.
49. Ibid., 340.
50. Ibid., 328f.
51. Johannes Strickler, ed., *Actensammlung zur Schweizerischen Reformationsgeschichte in den Jahren 1521–1532 im Anschluss an die gleichzeitigen eidgenössischen Abschiede*, vol. 1: *1521–1528* (Zurich, 1878), 207, no. 586.
52. Wackernagel, *Basel*, 344. His eventual appointment as *Leutpriester* in 1525 was also made with support from the community. See Strickler, *Actensammlung*, 208, no. 590.
53. Wackernagel, *Basel*, 329.
54. Ibid.
55. Numerous references in Wackernagel, *Basel*, 356ff.
56. All quotes are from the preaching mandate, which is printed in Dürr and Roth, *Aktensammlung*, vol. 1: 67.
57. Ibid., 66.
58. Wackernagel, *Basel*, 335.
59. Ibid., 367.
60. The events of 1525 in the weavers' guild are discussed by Hans Rudolf Guggisberg and Hans Füglister, "Die Basler Weberzunft als Trägerin der reformatorischen Propaganda," Moeller, *Stadt und Kirche*, 48–56.
61. The justification before the council in Dürr and Roth, *Aktensammlung*, vol. 1, 180–185, no. 316. The document is undated; on the question of its date see Dürr and Roth, 180 note 1.
62. Ibid., 181.
63. Ibid.
64. Ibid., 182f. (both quotes). For Zurich it has recently been calculated that the lights for the tombs of St. Felix and St. Regula in the cathedral (*Großmünster*) required 18 pounds of wax a year, which corresponded to 513 kilograms of grain, or approximately a master artisan's wage for about 65 days. Peter Jezler, Elke Jezler, and Christine Göttler, "Warum ein Bilderstreit? Der Kampf gegen die 'Götzen' in Zürich als Beispiel," *Unsere Kunstdenkmäler* 35 (1984): 281f.
65. Ibid., 182.
66. Wackernagel, *Basel*, 368; Dürr and Roth, *Aktensammlung*, vol. 2: 35f., no. 52, print the oath of truce (*Urfehde*) of Ulrich Leyderer (19 August 1525), who had played a leading role in these disturbances. On the life of Leyderer see R. Wackernagel, *Basel*, 367f.; for other witness testimony see Guggisberg and Füglister, "Basler Weberzunft," 54.
67. Wackernagel, *Basel*, 371.
68. The grievances are printed in Dürr and Roth, *Aktensammlung*, vol. 1: 242–257, nos. 407, 408. The individual villages and districts did not all present their demands jointly.

69. Ibid., 231f., no. 395.
70. Ibid., 234f., no. 398.
71. Dürr and Roth, *Aktensammlung*, vol. 2: 401f., no. 511; 390f., no. 306; Wacker-nagel, *Basel*, 269. The latter quote comes from a position paper of the council in its negotiations with the bishop's coadjutor. It is unclear to what extent the council pushed through its position.
72. Thus Wackernagel, *Basel*, 472, who also lists the setbacks. See also Bernd Moeller, "Zwinglis Disputationen. Studien zu den Anfängen der Kirchenbildung und des Synodalwesens im Protestantismus, II. Teil," *Zeitschrift der Savigny-Stiftung für Rechtsgeschichte, Kanonistische Abteilung* 60 (1974): 267.
73. Dürr and Roth, *Aktensammlung*, vol. 2: 504–545, no. 675. Additional responses passim in the same volume.
74. Ibid., 715f., no. 728.
75. Dürr and Roth, *Aktensammlung*, vol. 3, 197–202, no. 291 (23 December 1528). The guilds are not named but can be inferred from the reply of the council (203f., no. 293). See the slightly varying text in Vischer and Stern, *Basler Chroniken*, 67–71.
76. "And so, once . . . the disputation has ended we shall presently call together all our citizens and those who belong to the guilds into their various guild assemblies, and shall put the decision to the conscience of each person whether the Mass should be kept or abolished and shall follow the majority; and whatever shall be the majority at that time among the council, our common citizens, and the guild brothers shall be done in the name of God, in accordance with the majority, and the minority shall not resist it." Dürr and Roth, *Aktensammlung*, vol. 3, 235.
77. A detailed contemporary account of these events (and their background) is in Vischer and Stern, *Basler Chroniken*, 67–91; and see the account by Wackernagel, *Basel*, 511–515.
78. Recently scholars have interpreted the iconoclasm in Basel from a popular culture perspective as a carnivalistic ritual of release, but the chronological events show that this interpretation is not correct. See Robert W. Scribner, "Reformation, carnival and the world turned upside down," *Social History* 3 (1978): 303–329, here 307f., and Jezler et al., "Bilderstreit," 289. Scribner seems to have retracted his interpretation. See on this the minutes of discussion (by Peter Bierbrauer, Aendreas Holstein, and Heinrich Richard Schmidt) in Peter Blickle et al., eds., *Zwingli und Europa* (1985). Scribner took this into consideration when he decided not to characterize the events as a carnival ritual in the written version of his paper.
79. Dürr and Roth, *Aktensammlung*, vol. 3: 383–409, no. 473.
80. Gerhard Brendler, *Martin Luther. Theologie und Revolution* (Berlin, 1983), 299.
81. Quoted from Gerhard Pfeiffer, "Das Verhältnis von politischer und kirchlicher Gemeinde in den deutschen Reichsstädten," in Walther Peter Fuchs, ed., *Staat und Kirche im Wandel der Jahrhunderte* (Stuttgart, 1966), 88.
82. Strickler, *Actensammlung*, 226, no. 640.
83. Franz, *Quellen*, 510f., no. 173.
84. Quoted in Gottfried W. Locher, *Die Zwinglische Reformation im Rahmen der europäischen Kirchengeschichte* (Göttingen and Zurich, 1979), 469.
85. Kurt Kaser, *Politische und soziale Bewegungen im deutschen Bürgertum zu Beginn des 16. Jahrhunderts mit besonderer Rücksicht auf den Speyerer Aufstand im Jahre 1512* (Stuttgart, 1899), 192 (Frankfurt am Main, Colmar, Osnabrück); Franz, *Quellen*, 453 (Mainz), 483 (Mühlhausen); Locher, *Zwinglische Reformation*, 482 (Kauf-beuren), 495f. (Reutlingen); Marc Lienhard, "Mentalité populaire, gens d'église et mouvement évangélique à Strasbourg en 1522–1523: Le pamphlet 'Ein brüderlich warnung an meister Mathis . . .' de Steffan von Büllheym," in *Horizons européens*

de la réforme en Alsace. Mélange offerts à Jean Rott (Strasbourg, 1980), 55 (Strasbourg); Hans-Christoph Rublack, *Gescheiterte Reformation. Frühreformatorische und protestantische Bewegungen in süd- und westdeutschen geistlichen Residenzen,* Spätmittelalter und Frühe Neuzeit. Tübinger Beiträge zur Geschichtsforschung, vol. 4 (Stuttgart, 1978), 112f. (Salzburg); Rublack, "Reformatorische Bewegungen in Würzburg und Bamberg," in Moeller, *Stadt und Kirche,* 119 (Bamberg, Würzburg); Winfried Becker, *Reformation und Revolution,* Katholisches Leben und Kirchenreform im Zeitalter der Glaubensspaltung, vol. 34 (Münster, 1974), 89 (Stralsund).

86. Martin Brecht, "Die gemeinsame Politik der Reichsstädte und die Reformation," in Moeller, *Stadt und Kirche,* 87–90.

87. Bernd Moeller, *Reichsstadt und Reformation,* Schriften des Vereins für Reformationsgeschichte, no. 180 (Gütersloh, 1962); Heinz Schilling, "Die politische Elite nordwestdeutscher Städte in religiösen Auseinandersetzungen des 16. Jahrhunderts," in Mommsen, *Stadtbürgertum,* 235–307; Olaf Mörke, *Rat und Bürger in der Reformation. Soziale Gruppen und kirchlicher Wandel in den welfischen Hansestädten Lüneburg, Braunschweig und Göttingen,* Veröffentlichungen des Instituts für historische Landesforschung der Universität Göttingen, vol. 19 (Hildesheim, 1983).

88. Kaser, "Bewegungen im Bürgertum," 192. Hermann Wopfner, ed., *Quellen zur Geschichte des Bauernkrieges in Deutschtirol 1525,* Acta Tirolensia, vol. 3 (Innsbruck, 1908; reprint, Aalen, 1973), 88; Rublack, *Gescheiterte Reformation,* 112f. The references are a modest selection.

89. For Münster see H. Schilling, "Aufstandsbewegungen in der stadtbürgerlichen Gesellschaft des Alten Reiches. Die Vorgeschichte des Münsteraner Täuferreichs, 1525–1534," in Hans-Ulrich Wehler, ed., *Der Deutsche Bauernkrieg 1524–1526,* Geschichte und Gesellschaft, Sonderheft 1 (Göttingen, 1975), 205. In general Alfred Schultze, *Stadtgemeinde und Reformation,* Recht und Staat in Geschichte und Gegenwart, no. 11 (Tübingen, 1918), 21.

90. Franz, *Quellen,* 453.

91. See the evidence for Augsburg in Kießling, *Kirche in Augsburg,* 126–131.

92. Locher, *Zwinglische Reformation,* 460.

93. Ibid., 495f.

94. Hans-Christoph Rublack, "Politische Situation und reformatorische Politik in der Frühphase der Reformation in Konstanz," in J. Nolte, H. Tompert, C. Windhorst, eds., *Kontinuität und Umbruch. Theologie und Frömmigkeit in Flugschriften und Kleinliteratur an der Wende vom 15. zum 16. Jahrhundert,* Spätmittelalter und Frühe Neuzeit. Tübinger Beiträge zur Geschichtsforschung, vol. 2 (Stuttgart, 1978), 328.

95. According to Ozment, *Reformation in the Cities,* 128ff.

96. Ozment, *Reformation in the Cities,* 145, 148f.; Locher, *Zwinglische Reformation,* 154; Hans-Christoph Rublack, *Die Einführung der Reformation in Konstanz von den Anfängen bis zum Abschluß 1531,* Quellen und Forschungen zur Reformationsgeschichte, vol. 40 (Gütersloh, 1971).

97. For Wittenberg see Ulrich Bubenheimer, "Scandalum et ius divinum. Theologische und rechtstheologische Probleme der ersten reformatorischen Innovationen in Wittenberg 1521/22," *Zeitschrift der Savigny-Stiftung für Rechtsgeschichte, Kanonistische Abteilung* 90 (1973): 263–282, esp. 272–277. For southern Germany and Switzerland, see Moeller, *Reichsstadt*; Locher, *Zwinglische Reformation.*

98. See Bernd Moeller's essay, "Kleriker als Bürger," in *Festschrift für Hermann Heimpel zum 70. Geburtstag,* Veröffentlichungen des Max-Planck-Instituts für Geschichte, vol. 36,2 (Göttingen, 1972), 195–224, which claims general applicability, is based on these examples.

99. The dates for Strasbourg are from Moeller, "Kleriker," 210–217, with the quotes at 212. And see Lienhard, "Mouvement évangélique à Strasbourg," 55.

100. See Moeller, "Kleriker," 219.

101. The references for Nuremberg are from Moeller, "Kleriker," 220ff., as are the quotes.

102. Ibid., 216.

103. Ibid., 219.

104. For examples see the survey, of course not complete, by Pfeiffer, "Gemeinde," 81. For a detailed discussion of the problem see the case study by B. Rüth, "Biberach und Eberbach. Zur Problematik der Pfarrinkorporation in Spätmittelalter und Reformation," Zeitschrift der Savigny-Stiftung für Rechtsgeschichte, Kanonistische Abteilung 70 (1984): 134–169.

105. For Nuremberg, see Moeller, "Anfänge der Kirchenbildung," 256; and for Sélestat and Upper Swabia, see Schultze, Stadtgemeinde und Reformation, 13.

106. Dietrich Kurze, Pfarrerwahlen im Mittelalter. Ein Beitrag zur Geschichte der Gemeinde und des Niederkirchenwesens, Forschungen zur kirchlichen Rechtsgeschichte, vol. 6 (Cologne and Graz, 1966), 326–340.

107. See, in general, Schultze, Stadtgemeinde und Reformation, 14ff.; and for Frankfurt see Jahns, Frankfurt, 27f. Of course, we must not overlook the fact that in many cases the local church retained ways of exerting considerable influence, as the well-examined case of Augsburg shows. See Kießling, Kirche in Augsburg, 177.

108. Rublack, Nördlingen, 57.

109. The quote is from Kießling, Kirche in Augsburg, 320.

110. Pfeiffer, "Gemeinde," 86f.

111. Ibid., 79; Kießling, Kirche in Augsburg, 128.

112. See Kießling, Kirche in Augsburg, 126ff., with the quote at 128.

113. For demands for gratuitous sacraments, see Wilfried Ehbrecht, "Köln— Osnabrück—Stralsund. Rat und Bürgerschaft hansischer Städte zwischen religiöser Erneuerung und Bauernkrieg," in Petri, Kirche und gesellschaftlicher Wandel, 42–45; Heide Stratenwerth, Die Reformation in der Stadt Osnabrück, Veröffentlichungen des Instituts für Europäische Geschichte Mainz, vol. 61 (Wiesbaden, 1971), 36; Oz- ment, Reformation in the Cities, 35; Clemens von Loosz-Corswarem, "Die Kölner Artikelserie von 1525. Hintergründe und Verlauf des Aufruhrs von 1525 in Köln," in Petri, Kirche und gesellschaftlicher Wandel, 128; Johannes Schildhauer, Soziale, politische und religiöse Auseinandersetzungen in den Hansestädten Stralsund, Rostock und Wismar im ersten Drittel des 16. Jahrhunderts, Abhandlungen zur Handels- und Sozialgeschichte, vol. 2 (Weimar, 1959), 76. The demand for residence is documented by Rublack, Nördlingen, 62ff. The term "Pfaffenweiber" is attested for Osnabrück, where the papenwife are required to identify themselves by wearing striped mantles. Stratenwerth, Osnabrück, 21. Other examples are in Rublack, Nördlingen, 64f; Willy Andreas, Deutschland vor der Reformation. Eine Zeitwende, 6th ed. (1959), 84.

114. See the important essay by Moeller, "Kleriker," esp. 200.

115. For the figures on clerical properties, see Moeller, "Kleriker," 200; and Ozment, Reformation in the Cities, 25.

116. Ozment, Reformation in the Cities, 37; Ehbrecht, "Köln—Osnabrück—Stralsund," 33, 41; Dieter Demandt, "Konflikte um die geistlichen Standesprivilegien im spätmittelalterlichen Colmar," in Bátori, Städtische Gesellschaft und Reformation, 143ff.; Stratenwerth, Osnabrück, 19f.; Loosz-Corswarem, "Köln," 75; Kießling, Kirche in Augsburg, 97; Francis Rapp, Réformes et Réformation à Strasbourg. Eglise et société dans le diocèse de Strasbourg (1450–1525), Collection de l'Institut des Hautes Etudes Alsaciennes 23 (Paris, 1974), 410ff.

117. See Moeller, "Kleriker," 206ff.

118. Fuchs and Franz, Akten, vol. 2: 185, no. 1298.

119. Moeller, "Kleriker," 210.

120. Otthein Rammstedt, "Stadtunruhen 152," in Wehler, Der Deutsche Bauernkrieg 1524–1526, 264, based on the evidence from Frankfurt, Mainz, Wiesbaden, Oberwesel, Boppard, Friedberg, Limburg, Cologne, Münster, and Osnabrück. It is methodologically acceptable to bring in the evidence of later date, since in the above-mentioned cities the demands were only sporadically linked to the reformation. For Münster in Westphalia in particular see Schilling, "Aufstandsbewegung," 202; and Richard van Dülmen, Reformation als Revolution. Soziale Bewegung und religiöser Radikalismus in der deutschen Reformation (Munich, 1977), 265.

121. Kießling, Kirche in Augsburg, 97; Loosz-Corswarem, "Köln," 74f.

122. Moeller, "Kleriker," 200.

123. The references are scattered through the histories of the various cities, e.g., in Schildhauer, Hansestädte, 71f. (Stralsund); Loosz-Corswarem, "Köln," 123, 125; Demandt, "Geistliche Standesprivilegien," 136–154 (Colmar); Ehbrecht, "Köln—Osnabrück—Stralsund," 41, 44; Rapp, Strasbourg, 417.

124. At least this is shown by the relatively detailed study by Demandt, "Geistliche Standesprivilegien." For Strasbourg, see Karl Stenzel, "Die geistlichen Gerichte zu Straßburg im 15. Jahrhundert," Zeitschrift für die Geschichte des Oberrheins 29 (1914): 365–446.

125. See Ozment, Reformation in the Cities, 37 (Zurich); Rublack, Nördlingen, 56 (Nördlingen); Kießling, Kirche in Augsburg, 83–94 (Augsburg).

126. I must emphasize that efforts on the part of the cities to achieve such goals reach back into the thirteenth century. For a general overview see Moeller, "Kleriker." For a sophisticated case study see Kießling, Kirche in Augsburg.

127. See on this in general Hans Maier, Die ältere deutsche Staats- und Verwaltungslehre, 2d ed. (Munich, 1980).

128. Schultze, Stadtgemeinde und Reformation, 21ff.

129. Ibid., 22.

130. Schildhauer, Hansestädte, 69; Ozment, Reformation in the Cities, 35.

131. Quoted in Ozment, Reformation in the Cities, 178, note 62.

132. The most important viewpoints have been compiled by Rublack, "Forschungsbericht." See also Rainer Wohlfeil, Einführung in die Geschichte der deutschen Reformation (Munich, 1982), 118–123.

133. Kaser, Bewegungen im Bürgertum, 194.

134. Moeller, Reichstadt, 25; Ozment, Reformation in the Cities, 47. A similar use of the term "people" (Volk) can be found in Locher, Zwinglische Reformation, 460, 469, and elsewhere; Gottfried Seebaß, "Stadt und Kirche in Nürnberg im Zeitalter der Reformation," in Moeller, Stadt und Kirche, 75.

135. Brady, Strasbourg, 292.

136. Schilling, Konfessionskonflikt, 82.

137. Leonhard von Muralt, "Stadtgemeinde und Reformation in der Schweiz," Zeitschrift für Schweizerische Geschichte 10 (1930): 364f.; Schildhauer, Hansestädte, 98–110; Mörke, Rat und Bürger, 192f.; Moeller, "Anfänge der Kirchenbildung," 316.

138. The only exception in the recent scholarship is, in my view, the assessment of Rublack, which is limited, however, to Constance and Esslingen. Konstanz, 97. But Rublack also has examples of the importance of the community, 96–98; and similarly for Esslingen, "Reformatorische Bewegung und städtiche Kirchenpolitik in Eßlingen," Bátori, Städtische Gesellschaft, 218.

139. Moeller, Reichstadt, 25; similarly Muralt, "Stadtgemeinde und Reformation in der Schweiz," 372; Ozment, Reformation in the Cities, 124, 131; Locher, Zwinglische Reformation, 495f., and elsewhere.

140. Moeller, Reichstadt, 27; and see also Muralt, "Stadtgemeinde und Reformation," 363.

141. Brady, Strasbourg, 233f.; Turning Swiss: Cities and Empires, 1450–1550, Cambridge

Studies in Early Modern History (Cambridge, 1985), Chap. 5.

142. Bernd Moeller, "Stadt und Buch," in Mommsen, *Stadtbürgertum*, 27ff., and Thomas A. Brady, Jr., "The Social History of the Reformation between 'Romantic Idealism' and 'Sociologism': A Reply," in Mommsen, *Stadtbürgertum*, 40–43.

143. Brady, *Strasbourg*, 234f.; see also 291ff.

144. See the references in the introduction to Chapter 2; for southern Germany this has recently been more broadly attested to by Brady, *Turning Swiss*, Chap. 5; and for northern Germany by Mörke, *Rat und Bürger*, 298.

145. Strickler, *Actensammlung*, 225, no. 640.

146. Franz, *Quellen*, 483f., 455, no. 150.

147. Ernst Walder, "Reformation und moderner Staat," *Archiv des Historischen Vereins des Kantons Bern* 64/65 (1980/81): 521; Hans-Christoph Rublack, "Politische Situation und reformatorische Politik in der Frühphase der Reformation in Konstanz," in Nolte, Tompert, and Windhorst, *Kontinuität und Umbruch* 326; Heinz Schilling, "Dortmund im 16. und 17. Jahrhundert—Reichstädtische Gesellschaft, Reformation und Konfessionalisierung," in *Dortmund—1100 Jahre Stadtgeschichte* (1982), 178.

148. Rammstedt, "Stadtunruhen 1525." Rammstedt's model refers to the development in the cities in 1525, but I believe it can be applied to the entire reformation movement as such.

149. See the accounts of the development by Moeller, *Reichsstadt*, 28, and Ozment, *Reformation in the Cities*, 125–131 (see also the critique of Rublack, "Forschungsbericht," 124), which can be partially combined with Rammstedt's more abstract, but also more elastic model.

150. Franz Lau, "Der Bauernkrieg und das angebliche Ende der lutherischen Reformation als spontaner Volksbewegung," in Walther Hubatsch, ed., *Wirkungen der deutschen Reformation bis 1555*, Wege der Forschung, vol. 203 (Darmstadt, 1967), 82f. (Magdeburg), 86 (Braunschweig), 94 (Hannover); Rainer Postel, "Bürgerausschüsse und Reformation in Hamburg," in Wilfried Ehbrecht, ed., *Städtische Führungsgruppen und Gemeinde in der werdenden Neuzeit*, Städteforschung, vol. A 9 (Cologne and Vienna, 1980), 272f. (Hamburg); Schilling, *Konfessionskonflikt*, 76ff. (Lemgo); Moeller, "Anfänge der Kirchenbildung," 316 (Lübeck); B. Kroemer, *Die Einführung der Reformation in Memmingen. Über die Bedeutung ihrer sozialen, wirtschaftlichen und politischen Folgen*, Memminger Geschichtsblätter Jahresheft 1980 (1981), 106ff. (Memmingen); Van Dülmen, *Reformation*, 124f. (Mühlhausen); Schildhauer, *Hansestädte*, 103f. (Stralsund), 118, 120 (Wismar).

151. Guggisberg and Füglister, "Basler Weberzunft," 54f.

152. Johann Adam, *Evangelische Kirchengeschichte der Stadt Straßburg bis zur Französischen Revolution* (Strasbourg, 1922), 67.

153. Postel, "Hamburg," 372.

154. See on this Peter Eitel, *Die oberschwäbischen Reichsstädte im Zeitalter der Zunftherrschaft. Untersuchungen zu ihrer politischen und sozialen Struktur unter besonderer Berücksichtigung der Städte Lindau, Memmingen, Ravensburg und Überlingen*, Schriften zur südwestdeutschen Landeskunde, vol. 8 (Stuttgart, 1970), esp. 96–101.

155. Ehbrecht, "Köln—Osnabrück—Stralsund," 61; Loosz-Corswarem, "Köln," 100.

156. Moeller, *Reichsstadt*, 29, referring to the imperial cities.

157. Moeller, "Anfänge der Kirchenbildung," 250.

158. Ibid., 254.

159. Postel, "Hamburg," 374.

160. Moeller, "Zwinglis Disputationen," 304f., with the quote at 304. He situates the disputations within the framework of older traditions.

161. Moeller, "Zwinglis Disputationen"; "Anfänge der Kirchenbildung"; Ozment, *Reformation in the Cities*, 146ff.; Heiko A. Oberman, *Werden und Wertung der Reforma-*

tion. Vom Wegestreit zum Glaubenskampf. (Tübingen, 1977), 241–250; Locher, *Zwinglische Reformation,* 110–115. Moeller, "Zwinglis Disputationen," and "Anfänge der Kirchenbildung," shows how Zurich's model was imitated by other cities.

162. Von Muralt, *Stadtgemeinde und Reformation in der Schweiz,* 365; Pfeiffer, "Gemeinde," 90.

163. Oberman, *Werden und Wertung,* 246f. Independently of Oberman, similar conclusions have been formulated by Locher, *Zwinglische Reformation,* 110ff.; Ozment, *Reformation in the Cities,* 146.

164. Pfeiffer, "Gemeinde," 89f.

165. Franz, *Bauernkrieg Aktenband,* 186ff.

166. Peter Blickle, *Die Revolution von 1525,* 2d ed. (Munich, 1981), 168.

167. Franz, *Quellen,* 453ff., no. 149, concerning the "kurmainzische Viztum."

168. Ehbrecht, "Köln—Osnabrück—Stralsund," 39.

169. Some beginning attempts by Rammstedt, "Stadtunruhen 1525."

170. According to one of the central theses of Moeller, *Reichstadt.*

171. Moeller, *Reformation,* 113.

172. Pfeiffer, "Gemeinde," 96ff.; Ozment, *Reformation in the Cities,* 164f.; Schilling, *Konfessionskonflikt,* 142ff.

173. What are called in German "Ehe- und Chorgericht."

4

Communal Reformation—The Peasants' and Burghers' Reformations as a Unified Historical Phenomenon

Already a cursory comparison reveals that the peasants' reformation and the burghers' reformation shared common elements. It reveals chronological parallels between the two movements, but also divergent developments. A summary aimed at a more precise terminological definition of these two movements must examine specifically the following points: (1) the common structural elements; (2) connections between the actual historical events; and (3) the diffusion of the peasants' reformation and the burghers' reformation.

COMMON STRUCTURAL ELEMENTS

The bonds that link together the peasants' reformation and the burghers' reformation lie in the theological, ethical, organizational, and political spheres.

The gospel without human additions, the pure gospel, the gospel plain and simple represented for burghers and peasants the core of the reformation message. This point must be strongly emphasized, since it raises the fundamental question of the degree to which the rural and urban concepts of reformation were autonomous phenomena. Without an answer to this question we cannot hope to understand what the reformation meant to the broader masses. The central importance of this problem also explains why I devoted so much attention to uncovering and analyzing the words and concepts which peasants and burghers used to describe their notion of the reformation. This is not yet the place for a more detailed analysis of how the theology of peasants and burghers compares to the theology of the reformers. But even a cursory comparison reveals that not the entire core of reformation theology, the doctrine of justification, was appropriated, but only part of it, namely the principle of *sola scriptura*, justification through Scripture alone. The "gospel" stood chronologically always at the beginning of the reformation movement in the cities and villages, and it usually headed the list of demands and grievances drawn up by peasants and burghers. When the latter justified their support for the gospel, they argued that failure to do so would bring certain damnation and pointed out that the gospel could offer guidance in promoting brotherly love and the common weal. Of course, minor differences emerged between city and countryside. In the countryside, the gospel became more clearly relevant to practical concerns, as is reflected in the fact that the peasants developed, at least in rough terms, an ethical system derived from the gospel. In the city, on the other hand, the gospel was used more to support theological concerns and problems of church organization, such as the abolition of the Mass, the removal of images from churches and so on, issues which seem to have been rather secondary in the countryside. This is not surprising, since the burghers were literally closer than the peasants to the religious preaching of the reformers. Under these circumstances the theological thinking of the townsmen could not become as innovative as that of the peasants, a problem we will later examine in greater detail.

In the understanding of rural and urban society, the church realized itself in the community (*Gemeinde*). A sweeping and radical communalization of the church was one of the characteristics of the peasants' and burghers' reformations. The rights of patronage were seized more and more by rural and urban communities. The clergy was integrated into the community. The wealth of ecclesiastical institutions was confiscated. How that wealth was to be used and how the new evangelical clergy would be supported were issues decided upon by the community: through communal resolutions in the countryside, through church wardens—found in both the countryside and the cities—or through the cooperation of burgher committees with the city councils. The bonds that linked the new, young, aggressive evangelical church to the hierarchically structured Roman church were severed, and the many interconnections and links to the equally hierarchical world of the nobility were loosened, at least in principle. Neither the pope nor the emperor, neither a bishop nor a prince had any influence on, let alone control over, the internal church life of the community. It would be wrong to try and counter this argument by pointing to the fact that these ideas were only partially put into practice in the countryside and that they were effective in the cities for only a limited period. Given the actual historical course of the reformation movement in the empire, it is clear that the concept of reformation held by peasants and burghers cannot be reconstructed only from its concrete historical manifestations but must also take into account plans, ideas, and concepts. Only a few village communities succeeded in appointing their own evangelical pastors. For most communities the time between the emergence of this demand and the violent military suppression of the peasants was simply too short, often only a few weeks, to put it into practice. But this would not lead anyone to deny that the appointment of pastors was a crucial element in the peasants' idea of reformation. The importance which the community assumed in the reformation process in rural and urban society allows us, indeed, all but compels us, to use the term "communal reformation" as the overarching label for the peasant and burgher movements. Communal reformation meant reformation of the church and of society on a communal basis. Communal reformation thus has a theological as well as an ethical dimension.

The ethical substance of the peasants' and burghers' reformation becomes instantly apparent when we recall en bloc what so far have been rather scattered statements about notions of authority. Peasants and burghers voiced the demand—an uncompromising demand—that authority submit itself to the gospel. All incidents of rebelliousness in city and countryside, from the sacking of monasteries by the peasants to the expulsion of recalcitrantly Catholic councilors by the burghers, had no other purpose than to push through this demand. Submission to the gospel became the stamp of legitimacy. Lordship as such meant nothing. But if authority was willed by God—and this was never questioned—the political "theory" of burghers and peasants required that authority demonstrate that it was in accord with the divine will. It is not surprising that the age of reformation demanded from the authorities a commitment to the reformation, and wanted them to display that they were in line with the reformation and the gospel. The communal reformation posed a fundamental challenge to the legitimacy of political authority, such as had not been seen in centuries, at least not in any way approaching the same social breadth. This was a significant by-product of the communal reformation. It goes far in explaining the subsequent fate of the movement, and it is, in fact, a harbinger of the drama that was to unfold. Roughly speaking, about half of the empire pledged itself to this new criterion of legitimacy. Hence, the rebellions in city and countryside were also much more fundamental and deep reaching than ever before. In the cities they were not merely repetitions of older lessons learned in the late Middle Ages of how to express criticism to the authorities, and in the countryside they were not mere revivals of previous peasant revolts. Where the authorities were deaf to the gospel, peasants' and burghers' reformations could merge into a revolutionary movement.

Theologically and ethically, communal reformation was the demand to hear the pure gospel preached and to live accordingly; organizationally it was the desire to establish the church on the basis of the community; politically it was the wish to link the legitimacy of authority to the gospel and the community. Communal reformation is a term with a clear definition and content, built on questions about theological and ethical content, the social strata that supported the movement, and the legitimacy of political units. It is a much more accurate term than "storm years of the reformation," "wild growth of the reformation," or "people's reformation." Moreover, as we shall see, it also has much to contribute to explaining the subsequent development of the reformation into the princes' reformation.

If we wish to introduce the term "communal reformation," we must eliminate possible misunderstandings by taking another look at the meaning of "community" or "commune" (*Gemeinde*). If we use the term in connection with a religious movement, it suggests first of all a church community or parish. It would be wrong, however, to see the communal reformation as a movement focused on the parish.

In the cities it is more readily apparent than in the countryside that the reformation was carried by the urban commune, i.e., the political community, even though it could originate in the church parishes. Wherever the reformation movement entered its critical and clarifying phase, which usually occurred when committees were formed, it was a movement of the political community.

A closer look shows that this was also true for the peasants' reformation. It is striking that the so-called people's consultation in the Zurich and Bern countrysides solicited statements on the religious innovations not from the church communities but from the political communities, which is why they are more frequently and more appropriately called "consultations of the districts" (*Ämterbefragungen*). The political community and the church community could be identical, and in the countryside it often was, as is brought out by the literary allegory of the "church in the village." But when the peasants spoke of the election of pastors, they meant the political community, and this not only in Switzerland, but also in the southern German lands of the empire. When the famous Twelve Articles of the Upper Swabian peasants demanded that "an entire community" should elect the pastor, this was the same community that wanted to reclaim the forests from their lord and establish organs that would allocate the wood and supervise an orderly forest management.[1] In the Tyrol "every city and every district [wanted] to elect its own pastor," but also "every city and district its own judge."[2] The evidence is quite clear and compels us to view the peasants' reformation also as a movement of the political community. When the political community laid claim to the reformation and grounded the church in the community, it acquired a new ideological stature, new because it was now derived from theological principles.[3] By communalizing the church, burghers and peasants "sacralized" the community; no doubt this was an unconscious process, but one which corresponded to their needs. The urban and rural communes, previously a foreign body in the medieval schemes of world order, were legitimized, indeed consecrated, in the course of the reformation movement. This explains the new-found confidence of the communal associations, which, as the events showed, could now also attack the existing feudal structure of authority in a much more fundamental way.

Historical Connections

It is beyond doubt that the burghers' and peasants' reformations were closely interconnected and influenced each other. Numerous studies have shown that the evangelical movement was carried from the city into the countryside: from Zurich's principal church, the Grossmünster, into the Zurich countryside, from St. Martin's in Memmingen into the Upper Swabian countryside, from St. Aurelia's in Strasbourg into Alsace, and from St. Sebald's in Nuremberg into the city's territory.[4] But the spread of the reformation was not a one-way street, for it sometimes returned from the countryside to the city. In some cases this meant that the countryside hastened the reform process, as was the case in Kitzingen, Erfurt, Basel, Nuremberg, or Strasbourg; in some cases it initiated the process in the first place, as in Würzburg, Bamberg, Salzburg, and many other cities.[5] This deserves to be emphasized, since there is a widespread belief that the peasants' reformation was a mere derivative and continuation of the burghers' reformation, and for that reason alone can hardly lay claim to any special consideration or independent development. The closer a city's ties to the countryside, the more it was open to the movement carried by the peasants. This explains why the territorial cities rarely had any problems identifying with the programs of the peasants; why the suburbs, which were oriented toward agriculture, frequently became the reformation's point of entry into the larger cities;[6] and why those guilds with particularly close ties to agriculture were often the most committed supporters of the reformation in the imperial cities—the gardeners' guild in Strasbourg, the vintners' guild at Wissembourg, and the vintners' guild at Heilbronn.[7]

The burghers' reformation and the peasants' reformation already intersected in 1523 in Switzerland and in 1524 in Franconia and Alsace, and in 1525 they combined into a mighty, unified movement.[8] Contemporaries defined it as a movement of the common man, whose characteristic feature was precisely that it combined terminologically those strata in both city and countryside who had no share in the exercise of political power.[9] It is surely no coincidence that this choice of terms came to prevail especially in the reformation era; previously, in the late Middle Ages, the "common man" referred to the judge in the city, and later, during the late reformation period, the peasants were stuck with the term, which then hardly included the city at all.[10]

The merging of peasant and burgher vocabularies presupposes common elements of social and political status, and common interests and goals, among which was certainly the implementation of the reformation. In the 1520s the peasants and the burghers, as well as the princes and the lords, understood perfectly well that city and countryside pursued identical or similar goals. All saw how the common man joined together in "Christian Unions"—how programmatic a title!—and the lords called this the "revolt of the common man."[11]

An inside look at the converging peasant and burgher movements shows as another common goal the vague hope for more justice and love. This manifested itself negatively in the civic incorporation of the clergy, which received strong impulses from the peasant movement,[12] and in the sacking of monasteries by the peasants, frequently with the active participation of the burghers. In positive terms it expressed itself in aspirations to win economic, social, and political improvements, always at the expense of the authorities. The political extension of the communal reformation in city and countryside was the demand to assign offices of every kind through the principle of election. In the countryside this demand seemed newer and fresher than in the city, owing to the traditional rule by the nobility and the church; in the city, despite the oligarchic nature of the regimes, electoral principles had never entirely disappeared, and during the reformation they were merely reactivated in a new form. Of course, along with the emphasis on the electoral idea we see the first outlines of a new individualism within the framework of the corporative associations of the village, parish, and guild. In that regard the reformation had a disintegrating effect; the confessional split cut not only through the city, but also through the parish, the guild, the village, and eventually even through the family. In earlier times the corporative spirit had been so strongly developed that the majority vote was carried out, but now the latter was losing its binding power. The strongest evidence for this is the struggle for peace within the city, which was a constant companion of the reformation movement.

The convergence of the peasants' and burghers' reformation was, however, only a partial affair. Nothing shows this more clearly than the fact that in the cities, godly law had no important, and at best a marginal, place among the arguments invoked by the burghers. What this means, first of all, is that the godly law was a creation of the peasants. This comes as no surprise if we recall the demands which rural society raised with and through godly law: the principles of personal freedom and the freedom of nature (forest, meadow, hunting, fishing) are the distinct manifestations of the notion of godly law. In the cities, the ground was less well prepared for a comparable development, at least in the larger cities and the imperial cities. There the burghers enjoyed personal freedom, and their occupational involvement in the crafts and in commerce made them somewhat unaware of the late medieval feudalization of the uncultivated land, even though these developments did not go entirely unnoticed and were occasionally criticized.

The fact that the peasants were more strongly embedded in an authoritative political structure meant that the gospel was politically far more explosive in the countryside than in the city. Notwithstanding the traditional suspicions and the surprising scholarly ignorance that hinder a proper appreciation of the peasant programs,[13] we must emphasize that the godly law liberated considerable political-constitutional creativity, which culminated in the goal to create new political associations grounded in the village and city communes.[14] The "prophecy . . . that a cow shall stand on the Schwanberg, located in Franconia, and from there shall low or cry / and it shall be heard as though it were standing in Switzerland" seemed to be coming true, at least for a short while.[15] The reformation did in fact release forces which could have broken up the political system of the empire and which elevated the Swiss Confederation, the example that was always before the eyes of the burghers and peasants, to a guiding model. Not least therein lies the reason why the princes took much more vigorous and violent action against the villages than against the cities. As a result the communal reformation lost its coherence and unravelled into regional and socially isolated movements.

DIFFUSION OF THE COMMUNAL REFORMATION

Judged by its structural characteristics, the communal reformation was a unified movement. But very soon there set in the process of splintering, diffusion, and disintegration. The individual stages of this process can be roughly marked with the dates 1523, 1525, and 1532.

In 1523 it became clear that the peasants' and burghers' reformations in Switzerland were taking a course different from that of the empire, in that the Zurich Councils already at the first Zurich Disputation supported the new movement and gradually implemented it in city and countryside by means of legislative acts. Of course, one must not interpret this to mean that the reformation was imposed upon burghers and peasants. Quite the contrary, we must emphasize the undisputed fact that the reforms enjoyed broad social backing in city and countryside. But at the same time it is true that within a reformation guided by the council, the countryside, at any rate, could not develop any further independent theological and ethical ideas. Guided by the example of Zurich and conditioned by similar constitutional structures, the reformation in the Swiss city-states took place without any deeper social conflicts.

The year 1525 marked a serious setback for the communal reformation. With the military defeat of the rebellious peasants in Thuringia, Franconia, Swabia, and the Upper Rhineland, rural society was eliminated as a pillar of the movement. And by 1532 the burghers' reformation came to an end in most cities, as it culminated in the anchoring of the new doctrine in legal enactments. Evangelical councils and evangelical princes moved closely together and determined the subsequent fate of the reformation.

The year 1525 is undoubtedly most important for the fate and history of the communal reformation, and there is good reason why the question about the impact of the Peasants' War on the reformation is among the most passionate scholarly controversies.[16] We can contribute to this debate and its clarification in two ways: first, by calling attention to the qualitative changes in the communal reformation around 1525, which can be indicated with the term Anabaptist; and second, by pointing out the narrowing of the communal reformation to the reformation in the cities alone after 1525.

The Anabaptist movement represents in a sense the dialectical reversal of the communal reformation. The burghers' and peasants' reformation had the goal of improving the church and the world through the gospel, and the new society would embrace all burghers and all peasants, that is to say the entire community. The movement more or less turned this goal upside down by consciously and deliberately renouncing the transformation of all people and establishing a community on voluntary consent, a concept that ran counter to all previous practices and ideas. If we might call the reformation of the urban and rural communes a positive protest, the reformation of the Anabaptists became a negative protest.[17] We can briefly substantiate this assessment by examining the social origin and the theological-ethical statements of the Anabaptists.

The Anabaptist movement had two firm roots, one leading to Switzerland and Zwingli, the other to Thuringia and Franconia and Müntzer.[18] In both cases we are dealing with offshoots of the reformation, whose appearance must be explained from the particular character of the communal reformation in these two areas. It is no coincidence that the Anabaptist movement in Switzerland emerged in outline as early as 1523, took on clearer contours in 1524, and eventually became a significant force,[19] which was supported from the Franconian-Thuringian area by Müntzer's heirs. The numbers bear this out quite clearly: in 1525 there were forty-three Anabaptist communities; by 1529 the number had risen to 500, despite the persecutions which the Catholic and the Protestant authorities launched against them.[20] The Anabaptist movement in Switzerland must be seen as the struggle of a communal church against the emergence of the restrictive state churches and the consequent narrowing of church life. The emergence and resonance of the Swiss Anabaptists are explained by the theocratization of the reformation movement in Zurich, which excluded, or at least did not encourage, an independent communal life of the church. In any case, it did not accept any creative impulses "from below," and it ignored those that did arise. As a result the Anabaptist movement established itself alongside the traditional ecclesiastical and political associations. The ground had thus been prepared for a withdrawal from the social and political order.

This trend toward separation and disintegration was undoubtedly intensified by the crushing of the peasants' communal reformation in the empire and the repercussions in the cities. In social terms the Anabaptists were recruited from among the peasants and artisans. The connection between the Anabaptist movement and the Peasants' War has been so clearly demonstrated that it can hardly be doubted any longer.[21] Nor does it take a great exercise of imagination to realize that the failure to enforce the gospel as the fount of Christian life and conduct against the power of the authorities prompted the committed supporters of the reform movement in the cities and the countryside in a sense to withdraw from history.[22] The Anabaptists in Switzerland and spiritualists in Thuringia had already in 1524 discovered that they were kindred spirits.[23] Among their shared positions was their rejection of Luther, who "has tied his gospel" to the princes.[24] The linking of theology to established authority became in their eyes a dreaded vision of a renewed authoritarian and official church, something they had just been able to escape. It is interesting to note that in the same year when the first contacts were made between the Swiss and the Thuringians, the community of Männedorf complained to the Zurich Council that it had expelled preachers who "have preached nothing other than the holy Word of God: this they can prove through holy Scripture"; the community combined this with the demand that everyone had the right to preach, "preachers as well as peasants, who are enlightened by God to proclaim the holy gospel, so that the holy Word of God should be revealed."[25] The theological individualism of the "enlightened," who soon began to regard Luther and Zwingli as more papal than the pope and more dogmatic than dogma, has its counterpart in a social individualism that rejected the political structures. The established authorities were perceptive enough to understand this and realize the threat this posed to them. Their response was a merciless persecution of the Anabaptists, whose teachings said that

> no one shall carry a sword or shall collect money owed him by invoking the law and the courts, . . . no Christian, if he at all wants to be a Christian, shall collect from or give to another Christian interest or money for any kind of capital; also that all temporal goods shall be free and held in common, and everybody shall have complete possession of them . . . , no Christian shall be a figure of authority, . . . no Christian shall take or swear an oath (even to the authorities) nor to anyone else.[26]

The refusal to do military service could threaten the state's existence (especially in Switzerland, where this text comes from), the release of property its economic basis, the refusal to take the oath of allegiance its legitimacy. The Anabaptists drew the full consequences from a communal reformation which in the end never became a historical reality (cf. Fig. 2).

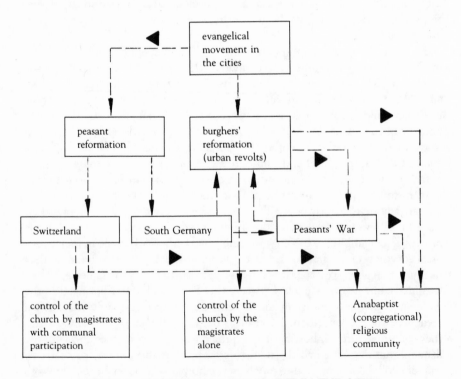

FIGURE 2   EVANGELICAL MOVEMENT IN THE CITIES

The year 1525 is prominent not only in qualitative but also in quantitative terms, for in the years following the communal reformation was reduced to the cities. In 1525 the peasants' reformation collapsed. This has lead Günter Franz to the verdict that in 1525 "the reformation lost its best vitality," and the path was taken "from a vibrant communal Christianity of the early Lutheran phase . . . to the ossified hierarchy of the established state churches"; henceforth the peasants were "indifferent, if not hostile, toward the reformation."[27] This assessment has been vehemently rejected as "wrong," as "an outrageous misrepresentation and distortion of reformation history," as "a biased falsification of history," a counterargument based on the course of the reformation movement in the northern German cities after 1525.[28] More recent, moderate positions concede that "the year 1525 constitutes a turning point in the history of the reformation," that regionally "the old church system could be reestablished," that "the tendency toward the institutionalization of the church with the help of the state gained the upper hand," although Luther did not lose his popularity.[29]

Can we settle the dispute between these opposing viewpoints with new arguments? Looking at the historical events, it is clear that rural society dropped out as a supporter of the evangelical movement, and in the region between Thuringia and Switzerland, Alsace and Strasbourg, the reformation as a whole suffered a distinct and irreversible setback.[30] A cursory glance at the map of the Holy Roman Empire of the German nation reveals that the reformation had lost, at least temporarily, between one-third and one-half of the territory of the empire. Given the high percentage of peasants in the overall population and the greater population density in southern Germany, it must have been roughly half the inhabitants of the empire who turned away from the reformation, who had to turn away because the lords labeled the peasants' reformation as "an uprising and a revolt." One can discount the importance of this fact and thus trivialize it only by characterizing the communal reformation as an aberration from the "real" reformation, that is to say the reformation of the theologians and the princes. Whether that would be justified and to what extent is a question we must settle later through a comparison of the theology and ethical ideas of the communal reformation with those of the reformers.

If we stay with the external events, it is also clear that the military suppression of the "Revolution of the Common Man" had repercussions in the cities. This was generally true for the territorial cities, which had to follow the pro- or anti-reformation stance of their respective territorial overlords—in the archbishopric of Salzburg and in the principality of the Tyrol, in the duchy of Württemberg and in the margraviate of Baden. But it also applies to a number of imperial cities that were more or less forcefully recatholicized—such as Heilbronn, Kaufbeuren, Memmingen, Sélestat, Schwäbisch Gmünd—or that returned more or less to the old church—such as Bopfingen, Mühlhausen in Thuringia, Nordhausen, or Rothenburg ob der Tauber.[31]

We can hardly speak of a continuous development of the reformation in the cities in general.[32] Apart from setbacks in some cases, for the cities as a whole we may speak at least of stagnation, if not an actual break in continuity, for in the years following 1525 the reformation made no visible progress in the urban areas.[33] Only in 1528 (Braunschweig, Goslar, Constance), 1529 (Biberach, Göttingen, Hamburg, Memmingen), 1530 (Lübeck, Ulm, Wissembourg), and 1531–1532 (Esslingen, Greifswald, Hannover, Heilbronn, Rostock, Soest) did the reformation achieve a breakthrough on a wider front.[34]

The character of the urban reformation between 1528 and 1532, and to some extent even thereafter, seems, from an inner-city perspective, comparable to its manifestations before 1525. And yet there were significant differences. Until 1525 the reformation in the cities was interlinked with the peasants' reformation, and not infrequently it received impulses from the hinterland and the surrounding countryside. We must also concede that it was more creative and courageous than the later urban reformation, which could count on the protection of a broader pro-evangelical front of princes, if not in its own territory at least in the empire.[35] In any case, with formation of the Schmalkaldic League (1531) at the very latest, the princely element assumed leadership of the reformation movement and the communal reformation came to an end.

The first phase of the reformation was a communal movement. This was its central and defining characteristic. The communal reformation was the response of the rural and urban societies to the appeal that had gone forth from the reformers. It remains to be examined what peasants and burghers got from the reformers and to what extent their theological and ethical positions overlap.

Notes

1. Günther Franz, ed., *Quellen zur Geschichte des Bauernkrieges*, Ausgewählte Quellen zur deutschen Geschichte der Neuzeit. Freiherr vom Stein-Gedächtnisausgabe, vol. 2 (Darmstadt, 1963), 174–179. The repeated use of the term "community" here and in other grievances does not allow us to make a distinction between the political community and the parish.
2. Hermann Wopfner, ed., *Quellen zur Geschichte des Bauernkrieges in Deutschtirol 1525*, Acta Tirolensia, vol. 3 (Innsbruck, 1908; reprint, Aalen, 1973), 37, 39.
3. See the interesting reflections by Gerhard Brendler, *Martin Luther. Theologie und Revolution* (Berlin, 1983), 297f.
4. The example of Zurich is documented above, Chapter 2, 16–20. For the others, see Martin Brecht, "Der theologische Hintergrund der Zwölf Artikel der Bauernschaft in Schwaben von 1525," *Zeitschrift für Kirchengeschichte* 85 (1974): 174–208; Franziska Conrad, *Reformation in der bäuerlichen Gesellschaft. Zur Rezeption reformatorischer Theologie im Elsaß*, Veröffentlichungen des Instituts für Europäische Geschichte Mainz, vol. 116 (Stuttgart, 1984), 49–56; Günter Vogler, *Nürnberg 1524/25. Studien zur Geschichte der reformatorischen und sozialen Bewegung in der Reichstadt* (Berlin, 1982), 83–95, 314.
5. Gottfried Seebaß, "Stadt und Kirche in Nürnberg im Zeitalter der Reformation," in Bernd Moeller, ed., *Stadt und Kirche im 16. Jahrhundert*, Schriften des Vereins für

Reformationsgeschichte, no. 190 (Gütersloh, 1978), 77; Thomas A. Brady, Jr., *Ruling Class, Regime and Reformation in Strasbourg, 1520–1555,* Studies in Medieval and Reformation Thought, vol. 22 (Leiden, 1978), 198ff.; Hans-Christoph Rublack, *Gescheiterte Reformation. Frühreformatorische und protestantische Bewegungen in süd- und westdeutschen geistlichen Residenzen,* Spätmittelalter und Frühe Neuzeit. Tübinger Beiträge zur Geschichtsforschung, vol. 4 (Stuttgart, 1978); and see also Bernd Moeller, *Reichsstadt und Reformation,* Schriften des Vereins für Reformationsgeschichte, no. 180 (Gütersloh, 1962), 21f.

6. Karl Czok, "Zur sozialökonomischen Struktur und politischen Rolle der Vorstädte in Sachsen und Thüringen im Zeitalter der deutschen frühbürgerlichen Revolution," *Wissenschaftliche Zeitschrift der Karl-Marx-Universität, Gesellschafts- und Sprachwissenschaftliche Reihe* 24 (1975): 53–68; Otthein Rammstedt, "Stadtunruhen 1525," in Hans-Ulrich Wehler, ed., *Der Deutsche Bauernkrieg 1524–1526,* Geschichte und Gesellschaft, Sonderheft 1 (Göttingen, 1975), 247, 255.

7. Peter Blickle, *Die Revolution von 1525,* 2d ed. (Munich, 1981), 175, 180, 185; and for territorial cities, see 183–188.

8. See Chapter 2, 16–20 (Switzerland); Günter Vogler, "Ein Vorspiel des deutschen Bauernkrieges im Nürnberger Landgebiet 1524," in Gerhard Heitz et al., eds., *Der Bauer im Klassenkampf. Studien zur Geschichte des deutschen Bauernkrieges und der bäuerlichen Klassenkämpfe im Spätfeudalismus* (Berlin, 1975), 49–81 (Franconia); Conrad, *Reformation in der bäuerlichen Gesellschaft* (Alsace).

9. Robert H. Lutz, *Wer war der gemeine Mann? Der dritte Stand in der Krise des Spätmittelalters* (Munich, 1979).

10. References in Peter Blickle, "Untertanen in der Frühneuzeit. Zur Rekonstruktion der politischen Kultur und der sozialen Wirklichkeit Deutschlands im 17. Jahrhundert," *Vierteljahrschrift für Sozial- und Wirtschaftsgeschichte* 70 (1983): 483–522, esp. 493–497.

11. Blickle, *Revolution,* 191–195.

12. Bernd Moeller, "Kleriker als Bürger," in *Festschrift für Hermann Heimpel zum 70. Geburtstag,* Veröffentlichungen des Max-Planck-Instituts für Geschichte, vol. 36,2 (Göttingen, 1972), 219.

13. The suspicions are discussed by Peter Bierbrauer, "Methodenfragen der gegenwärtigen Bauernkriegsforschung," in Horst Buszello et al., eds., *Der deutsche Bauernkrieg* (Paderborn, 1984), 23–37. For an example of scholarly ignorance, Walther Hubatsch, *Frühe Neuzeit und Reformation in Deutschland* (Frankfurt, Berlin, and Vienna, 1981), 148–156, 221f.

14. Blickle, *Revolution,* 196–223.

15. According to the pamphlet, "To the Assembly of the Common Peasantry" ("An die Versammlung gemeiner Bauerschaft"), quoted by Horst Buszello, *Der deutsche Bauernkrieg von 1525 als politische Bewegung,* Studien zur europäischen Geschichte, vol. 8 (Berlin, 1969), 191.

16. An overview is given by Blickle, *Revolution,* 274–278. I will have more to say about this discussion later; see also the references in the introduction.

17. I have discussed this at greater length in an essay, "Social Protest and Reformation Theology," in Kaspar von Greyerz, ed., *Religion, Politics and Social Protest. Three Studies on Early Modern Germany* (Stuttgart, 1984), 1–23.

18. See Hans-Jürgen Goertz, *Die Täufer. Geschichte und Deutung* (Munich, 1980), 13, although he places the accents differently.

19. Well documented by Leonard von Muralt and Walter Schmid, eds., *Quellen zur Geschichte der Täufer in der Schweiz* (Zurich, 1952).

20. Estimates are those of Richard van Dülmen, *Reformation als Revolution. Soziale Bewegung und religiöser Radikalismus in der deutschen Reformation* (Munich, 1977), 182f.

21. For Franconia, see Gottfried Seebaß, "Bauernkrieg und Täufertum in Franken," *Zeitschrift für Kirchengeschichte* 85 (1974): 284–300. For Switzerland, see James A. Strayer, "Die Anfänge des schweizerischen Täufertums im reformierten Kongregationalismus," in Hans-Jürgen Goertz, ed., *Umstrittenes Täufertum, 1525–1975. Neue Forschungen* (Göttingen, 1975), 19–49, esp. 44–48; C. A. Snyder, "Revolution and the Swiss Brethren: The Case of Michael Sattler," *Church History* 50 (1982): 278–287; H.-P. Jecker, "Die Basler Täufer," *Basler Zeitschrift für Geschichte und Altertumskunde* 80 (1980): 6–131, esp. 92ff. What is brought out, among other points, is how the leading Anabaptist Michael Sattler was shaped by his experiences of the Peasants' War, which he witnessed in Breisgau. Generally, see M. Haas, "Der Weg der Täufer in die Absonderung," in Goertz, *Umstrittenes Täufertum*, 50–78; van Dülmen, *Reformation*, 175; also, but more cautiously, Goertz, *Täufer*, 26.

22. It is in this context that we must see Goertz's characterization in *Täufer*, 99: "The voluntary association of the individual and the freedom from compulsion on the part of the authorities were thus the crucial characteristics of the 'Free Church.'"

23. Muralt and Schmid, *Quellen*, 13–21, no. 14.

24. Ibid., 19f.

25. Quoted by Kurt Maeder, "Die Bedeutung der Landschaft für den Verlauf des reformatorischen Prozesses in Zürich (1522–1532)," in Moeller, *Stadt und Kirche*, 96.

26. Heinold Fast, ed., *Quellen zur Geschichte der Täufer in der Schweiz*, vol. 2: Ostschweiz (Gütersloh, 1973), 3f.

27. Günter Franz, *Der deutsche Bauernkrieg*, 11th ed. (Darmstadt, 1977), 298f.

28. Thus the verdict of Franz Lau, "Der Bauernkrieg und das angebliche Ende der lutherischen Reformation als spontaner Volksbewegung," in Walther Hubatsch, ed., *Wirkungen der deutschen Reformation bis 1555*, Wege der Forschung, vol. 203 (Darmstadt, 1967), 71. Lau's argument is not directed explicitly at Franz, who is not mentioned in this context. Lau's position has been supported especially by Peter F. Barton, "Variationen zum Thema: Bauernkrieg und Reformation," in *Traditio—Krisis—Renovatio aus kirchlicher Sicht. Festschrift Winfried Zeller* (1976), esp. 125, 136–142; and by Thomas Klein, "Die Folgen des Bauernkrieges von 1525. Thesen und Antithesen zu einem vernachlässigten Thema," *Hessisches Jahrbuch für Landesgeschichte* 25 (1975): 65–116, esp. 111–115.

29. *Reformation*, 101, 111, with reference to the development in the cities.

30. For Alsace, see Conrad, *Reformation in der bäuerlichen Gesellschaft*, 165–175, who shows clearly that while the communities were still concerned about good pastors, their interest in the church declined noticeably, and older, pre-reformation practices of popular piety were taken up again.

31. The cities are mentioned, along with minor additions, in Moeller, *Reichsstadt*, 21f., and there, too, the quote.

32. Thus Lau, "Reformation als spontane Volksbewegung," 72f., who repeatedly stresses the unity of the period 1525–1532.

33. As far as we can tell, the only exception is Celle, which joined the reformation camp in 1526. Lau, "Reformation als spontane Volksbewegung," 72.

34. The lists have been compiled from the references in Moeller, *Reichsstadt*, 29, and Lau, "Reformation als spontane Volksbewegung," 72.

35. Perhaps we must place into this context a statement by Heiko A. Oberman, which he did not elaborate in greater detail: "The Peasants' War took place not primarily at the expense of the territorial expansion of the Reformation, but at the expense of the theocratic demands of the cities." *Werden und Wertung der Reformation. Vom Wegestreit zum Glaubenskampf* (Tübingen, 1977), 336f.

5

Church and Gospel in the Reformers' Theology

If we are to assess the degree to which the peasant and burgher reformations were either derivative or autonomous movements, we must first examine the ideas of the reformers concerning two central concepts, "community" and "gospel." I do not pretend, of course, that a historian can fully grasp and give an adequate account of the fine points and subtleties of reformation theology. But that is not necessary here. The question does not really concern the connection between the reformers' theology and ethical ideas as such and the peasant and burgher understanding of God and the world. What we must show is only the connection between the "published" theology and ethic of the reformers and the common man's concept of reformation. What the theologians wanted to tell the layperson of the sixteenth century is something the layperson of the twentieth century should be able to understand by using his hermeneutic skills.

This then is the task at hand: first, to sketch the essence of reformation theology and its pathways of communication; second, against that background to examine in greater detail the two central questions concerning the conceptions of the church and of the gospel.

THEOLOGY AND COMMUNICATION—PRELIMINARY REMARKS

Given the fact that rural and urban societies grounded the church in the community, the central question we must raise concerns the theologians' concept of the church. It is not sufficient, however, merely to reconstruct their notions of church and community; we must also determine what place they held in the various theological systems. Of course, we can never make such a determination with finality, since there are obviously no clear quantitative or qualitative criteria with which to assess individual aspects of a theology and their relationship to one another.

Two issues seem to arise from these considerations. The first is that in order to evaluate the place of church and community in the theology of the reformers, we must first give at least a cursory overview of their theology as a whole. The

111

second issue is that we must also consider the important fact that peasants and burghers had access to the theological thinking of the reformers only through the "published" theology that reached a wider audience. This leads us to the problem of communication, the question of how, in what way, and to what extent reformation ideas were transmitted to urban and rural society.

THE REFORMERS' THEOLOGY AND ITS
SOCIO-ETHICAL IMPLICATIONS—AN OVERVIEW

The essence of the theology of the reformers was the doctrine of justification. It received a particularly penetrating and profound formulation at the hands of Luther,[1] but in its fundamental features it was also advocated by the other reformers.[2] The maxims *sola gratia*, *sola fide*, and *sola scriptura* express first of all that grace, faith, and Scripture, as interconnected and interdependent concepts, constitute the theological core of the reformation. We can elucidate this concept of justification by pointing out how it deviated from the teachings of the Roman church. This seems a good approach, since contemporaries must have been struck above all by the differences that set it apart from traditional practice.[3]

Man was justified through his faith in God. Faith was the indispensable precondition for the grace of God. It arose from a person's act of humbling himself in imitation of Christ, but it required the active *virtus Dei* and was thus brought about by God himself. Grace without faith was unthinkable, and faith was always also an act of grace. The path to faith was the *logos*, Christ, the revealed Word of God as laid down in the gospel.

The contrast between the reformers' doctrine of justification and the teachings of the Roman church was sharp, and the implications were correspondingly profound. First of all, the Roman church in the late Middle Ages based itself on the Ockhamist doctrine of justification, which said that man was capable *ex suis naturalibus* of loving God above all else and could thus obtain God's grace through his own power. In contrast, the Protestant reformers, following Luther, emphasized that justification was a pure act of grace, for it was Luther's unshakable conviction and personal experience that man, because of the stain of original sin, could *ex suis naturalibus* produce nothing but evil. Compared to contemporary Catholic doctrine, mankind's role in justification was a modest one. A second difference lay in the teaching of the Roman church that the grace which brought justification came through the sacraments mediated by the institutionalized church. The doctrine of justification, by contrast, clearly pushed the sacramental character of the church into the background by infusing the sacraments with a different meaning. A sacrament was seen as a special manifestation of the Word; it was thus strictly dependent on the *verbum Dei*. The Word itself became sacramental. Strictly speaking, a sacrament could exist only because Christ himself is the Word. Contrary to the sacramental doctrine of the Roman church, the sacraments, which the reformers limited to baptism and the Eucharist, were to be more accurately defined as sacramental signs. A third and final difference lay in the fact that, unlike the reformers, the Roman church taught the dual authority of Scripture and tradition. More specifically, it tied the interpretation of Scripture to the exegesis by the church, thus granting to dogma an importance nearly equal to that of Scripture itself. Against this the reformers, basing themselves on the principle of *sola scriptura*, advocated the autonomy of Scripture and with it the idea that Scripture was *sui ipsius interpres*, "self-interpreting." It is clear what consequences these theological positions had for the Roman church. They deprived the church, which was founded on the doctrine that it alone could mediate divine grace and interpret Scripture, of its theological foundation and thus of its legitimacy.

As a "theory," the doctrine of justification as developed by Martin Luther did not invariably, through some inner dynamic, give rise to any practical implications for daily life. This was the point on which the theologians diverged. We can roughly divide them into three camps: the Wittenberg School around Luther, the Christian humanists, and the mystical spirit-theologians (*mystische Geisttheologen*). Both the Christian humanists and the mystical spirit-theologians drew stronger practical consequences and guidelines for behavior from the reform theology, while the Wittenberg reformers regarded it as inadmissible to derive from Scripture arguments concerning the political and social order.

The Christian humanists included Zwingli, Oecolampadius, and Bucer, along with some less prominent theologians. What sets them apart from Luther was their emphasis on Scripture as a source of law. This is perhaps the main reason why they are called Christian humanists. The aim of the humanists was to set up a kingdom of peace and harmony. What made this humanism "Christian" was its intention of achieving peace by realizing godly law as set down in Scripture. In other words, Christian humanism can be defined as "the effort to harmonize the order of the church and the world with the demands of the Bible."[4] A closer look at Huldrych Zwingli shall help us at least to sketch the position of the Christian humanists.

In Zwingli's view, the believer opts for a total transformation of social and political life.[5] Given his understanding of Scripture, the central question for Zwingli was how the will of God could be implemented in the world.[6] With reference to Acts 5:29, "We must obey God rather than men," Zwingli argued that the political order had to be brought in line with the divine will. Such a state of harmony became the true legitimating mark of lordship. The guidelines for the positive laws of the state were the natural law principle of respect for one's fellow man (Matthew 7:12), and its divine law counterpart of love for one's fellow man (Matthew 22:39). "You shall love your fellow man as yourself. If a law is not in accord with this Word of God, it is contrary to God."[7] The commandment to love one's fellow man as proclaimed in the Sermon on the Mount became the normative framework of positive law, and thus the serious effort was made to establish in real life one of the most striking principles of

Christianity. Love for one's fellow man, which Luther could conceive of only as an individual act arising from a state of justification, was assigned by Zwingli to the state virtually as a constitutional task. Of course we must qualify this by pointing out that Zwingli, in view of man's stain of original sin, believed that the divine will could only be realized at the relatively low level of natural law. Important for an assessment of his view of natural law is the fact that it was indissolubly linked to the spirit of God. "The law of nature," as Zwingli described it, "is nothing other than the direction and guidance of the divine spirit."[8] From this Zwingli then drew a remarkable conclusion with far-reaching implications: inasmuch as natural law was a creation of God, it was really only the believer who could understand it. Faith created the predisposition for forging natural law—whose aim was only in the most general terms defined through the principle of "respect for one's fellow man" (and its divine-law variant: love for one's fellow man)—into positive law. This gave a privileged position in political life to the believer and, of course, to the preacher, who was professionally concerned with Scripture. With Zwingli's approach the state fell under the supervision of the believers, who controlled the norms of life and the constitutional order. Scholars have occasionally used the term "theocracy" to describe this state of affairs. In any case, Zwingli developed a constitutional theory from his theology, and this set him fundamentally apart from Luther.

"Mystical spirit-theologians" is a makeshift term for the theology of Müntzer and of the early Thuringian Anabaptists and Spiritualists. They can be described as such owing to their belief that faith was constituted by a subjective experience, a mystical experience, as it were, which in turn was brought about by the spirit of God. I shall explain this idea in more detail by examining the theology of Thomas Müntzer.[9]

The common point of departure for Müntzer and Luther was that both originally started from a dialectic of the Word of God (Scripture) and the Spirit of God (Revelation). In developing his theological thinking, Müntzer shifted the emphasis to the "Spirit," Luther to "Scripture." Müntzer stressed the subjectivity of a faith experienced through the Spirit, while Luther accentuated the objectivity of a faith transmitted through Scripture.

For Müntzer, Scripture was evidence of the faith of those who wrote it, but in and of itself it did not constitute Revelation. It was objective, but had no subjective effect; it did not transform man. Revelation became a subjective experience solely through the experience of the Cross, which meant the overcoming of one's own humanness and creatureliness. Through the experience of the cross a person became Christlike, filled by the Holy Spirit and thus justified before God. Christ's redemptive act was still relevant, it was not merely a historic event that had occurred on Golgotha, but one that took place here and now. Whoever had experienced the Cross cleansed himself of the stain of original sin and returned to a state before Adam. Hence for Müntzer the world was divided into two groups, those who had experienced the Cross and the Spirit, and those who hadn't, the "chosen" and the "godless." This is the critical point where Müntzer's theology of suffering and the Cross was transformed into what scholars call a theology of revolution. For the chosen, inasmuch as they have become Christlike, know the will of God. Consequently they have the task of carrying out the divine will. Inasmuch as Müntzer interpreted the divine will to mean that the world had to be prepared for the coming of Christ and thus cleansed of the godless, the chosen became the ones who would eradicate the godless. Whoever remained mired in his creatureliness, that is, whoever resisted the chosen, would be exterminated. This provided the chosen with a means, although theologically not a very compelling one, of identifying attachment to the created nature: the princes, the rich, the old and the new "pharisees" of the Roman church and the reformation were still of the created nature because they refused to join the chosen, whose Christlike nature could not be perceived except through the subjective exchange of mystical experience among themselves.

THE TRANSMISSION OF REFORMATION IDEAS TO
BURGHER AND PEASANT SOCIETY—
PRELIMINARY METHODOLOGICAL REMARKS

"How did the common man come to know reformation ideas?"[10] In recent years this question has received increasing attention as a central problem in reformation scholarship.[11] And in fact this question poses itself with growing urgency once we look beyond the bare fact that society supported the reformation, and confront the problem that burgher and peasant societies developed their own ideas of the reformation. The task therefore is to explain not only the character of the reformation as a mass movement, but also the theological positions of the masses.

To begin with, the fact that we were able to identify the peasants' and burghers' reformation more precisely as a communal reformation underscores the uniform character of the concept of reformation. Of course, it is true that we can observe under the label "communal reformation" differences of social class (peasants versus burghers) and regional peculiarities (Switzerland, southern Germany). Nevertheless, from what has been said we may start from the assumption that the message of the reformers was apparently perceived and adopted as a relatively consistent system.

As the pathways along which reformation ideas were transmitted to society, scholars of communication have most recently emphasized oral communication (conversations, preaching), visual communication (images, broadsheets), "acting" communication (theater, carnival customs), and literary communication (books, pamphlets) as equally important or at least closely interconnected.[12] Pamphlets are the most useful type of source for helping us answer the question of how a peasant in the Salzkammergut and a burgher in Sélestat could develop similar notions of reform. They were the new propaganda medium of the reformation age, unequaled in intensity before or after this period. Their geographic range was essentially unlimited. In content they took up complicated theological issues, such as reformation preaching, and their formal structure was often that of a discussion or debate:[13]

> The pamphlet . . . introduced something new . . . Apart from the mere technical aspects, the greatest innovation was the agitational and partisan tenor of the pamphlets. This tenor was, however, derived from the tenor of the spoken word, from animated discussions among friends, acquaintances, and colleagues in taverns, on the street, or at home.[14]

The existence of the medium of the pamphlet dominates the current debate about the "reformation public," which Rainer Wohlfeil considers "among the most important preconditions for the phases of the reformation between 1517 and 1525,"[15] regarding "reformation public" and the "common man" as synonymous.[16] In Wohlfeil's view, both the emphasis on the importance of the common man for the reformation process as well as the chronological cutoff point in 1525 are elements that underly the concept of the reformation public. A few figures might underscore the importance of pamphlets for the process of communication, although we must keep in mind that the available estimates usually do not distinguish books and pamphlets. Lucien Febvre already estimated the total production of the sixteenth century at 150 million pieces.[17] In all likelihood more than 10 percent of these were of Luther's writings,[18] and the percentages shift even more clearly in Luther's favor if we look only at the publications of the time when the communal reformation was unfolding. It is believed that already in 1520, 500,000 copies of Luther's writings were in circulation;[19] Luther's New Testament, with twenty-two authorized and 110 pirated editions with an estimated number of 2,000 to 3,000 copies per edition, was one of the best-selling books during the first half of the sixteenth century.[20]

Bernd Moeller has said: "the fact that the original impulse of the reformation was a mass movement confronts us nowhere more clearly than in the incredible expansion of book production and the appearance of a new type of book, the pamphlet."[21] As an initial illustration of this, suffice it to point out that 527 pamphlets and tracts were published in the five years before 1517, while 3,113 appeared in the five years after 1517.[22] The published titles reveal that printed information spread like an avalanche. Of course the estimates on this point do diverge, primarily because so far we know only the approximate size of the corpus of pamphlets: estimates about the rate of increase, if we look only at the period 1518 to 1524, range from 600 percent to 1,000 percent.[23] At present we can say that the production of pamphlets between 1500 and 1539 came to at least 12,000 editions.[24] Since editions are commonly thought to have run to 1,000 copies, we are looking at 12 million pamphlets for a total population in Germany of 12 million. If we further take into consideration that "the number of pamphlets and editions in High German was far greater" than those in Low German, and that "the language boundary [acted] as a barrier to the spread of Lutheran ideas,"[25] this would mean in purely mathematical terms that there were about two or three pamphlets per person in southern Germany, the territory of the communal reformation. It follows that the market for pamphlets was in southern Germany rather than in northern Germany. If we leave aside Wittenberg, an outstanding publishing center inseparably linked to the person of Luther, printers were concentrated in the southern German region of Augsburg, Nuremberg, Strasbourg, Zurich, and Basel, to name only the more important centers.[26] This observation is strikingly confirmed if we look at the chronological distribution of pamphlets. The steadily rising output of pamphlets reached its zenith during the four or five years before 1525; the trend reversed itself in 1525, and thereafter began a strong decline.[27] By 1527 the total output of German pamphlets was barely 20 percent of the level of 1524.[28] If the break in the year 1525 has any meaning at all, it is surely that after the military defeat of the peasants in 1525, the market for pamphlets disappeared, or at least it shrank considerably. All this shows that pamphlets were read above all in southern Germany. The data we have also show that the level of education was much higher here than in the north. Saxony, for example, had only five schools in the 1520s, compared to eighty-nine in Württemberg.[29]

The importance of the pamphlet can be also measured by the care with which the authorities registered this development and eventually tried to control it through censorship. A letter of the imperial Governing Council (*Reichsregiment*) to the Swiss Confederates in 1523 pointed anxiously to

> . . . the dangerous and erroneous misunderstandings about our holy Christian faith that are now everywhere appearing among the common man through all kinds of thoughtless announcements [*ausschreiben*], pamphlets [*druck*], and teachings; where these things are not addressed with thorough counsel, they will undoubtedly in a short time grow into disturbances of such magnitude that they will give rise to considerable hatred, unrest, and revolt.

The main reason for this deplorable development was clearly "that all print shops now publish and sell, without permission from the authorities, not only many . . . frivolous and illicit libels, but also other pamphlets that demean and damage the holy Christian faith."[30] Strict censorship was said to be the only way to put an end to this. Which brings us to the question about the content of the pamphlets.

Although pamphlets have been studied for more than a century,[31] given the vastness of the material we cannot at present construct a precise picture about their content. And because of the limited capacity of any single scholar, this picture will not be free of inconsistencies. To begin with, Hans-Joachim Köhler's quantitative analysis shows that 98 percent of all pamphlets address the topics of theology and church, whereas—to pick a random number for comparison—only 43 percent discuss economic problems.[32] Bernd Moeller, currently one of the leading authorities on this material, has named three main themes of pamphlet literature: Luther's central teachings on faith, sin, and justification; the biblicist or Scriptural principle; and the polemic against the established church.[33] Heinz Scheible has placed the accents somewhat differently, weighing the doctrine of justification less heavily, and emphasizing rather more the biblicist principle and its ecclesiological consequences, which expressed themselves in criticism of the old church.[34] This agrees in part with older views, which were based on the belief that the pamphlets remained tied "to the principle of Scripture."[35] It thus seems indisputable that the pamphlets, so far as their content is concerned, emphasized the gospel and criticism of the old church. It is still debatable, however, how widespread was the key theological idea of the reformation, the doctrine of justification.

These more subjective verdicts have been given clearer contours by Hans-Joachim Köhler in a representative statistical analysis of the content of pamphlets. The findings showed "that the Scripture-principle was by far the most frequently discussed theme," addressed by more than 70 percent of the texts between 1520 and 1526; in second place was the doctrine of justification, and this finding is due to the fact that Luther's writings and reformation tracts were proportionally overrepresented in the sample.[36]

Based on the current state of research, we can say that the Scripture principle or "the pure gospel" and the associated church criticism were the theological themes of the pamphlets. Of course, we must not overlook the fact that these themes reached beyond a narrow theological concern:

> Every theological point of dispute led deep into the basic structure of the entire political and social existence and in fact touched the life of the people in all its manifestations . . . The disputes were not only about matters internal to the church, but concerned the total order of medieval life and thus a new image of the German person.[37]

Köhler has consolidated the various approaches to and findings on the problem of pamphlets into a new definition. He characterizes the pamphlet "as an early means of mass communication with propagandistic and agitational aims, which was used on such a large scale and with the clear intent of influencing the masses for the first time during the period of religious and social conflicts in the early modern period."[38] This definition includes the notion that the reformers and their supporters were the authors who gave the genre of the pamphlets its shape and content. The pamphlet was the primary, if not the exclusive, channel from which the common man got his information about the reformation, its theology, and its ethical ideas.

We can note in conclusion that the communal reformation and pamphlets overlapped geographically and chronologically. The geographic center of both was in southern Germany, and their common chronological focus was the four years prior to 1525. The production of pamphlets surely depended also on demand, and this would point to an especially strong interest in the reformation in southern Germany. It would seem that the authors of the pamphlets, the theologians of the reformation, knew full well that this was where their audience would be. But the pamphlets' propagandistic and agitational purpose also required that their authors, consciously or unconsciously, address the needs of the intended readers. This might explain the fact, puzzling at first glance, that there was apparently a gap between the theology of the reformers and the themes picked up by the pamphlets, as we have already seen in our cursory comparison of the theology of the reformers with the content of the pamphlets. This provides us with a methodological approach: we must examine the pamphlets to see whether we can find in them the demands raised by the peasants and burghers. Such a comparison alone can help us determine the extent to which the peasants' and burghers' reformations were dependent on the categories and ideas preformulated in the pamphlets, and the extent to which they were original and independent of them.

THE IDEA OF COMMUNITY IN THE REFORMERS' THOUGHT

To answer the question, "How did the common man come to know reformation ideas?" there are two conceivable methodological approaches. The first has been developed by Franziska Conrad in her study of the reformation in the rural society of Alsace, which includes some persuasive findings.[39] Her starting point was the peasants' local declarations, which were drafted in the form of petitions and grievances and contained statements on questions of faith. From here Conrad constructs the heuristic approach to the problem. She asks whether it is possible to find "opinion leaders" of the reformation, be they trained theologians or simple lay preachers, who can be shown to have had contact with the petitioning peasants. This method of inquiry proves for the most part successful, and a wealth of examples shows that preaching, pamphlet, and personal conversation could become the pathway by which reformation ideas were transmitted. The second stage of Conrad's approach consists in comparing the statements of each "opinion leader" at the time of his interaction with the peasants with the peasants' articulated notion of reformation. This makes it possible to grasp at a local level the divergence between high theology and popular theology, or more precisely, to uncover "peasant theology" at the village level. Only now, at the third stage of her interpretation, does Conrad compare the reconstructed "peasant theologies" in an attempt to isolate the common elements in the theological statements of the peasants in the Alsace. Apart from regional and local nuances, the final result is in fact a relatively uniform picture. For our purposes the value of Conrad's study lies in its demonstration that the structures and conditions of peasant life in the early sixteenth century (subjection to lordship, the economic situation, the development of a communal constitution, pious practices, and so on), played nearly as important a role in peasant theology as the theological ideas adopted from outside, which were adapted to the needs arising from the conditions of daily life.

This finding can in turn be used methodologically, inasmuch as we may assume that peasants and burghers grasped the reformation only in its central concepts. Our first look at the pamphlets has confirmed this, since it is one of their specific characteristics that they largely avoid detailed theological arguments. This may be one more reason why it would be methodologically misguided to explain Luther's concept of the church, for example, any other way than through his published writings. It would make no sense to reconstruct Luther's concept from sermons, lectures, and letters, for it was only as a published concept that it could have an effect on society.

Our task, then, is to filter from the corpus of pamphlets those that refer to the peasants' and burghers' idea of reformation. My aim has been to conduct a very comprehensive survey, and since the published pamphlets constitute only a modest portion of the entire corpus, I made use of the collection of pamphlets held by sub-project Z 1 of the Special Research Division 8 ("Late Middle Ages and Reformation") in Tübingen. The great advantage of this collection, which is being compiled for bibliographical purposes, is its comprehensiveness—in quantitative terms vastly exceeding the Gustav-Freytag collection—and the schematic classification of the pamphlets, which allows quick and systematic access to the material through computer programs.[40] A survey of the material suggested the following outline for our inquiry: first, the notion of community in Luther, who expressed himself very early and in some detail on this point; second, the positions of the other reformers; and third, the largely anonymous, popularizing ideas.

THE IDEA OF COMMUNITY IN LUTHER'S THEOLOGY

In 1523, Martin Luther composed what is the most comprehensive discussion and justification of the reformation concept of the church in a tract titled "That
• a Christian Assembly or Congregation Has the Right and Power to Judge All Teaching and to Call, Appoint, and Dismiss Teachers, Established and Proven by Scripture."[41] The tract came in response to a request of the community of Leisnig to Luther on 25 January 1523, asking him to give a biblical account of the place of the pastoral office. Luther himself probably thought of his reflections in more fundamental terms, since his tract says nothing about the concrete circumstances that led to its writing and avoids any reference to Leisnig.

In the title itself Luther stated his view in a precise and concise form. In the body of the argument he starts out from a definition of the Christian community. Just as the banner identified the army and the general, the preaching of the pure gospel identified the community: "The sure mark by which the Christian congregation can be recognized is that the pure gospel is preached there."[42] This first premise is followed by a second one:

> In the matter of judging teachings and appointing or dismissing teachers or pastors, it is not necessary to pay any attention to human statutes, traditional law, custom, usage, etc., even if they were instituted by pope or emperor, prince or bishop, if one half or the whole world accepted them, if they lasted one year or a thousand years.[43]

Luther then goes on to discuss and justify separately his rejection of any ecclesiastical or worldly authority concerning the judgment of teaching and the election of pastors.

In a fourfold exposition with references to Scripture (John 10, 14:21; Matthew 7:15; 1 Thessalonians 5; Matthew, 24:4), Luther explains that while everyone, including even popes and bishops, has the right to teach, judgment about the teaching belongs solely and exclusively to the pupils, the sheep, the congregation.[44]

> Thus we conclude that wherever there is a Christian community in possession of the gospel, it has not only the right and power, but also the duty—on pain of losing the salvation of its souls and in accordance with the promise made to Christ in baptism—to avoid, to flee, to depose, and to withdraw from the authority that our bishops, abbots, monasteries, religious foundations, and the like, are now exercising, since it is apparent that they are teaching and ruling contrary to God and his Word.[45]

The right of appointing pastors is expounded through a more extensive argument. Since the Christian community cannot perceive the Word of God, it needs teachers and preachers. But as the old church did not satisfy the evangelical doctrine, even preventing evangelical clergy from filling offices, and since God would not send any preachers from heaven, "we must follow Scripture and select and appoint from among ourselves those judged to be qualified [*geschickt*] and whom God has enlightened with understanding and endowed with abilities."[46] In principle every true Christian could be called upon, since he "possesses the Word of God and is taught and anointed by God to be a priest."[47] From this arises not only the Christian's right, but also his duty to proclaim the Word of God. Of course, Luther takes the view, which, like his entire argument, he supports very rigorously with biblical quotes, that the external situation must be taken into consideration. If a Christian finds himself alone among non-Christians, he is entitled and obligated to preach even without an appointment. But where "there are Christians who have the same power and right as he, he shall not call attention to himself, but shall let himself be called and chosen to preach and teach in the place of and by the command of the others."[48] The right of Christians to make their own appointments is specifically located in the •
community: "how much more right does a whole congregation have to call someone into this office";[49] "the community which has the gospel may and should elect and appoint from among its members someone to teach the Word in its place."[50] This principle Luther regarded as unrelinquishable, even if the bishops administered their offices in accordance with Scripture. Only in extraordinary emergencies could they choose and appoint preachers "without the will, the election, and the call of the congregation."[51] Election was indispensable, as was revealed not only by the history of early Christianity, but also by the history of the Roman church, in which bishops and popes were after all also elected. In both cases election had clear priority over appointment.

Luther never tired of affirming that the right of judging correct teaching and choosing a preacher, who occupied the highest office in the church, belonged to the community, as the gospel showed.[52] This point was rigorously and concisely spelled out, whereas the term "community"[53] remains relatively vague if we ask what precisely it was meant to correspond to in real life. If we call to mind the unnamed recipient of the pamphlet, the city of Leisnig, we may assume that the followers of the new doctrine there were granted the rights of the community, rights which were to apply also to all other communities.

At very much the same time when Luther was putting these thoughts to paper, in 1523, two other pamphlets appeared: "A Sermon Given at Candlemas in Wittenberg by Doctor Martin Luther, 1523,"[54] and "On the Appointment of the Ministers of the Church"[55] (De instituendis ministris ecclesiae) a work that appeared in both Latin and German. Both tracts are primarily concerned with expanding upon and justifying the notion that priesthood, "that is, preaching / praying / and administering the sacraments," belonged to all believers, "even though one single person of the community shall be charged with the outward office."[56]

What Luther described very forcefully and systematically in 1523 was, however, not new to his thinking. It had already appeared in outline in his tract "To the Christian Nobility of the German Nation Concerning the Reform of the Christian Estate," published in 1520. Here Luther already developed the notion
• of the priesthood of all believers as the basic condition of a Christian, but at the same time he also emphasized that the appointment to the office was the right of the community.[57] The Acts of the Apostles taught that

> it should be the custom for every town to choose from among the congregation a learned and pious citizen, entrust to him the priestly office, and support him at the expense of the community. It should be left to his discretion whether to marry or not.[58]

From the universal priesthood Luther further derived the right to judge the
• correctness of doctrine: "Besides, if we are all priests, . . . and all have one faith, one gospel, one sacrament, why should we not also have the power to test and judge what is right or wrong in matters of faith?"[59]

The extensive quotes from Luther's published writings are intended to show that he developed in the early 1520s a clear concept of the rights of the community, and by repeating it in many of his subsequent writings no doubt engraved it upon the public consciousness. "That a Christian Assembly" appeared in ten editions;[60] sixteen editions of "To the Christian Nobility" are attested.[61] To place all of this into the proper context, however, it is important to point out that Luther's statements on what constituted the church were not very numerous, and within his writings as a whole they account for only a modest fraction. Describing the concrete structure of the church was certainly not one of his prime concerns. This alone can explain why the term community has with him, to begin with, little connection to actual practice; in any case, it does not allow us to be more concrete than to say that the Christians gathered in the name of the gospel constituted the community. The implicit conflict with the actual constitution of the existing parishes and political communities was, at any rate, not expressly addressed. Every unbiased reader, after reading the texts I have cited, could assume that Luther was giving the community the right to decide doctrine and to choose its pastor, and that he did so against all traditional ecclesiastical and secular legal titles, as he had strongly and unmistakenly emphasized in "That a Christian Assembly."

How far the authority of the community should extend in a conflicting situation was a question Luther answered openly only at the time of the Peasants' War, and on this occasion he interpreted communal competence in a very restricted way. In his "Admonition to Peace in Response to the 'Twelve Articles' of the Peasants in Swabia," he did accept as legitimate the demand of the Twelve Articles that a community had the right to appoint and dismiss its pastor,[62] but he attached a string of conditions to this. First the authorities should be petitioned for a proper pastor; if they refuse, the community may choose one, but it had to support him from its own resources. "But if the authorities will not tolerate the pastor they have chosen and support, then let him flee to another city, and let anyone who wants flee with him."[63] This alone was the Christian and evangelical way of choosing a pastor. Can anyone deny that these are signs of a change in Luther's attitude? Are his instructions of 1525, to flee with the pastor if need be, still consistent with his call in 1523 to cast aside law, tradition and custom, along with papal, imperial, princely, and episcopal statutes, when it came to the matter of choosing a pastor?[64]

We can note that Luther granted very extensive rights to the community, virtually grounding the church in the community, but he did not define the concrete, worldly manifestation of this community with the desired clarity. We can note further that the formulation of a new concept of the church from the shambles of the Roman church he had smashed was not among his central theological problems, otherwise he would surely have devoted more space to it in his writings.[65] Nevertheless, among the reformers Luther spoke earliest and most clearly about the community.

THE IDEA OF COMMUNITY IN REFORMATION THEOLOGY

The year 1523 was a turning point in the development of the reformers' concept of the church. Before this time it is difficult, except for Luther, to find broader discussions of this theme; in 1523, however, they appeared in the pamphlet literature in remarkable breadth and reached a high point at about the same time. The basic beliefs were fairly uniform, although the theologians differed as to the practical consequences they drew from their theory.

A relatively restrained voice was that of Heinrich von Kettenbach, who shared with Luther the belief in the priesthood of all believers[66] and the notion that the church was strictly tied to the preaching of the Word of God and thus to the faith.[67] Even in his ecclesiological tract "A Sermon on the Christian Church," the formulation of positive norms for the church remarkably enough lags far behind the wide-ranging and trenchant criticism of the old church, and this goes for many, if not all of the reformers, not to mention the popularizing texts, which will be discussed below. Kettenbach, and with him other supporters of Luther, say rather what the church is not than what it truly is.

This holds true also for Johannes Brenz's tract, "A Sermon addressed to all Christians about the church and its Keys and Powers, and also about the Office of the Priesthood,"[68] which must have had a strong resonance since it appeared in eight editions. Against the official Roman church it defined the true church as a hidden body ruled by the Spirit of God; consequently the church could not err. Brenz's tract gets its own accent from the repeated emphasis on altruism as the mark of the true church. He goes beyond Kettenbach when he advocates even more clearly the priesthood of all believers, thereby granting the power of excommunication to all believing Christians, and when, in discussing the priesthood, he at least hints at the possibility of election by the community.[69] It is typical not only of Brenz, but of all the theologians, that they attempt to outline the new church through their biting criticism of the old. The business of the pastor, Brenz said, was to proclaim the Word of God and administer the sacraments, and "not to wear tonsure and cowl or to read Mass." Christ had sent out his disciples with the words "go forth, baptize and preach the gospel," and not "go forth, shave yourselves, wear long frocks, and have no wives."[70]

More clearly aimed at practical usefulness and implementation was the advice that Jakob Strauss addressed to Duke John Frederick of Saxony in 1523 under the title "That each Christian Assembly be given a Servant and not a Lord / Conclusion and Main Articles."[71] Already in the preface, Strauss emphasized "that it is needful to all the subjects and the entire land of Your Grace, that in every church or assembly the plain gospel is openly and purely preached."[72] The church was thus linked concretely to the existing parishes and church communities, and in keeping with the reformation concept of the church, these were given clearly defined rights: "The right and godly institution of the pastorate derives from the unanimous election of the assembly," thus the parish community was granted the right to choose its pastor.[73] However, this choice could be reversed if the preacher's proclaiming of the Word of God in the community no longer showed good results. In principle, the congregation was to be "free, unattached, and independent, from its servant," especially since he "who is permanently installed in a parish, wishes to be regarded not as a servant, but as a lord of the congregation."[74]

Martin Bucer expressed himself with similar clarity in 1523 in a tract he wrote to justify the sermons he had given in the Alsatian town of Wissembourg.[75] Without any hedging or reservations, Bucer granted the city of Wissembourg the right "that with you rests the judgment to decide who are true and who are false, • and also the power to remove the false and install the truthful";[76] the community thus decided about true doctrine and elected its own pastor. In a great variety of ways, Bucer underscored in particular the community's right and duty to appoint a proper preacher. As an aid in recognizing such a preacher, Bucer drew up a catalogue of qualities that were indispensable for the preachership: the

preacher must not seek his own self-interest, but must be content with simple •
food and clothes; he may not link salvation to good works, but only to faith in
Jesus Christ. The preaching of the pure gospel was thus emphasized as the core of
the true church. Bucer did not tire of warning the people of Wissembourg that
they would be risking their salvation if they allowed "human doctrine" or
"human fantasies" to be presented to them as the gospel, instead of the pure
biblical Scripture.

Along with Luther, the theologians who spoke most clearly when it came to
enumerating the rights of the community were Jakob Strauss and Martin Bucer.
By comparison, the statements of Balthasar Hubmaier, the Waldshut reformer,
seem rather feeble. In the "Eighteen Conclusions Concerning a Wholly Christian Life, Wherein it Consists,"[77] he listed merely the preaching of the pure
Word of God as the indispensable condition for the preachership. He obligated
the parishioners "to support and sustain [the preacher] with suitable food and
clothing";[78] in this way one could finally dispense with the *Frühmesser* (early
Mass priests), *Votiver* (priest who reads the votive Mass), *Requiemisten* (priests
who read Mass for the dead), and *Mittelmesser* (midday Mass priests), and get rid
of the "courtiers," *Pensioner* (pensioners), *Incorporierer* (incorporation holders),
Absentzer (absentee holders), "liars," and "windbags."

Finally, we must look at Huldrych Zwingli. Zwingli spoke only sporadically
about the form and structure of the church, and he developed his concept of the
community in greater detail relatively late, at the time when he was concerned
to draw a distinction between himself and the Anabaptists. His statements about
the church around the time of the Zurich Disputation of 1523 were inevitably
vague, since they were made solely by way of differentiation from the old
church. Pope and bishops with their pomp and power were not the church,
Zwingli said. Rather, "the church is nothing other than the number of all true
Christian believers assembled in the Spirit and Will of God."[79] Only in 1524 did
this general concept become more concrete when Zwingli gave certain rights to
the community. The community was entitled to depose a wrong shepherd,[80]
indeed, "the parish shall elect the preacher . . . for the same, and no one else,
will judge his teaching."[81] Zwingli had thus, relatively late as we can see, caught
up with Luther's position, which he reformulated again on other occasions
without adding anything of importance.[82]

Zwingli put forth the broadest outline of his concept of the church in his tract
"On the Preachership," published in 1525. Here Zwingli repeats and expands
his earlier view of the community: it elects the preachers, it decides on doctrine,
and it wields the ban. With the power of the ban Zwingli granted the community more authority than Luther did. But in explaining the election of the
preacher and the decision on true doctrine, he restricts this authority again. In
choosing the "teacher," the community had to solicit the advice "of wise
Christian prophets and evangelists, . . . since even a pure community by itself
does not have this right."[83] This qualification must be seen against the historical

background of the spread of the Anabaptists in Zurich. In a situation where his work seemed threatened, Zwingli took refuge in a stronger control of the community by the preachers.

The agreement between Zwingli and Luther in their concept of the church is clear, but there was also a notable difference. Whenever Zwingli spoke of the concrete rights of the community, he meant the church community, the parish. In Zwingli's thought, the spiritual-charismatic character that makes Luther's community so difficult to grasp blends with the real existing parishes. It was thus inevitable that the community included also unbelievers alongside the true believers gathered around the preaching of the gospel.[84] There is no doubt that Zwingli's statements concerning community were more like passing remarks. This is confirmed also by the scholarly literature, which, with the exception of Alfred Farner,[85] hardly addresses Zwingli's concept of the church.[86] It is no coincidence that the community was not mentioned in the quarrels between Luther and Zwingli on the occasion of the Disputation in Marburg.[87]

THE POPULARIZATION OF THEOLOGICAL IDEAS

The popularization of the reformers' theological ideas began on a broad front no later than 1521. Several elements set the "popularizing" pamphlets apart from the more theological pamphlets we have so far discussed: most of them were published anonymously, their formal structure was that of a dialogue, and in terms of content they combined the demand for a pure gospel with a harsh and often obscene criticism of the clergy. Of course, given the fact that the circle of authors is largely the same for both types of pamphlets, it is not possible in every case to come up with characteristics that set these pamphlets unambiguously apart from the "pamphlets of the theologians"; not all popularizing pamphlets appeared anonymously, and not all lacked deeper theological reflections. Nevertheless, the overall impression of these pamphlets is one of arguments reduced to particularly memorable slogans.

If we examine the popularizing pamphlets for their ecclesiological ideas, which even among the reformers did not occupy much space, we read these sources first with rising expectations, but soon also with rising disappointment. The fictitious discussions always lead right up to the point where we expect them to lay out the concept of the church. But that point itself is never reached, and the pamphlets fail to move beyond gross invectives against the pope, bishops, monks, and clerics of every stripe. The positive argument that was antithetically opposed to the old church was almost always the "gospel." This finds sufficient expression in the titles of the pamphlets, which strike up either the anticlerical or the evangelical argument, and mostly the former: "A nice dialogue between two good chaps [Gesellen] called Hans Toll and Claus Lamp concerning the Antichrist and his disciples";[88] "Of the benefice-market, the courtiers, and the temple slaves [Tempelknechte]";[89] "An invective and a revelation How the followers of the pope are driven by greed. A peasant and a knight have stood up against this. Read on and you shall hear more";[90] "A conversation of the pope with his cardinals how they can help the pope suppress the Word of God";[91] or finally, "Triumphus veritatis. The victory of truth, won by the Nightingale of Wittenberg with the sword of the Spirit."[92]

The argumentative structure of the pamphlets adhered to the following scheme. The supporters of the pure gospel were being hounded and cheated out of their salvation by the greedy church. In one dialogue "the layman" complains that the clergy, which was supposed to live off the tithe, did not dispense the sacraments without payment, and whoever could not pay died without them, while the laymen who concerned themselves with the gospel were denounced as clandestine preachers (*Winkelprediger*).[93]

Another tract outlined rules on how to recognize nonevangelical preachers, and gave instructions on how to evaluate their sermons. If the preachers refer to the Church Fathers, caution was advised, and it would be a good idea to let their words blow through one's ears like chaff in the wind. Anyone who only scolded and ranted from the pulpit without any justification from Scripture was "a very dangerous wolf, . . . and it would be good if he were driven out." Finally, "be on your guard"[94] against anyone who spoke only of miracles and saints. All manner of criticism against the clergy was very happily thrashed out and elaborated. Upright clergy could very well live off their benefices, and the shepherd could remain with his flock, "were it not for their great expenses for whores, rogues, and bastard children." This, together with their costly vanity, drove the priests to chase after benefices, "that is why they hurry to Rome as though chased by the devil. There they engage in every kind of fraud and trickery to get many benefices." The only answer was for princes and communes to prohibit courtiers from holding the priestly office; instead, the benefices were to be granted solely "to pious and learned priests, . . . who were born in your lands, cities, villages, and hamlets."[95]

The preaching of the pure gospel was demanded with the same frequency and urgency. "Indeed, it is necessary that we earnestly beseech God for proper preachers, who will preach the gospel to us purely, and will leave their fairy tales at home," a speaker tells his friend.[96] A pious man is characterized in these words: he "reads the gospel and St. Paul, so that he may be saved by the truth."[97] The true Christian congregation wants to hear the gospel and not "other drivel and fraud [*lupperei*]."[98] From here it was then only a small step to granting the laity a higher authority than the clergy when it came to dealing with Christian truth. That the Word of God was "used more among the common man than among the learned"[99] was a fairly common stereotype. In a conversation with a nobleman and a courtier, a monk complained that the peasants "could talk about Scripture. They are too clever for me, wherever I go." Ban and anathema (*Bann und Acht*) were of no more use against them; among the peasants these mattered no more than "if a duck had quacked them." In truth, the monk admitted to the nobleman and the courtier, it was the peasants who professed the Word of God, which had been taught to them by "learned priests with a true conscience or understanding," who had escaped from the monasteries.[100] It is therefore not surprising that the priesthood of all believers was also invoked on behalf of the peasants and turned against the consecrated caste of priests. In a "Complaint and Answer of Lutheran and Popish Priests," the "Lutheran pastor" warned that "the peasants will now also make priests," to which the "popish priest" responded dejectedly, "the peasants say that they are also consecrated, and yet they have no tonsure, and they beat us like dogs."[101] When such ideas were taken further, we occasionally also get a rough glimpse of the community.[102] Most clearly so in the liturgical ordinance from Ellenbogen.[103] It unmistakenly granted the community the right to elect its pastor, although at its own expense, bound preaching to "the clear, bright and pure gospel, as Christ the Lord created it and left it behind," and gave the priest (not the preacher) no other rights toward the community other than his official duties, since the community bore the burden of maintaining the church.

Pamphlets with a higher intellectual level also experienced a wider circulation. They include those tracts that can be attributed, either with certainty or in all probability, to Martin Bucer or Eberlin von Günzburg. A good case has been made that Bucer is the author of two of the most widely printed pamphlets of 1521: the "Dialogue" and "Neukarsthans," although final certainty is not possible in this question. With 13 editions, "A pleasant dialogue and conversation between a priest and a village mayor"[104] was certainly among the most widely read pamphlets of the early reformation.[105] The "Dialogue" develops its positive concept of the new doctrine based on a catalogue of the vices and omissions of the Roman clergy. By way of contrast it paints the ideal of a pastor who acts as the servant of the community and does not set himself up as lord over the parishioners; the justification is indirectly supplied through the repeatedly invoked argument of the royal priesthood of all Christians, which in turn is derived from Scripture. This prompts us to point out once again the great importance of the gospel. The "Dialogue" leaves no doubt that the Roman church had improperly attached doctrines "to the gospel and the Word of God, which did not belong there," whereas "not one iota of one letter should be added to or taken away from the law of God." But the conception of the gospel developed here went beyond the connotations usually associated with it. One could deviate neither to the right nor to the left "from the law of God." God does not "wish to have human law next to his law." Whoever kept the commandments, repented his sins, and kept up "the works of charity," "will not die the eternal death." No question, the gospel has here become virtually interchangeable with the Lex Christi, the legalistic character of Scripture is emphasized, and the worldly implications of the reformation message are underscored or even justified in the first place.[106]

The "Conversation booklet New Karsthans,"[107] which the majority of recent scholarship has attributed to Bucer, appeared in 10 editions and was thus also among the pamphlets that enjoyed a fairly wide circulation.[108] The author no doubt deliberately echoed the "Karsthans" published in the same year, a work possibly from the pen of the St. Gall humanist Vadian,[109] seeing that in this tract Karsthans, a symbol of the violence-prone peasant, was won over by Luther to a peaceful implementation of the reformation. "New Karsthans" is unique in that it developed and justified, at a very early time and without parallel in its genre, the election of the pastor by the community, whereas "Karsthans" advocated only the common priesthood.[110] This is all the more remarkable, as preliminary work in this direction existed only in Luther's "To the Christian Nobility," and no one had yet undertaken a systematic exposition of this problem. Franz von Sickingen, the partner of Karsthans in the dialogue, at first merely suggests cautiously that "the common people are not excused if they have an unsuitable bishop" (which means the same as pastor), since they have to pay attention to "who was chosen as shepherd and how the election took place." Karsthans agrees enthusiastically and accuses the priests of denying the people such rights; in their eyes, Karsthans complains, the common people were nothing but "rude rascals and blockheads, and they look upon us as though we were merely stupid beasts."[111] Von Sickingen picks up this complaint and responds that the priests should "exclude no one from the churches, we all are the church, and no one more so than anyone else. Moreover, we (whom they call the laity) should help elect the bishops and the priests and should provide ourselves with clergy."[112] Rarely had this been expressed with such clarity prior to 1523. In an appendix of 30 articles, to which Karsthans and his friends pledged themselves on oath, the open hatred of the priests is celebrated almost in the form of a litany; against this background of invective, the true pastor could be made to stand out all the more effectively. Priests, we are told, should not be called "spiritual fathers but scoundrels of the flesh,"[113] the "pope in Rome [should be] regarded as an Antichrist," the cardinals and bishops are "apostles of the devil." The courtiers should be considered mad dogs, "whom it would be fit to beat, capture, choke, and kill." We could expand this list with additional articles. The positive counterpart is the model clergyman, whom they "wish to look upon and judge according to his works, like any other man," who resides in the community, and who is eager "to preach the gospel and Christian law" lest he wants to be dismissed from his office.

Johannes Eberlin von Günzburg was a vastly more productive pamphleteer than Bucer, although he undoubtedly did not match the latter's incisiveness when it came to formulating his new concept of the church. In his "Seventh Confederate" (*Siebenter Bundesgenossen*) under the title "The praise of the priests,"[114] he did develop his ideas of the conscientious administration by a priest of his office and the necessary preconditions—proper income from parish dues and tithes—but he also used this occasion to launch into a long-winded polemic against the endowment of Masses by the common people, which served no other purpose than "to fatten so many people in the monasteries." Proper Masses should be read in the parish churches, the Mass for the dead could also be celebrated, but beyond that one should refrain from all endowments and thus render monkdom dispensable. "Be brave and take the matter courageously into your hands," Eberlin encouraged his readers,

deprive the fire of its wood / that is, take away the daily nonendowed [ungestiftte] support from the useless / ignorant / lecherous / lazy / gluttonous / greedy monks and priests / you will see that there won't be so many idlers and fabricators of vices / and where this sort declines in number / vices will also decrease and the daily food will increase.[115]

Two years later, in 1523, Eberlin von Günzburg developed his notion of the church more clearly and drew closer to Luther's position in two printed tracts addressed to the city of Ulm.[116] Christians were now unquestionably given the right to

judge the teachings of councils, the pope, and the church Fathers, and we do not allow the objection that any fool now becomes judge over sermons, since a Christian is not just any person but a very special person, of whom there are few, even Christ calls them a small flock.[117]

Of course, Eberlin clearly reveals here that he had no useful criteria on who concretely was to judge doctrine. In his second writing to Ulm, he took a strong stance on behalf of the city's right to appoint a preacher. It was irrelevant whether the candidate had previously been a secular or regular cleric; the sole criterion of his appointment should be a readiness to embrace an unquestioned "evangelical doctrine," which should be presented for popular judgment in the form of theses, and recommendations "from other famous evangelical preachers."[118] In contrast to Bucer, with Eberlin it was not the community which chose the pastor but the council of the city, as the title sheets clearly show.

Perhaps the most revealing example of how reform theology was appropriated at the communal level is the 1523 tract titled "A short account how the village mayor and the community of the village of Friedhausen on Gnodenberg have jointly chosen and elected a juror [Schöffe] of their village, by name of Hans Knüchel, that he shall, in their pastor's stead, proclaim and preach the evangelical doctrine and the path of salvation, until their pastor returns."[119] The tract came from the print of Pamphilius Gengenbach in Basel. It seems rather unlikely that the printer himself was the author, but for our purposes that is of no great importance.[120] The special character of this tract is precisely that it can be read like an instruction manual for communities for making theological decisions.

The pamphlet introduces itself formally as a charter issued by the village mayor and the community.[121] It notes that the priest did not reside in the village; instead, he provided underpaid monks and vicars as short-term substitutes, who preached contradictory doctrines, "one was Lutheran, the other popish," with the result that many quarrels had arisen in the community. In two communal meetings it was decided to forbid the substitutes to preach. As preacher they appointed Hans Knüchel, who as a Schöffe was no doubt a respected member of the community. Knüchel was known among his fellow villagers for his knowledge of the Bible, and he had up to that time "told them the word of the holy gospel and had instructed them on the path of eternal salvation."[122] This decision was backed up by the communal ban: "A great penalty has been set for anyone who mocks this teaching." It was clear what the community wanted: in the first place, evangelical preaching for the sake of their salvation, but second, also peace in the village. The rights of the pastor were not abolished; he could assert them if he decided to reside in the village. Correspondingly, Knüchel's preaching commission to preach granted to Knüchel was definitely one of limited duration. After the community had made these decisions, the village mayor began negotiations with Knüchel. The attempt to persuade him to accept the commission takes up the larger part of the pamphlet. After he finally agrees, "Hans Knüchel is led into church accompanied by the entire parish and followed by young and old."[123] The village mayor gave a brief speech in which he once more outlined the duties of Knüchel until such time as the absent pastor would assume his pastoral responsibilities in a proper manner. Then, before the entire community, the mayor affirmed once again the binding force of the decisions under threat of punishment: "Thus it is also decreed that whosoever, no matter who it may be, shall dare to obstruct him [Knüchel] in this, to impede, mock, or reproach him, if that should happen, they shall punish him or her in life and limb; let everyone act accordingly."[124] This was followed by a brief prayer from Knüchel and by his first sermon, which can with little effort be deciphered as the author's profession of faith. In good reformation fashion Knüchel advocated the idea that "faith is a gift and a grace, which is not bestowed on anyone"[125] who did not possess certain virtues. These virtues are not identified, but if we may draw on the broader context for our interpretation, Knüchel was probably thinking of humility and love for one's fellow human being. But something else is more important for Knüchel: the preconditions for attaining the grace of faith he deliberately sets aside to emphasize the notion "that faith alone is not enough for salvation." "Faith without works is totally useless and dead"—this becomes the programmatic slogan of his discourse. Knüchel backs this up with scriptural passages, and the congregation is told to follow it as a way of abiding by God's commandments. "A short account" is very close to the common man's concept of reformation. It demanded the preaching of the pure gospel and a corresponding way of life. After repeated, unsuccessful attempts to convince the village priest to dwell within the community, it set into motion the decision-making mechanisms of the political community in order to remedy inadequate pastoral care—perceived as a grievance and a source of conflict—by having the community elect a preacher, whom it protected through the legislative and policing powers of the village ban.

Theologically, "A short account" is certainly sophisticated, for despite noticeable emphasis on Scripture as the Lex Christi, Knüchel's presentation of the doctrine of justification is basically correct. The theological level is splendidly reflected in the discussion between Knüchel and the village mayor, both of whom prove to be very knowledgeable about Scripture and church life. In the course of the dialogue, which is not without its dramatic moments, they eventually arrive at the point where a reluctant Knüchel yields to the better theological arguments of the village mayor. In reading this dialogue, we invariably think of Luther's demand that the preacher should let himself be "drawn forth" by the community.

With their concern for the common people, pamphlets are, in the verdict of Paul Böckmann,

> the clearest expression that the hierarchical order of estates was being replaced by the communal idea. Not the lords as such matter, but the community as a whole, since a truly Christian life among people was possible only within the community.[126]

GOSPEL AND WORLDLY ORDER IN THE WRITINGS OF THE REFORMERS

Wherever the authorities refused to yield ground to the reformation, the common people, unless they wanted to give up "their" reformation, had to develop concepts of a new political order, one which at least allowed the possibility of preaching the Word of God, thereby ensuring the salvation of the soul. Given the twofold reformation concept of the common man, such a move was intimately linked with notions of a better, more Christian world, which the people believed could be realized with the help of godly justice or godly law, as the peasants frequently expressed it.

As I have repeatedly indicated, theologically such notions were prepared above all in Zurich. This entails three things for our discussion: (1) We must look again at Zwingli's concept of authority and his elaboration of the term godly justice, especially in view of the fact that scholarship has so far overlooked that Zwingli was the only one among the reformers and theologians who developed in a broader way this central legitimizing concept of the Revolution of 1525. (2) We must examine once more and more closely whether and to what extent the peasants—and the burghers in so far as they speak of godly law—referred back to Zwingli. (3) The question concerning authority and godly law became a fundamental conflict through the opposition of Martin Luther, who in his pamphlets of 1525 concerning the Peasants' War argued not only against Müntzer but also against Zwingli.

GODLY JUSTICE AND AUTHORITY IN ZWINGLI

Zwingli presented his ideas about authority primarily in two main tracts: "Exposition and Basis of the Conclusions"[127] and "On Godly and Human Justice."[128] Even though both tracts were written in 1523 and discuss a common problem, the circumstances leading to their composition were very different. "Exposition" presents a written version and broader elaboration of his arguments on the occasion of the First Zurich Disputation of 1523, and it constitutes "the first evangelical dogma in the German language."[129] "Justice," on the other hand, was rather an occasional tract, arising from a sermon with the goal of putting the radicals in Zurich in their place.[130] Whereas in "Exposition" Zwingli outlined the tasks and limitations of authority in brief and clear strokes, he became more cautious, defensive, and wordy when he wrote "Justice" a few months later. The concept of "godly justice" played no role in "Exposition," while it became virtually the *leitmotif* of "Justice." In view of this, it is advisable to present Zwingli's ideas about authority and godly justice separately and in this order, all the more so since Zwingli himself repeatedly referred to "Exposition" as important for an understanding of "Justice."[131] Since both tracts appeared in several editions, there can be no doubt about their impact.

In stark contrast to Luther, Zwingli did not separate law and gospel: "Now the commands of God are not advice . . . , but are true commandments of God, which he demands of us, and he does not allow us to come to him unless we are as innocent, pure, and pious as his will demands."[132] Christ alone fulfilled "the commands," the commandment, the law, from which it followed, on the one hand, that man is incapable of living up to the laws of God, and, on the other, that the death of Christ has relieved human despair and imperfection.[133] Zwingli's attempt to draw the gospel into the concept of law can be illustrated by his interpretation of Matthew 5:17. Christ did not come into the world to dissolve the law, the concrete expression of God's will; rather, he came "to open [*offnen*] that which previously has not been opened in the law."[134] In Switzerland, *offnen* is a legal term and refers to the correct interpretation of the law.[135] What this means is that Zwingli has here all but equated law and gospel. Since the law was understood as an imperative, the confluence of law and gospel naturally entailed that Zwingli's theology was much more relevant for life in this world than Luther's. "Faith in the gospel" means in Zwingli not only a personal decision for the blessed promise of eternal salvation, but also a decision for a total transformation of social and political life.[136] This is clearly expressed when Zwingli contrasts two correlated concepts: the decision for the "gospel" is also a decision for the "common weal"; and adherence to "human doctrine" produces only "self-interest" (*Eigennutz*). Zwingli's concept of the gospel determined his concept of authority. His notion of authority starts from the same axioms as Luther's: in principle every person is subject to authority, and in principle all authority is ordained by God. Zwingli proceeds from the basic assumption that authority has a double function: to punish the evil-doers, the godless, and to protect the faithful.

Given Zwingli's conception of the gospel, the central question that arose for him was how the Will of God could be unfolded and perfected in the world. The starting point of his reflections was the relationship between this life and the hereafter, between obedience to God and obedience to authority. In a reference to Acts he notes: "If the law of the princes is contrary to God, we have heard it said that Christians will say: one must be more obedient to God than to man."[137] Luther had concluded from this that obedience to God, which stands above obedience to authority, permits and demands passive resistance in matters of the faith. From the same passage in Acts, Zwingli drew a very different conclusion when he went on to argue: "This is why Christian princes must have laws that are not contrary to God, otherwise their subjects will refuse to obey them, and this will give birth to unrest."

We must grasp the full import of this sentence. It follows from it that the law—or more generally: the political order—must conform to the Will of God; where that was not the case, the subjects reject authority, refuse obedience, cause uproar and unrest. The conformity of the worldly order to the Will of God thus became the mark of legitimacy for authority. Of course, that immediately raised the question of how one could recognize whether the acts of authorities conformed to the Will of God. Zwingli first gave a general answer:

> In order that you [i.e., person of authority] do not cut off a healthy limb as though it were a rotten one, or let a rotten one stand as though it were a healthy one, it is necessary that you should actually know what health and what sickness is. But that you can only learn through the law, the law which God has given. That must be your guideline to follow; and you shall not make the guideline, but shall simply follow it. Therefore, if you find that your law is not in conformity with Godly law, do not follow it.[138]

As an example Zwingli pointed to the prohibition of marriage for clerics, a purely human law, as he says: "Therefore all the authorities sin who punish what is not unjust before God."[139] Zwingli emphatically underscored that this single example had general applicability:

> On the basis of this example one should approach all other disputes, on account of which there has been quarreling to this very day. If one finds the relevant Word of God, it shall settle all discord. If one does not find it, let no one care about the quarrel; for we shall neither add to nor subtract anything from the Word of God.[140]

The first thing that emerges from these passages is that Zwingli bound authority to a strict legality. Since he distinguished between a law made by man and a law given by God, we must ask how the two are related. "In short, remember," says Zwingli,

> all laws concerning your fellow man should be grounded in the law of nature. Whatsoever you wish done unto you, do so unto others Matt. 7 [Matthew 7:12]. Matthew later expressed this even more clearly: Matt. 22 [Matthew 22:39]: "Love your neighbor as yourself." If a law is not in accord with this Word of God, then it is against God.[141]

Zwingli here took the demand of natural law: "Do unto your fellow man as you wish to have done unto you," and raised it to a higher level through the divine commandment of love for one's fellow human beings. Zwingli used a second, comparable example to explain the difference between godly law and human law. One part of the law, godly law, "looks solely at the inner person," while human law looks at "the outer person."[142] "'Thou shalt not steal' is a commandment concerning the external life and piety. 'Thou shalt not covet thy neighbor's possessions' is a commandment concerning inner godly righteousness."[143]

But experience showed that the authorities' actions in no way conformed to this concept of the law. Rather, they believed they stood above those whom they ruled. This haughtiness was traced back to Adam and thus grounded in original sin and its consequences. It followed from this that humankind, burdened with the stain of original sin, tended toward arrogance, toward self-interest, in short, toward the negation of natural law, not to mention godly law. This called for an explanation and a more precise definition of natural law, the law of nature. Zwingli offered the following: "the law of nature is nothing other than the instruction and the guidance of the godly spirit," and he adds by way of clarification that "nobody understands the law except the believer."[144] Thus faith was also demanded of authority. Eventually all this led to the conclusion that authority had been established so as to act in accordance with godly law.[145]

Zwingli thus clearly placed authority under obligation of being a Christian authority, whereas Luther left the worldly orders untouched in their historical rights, Zwingli did not. The positive law of the state had to be harmonized with the law of nature. That could be achieved only when "all old and previous laws" (the existing positive laws) were examined to see "whether they are in accord with or contrary to the godly law of love for one's fellow man and the law of nature, both of which form one law."[146]

What this entailed, in principle, was a recodification of the existing legal order where it did not conform to the order of natural and godly law.

This call for a Christianization of positive law and thus for a Christianization of the state had a parallel in Zwingli's demand that the people had to be led to an understanding of natural law. Where that was done—and according to Zwingli, it could never be more than an approximation[147]—the optimal state would be created.

> Thus it follows that no regime can be more quiet and pious than when the Word of God is preached most purely in it; also, that nothing strengthens a government more; for the most pious regimes know for certain that they are the most firm. Whence it is certain that they are nothing but tyrants who do not allow the gospel to be preached among their people.[148]

Zwingli stated with the desired clarity what should be done if the authorities resisted Christianization:

> If the king or lord is chosen by the common hand [*von gemeiner hand*] and commits evil, the common hand shall get rid of him; otherwise, the people will be punished along with him. If a small number of princes has chosen him, one shall inform the princes that one no longer wishes to tolerate his vexatious life, and shall order them to depose him.[149]

This doctrine of resistance embraced even heritable monarchy, which in Zwingli's view was particularly in danger of degenerating into tyranny since there were no elective bodies to which such authority was answerable; the tyrant could be removed if "the entire mass of the people unanimously" desired it.[150] Zwingli's thoughts on the right of resistance are found in "Exposition"; "Justice" no longer made any mention of it. If the authorities do not improve themselves, we read there, "God will surely look for a judge of his people; he will bring him to them from far-away lands."[151] Here we see once again that Zwingli's "theory of the state" was in the final analysis not a very solid one.

If the state could fulfill its true purpose only by adhering to natural law, and if natural law itself could be understood only by the faithful through "the instruction and guidance of the Spirit," then the church community and the political community were one and the same. This is a position which diverged dramatically from that of Luther, and it met with a very broad resonance in society.

The talk of godly justice also enjoyed a broad resonance. I must preface my discussion by saying that it is far from easy to make out the main line of argument in the lengthy tract, "On Godly and Human Justice." Moreover, the fact that this work overlaps only partially with "Exposition" makes it more difficult to present Zwingli's thoughts as tightly constructed. Finally, a terminology that is not always sufficiently clear creates additional complications for any attempt to explicate the meaning of "godly justice" in Zwingli's writing.

We can gain access to Zwingli's thoughts about the exercise of authority by looking at the way he used the concept of "human justice," the counterpart to godly justice. For Zwingli speaks repeatedly of "human justice or authority."[152] In contrast to "spiritual power," which Zwingli vigorously rejected as unjustified, it becomes clear that worldly power can be equated with human justice: "Human justice or authority is nothing other than proper power, which we call worldly power."[153] In view of this equivalence, it is quite self-evident that human justice also has its source in the divine Will: "One must also be obliging and obedient to human justice owing to the commandment of God."[154]

But not only human justice and authority were used analogously; the same applied to human justice and human law. This gives us our first approach to the concept of godly justice. "Therefore there are two kinds of law, just as there are two kinds of justice: one godly and one human."[155] Human and godly justice do not represent two fundamentally different modes of being in Zwingli's thought, as was the case in Luther's thinking about the two kingdoms. Instead, they are complementary concepts, divided and separated by humankind's original sin but arising from a common source: the divine Will. This explains Zwingli's conviction and claim that "authority has been established in order to strive for divine justice to the extent that it is within its power."[156]

GODLY JUSTICE AND GOSPEL AS AN ARGUMENT
FOR THE COMMON PEOPLE

What the peasants and burghers could learn from Zwingli was his conviction that one could derive practical guidelines for social and political life from the gospel and that one could gradually get closer to godly justice if one had a Christian authority and corresponding governmental measures. This godly justice was perfect justice, even though in the end human beings, tainted with the stain of original sin, would never be able to attain it fully. Zwingli's texts are difficult to understand even for a modern reader who has some familiarity with the kind of arguments used in theology and political theory, and they must have been hardly more accessible to sixteenth century peasants. Zwingli could not really claim to have presented the practical application of the gospel and the content of godly justice with such precision that his followers could use them as a springboard for political action. If we inquire of Zwingli how the gospel was to be applied, we come away in the end without any concrete instructions. In any case, the category of godly law as it was developed primarily by the peasants was certainly in no way inferior in clarity and incisiveness to Zwingli's ideas.

Of course it cannot be denied that Zwingli's basic idea about the practical relevance of the Word of God literally "made reformation history," namely in the way society reacted to Zwingli and in the way Luther eventually reacted to society. Luther's rejection of the peasants in 1525, with its world-historical consequences for the reformation as such, is not thinkable without Zwingli's writings of 1523.

In order to clarify the impact of the opposing positions of Zwingli and Luther, it is necessary to show that Zwingli was more important than Luther for the common man's concept of reformation. In other words, we must localize more precisely the peasant (and burgher) notions of gospel and godly law, and examine them for possible derivations from Zwingli.

It is remarkable that the ideas about the gospel's binding force in this world and about godly justice or godly law arose simultaneously (end of 1524/ beginning of 1525) in several areas: the Allgäu, the upper Rhine, and in mid-Upper Swabia.

We have an exceptional source from the Allgäu, the register of serfs (*Leibeigenschaftsrodel*) of January 1525,[157] which is notable because it records for the most part the individual complaints of three categories of peasants on the lands of the imperial abbey of Kempten, namely, the *Muntleute* (free tenants under the protection of a *Vogt*), the *Freizinser* (free rent-paying tenants), and the serfs. Arranged by parishes, it lists a total of 335 individual complaints, which together document about 1,220 cases in which someone suffered a degradation in social status as a result of the abbey's actions. The peasants complained that free men had been depressed into rent-tenancy (*Zinserschaft*), while the free leaseholders (*Freizinser*) had been forced to make their wives and children over to the monastery as serfs. "Item, Nesa Hainzelmännin von Bachen, a free woman," a typical complaint runs,

> they took my late husband, who was a serf. He was arrested, and when I wanted to get him out of the prison, I had to give up my letter of freedom, and deliver up myself and my children as serf. This happened under the former lord [Abbot Johannes Rudolf of Raitnau, 1507–1523], this I protest before God and the law.[158]

By imprisoning her husband, the abbot forced the woman to relinquish her higher legal status. Equally dubious in legal terms was the way in which the abbey put its rights over serfs into practice. With no concern for the livelihood of younger children, half of the inheritance was confiscated if one of the parents died, which could lead to ruin especially if several marriages had been contracted within the same family due to the death of one of the partners. "Item, Peter Boneberg, serf: when my mother died, we the children had to divide [the inheritance] with the current lord, and gave him ninety lbs. and now the children have to beg for holy charity, this I protest before God and the imperial majesty."[159] In addition to individual complaints about a degradation of legal status, improper inheritance demands, increased exactions from landholdings, and more, there are also complaints from the various communities, as for example from the inhabitants of Günzburg, who stated that the abbot had seized their royal patents of liberty (Freiheitsbriefe).[160]

This brief sketch of the monastic abuses the peasants complained about shows that the traditional law was apparently failing completely. The closing words of the cases I have cited reveal the helplessness of the plaintiffs. When the peasants do more than recite the bald facts of the case, they place their complaints before "God and justice." These two terms could merge into the concept of "godly justice." Jakob Beggell took this conceptual step: with the abbot's permission he had bought a mill, and was complaining that he had to pay the abbot a carting fee (Auffahrtsgebühr) in addition, which was nearly as high as the purchase price itself. This seemed thoroughly unjust to him, and he "therefore requests godly judgment on whether he owes [it] or not."[161]

The formula "this I complain to God and justice" in itself is unusual. It probably reflects not only the real hopelessness and uselessness of the "good old law," but also indicates reformationist influences. It is striking to observe that this line of justification was hardly used in most villages, while it was very common in two specific parishes. These were Thingau and Günzburg,[162] two neighboring parishes and both about 14 kilometers from the nearest imperial city in which evangelical preaching could be heard: Kaufbeuren. The striking finding that among more than twenty parishes only the two closest to Kaufbeuren denounced the actions of the abbots of Kempten as "against God and justice" suggests that we ought to take a closer look at the reformation preaching in Kaufbeuren. Jakob Lutzenberger, the pro-reformation activist in the city, is regarded as a follower of Zwingli.[163] Kaufbeuren's orientation toward Zurich is underscored by the fact that the Constance reformer Wanner attended the

Disputation at Kaufbeuren on 30 January 1525, and that the Memminger preacher Schappeler had also been invited; both men were very close to Zwingli. Even though the interpretation I am offering suffers from a lack of incontrovertible evidence, it can still lay claim to a certain degree of plausibility. In any case, the notion of godly law was spread by the Kempten peasants to the Allgäu, and it is possible that it originated from Thingau and Obergünzburg.

An example which reveals the connections between the peasants' justifications and Zwinglian doctrine much more clearly is supplied by the landgraviate of Klettgau, located on the upper Rhine. On 23 January—hence at the same time as their counterparts in the Allgäu—the Klettgau peasants announced to their lord, the Count of Sulz, that henceforth they would render only what "is godly and just and also Christian," and that they expected him to let them "live in the word and justice of God."[164] This still vague formulation underwent its final elaboration in March. The envoys who were being sent to Zurich for the negotiations between the authorities and the peasants received their powers with the following restriction:

> . . . they shall not act contrary to the only guideline (which is the Word of God), and they shall not have any judge, and shall not begin the talks unless the Old and the New Testament are the judge, for there is no true judge in heaven and on earth other than the Word of God.[165]

The correspondence between the Klettgau peasants and the city of Zurich—Klettgau shared citizenship rights with Zurich—shows without a doubt that the Klettgau peasants, during their repeated stays in Zurich, became acquainted with the idea that the pure gospel had to be put into practice. For the council of Zurich tried to convince the Klettgau peasants to introduce Zurich's religious mandates in their county as well. Eventually these efforts strengthened the notion among the Klettgau peasants—or perhaps even suggested it in the first place—that the pure gospel was to be the measure also of all worldly order. It has been argued that the Klettgau peasants' idea about the gospel passed into a Federal Ordinance that was circulating along the upper Rhine, and that in this way it was more widely spread throughout the upper Rhine region.[166]

In mid-February, at the latest, the Upper Swabian peasants around Ulm declared, in their negotiations with representatives of the Swabian League, that "godly justice"[167] would tell each order what it could and could not do. By extending this principle further, the Upper Swabian peasants eventually demanded that the gospel be made the measure of all worldly order. Through the formulation in the Twelve Articles, this notion had considerable influence on the entire region engulfed by the Peasants' War:

> It is our conclusion and opinion that if one or more of the here formulated articles should go against the Word of God, which we do not believe, we reject that article, if such can be proven to be the case in the Scriptures . . . Likewise, we reserve the right to make further demands should they be found to be justified in the Scriptures.[168]

GOSPEL AND SOCIAL CHANGE IN LUTHER—
A REJECTION OF ZWINGLI VIA THE PEASANTS

The printing of the Twelve Articles and the mention by name of leading reformers prompted Martin Luther to publish an "Admonition to Peace in Response to the 'Twelve Articles' of the Peasants in Swabia."[169] In it Luther spoke his mind bluntly, first to the princes and then to the peasants. Despite all the criticism aimed at the princes, Luther underscored that he had never really questioned princely authority:

> You and everyone must bear witness that I have taught with all quietness, have striven earnestly against rebellion, and have energetically encouraged and admonished people to obey and respect even you wild and dictatorial tyrants. This rebellion cannot be coming from me.[170]

But how was rebellion to be avoided? Through understanding and concessions, Luther told the princes; through modesty and the retracting of excessive demands, he told the peasants.

This appeal, which urged compromise and settlement, reveals how severely Luther disapproved of the actions of the peasants, refusing to grant them even the appearance of legitimacy. Luther rejected the Twelve Articles with four arguments drawn from Holy Scripture: he who lives by the sword will die by the sword; only the authorities, as divinely instituted powers, have the right to punish the evil in the world; and no one can be his own judge.[171] He aimed his sharpest and most resolute objection, of course, at the peasants' invocation of the gospel and godly justice.

> Leave the name Christian out of it. Leave the name Christian out, I say, and do not use it to cover up your impatient, disorderly, un-Christian undertaking. I shall not let you have that name, but so long as there is a heartbeat in my body, I shall do all I can, through speaking and writing, to take that name away from you.[172]

In fact, the peasants were not even worthy "of being called heathens or Turks . . . , for you rage and struggle against the divine and natural law, which all the heathen keep."[173]

Reformation scholarship has shown beyond a doubt that these positions, clear in meaning and put forth in strong words, stand in an unbroken line of continuity from Luther's theology and social ethics.[174] In his doctrine of the two kingdoms or the two governments, Luther had defined authority, which he regarded as instituted by God, as a necessary order against sin, whose task it was to protect creation from the destructive power of sinful man. True Christians, who as believers followed in Christ's footsteps and lived the commandment of love, didn't really need any authority, yet they submitted to it and placed themselves in its service precisely because of the New Testament commandment of love for one's fellow man. What is decisive for Luther's understanding of authority and the state is that he located it between the divine will of creation on the one hand and the *natura corrupta* of man on the other. Two things followed from this: authority became sacrosanct, and active resistance to it was strictly and in principle denied.

Nevertheless, Luther's "Admonition to Peace" also shows uncertainties of judgment, although they were worked into the text in a rather indirect and concealed manner.

Luther began by making it clear to the peasants that in their acts and course of action they had to take into account not only how strong they were militarily and how unjustly the authorities were treating them. The very first thing to consider was whether they could defend their actions with good conscience.

If you have a good conscience, you also have the comforting advantage that God will stand by you and help you. Even though you may be defeated for a while or even suffer death, in the end you would win, and you would preserve your souls eternally with all the saints.[175]

Here, at least, Luther left it open whether a resistence to the princes which arises from conscience and not from economic and social interests might not be justifiable. However, this certainty of conscience had to prove itself as inspired by God, since neither the Old and New Testaments nor godly and human justified the actions of the peasants—on this Luther was adamant. Consequently he demanded that the peasants "produce a new and special command from God, confirmed by signs and wonders, which commands you and gives you power to do such things."[176] The Peasants' War would need its Moses in order to be justified.

For a brief moment Luther made room here for an interpretation of the Peasants' War which, formulated into a question, reads as follows: Could the peasants' insurrection not be understood as God's punishment for the godless? Or, are the peasants not the tools of a providential plan? Here Luther's apocalyptic expectation, an ever-present latent undercurrent, breaks through: "It is not the peasants, dear lords, who resist you, it is God himself who resists you to punish your tyranny."[177]

Of course, Luther himself energetically opposed the possibility of such an interpretation and eventually excluded it altogether. To do so he used two lines of argument that allowed him to brand as un-Christian the peasants' concept of the gospel, which linked the yearning for the salvation of the soul to the desire for more altruism and common good in the world. The first argument works with the assumption that the peasants had become victims of "false prophets" who were really "prophets of murder."[178] Luther's characterization of the false prophets as prophets of murder was based on his conviction that they were intent on transforming the structures of authority and thus the world, which could be accomplished only in opposition to the authorities, hence with rebellion and murder. The label of "prophets of murder" grew from Luther's conviction that a wrong and perverted idea of the gospel was being preached, one which in the final analysis was driven by the aim of suppressing the true gospel. The prophets of murder were a manifestation of the devil, whom Luther saw as a definite reality threatening his own work in a variety of personifications—in the pope, for example, or in the zealots (*Schwärmer*). To see the peasants as the victims of the devils' seduction meant, in the final analysis, to brand their actions as diabolical. Two things were diabolical in the peasants' actions: their perversion of the gospel for their own interests and their guilt, incomparably greater than that of the tyrannical lords because they were engaged in rebellion.

> The rulers take your property unjustly, that is one thing. In return you take from them their authority, which is the source of all their property, life and being. Therefore you are far greater robbers than they, and intend to do worse things than they have done. "Indeed not," you say, "we will leave them their lives and enough to live on." Let him believe it who will, I don't . . . If your undertaking were right, any man might become judge over another. Then authority, government, law, and order would disappear from the world; there would be nothing left but murder and bloodshed.[179]

Luther's suspicion that the peasants would leave the lords neither life nor livelihood was an accusation which had so far not been confirmed by events up to that point and would not be in the future. Was Luther driven by the dynamic of his own argument when he drew this forced parallel between the practice of the peasants and his theory about the prophets of murder? At any rate, Luther interpreted the Twelve Articles not within the framework of his own concept of the two governments, according to which the worldly orders followed their own logic and reason, but clearly from an eschatological perspective. In his view the Peasants' War was either the work of God—an interpretation which he eventually dismissed—or the work of the devil—an interpretation which he eventually came to advocate. Consequently, Luther was not fighting against the peasants in his "Admonition to Peace," but against a theology he regarded as a threat to himself.

Two irreconcilable concepts of the gospel stood face to face: on the one hand Luther's notion of the gospel, which was focused on justification, and which in principle left the secular sphere to its own rules and laws; on the other the peasants' symmetrically structured concept of the gospel, which saw in Scripture a guide both to eternal salvation and to a Christian and more just world.

What Luther demanded of the peasants was resigned submission to the will of the lords and authorities, the abandonment of a decades-old tradition of peasant resistance, and the renunciation of their self-assertiveness and identity. Small wonder that they could not and would not choose that path.

When the Peasants' War reached its furthest geographical extent and, with the rising in central Germany, struck close to home, Luther penned his second tract on the Peasants' War, "Against the Robbing and Murdering Hordes of the Peasants."[180]

The dismay which this tract aroused even among Luther's friends resulted not from his analysis of the Peasant War, but from the conclusions he drew and urged on the rulers. Analytically this second tract offered little that was new over the first one. The criticism of the peasants moves on three known levels:

they refused to obey their authorities, they robbed and plundered, and they cloaked their actions with the gospel. What Luther saw at work were "bloodthirsty peasants and prophets of murder."[181]

Pointing out "that they [the peasants] have sworn to be true and faithful, submissive and obedient to their rulers," he condemned the rebels as "faithless, perjured, lying, disobedient scoundrels and villains."[182] Of course, Luther overlooked the fact, deliberately or not, that the peasants' oath of obedience had its counterpart in the lords' promise to protect their subjects in their old rights and liberties, to adhere to the norms of law and justice, and not to raise the economic burdens above a level that could be morally justified. Precisely the oath of allegiance which Luther brought up is excellent evidence that the peasants had a basic right of resistance.[183] Allegiance could be refused by the subjects. There are many instances in the pre-reformation period where allegiance was denied or given as a conditional promise. Authority in the tradition of the Middle Ages was not absolute authority, and Luther shows a lack of all objectivity and sense of reality when he obliges the peasants to act in accordance with his own concept of authority, which was oriented toward absolute obedience.

The structure of Luther's argument is the same in "Against the Robbing Hordes" as it was in "Admonition to Peace." To prove that practice and theory were identical, or, to put it differently, in order to equate the actions of the peasants with the theology of the prophets of murder, Luther portrayed the stages of the Peasants' War far more severely and bleakly than they in fact were. Not objectivity but subjectivity marks Luther's picture of the Peasants' War. Only in this way was it possible to remove the conflict from the framework of secular law as an expression of opposing interests and to see it instead as the devil in action. Only thus can we explain the consequences which Luther derived from his analysis for the action the princes should take.

Although he appealed to the "Christian" authorities to make another effort at resolving the conflict through agreements and court settlements, Luther reminded them of their office and called upon them to crush the peasants.

> A prince and lord must remember that he is the officer [*amptmann*] of God and the servant of his wrath . . . If he has the power to punish and does not do so, be it by shedding blood or killing someone, he becomes guilty of all murder and evil . . . Thus the authorities shall now confidently advance and strike with good conscience, as long as their hearts still beat. Thus, anyone who is killed on the side of the rulers may be a true martyr in the eyes of God . . . Therefore, dear lords, here is a place where you can release, rescue, help. Have mercy on the poor people! Whoever can do so, let him stab, strike, slay. If you die in doing it, good for you, for you can never more obtain a more blessed death.[184]

There is no question that Luther always opposed rebellion and consistently emphasized authority as divinely ordained; in this respect he remained faithful to his convictions. Historians and theologians have praised this faithfulness as greatness: "Luther was nowhere greater in his combative fury than on such occasions. He . . . remained fearless as ever . . . He remained true to himself at every step,"[185] Gerhard Ritter wrote, and Paul Althaus faithfully extended the notion: "The Luther who risked everything on this occasion, his standing with the people, indeed his life, for the sake of his conscience, is of no less stature than the Luther confronting the emperor and the empire in Worms."[186]

Greatness and consistency often exact a high price. Luther paid the price by literally demonizing people. "I think," we read in his appeal "Against the Robbing Hordes," "that not a devil is left in hell; they have all gone into the peasants."[187]

> Behold what a mighty prince the devil is, how he has the world in his hands and can throw everything into confusion, when he can so quickly catch so many thousands of peasants, deceive them, blind them, harden them, and throw them into revolt, and do with them whatever his raging fury undertakes.[188]

The essence of Luther's view of the Peasants' War is its eschatological interpretation. He did not see in it the clash between two conflicting concepts of authority, on the one side the traditional feudal model of lordship inherited from the Middle Ages, on the other the modern, communal model of participatory lordship, which pointed the way to the future. Instead, Luther interpreted the war as a worldly manifestation of the *regnum diaboli*.[189] The devil's tools were the false prophets, the prophets of murder.

Who were the prophets of murder? In "Against the Robbing Hordes," Luther spoke very bluntly. The peasants were "doing the devil's work. This is particularly the work of the arch-devil who reigns at Mühlhausen and does nothing except stir up robbery, murder, and bloodshed."[190] The clear target of Luther's invective in "Against the Robbing Hordes," was Thomas Müntzer. He wrote against the Müntzer for whom Christ's lordship in the world was realized in the devolution of rule (a *translatio imperii*) to the common people, as well as against the Müntzer whom thousands of peasants were following in Thuringia, while Luther was reviled, even threatened, by them. This leaves the question of who the prophets of murder were in the "Admonition to Peace." That he was not talking about Müntzer is suggested already by the full title of "Against the Robbing Hordes," for he was speaking of the "hordes of the *other* peasants." The only edition which combined the two tracts on the Peasant War makes it even clearer that Luther aimed his two writings at different people: "Admonition to Peace in Response to the 'Twelve Articles' of the Peasants in Swabia, Also Against the Robbing and Murdering Hordes of the Other Peasants."[191] The "Admonition to Peace" refers to Upper Swabia, "Against the Robbing Hordes" to Thuringia. Who was the prophet of murder in Upper Swabia whom Luther sought behind the Twelve Articles but did not name?

Luther's line of argument in "Admonition to Peace" was aimed squarely against the *a priori* claim in the Twelve Articles that the gospel could and should establish the parameters for shaping the secular order. If we look for the theological source of this political theory we come upon Huldrych Zwingli. A comparison of Zwingli's ethics and concept of state with the political theory of the Twelve Articles reveals that they are highly congruent. If one wants to locate the Twelve Articles theologically, they belong to Zurich.

In his tracts on the Peasants' War Luther did not argue against the peasants as such but against those reformation theologians whose interpretation of the Word of God diverged from his own. In striking out against Müntzer and Zwingli, Luther, with his customary analytical brilliance, opposed precisely those offshoots of the reformation which, by virtue of the rigor of their alterna-tive blueprint and the consistency of their theological systems, presented a serious threat to his own theology and ethics; and what was even worse, they found the necessary followers. The peasants and burghers of Thuringia were in Müntzer's camp, those of southern Germany in Zwingli's. By 1525, Luther's influence had shrunk to Saxony and Hessia.

Luther's success is obvious. Müntzer's execution in 1525 determined that there would be no Müntzerian church. In the same year it was also determined that there would be no Zwinglian church in the Holy Roman Empire of the German nation. Luther's suggestion, that there was a prophet of murder in Zurich, was diligently seconded by the emperor and the imperial estates, and after 1525 the conceptual link of Zwinglianism and revolt was common.[192] Now in retreat, Zwinglianism was forced to give up one stronghold after another.

Notes

1. Instead of listing the specialized literature in detail, I shall refer summarily to Gerhard Ebeling's article "Luther" in *Die Religion in Geschichte und Gegenwart*, vol. 4, 3d ed. (Tübingen, 1960), cols. 495–520.
2. On the reformers who embraced this doctrine, see Gottfried W. Locher, "Grund-züge der Theologie Huldrych Zwinglis im Vergleich mit derjenigen Martin Luthers und Johannes Calvins," in Gottfried W. Locher, *Huldrych Zwingli in neuer Sicht. Zehn Beiträge zur Theologie des Zürcher Reformators* (Zurich and Stuttgart, 1969), 173–274.
3. In part I am reworking here the summary from my *Die Reformation im Reich*, Uni-Taschenbücher, vol. 1181 (Stuttgart, 1982), 36–64.
4. Wilhelm Maurer, article "Reformation" in: *Die Religion in Geschichte und Gegen-wart*, vol. 5, 3d ed. (Tübingen, 1961), cols. 858–873.
5. Locher, "Theologie Zwinglis," 180.
6. Zwingli developed the central arguments in 1523 in "Auslegen und Gründe der Schlussreden," on which the following interpretation is based. The text in ZW, vol. 2: 21–475; here esp. 318–345.
7. Ibid., 324, lines 22ff.
8. Ibid., 325, line 16f.
9. I am largely following Thomas Nipperdey, "Theologie und Revolution bei Thomas Müntzer," in Thomas Nipperdey, *Reformation, Revolution, Utopie. Studien zum 16. Jahrhundert* (Göttingen, 1975), 38–84, and Hans-Jürgen Goertz, *Innere und äußere Ordnung in der Theologie Thomas Müntzers*, Studies in the History of Christian Thought, vol. 2 (Leiden, 1967).
10. Thus the subtitle of Robert W. Scribner's essay, "Flugblatt und Analphabetentum.

Wie kam der gemeine Mann zu reformatorischen Ideen?" in Hans-Joachim Köhler, ed., *Flugschriften als Massenmedium der Reformationszeit. Beiträge zum Tübinger Symposion 1980*, Spätmittelalter und Frühe Neuzeit. Tübinger Beiträge zur Geschichtsforschung, vol. 13 (Stuttgart, 1981), 65–76.

11. For the recent discussion I refer especially to Köhler, *Flugschriften*, and the relevant essays in Wolfgang J. Mommsen, ed., *Stadtbürgertum und Adel in der Reformation*, Veröffentlichungen des Deutschen Historischen Instituts London, vol. 5 (Stuttgart, 1979). Less useful, despite its promising title (*Laienbildung*) is the volume edited by Ludger Grenzmann and Karl Stackmann, eds., *Literatur und Laienbildung im Spätmittelalter und in der Reformation. Symposion Wolfenbüttel, 1981* (Stuttgart, 1984).

12. See Scribner, "Flugblatt und Analphabetentum," 66ff. for a first overview. Recently more broadly discussed by Robert W. Scribner in *For the Sake of Simple Folk. Popular Propaganda for the German Reformation*, Cambridge Studies in Oral and Literate Culture, vol. 2 (Cambridge, 1981).

13. In addition to the works of Robert W. Scribner, see also M. Rössing-Hager, "Wie stark fand der nichtlesekundige Rezipient Berücksichtigung in den Flugschriften?" in Köhler, *Flugschriften*, 77–137, who shows through an analysis of the form of the language that the pamphlets were also intended to reach illiterate people.

14. Scribner, "Flugblatt und Analphabetentum," 69.

15. Rainer Wohlfeil, "'Reformatorische Öffentlichkeit,'" in Grenzmann and Stackmann, *Literatur und Laienbildung*, 47.

16. Ibid., 48f.

17. Richard G. Cole, "The Reformation Pamphlet and Communication Processes" in Köhler, *Flugschriften*, 147.

18. The estimates concern only pamphlets and are based on the Gustav-Freytag collection; cf. Cole, "Pamphlet," 147.

19. Bernd Moeller, "Stadt und Buch," in Mommsen, *Stadtbürgertum*, 30.

20. Moeller, *Reformation*, 89f.

21. Moeller, "Stadt und Buch," 30.

22. The dates according to Helmut Brackert, *Bauernkrieg und Literatur* (Frankfurt am Main, 1975), 66.

23. The lower number is derived from the data in Moeller, *Reformation*, 87f., who gives 150 editions for 1518 and 990 for 1524. Cole, "Pamphlet," 149, advocates the higher number, based on a quantitative analysis of the Gustav-Freytag collection.

24. For this information I am indebted to Dr. Hans-Joachim Köhler (Tübingen), whose bibliography of German and Latin pamphlets between 1501 and 1530 has begun to appear. Hans-Joachim Köhler, ed., *Bibliographie der Flugschriften des 16. Jahrhunderts*, Part I: *Das frühe 16. Jahrhundert*, vol. 1 (Tübingen, 1991). The dates are from Hans-Joachim Köhler, "Erste Schritte zu einem Meinungsprofil der frühen Reformationszeit," in Volker Press and Dieter Stievermann, eds., *Martin Luther. Probleme seiner Zeit* (Stuttgart, 1985), 244–281.

25. Moeller, *Reformation*, 88.

26. See, for example, the analysis of the pamphlets published in 1523 (Gustav-Freytag collection) by Cole, "Pamphlet," 161.

27. Ibid., 149ff.; Moeller, *Reichsstadt*, 34.

28. Köhler, "Meinungsprofil," appendix of graphs: "Chronologische Übersicht über die FS-Produktion."

29. Scribner, *For the Sake of Simple Folk*, 1f. See on this also the impressive work by Rudolf Endres on Franconia, most recently, "Das Schulwesen in Franken im ausgehenden Mittelalter," in Bernd Moeller et al., eds., *Studien zum städtischen Bildungswesen des späten Mittelalters und der frühen Neuzeit* (Göttingen, 1983), 173–214.

30. Letter of the governors, *Statthalter*, prince electors, etc., to the Swiss Confederates, dated 21 January 1523. Printed in Johannes Strickler, ed., *Actensammlung zur Schweizerische Reformationsgeschichte in den Jahren 1521–1532 im Anschluss an die gleichzeitigen eidgenössischen Abschiede*, vol. 1: *1521–1528* (Zurich, 1878), 193f., no. 540.

31. The state of scholarship on this topic can be quickly surveyed in Köhler, *Flugschriften*.

32. Köhler, "Meinungsprofil," 13f.

33. Moeller, *Reformation*, 89. Moeller has a similar analysis, though with modifications for a select corpus of thematically related pamphlets, in "Stadt und Buch," 36.

34. Heinz Scheible, "Reform, Reformation, Revolution. Grundsätze zur Beurteilung der Flugschriften," *Archiv für Reformationsgeschichte* 65 (1974): 108–133, here 131.

35. Paul Böckmann, "Der gemeine Mann in den Flugschriften der Reformation," *Deutsche Vierteljahrschrift für Literaturwissenschaft und Geistesgeschichte* 22 (1944): 189.

36. Köhler, "Meinungsprofil," 10.

37. Böckmann, "Der gemeine Mann in den Flugschriften," 187.

38. Köhler, Preface in *Flugschriften*, x. He discusses this in greater detail in "Die Flugschriften. Versuch der Präzisierung eines geläufigen Begriffs," in *Festgabe für Ernst Walter Zeeden* (Münster, 1976), 36–61.

39. Conrad, *Reformation in der bäuerlichen Gesellschaft*. This approach was taken up again in her essay entitled "Die 'bäuerliche' Reformation. Die Reformationstheologie auf dem Land am Beispiel des Unterelsaß," in Peter Blickle et al., eds., *Zwingli und Europa* (Göttingen and Zurich, 1985).

40. The kind co-operation of the project director Dr. Hans-Joachim Köhler and his assistants, who invested much time and patience in locating the relevant pamphlets, deserves special acknowledgement. All the more so, as their efforts are hardly reflected in the subsequent notes, since it made sense to cite the pertinent pamphlets, wherever possible, from critical published editions that are more readily accessible. Where I have made use of the Tübingen collection, references are identified by the code Z 1 and the Tübingen serial number.

41. WA, vol. 11, 401–416.

42. Ibid., 408.

43. Ibid., 408f.

44. Ibid., 410f.

45. Ibid., 411.

46. Ibid.

47. Ibid.

48. Ibid., 412.

49. Ibid., 413.

50. Ibid.

51. Ibid., 414.

52. Ibid., 415f.

53. Contrary to a widespread opinion, a passage (ibid., 415) where Luther points out that magistrates and princes hired preachers, yields nothing on this issue.

54. Ibid., vol. 12: 420–426.

55. Ibid., 160–196.

56. Ibid., 423; and see also 178f., 189.

57. Ibid., vol. 6: 408.

58. Ibid., 440.

59. Ibid., 412.

60. Ibid., vol. 11: 402ff.

61. Ibid., vol. 6: 397–402.

62. Ibid., vol. 18: 325.

63. Ibid.

64. See among more recent studies Wolfgang Stein, *Das kirchliche Amt bei Luther*, Veröffentlichungen des Instituts für Europäische Geschichte Mainz, vol. 73 (Wiesbaden, 1974); also esp. p. 172 for the vague term "community" (*Gemeinde*). See also the survey of the scholarly literature in Bernhard Lohse, *Martin Luther. Eine Einführung in sein Leben und Werk* (Munich, 1981), 180–190.

65. For all that, it is noteworthy that one of the more interesting recent biographers of Luther has asserted that Luther raised "the community's right of deciding to the principle of the reformation," Brendler, *Luther*, 297.

66. "Ein Sermon zu der löblichen Stadt Ulm zu einem Valete," printed in Otto Clemen, ed., *Flugschriften aus den ersten Jahren der Reformation*, 4 vols. (Halle, 1907–1911; reprint: Nieuwkoop, 1967), vol. 2: 113.

67. "Ein Sermon von der christlichen Kirche." Ibid., 95f.

68. Printed in Martin Brecht and Gerhard Schäfer, eds., *Johannes Brenz, Frühschriften*, part 1 (Tübingen, 1970), 17–22; the various editions are documented, 16.

69. Ibid., 22, line 23.

70. Ibid.

71. Facsimile edition in Joachim Rogge, *Der Beitrag des Predigers Jakob Strauss zur frühen Reformationsgeschichte*, Theologische Arbeiten, vol. 6 (Berlin, 1957), 157–166.

72. Ibid., 159.

73. Ibid., 163 (article 15).

74. Ibid., 164 (articles 26, 28).

75. "Martin Butzers an ein christlichen Rath und Gemeyn der statt Weissenburg Summary seiner Predig daselbst gethon," printed in Robert Stupperich, ed., *Martin Bucers Deutsche Schriften*, vol. 1: *Frühschriften 1520–1524*, Martini Buceri opera omnia, Series I (Gütersloh and Paris, 1960), vol. 1: 79–147.

76. Ibid., 135.

77. Printed in Gunnar Westin and Torsten Bergsten, eds., *Balthasar Hubmaier. Schriften*, Quellen und Forschungen zur Reformationsgeschichte, vol. 29 (Gütersloh, 1962), 71–74.

78. Ibid., 74.

79. ZW, vol. 1: 537, line 18, to 538, line 1.

80. According to "Der Hirt," based on a sermon delivered in October of 1523, printed in 1524. Ibid., vol. 3: 64.

81. According to notes to "Der drei Bischöfe Vortrag an die Eidgenossen." Ibid., vol. 3: 78, line 27f.

82. "Adversus Hieronymus Emserum antibolon." Ibid., vol. 3, 262, lines 11f.: "Harum [ecclesia] est de pastore iudicare . . . et de doctrina." "De vera et falsa religione commentarius." Ibid., vol. 3, 756, line 23f.: "Ecclesia, quae est Christi sponsa, et pastorem et verbum eius iudicat."

83. Ibid., vol. 4: 427, lines 12f.

84. On this see the attempt by Alfred Farner to work out different phases in Zwingli's understanding of the church, *Die Lehre von Kirche und Staat bei Zwingli* (Tübingen, 1930), 3–6. See also the relevant articles of the First Helvetic Profession (Erstes Helvetisches Bekenntnis) as given by Fritz Büsser, ed., *Beschreibung des Abendmahlstreits von Johann Stumpf* (Zurich, 1960), 68ff.

85. Farner, *Kirche bei Zwingli*.

86. See, for example, Gottfried W. Locher, *Die Zwinglische Reformation im Rahmen der europäischen Kirchengeschichte* (Göttingen and Zurich, 1979), 218, where Zwingli's notion of the church is discussed only once in passing.

87. Büsser, *Beschreibung des Abendmahlstreits von Johann Stumpf*.

88. Oskar Schade, ed., *Satiren und Pasquille aus der Reformationszeit*, 3 vols. (Hannover, 1863), vol. 2: 132ff.
89. Ibid., vol. 3: 60f.
90. Ibid., vol. 2: 180.
91. Ibid., vol. 3: 80.
92. Ibid., vol. 2: 210.
93. Ibid., vol. 3: 209.
94. Ibid., 24.
95. Ibid., 60f.
96. Ibid., vol. 2: 132.
97. Ibid., 180.
98. Ibid., vol. 1: 28.
99. Ibid., vol. 3: 80f.
100. Ibid., 101f.
101. Ibid., 147.
102. Ibid., vol. 2: 210; vol. 3: 209f.
103. ZI no. 7403: Ordnung / wie es soll mit dem gottes // dienst / vnd desselben dienern in der Pfarr // kirchen der Stat Elbogen / gehalten // werden / durch den wolgebornen Graf // fen vnd herren / herren Sebastian Schlick // Grafen zu Passaw / herren zu Weyß- // kirchen vnnd Elbogen etc. Mit // sampt dem Ratt da selbst vnd // jrer gemain in Christo be // schlossen vnnd // auffgericht.// Anno domini M.D. XXiij.
104. ZI no. 958. Printed in the section titled "Dubiosa" in Stupperich, *Bucers Deutsche Schriften*, vol. 1: 445–495. For the attribution to Bucer, see most recently and in detail Herbert Demmer, in Stupperich, 396–400, who considers Bucer's authorship to be clearly established.
105. For the number of copies per edition and the printing sites, see Stupperich, 396.
106. All quotes after the version ZI, no. 958, fol. B 3.
107. Printed in Stupperich, *Bucers Deutsche Schriften*, vol. 1: 406–444; and Schade, *Satiren*, vol. 2: 1–44.
108. On authorship, the editions, and the places of printing, see Demmen, in Stupperich, *Bucers Deutsche Schriften*, vol. 1: 392–396.
109. Hans Rupprich, *Die deutsche Literatur vom späten Mittelalter bis zum Barock*, Geschichte der deutschen Literatur, vol. IV, part 2 (Munich, 1973), 116f.
110. Clemen, *Flugschriften*, vol. 4: 116: "das wir al priester, pfaffen vnnd pfeffin send."
111. Schade, *Satiren*, vol. 2: 20.
112. Ibid.
113. All quotes are from ibid., 42ff.
114. ZI no. 2832. The complete, programmatic title, which gives a good summary of the content, reads as follows: Dz lob der pfarrer // Von den vnnützen // kosten der gelegt wirt von dem // gemeinen vnuerstendigen volck // vff maß lasen / volgungen / begreb- // nüß / sybend / drysigst / jartag etc. Vnd // vom lob der Pfarrer vnd irer nötigen Caplon."
115. All quotes are from ibid., next to last and last folios.
116. These are "Ain kurtzer gschriftlicher bericht etlicher puncten halb Christlichs glauben, zugeschickt der hailgen samlung außerwelten Christen zu Vlm in schwaben . . . ," printed in L. Enders, *Eberlin von Günzburg 2*, 171ff., as well as "Die ander getrew vermanung Johannes Eberlin vonn Guntzburg, an den Rath der loblichen stadt Vlm," printed in L. Ender, *Eberlin von Günzburg*, vol. 3: 1ff. From this are taken the following quotes.
117. Ludwig Enders, ed., *Johannes Eberlin von Günzburg, Sämtliche Schriften*, 3 vols. in 2, Flugschriften aus der Reformationszeit, vols. 11, 15, 18 (Halle, 1896–1902), vol. 2: 181.

118. Ibid., vol. 3: 18f.
119. ZI no. 1699, printed in Clemen, *Flugschriften* 1, 225ff. The quotes from ZI, no. 1699.
120. See Karl Lendi, *Der Dichter Pamphilius Gengenbach, Beiträge zu seinem Leben und seinem Werk*, Sprache und Dichtung, vol. 39 (Bern, 1926), 69, where the question of authorship is discussed in detail.
121. The text begins with the words: "Wissend sei menglichem / das in dem Jar als man zalt. M.D. xxiij." ZI no. 1699, Aij.
122. Ibid., Aiij.
123. Ibid., Cij.
124. Ibid.
125. Ibid., Ciij.
126. Böckmann, "Der gemeine Mann in den Flugschriften," 213f.
127. ZW, vol. 2, 21–457.
128. Ibid., 458–525, with the text proper at 471–525.
129. Locher, "Theologie Zwinglis," 183.
130. See the introduction of the editor Emil Egli to "Justice" in ZW, vol. 2, 458–468.
131. Ibid., 478, lines 17ff.
132. Ibid., 481, lines 18–21.
133. Ibid., 481, lines 22–31.
134. Ibid., 495, lines 26f.
135. This interpretation deviates somewhat from the reading suggested by the editor. In my opinion *offnung* must not be read as *Offenbarung*, "revelation."
136. Locher, "Theologie Zwinglis," 180. See also Erik Wolf, "Die Sozialtheologie Zwinglis," in *Festschrift Guido Kisch* (Stuttgart, 1955), 167–188, esp. 179–187.
137. ZW, vol. 2, 323.
138. Ibid., 324, lines 11–18.
139. Ibid., 505, lines 14f.
140. Ibid., 505, lines 17–21.
141. Ibid., 324, lines 18–24; and see also 429, lines 10–20.
142. Ibid., 484, lines 17, 22.
143. Ibid., 484, lines 25–28.
144. Ibid., 325, lines 10, 16f.
145. Ibid., 520, lines 11ff.
146. Ibid., 329f.
147. On this see Arthur Rich, "Zwingli als sozialpolitischer Denker," *Zwingliana* 13 (1969–1973): 67–89, esp. 81–86.
148. ZW, vol. 2, 331, lines 8–13.
149. Ibid., 344, lines 20–25.
150. Ibid., 345, line 20f.
151. Ibid., 510, lines 15ff.
152. Ibid., 494, line 26.
153. Ibid., 497, lines 28ff.
154. Ibid., 497, line 23f.
155. Ibid., 484, line 15f.
156. Ibid., 520, lines 11ff.
157. "Der Kemptener Leibeigenschaftsrodel," ed. by Peter Blickle with H. Besch, *Zeitschrift für bayerische Landesgeschichte* 42 (1979): 567–629.
158. Ibid., 586.
159. Ibid., 594.
160. Ibid., 605.
161. Ibid., 593.

162. Ibid., 590ff. A systematic analysis of the *Leibeigenschaftsrodel*, which would be interesting from many different aspects, is still lacking.
163. Justus Maurer, *Prediger im Bauernkrieg*, Calwer Theologische Monographien, vol. 5 (Stuttgart, 1979), 399f.
164. Staatsarchiv Zürich, A 192.1, fol. 123f.
165. Ibid., fol. 135.
166. Peter Blickle, "Nochmals zur Entstehung der Zwölf Artikel," in Peter Blickle, ed., *Bauer, Reich und Reformation. Festschrift für Günther Franz zum 80. Geburtstag* (Stuttgart, 1982), 288–300.
167. Franz, *Quellen*, 147.
168. Ibid., 178f.
169. WA, vol. 18, 279–334; the text itself (without introductory commentary) is from 291–334.
170. Ibid., 295, line 34; 296, line 21.
171. Ibid., 302–305.
172. Ibid., 314, lines 30–34.
173. Ibid., 307, lines 34–36.
174. The topic of Luther and the Peasants' War is treated in almost all larger works dealing with Luther and the reformation. Among the more important specialized studies are Kurt Aland, "Luther und der Bauernkrieg im Lichte des Marxismus," in Kurt Aland *Apologie der Apologetik. Zur Haltung und Aufgabe evangelischen Christentums in der Auseinandersetzungen des Gegenwarts* (Berlin, 1948), 94–111; Paul Althaus, "Luthers Haltung im Bauernkrieg. Ein Beitrag zur lutherischen Sozialethik," in Paul Althaus, *Evangelium und Leben* (Basel, 1953); Carl Hinrichs, *Luther und Müntzer, ihre Auseinandersetzung über Obrigkeit und Widerstandsrecht*, Arbeiten zur Kirchengeschichte, vol. 29, (Berlin, 1959); Franz Lau, "Die prophetische Apokalyptik Thomas Müntzers und Luthers Absage an die Bauernrevolution," in Friedrich Hübner, ed., *Gedenkschrift für Werner Elert. Beiträge zur historischen und systematischen Theologie* (Berlin, 1955), 163–170; Hartmut Lehmann, "Luther und der Bauernkrieg," *Die Geschichte in Wissenschaft und Unterricht* 20 (1969): 129–39; Friedrich Lütge, "Luthers Eingreifen in den Bauernkrieg in seinen sozialgeschichtlichen Voraussetzungen und Auswirkungen," *Jahrbücher für Nationalökonomie und Statistik* 158 (1943): 369–401. For a comprehensive bibliographical essay and a critical review of the literature, see most recently Gottfried Maron's article "Bauernkrieg" in *Theologische Realenzyklopädie*, vol. 5 (1979), 321–338. See the critical remarks by Hans-Joachim Gänssler, *Evangelium und weltliches Schwert. Hintergrund, Entstehungsgeschichte und Anlaß von Luthers Scheidung zweier Reiche oder Regimente*, Veröffentlichungen des Instituts für Europäische Geschichte Mainz, vol. 109 (Wiesbaden, 1983), 152ff. Mark U. Edwards, Jr., *Luther and the False Brethren* (Stanford, 1975), 60–81.
175. WA, vol. 18, 33, lines 22–26.
176. Ibid., 304, lines 29–31.
177. Ibid., 295, lines 22–24.
178. Ibid., 308, 320, and more.
179. Ibid., 305, line 3 to 306, line 27.
180. Ibid., 344–361, with the text proper at 357–361.
181. Ibid., 361, line 16.
182. Ibid., 357, lines 23f., 28f.
183. On this problem see Saarbrücker Arbeitsgruppe (Saarbrücken Colloquium), "Huldigungseid und Herrschaftsstruktur im Hattgau (Elsaß)," *Jahrbuch für westdeutsche Landesgeschichte* 6 (1980): 117–155. For two well-documented cases in pre-reformation southern Germany where allegiance was refused, I can point to

Ochsenhausen in 1498 (Ewald Gruber, Geschichte des Klosters Ochsenhausen von den Anfängen bis zum 16. Jahrhundert, unpublished dissertation, Tübingen, 1956) and Kempten in 1523 (Franz Ludwig Baumann, ed., *Akten zur Geschichte des deutschen Bauernkrieges in Oberschwaben* [Freiburg im Breisgau, 1877], 336).

184. WA, vol. 18, 360, lines 1f., 5f., 11f., 28f.; 361, lines 24ff.
185. Quoted by H. Lehmann, "Luther und der Bauernkrieg," 134.
186. Althaus, "Luthers Haltung," 39.
187. WA, vol. 18, 359, lines 11f.
188. Ibid., 358, lines 28–32.
189. Compare on this Luther's later interpretation in Siegfried Bräuer, "Luthers Beziehungen zu den Bauern," in Helmar Junghans, ed., *Leben und Werken Martin Luthers von 1526 bis 1534*, vol. 1 (Berlin, 1983), 457–473, here at 462; Edwards, *Luther*, 199.
190. WA, vol. 18, 357, lines 12–14.
191. See on this the prefaces of the editors, WA, 279–290, esp. 282, and 344–355, esp. 345–348.
192. Broad documentation in Heinrich R. Schmidt, *Reichsstädte, Reich und Reformation. Korporative Religionspolitik 1521–1529/30*, Veröffentlichungen des Instituts für europäische Geschichte Mainz, vol. 122 (Wiesbaden, 1986).

6

The Communal Reformation in the Tradition of Late Medieval Political Culture

The common people in the countryside and in the city developed concepts of the reformation that were identical in their basic principles. They adopted the reformers' concept of church, the idea of a church that should be grounded in the community; and yet they added something to the theologians' concept by concretizing the church within the political community. The common people adopted the reformers' category of the pure gospel, although in the southern German version the gospel was also socially and politically relevant. Yet they added something to this concept by insisting that it imposed an obligation for concrete action. Abandoned by Zwingli and other southern German reformers, who could not solve the dichotomy between the imperative of realizing the gospel in the world on the one hand, and the gospel's promise of peace on the other, the common people concretized the pure gospel in the theory of a Christian Republic in which godly law had normative force. The common people in country and city listened to the reformers when they talked about the realization of *ecclesia*, they listened to the southern German reformers when they talked about the realization of the gospel, but they were not merely imitators. Their struggle for the Christian Republic was the qualitative leap from the theory of the intellectuals, who shied away from responsibility, to the concrete, day-to-day practice of the common people. And this practice was not nourished by religious faith; rather, its explanation lies in the actual living conditions, in the village and the city, in the political culture of the late Middle Ages.

The political culture of the high Middle Ages was dominated by the nobility and the church. In the late Middle Ages, the burghers and peasants made themselves heard, they competed with, indeed they threatened and endangered, the world of noble and clerical lordship by creating their own organizational forms. At the end of the thirteenth century, new political associations arose in the north of the empire, such as the Ditmarsh association, and in the south of the empire with the Confederacy of Uri, Schwyz, and Nidwalden. Arising from peasant communities, these associations were later joined by cities. The experiment in the south seems to have captured the imagination of contemporaries in a special way. Sometimes successfully, sometimes unsuccessfully, burghers and peasants rose to oppose their lords, with mixed results. They were unsuccessful at the beginning of the fifteenth century between Lake Constance and the Tyrol, successful in the archbishoprics of Chur and Sitten. Of course, change was not always violent; some bishops left their former estates (*Domhöfe*) and the nobles their manors, and thus the cities and villages gained more room for political action. The reception of Aristotelian thought by Thomas Aquinas and his students imparted a new meaning to life in the late medieval world. While Aquinas himself had already distinguished two modes of being, that of the burgher and the noble, his students believed that a person found his full realization in the urban world: "si non es civis, non es homo." Now the "felicitas politica" stood higher than the "felicitas contemplativa." From here there are links to humanism, which was also a highly civic culture, and which from the basis of the civic *res publica* reflected on the bonum commune. But even the peasants' world increasingly attracted attention, especially in the empire. The literature of writers such as Johannes Tauler, Peter Suchenwirt, and Hans Rosenplüt began to respect the peasant and to praise his virtues. In the debate over imperial reform, as we see it in the writings of Peter von Andlau, of the Revolutionary of the upper Rhine, and finally in the utopian blueprints of the early years of the reformation era, there was at least a discussion about what the peasant meant to the empire.

All this is well known. But what is too little part of the historical awareness are the preconditions that formed the background to these phenomena. First, cities and villages were emerging, a process which we can call the communalization of society, since the daily lives of the people were now shaped by the urban and rural communes. Second, this process of communalization had far-reaching consequences, since the lower orders organized in the communities developed a self-consciousness which the Middle Ages did not know. Communities resisted their lords, and they strove for participation in political decision-making bodies at the highest levels, the provincial and imperial diets. In both areas they were not without success. Third, from the daily cares and joys of life in the villages and the cities, and from the confrontations with lordship, whether in armed conflict or in the cooperative setting of the estate assemblies, independent norms and values arose among the common people. These are the preconditions for understanding the reformation as a social and political phenomenon.

THE COMMUNALIZATION OF LATE MEDIEVAL SOCIETY

The communalization of society had its roots in certain economic changes at the end of the High Middle Ages. First, the manorial structure disintegrated. Second, the formerly unfree tenants, who now had to take economic responsibility for themselves, developed special political associations in the form of urban and rural communes with a large degree of autonomy. Third, this emergence of communal administrative and legal practices offers a particularly good insight into the growing process of communalization, which eventually also drew the church into its wake.

THE DISSOLUTION OF HIGH MEDIEVAL STRUCTURES

The late Middle Ages is universally regarded as a time of profound change, reflected, for example, in the movements for imperial reform, the conciliar efforts, and the territorial ambitions of the imperial princes. One process whose importance has so far been underestimated was the dissolution of the high medieval social structure. In negative terms it was the break-up of the manorial units, in positive terms the formation of two new social forms, the village and the city, as the primary bases of governance for the overwhelming majority of the people.[1]

A cursory look at how the manorial system functioned can sharpen our awareness for the new entities, the village[2] and the town.[3] The term "manorial system" (*Villikationssystem*) describes an arrangement in which agricultural and artisanal work was centered on a manor supervised by the lord himself (*Fronhof*) or by his representative (*villicus*).[4]

This system entailed that the extensive lands of the lord (the demesne) were cultivated through the labor dues of the unfree peasants. At the end of the High Middle Ages this system entered into a profound process of change. The final outcome of this process in regard to the organization of agriculture was the distribution of the demesne among the unfree peasants in parcels the size of family farms to be worked independently. Payments in kind and in coin replaced the former labor services; rentier lordship based on rents displaced the manor. The landlord withdrew from the organization of agriculture, and, if he was a nobleman, built his castle in some prominent location. These were the beginnings of the autonomy of the rural commune (*Landgemeinde*). We can describe these beginnings particularly well by looking at the village, which was, after all, the most widespread form of the rural commune.

The nobility's disinterest in agriculture invariably led to a distribution of the lands, fields, and meadows among the tenants. Field and rotation systems emerged, a widespread method being the three-field rotation. These systems subjected the farm holders to compulsory tillage (*Flurzwang*) and directed them toward cooperative behavior, since the land had to be sown and harvested in a communal effort, and the commons were used collectively by the livestock of the entire village. This relatively complicated system of agricultural work could not draw upon any previous models; it had to be managed by the very people involved in it.

What favored and hastened this process was the fact that the village, which was emerging at the same time, represented a new social entity. The intensification of social relations and the growing complexity of economic arrangements demanded that the spheres of life which were of vital importance to rural society be regulated and safeguarded. Norms for communal living had to be devised, organs for supervising adherence to the norms had to be established, institutions for settling violations of the norms had to be created. After the dissolution of the manors, the framework for these steps—which I will shortly discuss in greater detail—could only be the village. To regulate communal life the village commune developed a communal right of legislating; administrative organs for enforcing village laws were created in the form of village offices; and the adjudication of violations was handled by the village court.

Two things follow from the transformation that society underwent at the end of the high and the beginning of the late Middle Ages. On the one hand, older ties of lordship, reflected, for example, in the fact that property was still tied to the landlords' authority (and this normally involved also rights of jurisdiction), continued to shape the life of the village, and to that extent the village was by no means a sphere free of all feudal lordship. On the other hand, something new arose with the village in the form of the village commune, a social and political entity based on new ways of working and living together, with the rural community itself responsible for its organization. The older rule by outside people was replaced by a new, if limited, self-determination. The emergence of village communes thus marked a qualitative change for agrarian society. It is surely no coincidence that it is only from this time on that we begin to encounter the term "peasant" in the sources,[5] and that freedom and unfreedom were being displaced as criteria of social differentiation by occupational characteristics; society differentiated itself into those who prayed, those who fought, and those who worked, into clergy, nobility, and peasants.[6] The unfree serf became a peasant. What did that mean for rural society?

The feudal world of the High Middle Ages was determined by vertical relations, by a pronounced, differentiated hierarchical order. According to the military order of precedence (Heerschildordnung), this hierarchy comprised six of seven categories, from the emperor down to the knight.[7] Every place in the hierarchy had corresponding political rights. This meant for rural society that it had no political rights, it lived in a legal or factual state of unfreedom. We can document this empirically in eastern Germany, where we can observe a process of refeudalization in the fifteenth and sixteenth centuries. The result was that the commune as a political unit was dissolved in the domain of manorial rule (Rittergutsherrschaft), while forms of unfreedom were reintroduced through heritable serfdom and Gesindezwangsdienst for peasant children, forms that had been characteristic of the manorial system.[8]

In contrast to the feudal world, the village commune was shaped by horizontal relations, by the equal status of the owners of the farms within the communal group and their political self-determination. This communalism was most strongly developed where feudalism was weak or had lost strength. That applies especially to southwestern Germany and Switzerland, where the nobility was quantitatively and qualitatively of far less importance than in the east. At the same time this was the region with a close-knit network of cities.

A comparative look at the city is intended only to complete the picture I have so far painted. Since scholarship on the history of towns has been pursued for far longer and in greater depth, the late medieval development of the town is much better known than that of the village. As a result we can make do with a brief sketch, whereby the focus will be above all on explaining and justifying the comparability of the developments in village and town.

The emancipation of the urban communes, away from the authority of the town lords and toward the autonomy of the city republic, was a protracted process. In some cases it could take centuries, but as a rule it began at the end of the Hohenstaufen period and culminated in the course of the fifteenth century. The process can be illustrated particularly well in the cities of southern Germany that once fell under the jurisdiction of the Hohenstaufen, the Welfs, the Zähringers, or various bishops. By around 1500 they were free or imperial cities, a status that allows us to rank them alongside other so-called immediate powers, who exercised real political authority.

The stages in the urban community's path toward a very high degree of political independence can be summarized as follows: exemption from the jurisdiction of external courts; curtailment of the power of the royal or episcopal bailiffs; participation in choosing the warden (*Ammann*), and eventually the acquisition of the exclusive right of appointment; acquisition of the right of high justice; and elimination of serfdom in favor of personal freedom.[9]

To illustrate what I have just said we can turn to the episcopal city of Augsburg. As early as the late thirteenth century there were conflicts between the bishop and the *cives* or the *universitas*. Eventually, with royal consent, the "oldest and . . . wisest councilors of Augsburg" drew up a code of law and had it confirmed by the king.[10] The code clearly distinguished three legal spheres, that of the bishop, represented by the castellan, that of the king, represented by the bailiff, and that of the city. The growing interest of the German kings and emperors in the rising cities led in Augsburg to a progressive and irresistable decline of the castellan's authority, so that the struggle over the city's degree of autonomy was eventually fought out between the urban commune and the bailiff. By the fifteenth century, at the latest, Augsburg had decided this unstable situation in its own favor. In 1426, King Sigismund issued a charter which declared that if the citizens of Augsburg

> petition us or our successors in the empire for a bailiff, or request that we give them a different one, whom they shall then name to us, we will and ought to give them the same without delay . . . and shall also support, maintain and protect him in the bailiff's office during his lifetime, or for such time as it shall be to the above-mentioned pleasure of the city of Augsburg.

The bailiff, for his part,

may then in our stead grant to his under-bailiff, who is called the city bailiff, whom the same Augsburgers shall also choose, the ban to sit in judgment over dangerous people and other matters, whatever seems fitting for him to do, in accord with the law of the city.[11]

With this charter the royal rights in the city had been in a sense communalized. Memmingen is an example for a second type of city. Founded by the Welfs and taken over by the Hohenstaufen, its development took a less complicated course than that of Augsburg, since the overlordship, which in Augsburg was divided between the bishop and the royal bailiff, was here combined in one hand. While during the post-Hohenstaufen period the governor (Landvogt) of Upper Swabia was still entrusted with legal jurisdiction over the city in the name of the king, this situation changed in the course of the fourteenth century. In 1312 Memmingen obtained the right of appeal in the appointment of the mayor (Ammann), who until then had been appointed by the governor. In 1350 the town was granted the nomination of the mayor; and finally, in 1403, the mayor's earlier rights of low justice were expanded by the right of high justice in matters of life and death (Blutbann).[12] The royal rights had thus passed into the hands of the town. Parallel to this process there occurred a progressive undermining and elimination of the feudal legal titles that invariably existed in a city that had originally been under the administration of Welf and Hohenstaufen ministerials. Under the heading "To abolish serfdom," the town's legal code stated:

> The following is decreed and in accord with ancient law: in regard to those who become our citizens and have lords . . . he [the lord] shall seek his rights before the year and a day shall arrive . . . But if the lord lets the matter slide until a year has passed since they became citizens, he shall henceforth have no right to them.[13]

This general outline and the examples of Augsburg and Memmingen serve merely to focus our attention on a process that holds true for town and country alike, a process that began at the end of the High Middle Ages and concluded at the beginning of the reformation period. The very first thing that separated the peasant and the burgher from the unfree man of the High Middle Ages was the opportunity to organize his own work and dispose relatively freely the fruits of his labor. To use a modern comparison, one might see the late medieval system of dues as a modified tax system. The point of this comparison is to call attention to the fundamental difference between the conditions of work in the High Middle Ages and those in the late Middle Ages. In the High Middle Ages the unfree person worked on the estate of his lord, and was fed, clothed, housed, represented, and protected by him, at least in theory. If he worked any land on his own, it returned to the lord upon his death, along with all movable property, if he had been able to accumulate any during his lifetime. A very common word in southern Germany for describing this state of affairs was Eigenschaft, which expressed the lord's extensive authority.[14] After the nobility (and the church) had ceased to claim the fruits of the labor of the politically disenfranchised classes, the entire system began to falter, and it fragmented into a great array of lordly privileges: from serfdom to landlordship to judicial lordship. At the same time, there arose structures in villages and towns which opened completely new dimensions of human existence for late medieval people. As we shall now see, late medieval people began to assume responsibility for their own lives.

COMMUNAL ADMINISTRATION AND JUSTICE

The common focal point for the village and the city is the community. Two things set the community apart from the manorial estates of the High Middle Ages. First, the village and the city had a spatial focus, unlike the personal ties that constituted manorial units, and, second, they took over what were formerly functions of lordship. What we mean by a rural community can be most quickly grasped by looking at the communal assembly.[15] At least once a year the owners of agricultural farms met in the village, the district, or the valley to deliberate on village matters. The communal assembly undoubtedly decided matters that were of some political importance, for example, whether the community should bring a court case against the landlord or maybe even oppose him with violence in an effort to push through its own claims.[16] This example highlights the self-conception of the community, which saw itself as an association capable of taking political action. Of course, the jurisdiction of the community is reflected even more clearly in the usual topics of deliberation that came up year after year. The most important affairs of the communal assembly were legislation as well as the election of the village organs. The customaries (*Weistümer*) from the German-speaking regions, which number in the thousands, show that the legal corporation (*Rechtsgenossenschaft*) had the right of issuing directives, and that the statutes derived from this referred ever increasingly to the village, the rural district, or the inhabitants of a valley—in short, that the daily problems were taken care of via the statutes of the community itself. The communal charter from Pfalz in the Tyrol from the year 1471, which regulated wood use, irrigation, and problems of the commons, can be considered quite representative of the situation I have sketched:

> Let it be known to all who see, read, or hear this open declaration, that we, the neighbors who reside in the village of Pfalz, have jointly, unanimously, with good deliberation and freely drawn up and made a statute, in particular for our honor and benefit and those of our descendants, and we have . . . devised and decreed the same.[17]

In Mähringen in Upper Swabia, "a community came to an agreement" in 1484 and 1506 about tree felling, damage caused by animals, and encroachments in fencing, plowing, and mowing, and it did so without any involvement on the part of the lord.[18] In the late Middle Ages, such communal jurisdictions were respected by the authorities even in situations where the lordship had the political power and the moral competence to restrict communal rights. Despite the uprising of the peasants of St. Gall in 1490, the subsequent arbitration conceded:

> . . . but if or when it should happen that some community wants to settle or regulate the affairs of the same community—deciding compulsory tillage, setting boundaries, and other such things, the same community may do this with an assembly of those who belong to said community, as often as is necessary.[19]

If we move to a description of the authority of the village organs, we can grasp in even greater detail the spectrum of communal jurisdictions. One important administrative organ of the community was a collegially operating committee, which we find in various compositions. The names Two, Three, Four, Six, and Twelve designate councils which were composed respectively of two, three, four, six, or twelve peasant jurors. Their jurisdiction consisted in safeguarding the village territory (Dorfmark) and the individual plots within the village lands; monitoring fire safety regulations; supervising the commercial establishments like the smithy, the mill, the baths, and the taverns; and controlling weights and measures. In order to accomplish its tasks effectively, this organ was not infrequently equipped with regulatory and prohibitory authority, which we might compare to modern-day statutory authority.

As the size of a village increased, the duties of this committee could be assigned to officers with specific functions: a field guard to inspect and supervise the fields and commons or a watchman to watch over the village during the night and prevent fires.

In the communal court the village had an organ for supervising the norms, which could be codified, but did not have to be, or which had been promulgated by the community or its officeholders.[20] As a jurors' court (Schöffengericht) it was staffed with between six and twenty-four peasant jurymen. It extended its competence to administrative jurisdiction, involvement in keeping land registers, issuing of birth certificates or drafting of last wills, as well as to civil and criminal cases, such as violation of property boundary lines or disturbances of the village peace through insults, brawls, or bodily injury. In other words, we are talking about that sphere which is described, in contemporary and scholarly terminology, as "low justice." In Ulten in the Tyrol, this situation was described in 1521 with the following stipulation: "the said subjects shall settle and arbitrate minor matters, which do not touch upon immoral acts [inzicht] and felonies."[21] High justice over murder, theft, and arson was usually reserved for the seigneurial organs, but even in this area the participation by the communities occasionally increased in the late Middle Ages. In the Engadin in 1519, the councils of Emperor Maximilian and the bishop of Chur along with the communities worked out a code of high and low justice, as is clearly evident from the concluding passage: "This statute charter has been written in two identical copies, one given to His Royal Majesty and Honor and to the bishop of Chur, the other to all the communities of the Lower Engadin."[22]

At the top of the communal administration and the administration of the law stood the warden (*Ammann*), the village mayor (*schultheiß*), or the bailiff (*Vogt*). He presided over the communal assembly, was usually the chairman of the court, and functioned as the head of all the other administrative organs.

What the communal organs had in common was that they were always staffed by the peasants themselves. The rural commune had little or no acquaintance with seigneurial or state officials. Wherever individual and communal interests came into contact, the community used its own, self-appointed organs to take regulative, administrative, legislative, adjudicative, and punitive action. In general, the starting points of peasant self-government were and remained agriculture with its attendant problems, as well as the issues that were bound to arise when people live closely together in a small, closed settlement area.

In all this we must not, of course, overlook the fact that village interests frequently overlapped with those of the village authorities or the village lord. Quarrels over land, for example, invariably also involved seigneurial interests. Since the landlord received dues in kind from the village, he, too, was concerned about inspecting weights and measures. This explains why the local authorities were involved in the appointment of the communal organs. The local lord undoubtedly exerted the greatest influence over the appointment of the communal leader (*Gemeindevorsteher*); he reserved for himself at least the right of confirming the person chosen, but more frequently he selected from a slate of three or four men proposed by the community the candidate who seemed particularly suitable to him. In the Tyrolean district of Stubai, the following was confirmed on oath in 1421:

> . . . if a judge is to be appointed in Stubai, the neighbors themselves [*die nachpaurschaft*] have the authority and the right to select three men from amongst themselves and propose them to a representative [*phleger*] (representative) of the territorial lord; the representative then has the choice to pick one judge from the three, whichever he likes best.[23]

The same procedure is also found in Switzerland and elsewhere in southern Germany: "Item, those of Altlicken," we read in a customary of this village in the Zurich region,

> shall give to me [the lord] a bailiff if I so desire and need one; thus I shall call together an assembly and place this matter before them, after which they shall have an election for a bailiff . . . and shall propose three to me; I may then take from the three whomever I want.[24]

It was probably comparatively rare that a community could itself appoint the local headman, as was the case in Birmensdorf in the Zurich area, where a notice of the late fifteenth century confirmed to the members of the community "that they have appointed a sub-bailiff through majority vote."[25]

The influence of the higher authorities remained much weaker when it came to the appointment of the jurors (*Schöffen*). Even though the jurymen usually also had to be confirmed by the judicial overlord, under the best of

circumstances for the authorities the village community and the lordship alter-
nated in appointing a juror. Interference from the higher authorities was least
with the organs that were more narrowly administrative, and whose election by
the community was usually accepted by the lordship. Frequently the "communal
neighbors" were given confirmation "that they shall every year . . . appoint two
or four,"[26] or that "it [is] the law and old custom of our manor [hof] that we shall
appoint three village mayors [dorffmeyer] . . . These same village mayors shall
have the authority over bridges and roads, and the right to determine compulsory tillage."[27] In Ersingen in Upper Swabia,

> the communal wardens [gemeindspfleger] and the fours and the village warden
> [undergänger] are chosen. Their election is carried out, in the presence of the
> lordship, by the community and every member of the community by writing
> down the votes, and whoever has been chosen to be one of the fours or a
> warden by the majority shall remain in his office for two years.[28]

•   We can note as our finding that a political autonomy of the community did
exist, but it was an autonomy restricted by the local overlord.

The expansion and deepening of the range of action available for rural society
had its parallel in urban society in the changes that city and town constitutions
underwent in the late Middle Ages.[29] It may be assumed that this development
is sufficiently known, so that a cursory sketch should suffice for the southern
German area. Moreover, this sketch will limit itself to generalizations about the
development in the imperial cities, since the far more modest work on the
territorial cities precludes general statements at this time.

The older scholarship devised the less than happy term "guild democracy"
(Zunftdemokratie) to describe an essentially accurate development in the German cities, primarily those in the south: the dismantling of old administrative
and governing structures that had been inherited from the time of "feudal" city
lordship and were dominated by the patriciate in favor of the homeowner and
family man who enjoyed full citizen rights and was corporatively organized in his
guild. This process—beginning in the middle of the fourteenth century and
frequently not ending until around 1500—belongs chronologically to the period
during which the political rights of rural communities also developed and
stabilized.

From about 1350 to 1550, the guild as an organizing principle dominated
urban political life.[30] If the patriciate wanted and was able to exert influence on
the political constitution of the city, it accommodated itself to the guild. The
guild as a corporate association of artisans and tradespeople in related trades
grew from primarily economic interests. But like all medieval corporations, it
deepened its raison d'être by binding its members to a common ethos (quality and
price of the products) and by bringing them together beyond their professional
interests through religious and social activities (guild feast, care of the sick,
burial funds). If we wish to make comparisons with the countryside, the crucial
thing was that membership in a guild, which presupposed ownership of a house,

constituted citizenship, just as in the countryside communal membership was linked to ownership of one's own farmstead or at least "one's own hearth." Since in the city only the guild as a corporation had the right to political representation, political goals could be attained only through the guild. By participating in forming guild policy and taking part in the election of the guild brothers, a burgher could realize his claim to political maturity.

Where the council and the court were appointed via the guilds, the patriciate also had to organize itself, into societies, as in Lindau and Augsburg, or into guilds as in Kaufbeuren, Kempten, and Memmingen. The patrician organizations could not claim any special privileges, but they did possess the necessary financial means and time to devote themselves to the political and administrative affairs of the city. Since city offices were honorary posts without salary, they were largely the preserve of the wealthy, the more so, the more time-consuming political affairs became. In this way the oligarchic character of the urban councils strengthened again, especially from the second half of the fifteenth century on. For practical reasons, the positions won by the guilds could not be maintained and defended to their full extent.[31]

Of course, there can be no doubt that right up to the eve of the reformation, the council, as the key organ of political decisions within the city, was elected primarily from among the guilds and with the participation of the community. Where patricians did get positions on the council, the electoral procedure with the attendant dependence on the will of the electorate offered some assurance that the magistrates would not pursue solely their own political ideas and serve only the interests of their own social class. Even though the emergence of so-called privy councils promoted oligarchic tendencies and a separation from the community, there still was a committee of supreme political effectiveness in the existing institution of the Great Council. It assembled for particularly important issues: in Augsburg, for example, to revise the election procedures for the council in 1476, and in Zurich for the disputation in 1523 between Zwingli and representatives of the bishop of Constance.

Examples which illustrate the extensive rights of the rural communities come from the same region in which the reformation was also a peasant movement. It would certainly not have been easy to marshal similar source passages for western or central Germany during the pre-reformation period. What we have known since the work of Karl Siegfried Bader, namely that the southern German region was particularly highly developed in regard to its communal autonomy, has been confirmed by all subsequent studies outside the area examined by Bader.[32] For the Saar-Mosel region, it has been shown that local administration and justice remained much more deeply rooted in older traditions of the manorial system, and consequently it was "the sole right of lordship to select and appoint jurymen and court officials."[33] Under these conditions, the village could not develop any noticeable life of its own. A recent study examining the village community in Hessia gives a striking account of its jurisdiction, which was limited to petty cases.[34] It is hardly necessary to call to mind the decline of the eastern and, to some extent, of the central German communities to the level of purely economic associations in the fourteenth and fifteenth centuries.[35]

Within the area of German legal traditions, the Franconian-Alemannic as well as the Swiss-Austrian region thus took a separate line of development during the late Middle Ages. It was here that administration, together with the administration of justice that was linked to it, shifted from the older seigneurial manor to the more recent corporative community, with all the logical consequences this shift entailed: communal statutory sovereignty, communal administration, and communal administration of the law.

A comparison with western Europe also underlines the special, if not unique, position of the southern German region. Although there are considerable parallels to the rural communities in France, since they also participated "à la législation, à la police, à l'administration,"[36] they apparently lacked juridical competence. Juridical authority was a crucial part of the southern German rural community, and its presence underscores the eminently political character of this community. Clearer still is the difference to England, where the medieval organizational type of agricultural and agrarian society was preserved in the form of the manor; in any case, "the English village . . . was in a purely formal way never a community in the sense that the German villages were."[37]

This observation does not apply to an equal extent to the cities, since they were numerous in the north and especially in the northwest of the empire. Nevertheless, it cannot be denied that the network of cities in Franconia, Swabia, Alsace, and Switzerland was denser, and especially that the autonomy of the city was more extensive in these areas; the imperial cities confirm this. Looking at Europe as a whole, one cannot deny that the empire—next to Italy—brought forth an urban culture that was unique in regard to its political components, owing to the extensive autonomy of the community based on the guilds.[38]

The far-reaching communalization process in the rural and urban society of southern Germany eventually extended also to the church.

TENDENCIES TOWARD A COMMUNALIZATION OF THE CHURCH

Hans Erich Feine once pointed out "that in the rural communes of Inner Switzerland the ecclesiastical emancipation began only in the fifteenth century in the wake of the political emancipation." At that time began the development which approached its high point in the 1520s and made Switzerland into the "classic land of rights to elect pastors and of communal lay patronage."[39] A connection is suggested here between political and ecclesiastical "emancipation," one that reached its conclusion—with a geographic applicability that was initially limited to Switzerland—in the reformation period. Karl Siegfried Bader observed that "a village without its own parish church . . . simply was not a real village deserving of the name," and he corroborated that view with the efforts of the villagers to gain control first of all of a chaplaincy or a vicariate, which gave them at least a chapel. It has rightly been noted that the medieval village was more attached to its own chapel, which belonged only to the village, than to the distant, impersonal parish churches of a larger parish.[40]

Two strands of motives intersect in a process we could call the communalization or localization of the church: an adjustment of the church to the existing political culture of rural society, and an equating of the political with the ecclesiastical community. These trends can be attested to above all in southern Germany, which is also where they were particularly successful. Dietrich Kurze has distinguished three levels in this process: the right of the community to complain about the minister or pastor and to request his dismissal; the right of the community to be heard when an appointment was made by the lay patron; and the right of the community to freely elect its pastor.[41]

The community's right to lodge complaints was very widespread, and it was in a sense institutionalized in the office of the church wardens (*Kirchenpfleger*). These were mostly representatives chosen from the community to administer the church endowment, the patrimony of the "saint." Pastor and church wardens supervised the moral and religious life of the members of the community, but with the growing communal self-confidence, the church wardens and the community also supervised the moral and religious life of the pastor.[42] As a rule the church wardens were elected to a limited term and had to answer to the community. We frequently encounter formulations like the ones used in the statutes of the South Tyrolean community of Kaltern:

Item, if a community appoints a church provost [*kirchprabst*], when his year is over, he shall settle accounts with the community leader [*tschiniken*], the jurors [*gesworn*] and the entire community, on pain of a fine of 10 lbs.[43]

We can work on the assumption that this institution was widely known throughout southern Germany.[44] In so far as the election of church wardens gained ground, and their controlling function over the local church expanded, they attest on the lowest level, as it were, to the advancing process of the communalization and localization of the church.

The myriad ways in which a community participated in filling pastoral offices have not yet been sufficiently examined.[45] The example of the community of Wendelstein, with which we began our discussion of the peasants' reformation, was surely not an isolated case. The Tyrolean community of Villanders laid down the following in its statutes at the end of the fifteenth century: "whoever is patron of the parish in Villanders, if he wants to appoint a vicar, he shall appoint him with the consent and agreement of the parish, and if the community does not like the vicar, he shall appoint a different one."[46] This expresses a situation which scholarship has been able to confirm also for other locations.[47] What becomes visible here is a trend that can be exemplified particularly in the elections of pastors, which can claim special attention since they represent the highest form of communal influence on the church.

"The most important thing separating the history of the elections of priests in the two periods," the high and the late Middle Ages,

is the spread of communal participation to regions which earlier had not known the right of electing priests or had not been able to push it through: to Ditmarsh, to the Swabian-Alemannic region in southwest Germany, to the original Swiss cantons, as well as to the Austrian alpine regions.[48]

If we leave Ditmarsh aside, these areas mark off a region that is virtually identical with the region in which the communal reformation occurred. Elections of pastors are attested from the upper Rhine all the way to the Tyrol, elections which the communities generally were able to push through in the fifteenth century. The village law of Ehringen, near Nördlingen, laid down "that the community in Ehringen has the power to elect a pastor . . . and where a pastor is not amenable to a community, it may give notice on a quarterly basis."[49] The community of Davos in the Graubünden declared around 1500, "item, firstly we have a free parish, which we grant to a pastor on a yearly basis."[50] The practice reflected in these passages is one we can also observe above all in central Switzerland, namely that "the communities not only appointed their pastors but could even dismiss them, and conducted yearly re-elections or new elections."[51] This meant that the office of the pastor had moved very close to that of the warden (Ammann), at least in regard to the way in which these two officeholders were appointed and supervised. The communities acquired patronage or presentation rights, either through outright purchase or by endowing, founding, or building their own church.[52] The first approach shows the people's interest in controlling the church located in the village; the second approach their desire to have a church in the village and not outside of it. In both cases considerable financial resources were needed, which few communities probably commanded. In both cases there were also high "political costs," because the patrons always fought vigorously against the advance of communal rights and likewise against the separation of filial churches from the mother parish, since that always entailed a financial loss for the old patrons. The argument that a more tightly knit network of parish churches also improved pastoral care seems to have carried little weight with the established church.

It is important not to create the impression that the right of electing pastors was fairly widespread in any larger region of southern Germany. Communal patronage and nomination rights were and remained the exception. For Vorarlberg, where more precise figures are available, historians were able to calculate that, with the addition of the patronages acquired by communities in the sixteenth and seventeenth centuries, only twenty percent of the communities controlled the right of presentation and nomination, and even then only for part of the time.[53]

From all this we can at least draw the important conclusion that the communities were well on their way to vigorously expanding their rights over the church, but that they were also far from having achieved that goal. Dietrich

Kurze, the leading authority of parish conditions in the Middle Ages, formulated in this context a general verdict that is suited to corroborate the concept of the communal reformation:

> It is true that all these manifestations breathe the same spirit of communal self-government, that this spirit was strongest where these rights appeared together, and that in precisely those places the pressure for election of the pastor was most powerful.[54]

What is more, it is tempting to speculate—a speculation I shall hint at but not pursue further at this point—whether there is a causal connection between the observation that central Switzerland, on the one hand, had the highest concentration of communal patronages, and, on the other, took relatively little interest in Zwingli's reformation.

Finally, if we end by taking a look at the election of pastors in the cities, we see that barely one hundred cities had been able to push through that right by the eve of the reformation.[55] This seems like a small number, considering that there were about 3,000 cities in the empire around 1500. Of course, in the cities we must take into consideration the countless foundations of guilds, brotherhoods, patricians, and merchant families, which greatly improved pastoral care in the sense of a localization of the church. We may support this with an important pronouncement by Dietrich Kurze, who drew from his studies the following conclusion: the "congruences show that the basic lines of the history of the election of pastors in city and countryside were substantially the same."[56] And in the view of Karl Siegfried Bader, these basic lines of development led into the reformation:

> With typical variations among the different confessions, the reformation merely acknowledged as a fundamental legal form what had long since sprouted forth on the tree of the church from the constitution and popular piety of the late Middle Ages, for the most part as a wild growth.[57]

A comparative survey of Western Europe shows that the intermediate and highest stages of communal control over the church were reached neither in France nor in England. Only the institution of the church warden, the lowest form of communal participation in religious life, underwent a comparable development in the rest of western Europe.

All of these observations about German rural parish life help to bring into sharp focus the role of communities in Germany, particularly in southern Germany. For, according to the most recent studies—still limited to Spain although presumably of broader validity—a significant characteristic of the Roman church in the late Middle Ages and early modern period was the fact that the faithful strove for a localization of the numinous, which found expression in the many chapels that stood as religious centers outside the parish churches and monasteries. In any case, there were more than 900 chapels for the approximately 500 villages and cities examined in Castille.[58] Of course, this is only one particularly significant aspect of a broader phenomenon: within the Catholic church, the faithful, in addition to making use of universal rites and practices (the Mass, the profession of faith), were pressing for a localization of the sacred.[59]

COMMUNITY AND THE OUTSIDE WORLD:
COMMUNITY AND LORDSHIP

It goes without saying that the community was not an isolated political entity. Its mere existence, and its tendency to expand, had an impact on the principalities, counties, bishoprics, monasteries, and city-states of which it was a part. The new organizational forms in economic life, society, and law invariably led to tensions, disagreements, and even outright clashes with the feudal authorities. In the long run these conflicts could be muted or resolved if it proved possible to assimilate the political aspirations of rural and urban society into the territorial state in an institutional way.

Communities and authorities had a characteristically tense relationship, and it is understandable why that should have been so. The community, with its horizontal structures and equality among all its members, competed with lordship, which in the late Middle Ages manifested itself primarily as feudal lordship and thus as a vertical structure. The city-states north of the Alps also followed very much these medieval traditions in the way they administered their territory. This explains why, on the one hand, the community was never entirely without threat to its existence, and, on the other, it did not seem wise to dissolve the community once it had constituted itself. Some striking events in Switzerland can serve to illustrate this. In 1477, younger people, primarily from Inner Switzerland, had decided on a military expedition to Geneva against the will of their authorities, for the purpose of collecting by force the contributions from the Burgundian wars that Geneva still had not paid.[60] As "foolish people" (*torechte Leute*), as they called themselves with a touch of irony, they marched out in warlike formation, nearly 1,800 strong, under a banner depicting clubs and a boar, which earned the entire expedition the name "the foolish life" or "boar-banner expedition." The expedition had a harmless outcome. It did not lead to a military confrontation, but it deeply disturbed the authorities of the Swiss confederate cantons. The response came in the form of the Compact of Stans in 1481. With this pact the confederate cantons assured themselves of mutual aid in case of "willful violence" and prohibited henceforth "all dangerous assemblies, gatherings, or petitions," if they took place "without the consent and permission" of the authorities. But apparently it proved very difficult to enforce these regulations in the peasant cantons of Inner Switzerland. In any case, at the meeting of the confederate members in 1489, Schwyz moved that the article "in the agreement of Stans to the effect that the communities shall not assemble" be abolished, for it was quite an urgent necessity "that all these communities gather," especially since "hitherto the confederacy had not fared badly with this practice."[61]

A fundamental conflict manifests itself here: to what extent were the communities, all of which, after all, had authorities above them, entitled to make decisions independently? Or to put it differently and more basically: in political decisions of a general nature, did priority in the final analysis lie with the jurisdiction of the community or with that of the authorities?

Among the more striking phenomena of the late Middle Ages is the resistance of the lower orders, the peasants and the burghers. Marc Bloch has acknowledged the importance of this situation by likening the peasant revolts in the old feudal system to the workers' strikes in industrial society.[62] This blanket statement, which is undoubtedly illuminating for Europe as a whole, requires more detailed discussion in the case of the empire.[63] Four aspects deserve to be singled out from the perspective of the community. First, a chronological sequence is apparent. For example, no peasant revolt occurred prior to the formation of peasant communes. Second, we notice a geographic concordance. Of the documented cases of revolt and unrest—approximately sixty—only one did not occur in the south of the old empire, and about fifty are located within the zone of the communal reformation. Third, it is not difficult to show a rising curve of unrest. While at the end of the fifteenth century there was one revolt within the space of one generation (twenty-five years), between 1500 and 1525 the number rose to eighteen. Fourth, it is quite apparent that in the late medieval empire we are by no means dealing primarily with separate acts of peasant and burgher resistance, even though these also did exist. On the contrary, the common picture is one of a combined uprising of city and countryside, in Europe as well as in the empire. The English Peasants' War of 1381 and Kett's Rebellion of 1450 owe their character not least to the participation of the cities, as was also the case in the Appenzell war of the early fifteenth century, the Salzburg revolt of 1462, or the Poor Conrad uprising in Württemberg in 1514.

These observations reveal that there was a geographic, chronological, and factual overlap of community and resistance. Resistance was, in a sense, the continuation of the commune's emancipation by other means. In 1401, the four communities in the region of Appenzell united with the city of St. Gall to form an alliance. The upshot of this was that the aristocratic castles in the Rhine valley were destroyed, attacks were carried out into the Tyrol and the Allgäu, and finally the League on the Lake (*Bund ob dem See*) was established as a sister foundation to the Swiss Confederacy. In 1462 the rural (peasant) district and hamlets in the archbishopric of Salzburg united against the archbishop and achieved in this way at least a temporary incorporation into the political estates of Salzburg. In 1469, all the villages of the monastery of Ochsenhausen joined together to push through their interests, an act that eventually led to the military intervention of the Swabian League in 1502.

Such observations force us to accord the commune a very important place in the late Middle Ages. With the help of communal organization—and only in this way—did peasants and the burghers learn to say no, to protest, to question the demands of lordship and the claims of the authorities. The protest of the faithful against the church in Rome was rehearsed in the protest of the subjects against their lords.

Ever since the more recent ethnological scholarship has described the village as a "community of necessity and terror,"[64] a portrayal the intellectuals have enthusiastically adopted, any attempt to assign positive values to the community is likely to be dismissed and tossed aside as one more obsolete scholarly idea. The usefulness and utility, if not to say the aesthetic, of a positive model of the community must be substantiated and justified more vigorously than might have been the case some time ago. Of course, it would be a fundamental misunderstanding to assume that the community portrayed in the preceding pages was without internal tensions. But it is surely a fundamental misunderstanding to take the negative picture of the community which has been elaborated on a narrow empirical basis for the more recent history of Württemberg and apply it to the situation in the late Middle Ages. Most recently—evidence for the short life span of scholarly fashions—it has become fashionable again to regard "the village" with a good deal of nostalgia. What can we say for the late Middle Ages?[65]

Of course, the community, like every human social group, had its share of tensions, rivalries, and conflicts. But for the late Middle Ages, we must strongly emphasize the fact that the solidarity-producing effects of the community were far greater than the divisive effects of divergent social groups. As far as we know, the only pre-reformation source in which peasants described their troubles and problems is the already mentioned grievance list from Kempten with its 335 individual complaints. In it there is not the least hint which would lead us to suspect that inner-village social tensions existed. In general it must be remembered that it would have gone beyond the mental world of late medieval people to undermine a communal decision with independent actions. In the seventeenth and eighteenth centuries, on the other hand, it is quite possible that subgroups formed within the villages—associations of interest, as it were, in the form of "syndicates"—which pursued their goals through the court system all the way up to the highest imperial courts.[66] We know from the few better documented cases that the commune often had a hard time persuading its mayor or headman (Ammann) to join an alliance with neighboring communities. Conversely, there are instances in which the headman himself had to persuade and convince his community to make common cause with other communities.[67] In all cases, however, the communal decision was carried out, and whoever dared to oppose it was threatened with the communal "ban"—which meant the exclusion from the communal institutions of the commons, the bath-house, the well, and so on. If we recall that the Ammann was also the seigneurial representative in the village, the joint actions undertaken by the communities and their officers express the integrating power of the community. We can corroborate this with the observation that the various social groups in the village had an appropriate participation in the allocation of the village offices. In Swabian villages, for example, it was customary to fill the office of the Four in such a way that two men were selected from the peasantry and two from the small tenants (*Seldnerschaft*).[68] For the area of Austro-Bavarian law it can also be accepted as certain that officeholding and wealth did not overlap; rather, the officeholders mirror relatively faithfully the social structure of the village.[69] In the scholarly literature, only David Sabean has put forth the view that inner village social tensions predominated over the integrating powers of the community in the pre-reformation period,[70] although his empirical basis rests on two exceedingly thin and even controversial source passages.[71] Nothing today permits us to dispute and deny the community's integrating and solidarizing function. This is all the more understandable since the community provided the institutional framework in which individual, personal rights could flourish.[72] The community supplied also the institutional framework, with the requisite political counterweight to lordship, that allowed people to buy or wrest from the authorities the rights they had hitherto possessed.

As early as 1919, Konrad Beyerle pointed out in the Weimer National Assembly that there were "positive historical models for the modern basic rights," and together with his student Robert von Keller he looked for these rights in the medieval urban liberties (*Stadtfreiheiten*).[73] What he had in mind were in particular the "guarantees of liberty" that were part of the basic rights of the burgher and which could develop in the corporative-cooperative association of the city, as is expressed in the saying that "city air makes free."

Of course the slogan "city air makes free" merely reminds us of a development which began particularly early in the city and was quickly successful, but which undoubtedly also occurred in the countryside. The logical inversion of this dictum would have to read "country air makes unfree," and this would certainly be false. For we can show that in the late Middle Ages a process got under way, precisely in southern Germany, which eventually found its logical endpoint during the reformation period in the theologically based demand that serfdom be abolished. Rural society laid hold of personal freedom in piecemeal fashion, without fully attaining it. But at least it won—admittedly with repeated setbacks—remarkable advances, which make it possible to classify the differences to the urban situation as one of degree and not of kind. Apparently it was not the "city" which formed the precondition for personal freedom, but the "city-commune." It follows from this that wherever communities were highly developed—hence also in the countryside—there was the possibility of winning emancipation from older forms of unfreedom and serfdom.

In the chronicles of Switzerland, the separation of the county of Appenzell from the monastic seigneurial landlordship of St. Gall and its emergence as the eight members of the Swiss Confederacy reads as follows. Before the Appenzellers

> . . . had become a member of the confederacy, there was an abbot of St. Gall who thought that every time someone died in Appenzell he should

inherit his estate. It so happened that a poor man died, and the Appenzellers buried him in his best clothes. The abbot came and forced them to exhume the man and give him the good clothes.

"The abbot and the Appenzellers . . . quarreled" over the monastery's seigneurial claims to the estate of a bondsman.[74] According to the interpretation of the chronicler, the events in Appenzell at the beginning of the fifteenth century represented a "war of liberation." Despite the necessary corrections to such a monocausal explanation, it is true that ideas of liberty did indeed play a large role in giving the resistance movement of the Appenzellers direction and a goal. For the starting point of the peasant demands was freedom of movement, which the lord could deny by invoking the seigneurial rights over bondsmen. The Appenzellers justified their demand for freedom of movement by arguing that they were free to move into the town of St. Gall. That was certainly correct, since St. Gall had originally belonged to the monastic territory. But in the meantime it had become an imperial city, and from this the Appenzellers deduced, first, freedom to move into all imperial cities, and then general freedom of movement, an undoubtedly forced peasant logic.

In 1415 the abbey of St. Gall entered into an alliance (*Burg- und Landrecht*) with four members of the confederacy, but found it difficult, surprisingly enough, to obtain the necessary consent of its peasants. Eventually the monastery bought their consent by conceding that

> henceforth and for all eternity [we] shall be entirely quit of *gwandfall* [right to claim the best piece of clothing upon a bondsman's death] and of rights of inheritance or bequest, as we and our monastery have had toward the above-mentioned tenants of the abbey.[75]

Henceforth the monastery would content itself with the best animal in the stable [heriot], from which it followed that "each and every one of the above-mentioned tenants of the abbey, man or woman, may arrange, give, and bequeath his immovable and movable goods . . . in any way he desires and to whomever he wishes."[76] One of the central legal implications of unfreedom and serfdom, the inability to own property, was here removed. The peasant could now pass on the fruits of his labor. Within the context of the events of 1489 in the territory of St. Gall—which have come to be known as the *Rorschacher Klosterbruch* (the wrecking of the monastery of Rorschach)—military actions against the monastery were demanded with the argument that this was the only way "to remain free tenants of the abbey" and "shake off all burdens." The idea of freedom was linked, finally, with the dream of a republican state: "We don't want to hear of the Confederacy, bailiffs, or lords; we want to be lords and liberate ourselves."[77] The peasants strove not for affiliation with the confederacy adjoining St. Gall, which would have been the obvious thing to do, but for freedom, understood as political autonomy.

The three examples from the territory of the imperial abbey of St. Gall are merely meant to document a trend, and the passages themselves must be seen within their respective, more complex contexts. Broadly speaking, this trend was oriented toward freedom or, formulated more carefully, toward the dismantling of serfdom. To this we must add the important fact that the movement was not set in motion by growing pressure on the part of the lordship; instead, it was the monastic tenants who step by step curtailed the monastery's seigneurial rights over people. Is it permissible to generalize this observation?

Medieval unfreedom was defined by the fact that the lord had a claim—although limited by ethically binding norms—to the labor of his serfs and the fruits of their labor. The lord's right of inheritance in case of death and the serf's labor dues were derived from this claim of lordship. In order to secure this claim, there had to be some guarantee that the peasant would not alienate his person from the lord; the prohibitions against free movement and against contracting marriages outside one's own group of serfs are explained by this legal title. When the lords in the late Middle Ages laid claim to a tenant as serf, they had precisely this right of lordship in mind.

As the lords abandoned the direct cultivation of their lands, the need for labor declined, and the problem of labor dues became a relatively marginal one, since the lords no longer had the same direct need for labor. Henceforth the conflicts revolved around the freedom of movement and the right of inheritance. The peasants ignored the prohibition against freedom of movement on a massive scale, as is corroborated already by the fact that the urban population grew considerably over the long run despite devastating plague epidemics. This rise in population could not have been based on the natural population growth of city dwellers themselves. It was a necessary, if reluctantly undertaken adjustment to actual conditions when the prohibition against freedom of movement was lifted by the lords—in 1451–1459 in St. Gall, in 1502 in Ochsenhausen, and in 1514 in the duchy of Württemberg.[78] In 1298 the subjects of the monastery of Ottobeuren procured from King Albrecht a mandate which prohibited the abbot from seizing the "inheritance" of his bondsmen, limiting his rights instead to the *heriot*. The same was achieved by the peasants of the Black Forest abbey of St. Blasien step by step between 1370 and 1455, by the rebellious subjects of the monastery of Steingaden in 1423, and by the peasants of the imperial monastery of Ochsenhausen in 1502.[79] These examples show that the lords' claims to rights of inheritance were increasingly difficult to enforce.

This development was also mirrored in the language. The peasants no longer wished to be called "bondsmen" or "serfs," but instead "free tenants of the abbey" or "free subjects" (*Herrschaftsleute*), whereby the accent was naturally on the adjective "free."

No feudal right of lordship that was handed down from the Middle Ages was attacked by society more vigorously than that of serfdom. There were good and understandable reasons why that should have been so. When people themselves organized and took responsibility for their work, it was difficult to understand why one should not pursue work wherever it promised the highest profit—in the city, for example. And the right of inheritance as claimed by the lords, their laying hands on what the peasant had worked for during his life, proved simply utterly incompatible with the new labor system. This explains the many complaints about the seizure of "inheritance," "a part," and "bequests." In all likelihood the prince-abbot of Kempten was enforcing a traditional right when he seized from his bondsmen the "half-share" in case of death. But the peasants were now contesting his rights as unjust. "The people are complaining," we read in the register of serfs (Leibeigenschaftsrodel) from Kempten,

> that when their fathers died, my Gracious Lord has always taken the half-share of the possessions and whatever else there was, and when the mother died after that, he once again divided all with them and my Lord always took half of the possessions.[80]

Among the most remarkable developments in late medieval agrarian history is surely the fact that the peasants' right of inheritance increasingly gained ground. Assuming the necessary qualifications, it is possible today to make the general statement that we can observe "for the fifteenth century . . . a clear shift from the temporary lease [Zeitleihe] to the heritable lease [Erbleihe]."[81] The peasant's demand to be able to bequeath the fruits of his labor to his children or closest relatives was not limited to movable goods but included also immovable property that was usually subject to the landlord's rights and titles.

This process of a fundamental improvement in peasant living conditions is utterly unthinkable without the existence of the community, even though there were arrangements involving individuals. Wherever we can substantiate in greater detail the transformation process from a lease limited to a certain number of years or to a lifetime to a right of inheritance, we are dealing with events in which the communities were involved in some way or another. Sometimes they used the provincial diets as a forum for pushing through such interests, as in the Tyrol; sometimes all the communities under a given lordship petitioned the authorities and, if necessary, underscored the seriousness of their concerns with the threat of resistance and military force, as happened in southern Germany.[82]

To this day it is difficult to gauge what kind of mental transformation was actually connected to the changes we have described, and which had their agitational and organizational focus in the community. Undoubtedly the once coherent order of the High Middle Ages had not yet been replaced by a new, universally accepted world order and world view. The fundamental change that occurred with the transformation from the manorial system to the village and the city, from the unfree to the peasant and burgher, from dependent compulsory labor to the independent work of the peasant and artisan, required a fundamentally new order of things. The critical concept whose definition and meaning were at stake was, it would seem, that of Eigentum (private property).

Even though the word has a high medieval precursor in the form of Eigenschaft, Eigentum surely meant something completely different. Eigenschaft described a form of life in which the peasant and the lord had equal rights—to the goods, the forest, the water, but also in shaping the nature of seigneurial lordship and the legal order. The estate records of the Middle Ages express this clearly by recording what sort of dues and rights the peasants "issued" (*gewiesen*) or "granted" (*geöffnet*) to the lord. Thomas Aquinas reflected this situation on a theoretical level when he discussed the question of private property.[83] There was such a thing as private property, but only in trusteeship, not for personal use; the *potestas procurandi* came with the proviso to treat *res ut communes*.

Eigentum is the opposite of *Eigenschaft*. *Eigenschaft* meant common use and common ownership; *Eigentum* meant private use and private ownership. In the reformation period, Thomas Müntzer and Thomas More sharply denounced the beginnings of this development. "The dregs of usury, thievery, and robbery," says Müntzer, "are our lords and princes, they take all creatures as their personal property. The fish in the water, the birds in the air, the plants in the earth, all must be their own."[84] Thomas More developed his social model in Utopia out of a biting critique of private property. For what More attacked was property stripped of its social bonds and obligations, and the appropriation of the soil in the form of enclosures for the purpose of a capitalistically organized agriculture, which drove the people from the land or at least deprived them of their existing rights of usufruct. An agricultural economy run under the category of *Eigenschaft* in principle made it impermissible to drive a peasant from his homestead; at the most he could be moved to a different homestead on the same lands. Had More been writing in German, he would have demanded that society return to *Eigenschaft*.[85]

The act of appropriation in the sense of privatization was therefore noted by late medieval people with great sensitivity and criticized with corresponding vehemence. When the *Reformatio Sigismundi* accused the lords of placing woods and waters under their jurisdiction without justification for doing so, it was saying that the lords were arrogating forests and rivers as their private property. And the same thing was done to people: "It is an incredible outrage that there should be in Christendom today a state of affairs which allows one man to say to another, before God, 'You are my property!'"[86] Erasmus of Rotterdam eventually supplied this critique with a justification based on natural law: "since nature gives birth to all men in a state of freedom," serfdom was contrary to nature.[87]

Behind the discussion over property in the late Middle Ages stands the fact that work and lordship were no longer mutually dependent. Rather, work and lordship had become "two property-creating principles."[88] As soon as work could organize itself under the protection of town and village and was uninfluenced by orders from lordship above, it was no longer bound to lordship. Peasants and burghers gave increasing validity to the notion that work created personal property. Where a farm had been *de jure* or *de facto* passed on from father to son for generations, such a notion could and invariably did consolidate itself. It was part of the logic of this development that the lords, too, erected everywhere signs reading "Private—Keep Out", in the forests and commons, on the waterways, and finally also with human beings.

No one would want to doubt that the legal order depends to a large degree on the organization of property; modern political systems are sufficient evidence for this. The early sixteenth century had outgrown the security of the high medieval model of *Eigenschaft*, but it had not yet acquired the security of modern property relations. The result was a high level of legal instability. Fairness, custom, good law, old law, all were put to the test of fundamental changes in all conditions of life, and eventually they proved incapable of coping with them. This explains the call for a new law marked by dignity and authority. That law was godly law.

COMMUNAL REPRESENTATION

The late medieval discourse about basic questions of the human condition and the social order presupposed the existence of the commune. The innovations that could come from the community eventually exerted a considerable influence on late medieval culture. For obvious reasons the community could not be content to order its internal affairs; it also had to make sure that the principles of its existence and its interests would be respected within the larger political-governmental structures. As a result, the communities penetrated into one of the most important political corporations of the late medieval and early modern state—into the imperial and regional diets of Germany, the *états generaux* and the *états provinciaux* of France, and the Parliament of England. All these institutions had originally been assemblies of the prince with his magnates. In the late Middle Ages town representatives sat in all of them.

One could follow the widespread lead of scholarship and explain this development with the crude fact that monarchs and princes had rising financial needs. In principle taxes had to be authorized, and the cities were financially the strongest corporations. It is probably more correct to accord the right of approving taxes secondary importance behind the European legal principle "quod omnes tangit ab omnibus approbari debeat" ("what concerns all must be approved by all"). That all had to approve what concerned everyone had far-reaching implications. It was not only the financial operations of the princes that had to be "approved" but also their legal measures; it was not only the nobility, the prelates, and the burghers who were "concerned" but also the peasants.

I shall briefly highlight these two aspects—the actual extent of peasant representation in parliamentary and other assemblies of estates.[89] Among the conspicuous facts about parliamentary assemblies in the empire is that in southern Germany the peasants sent representatives to the regional diets or to specially constituted assemblies (*Landschaften*). Although there are similar phenomena along the North Sea coast, in central and northern Germany we do not find anything comparable to the imposing territorial representation that developed under the archdukes of Austria, the dukes of Württemberg, the archbishop of Salzburg, or the bishops of Basel. The answer as to why that was the case is to be found in the powers and instructions given to the peasant representatives to the regional diets. For what we are dealing with was not, to be more precise, a representation of the peasants, but a representation of the communities. And these communities had to exercise functions that were closely related to those exercised by the nobility and the church, which implies that they had reached a high degree of political autonomy. This explains why in the city it was frequently the mayor, the council, and the community, or in the village the headman (*Ammann*) and the community who put their seal to the powers of the delegates. Where no parliamentary representation existed for the rural communities, they were deprived of their political rights already in the late Middle Ages, as in Brandenburg, or they attained a level of autonomy that barely went beyond trivial matters, as in Hesse.

It is obvious that peasant representation overlaps with a zone of highly developed communes. The communal reformation occurred precisely in the area where we can speak of a political representation of the communities: between Alsace and Salzburg, between Franconia and Inner Switzerland. A further conspicuous fact is that peasant representation on a regional level developed essentially during the three generations preceding the reformation, the representation of urban communities only shortly before that. This meant, first of all, a hitherto unknown expansion of the horizon of political experience for the peasants and of course for the burghers. The issues discussed at the regional diets had to be deliberated on in the town and the village. No deputy to the regional diet from the towns or the villages had a free mandate. The decisions made at a regional diet in a territory that had peasant and burgher representation took effect only when they had been ratified by the communities. Politics in a territory thus became dependent on a "public." This public then vigorously exerted its own ideas. We can substantiate this by looking at the territorial constitutions and administrative ordinances (*Polizeiordnungen*), which were far from being expressions of the princes' political ambitions, at least in the south of the empire. What the territorial constitutions and early administrative ordinances laid down as positive law were the grievances that urban and rural communes presented to the regional diets. This can be corroborated wherever the existing sources allow us to reconstruct the drafting process. Several examples can be found in the county of Tyrol. Here we can observe this process at work in the passing of decrees and mandates dealing with taxation and the administration of justice in the archbishopric of Salzburg in 1462; of decrees dealing with territorial defense and the system of dues and inheritance laws in the prince-abbey of Berchtesgaden in 1506; of decrees dealing with the constitution of the courts in the bishop of Augsburg's ward (*Pflege*) of Rettenberg in 1518; and finally, of decrees dealing with the management of estates, questions of serfdom, the legal stages of appeal, the maintenance of peace, and obligatory military service in the lordship of Rötteln-Sausenberg in Baden in 1517. These are a sample and do not sufficiently express the fact that, for example, a series of Tyrolean territorial constitutions after the early fifteenth century were little more than the Innsbruck government's editorial adaptation of the grievances of the "third estate."

The constitution of Rötteln-Sausenberg was drawn up "in the presence and with the advice of the committee of our landgraviate of Sausenberg and our lordship [Rötteln], specially summoned and assembled for this purpose." The court constitution of Rettenberg was drawn up "upon hearing and diligently heeding your [the subjects'] submitted complaints and advice." In the prince-bishopric of Sitten in the Valais, changes to the territorial law "shall be passed by those who are appointed councilors at that time by the common man."[90]

The important role that burghers and peasants played in the drafting of territorial constitutions, decrees, and mandates has so far been attested only for territories which had a parliamentary constitution. But the same can be shown also for other lordships. For example, the subjects of the monastery of St. Gall complained that "it used to be custom that when a lord of St. Gall wanted to do something with regard to his common tenants [gmeiner gotshuslüten], he would call them together on it,"[91] referring thus to the fact that measures affecting the entire domain required the consent of all. In some of the smaller monastic lordships of Swabia, as well, we can attest to the participation of the subjects in the drawing up of comprehensive regulations about inheritance law, serfdom, and property law, which were valid throughout the domain. In 1456, the "subjects and common people as a whole and individually" were party to an agreement with the abbess of Rot an der Rot,[92] while "the subjects, dependents, and Gerichtslütte [subjects of the court jurisdiction]" were party to an agreement with the abbot of Ochsenhausen in 1502.[93] Twelve other, similar cases, which have so far been corroborated, confirm the breadth of peasant participation in the redaction of larger codifications.

The participation of the common people in the drafting of territorial laws, territorial constitutions, and administrative ordinances, and in the making of individual regulations on questions of inheritance law, property law, serfdom, or the administration of civil and criminal law, clearly documents the will of the social groups to push through their own interests beyond the sphere of town and village. It was not the authorities who presented their ideas for deliberation. Rather, for the most it was the subjects who were insistent that their ideas should become positive law within the territory. Of course that could be achieved only partially and by lowering their sights on certain demands. But was it not a small step from here to demand for oneself the supervisory function, which traditionally had belonged to the lords? Would it not be possible to turn the traditional order upside down and thus put it into its proper alignment?

COMMUNAL VALUES AND THE ADOPTION OF REFORMATION IDEAS

Norms and values have distinct social origins. Assuming that communalism as a way of life existed—which I think has been sufficiently proved—it must have also developed norms and values that set it apart and distinguished it from feudalism, from the aristocratic world with its norms and values. To elaborate on these norms and values is difficult for a variety of reasons. One difficulty is the historiographical situation, another concerns methodological problems. Whereas it is relatively easy to talk about the norms and values of the nobility, given a long and rich tradition of scholarly work in this area, the situation is quite different in regard to the value system of the burghers, not to mention that of the peasants.[94] Both because the concept of communalism is a new one, and because it has only recently been noticed that burghers and peasants formed a single group, the necessary preparatory work has simply not been done.[95] In terms of method we face the well-known problem that the common people did not give explicit expression to their values and norms, least of all in the pre-reformation period. For example, before 1525 it was almost never stated that personal freedom was among peasants a norm relevant for concrete action, but we can infer as much from the actions undertaken against serfdom. The entire structure of norms and values of the common people can be methodologically accessed more readily by decoding actions than by referring directly to articulated norms and values. Under these conditions the best we can produce at this time is a first sketch, which is furthermore guided by the question of how we can explain in the final analysis the process by which reformation ideas were adopted within society. We shall start from the heuristic assumption that values and norms develop both within a system (here communalism) as well as through a confrontation of the system with the outside world.

As a "self-contained system" communalism is characterized by the fact that independent labor gives rise to an autonomous organizing of the people's life and livelihood (see Fig. 3). The organization of day-to-day life, the economic, social, and legal problems of the small community that is a village or town, are expressed in communal administration, communal statutory sovereignty, and communal jurisdiction. This has already been discussed at length; all that remains to be answered is the question of what the consequences were for the value conceptions. It should be apparent that village and town could function only with the existence of a developed neighborliness, in the positive sense of an obligation of mutual aid in cases of recognized individual need. Let me briefly illustrate this once more with two examples. The system of defense in the town and the common pasture in the village commons lived from a functioning neighborliness, and the same is true for all its institutional derivatives: administration, legislation, and administration of justice. What we still need to address is the hitherto undiscussed securing of the people's livelihood.

We must bear in mind the well-known fact that resources were limited in preindustrial society, and thus naturally also in late medieval society. As Peter Laslett has said,

> . . . this society knows the firm rule that a new household may be established only when an existing household has been dissolved or when additional resources have been created, which allow the entire society to expand by adding a new household, in other words a new basic social unit. Such a rule of household establishment is a principle of family structure, and it also acts to regulate the age and conditions of marriage for both sexes.[96]

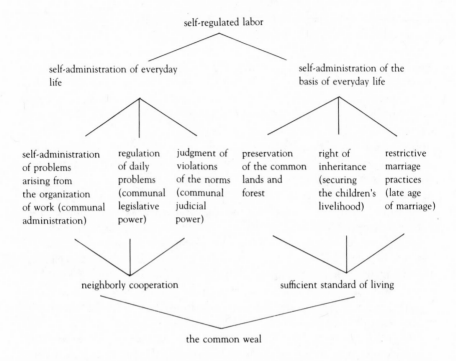

FIGURE 3   INTERNAL ORGANIZATION AND VALUES OF COMMUNALISM

The "household establishment rule" had the effect that the families were kept relatively small at an average size of five persons. We can ignore the differences between town and village here because they are negligible compared to the size of noble families. It also meant that the age of marriage was high. One could hold "primarily economic needs"[97] responsible for this kind of behavior, but from a different perspective we might also speak of a responsible management of the livelihood of future generations. We find this reflected above all in the efforts to secure the right of inheritance. This right would benefit only the following generation and not the living generation, which not infrequently made considerable sacrifices in order to push through these improvements against the opposition of their lords. To give two examples: the tenants of the monastery of Weissenau paid 1,550 fl. in the mid-fifteenth century to improve their inheritance right, while the tenants of the monastery of Schussenried paid a cash sum equivalent to 50 percent of the yearly dues for the same purpose.[98] Further evidence for this generation-spanning concern for the livelihood is furnished by the usually careful way in which the communities managed the forests and commons. The fact that a proper village normally had a forest warden (*Holzwart*) shows that no one could simply help himself to lumber, firewood, or fencewood from the communal forest; rather, out of a concern for securing this important raw material also for one's children and grandchildren, wood was allotted to everyone as sparingly as possible. The guiding concern in securing the conditions of life was to provide an adequate livelihood for present and future generations.

Neighborliness and adequate livelihood gave rise—inevitably, we might say—to the notion of the common weal, the principle which allowed people in city and village to live together productively in the first place. The solid anchoring of this value in peasant and burgher society found expression during the reformation period in the fact that it was now turned outward, as it were, and applied as a measuring rod to the great lords. The common man demanded that they, too, should submit to the common weal.

Every historian who has any familiarity with early sixteenth century sources will confirm that the common weal held an extremely important place in the letters, gravamina, and demands of the common people; already the mere fact that it appears so often indicates its importance. It may be objected that we are dealing with a vague and imprecise phrase, one that was invoked at all times to legitimize political structures. We can respond by pointing out that aristocratic society of the Middle Ages did not explicitly know the common weal as a recognized social value or norm of political action. No exercise of authority, no matter what kind, justified itself by arguing that it promoted the common weal;[99] rather, lordship gained its legitimacy exclusively from its protective function, concretely from safeguarding the law and maintaining the peace at home and abroad. Although the Middle Ages may have understood the common weal as the natural by-product of peace and law, the only thing we can state with certainty is that the political language hardly knew the common weal or related formulations, apart from the vague, and in our context not very helpful, title of the emperor as the "Augmenter of the Empire" (*Mehrer des Reiches*). Although the *bonum commune* did have a place in the theological discussions and theories about the state from Thomas Aquinas on, it was absent from practical politics as a normative category. Until it can be proved otherwise, we may argue that the common weal was a category developed within the peasantry and burgher class. It was picked up by the German princes only in the course of the sixteenth century; in the form of welfare, later of happiness,[100] it was presented as the chief function of the state, which rulers sought to achieve through "good policy." Ironically, the early modern *raison d'état* of the common good provided the princes legitimating cover for their policies which eventually reduced the common man to the status of a subject. The common good derived its theoretical justification—and this, too, is ironic—from the reception of Aristotelian thought in Lutheran Protestantism, for which Melanchthon was responsible. The peasants and burghers, who elaborated the common weal as a value of the utmost dignity, found no existing, theoretical justification for this concept in the pre-reformation period.

The common weal harmonizes extremely well with the New Testament notion of love for one's fellow man. Peasants and burghers confirm this in their use of the succinct phrase about the "common good and Christian, brotherly love," which were to be put into practice now that the "pure gospel" had once again come to light. Brotherly love no longer manifested itself primarily toward the poor, as was the practice in the old church, but toward one's immediate neighbor.

If we return once more to the categories of neighborliness and adequate livelihood, which constituted the common weal, we can make a good case that they, too, shaped the adoption of reformation ideas. It was in keeping with the principle of neighborliness that the pastor should reside in the community and look after his pastoral duties conscientiously and in person. It was in keeping with the principle of adequate livelihood that he should draw a decent income from the generally financially solid benefices and should not have to secure his livelihood by charging surplice fees. The universal belief of peasants and burghers that the pastor should exemplify his calling in his own life and conduct and should be worthy of his task makes sense against the background of the binding norms of neighborliness and adequate livelihood.

The closed system of communalism was not an isolated system. It interacted with an outside world that was structured on fundamentally different terms, and which, in its concrete manifestation of the aristocratic world, also adhered to different norms and values. In the confrontation with the outside world the peasants and burghers developed additional values beyond those of neighborliness, adequate livelihood, and the common weal.

Nobility was defined by lordship. As a form of authority that was exercised by a single person, lordship clashed with the notion of neighborliness as I have described it. The community as an organizational form increasingly excluded aristocratic lordship on a local level from administration, lawgiving, and the administration of justice; in other words, it weakened it. Parallel to this development was the integration of the community into territorial representational bodies, as discussed earlier. Participation on the territorial level became the demand of peasants and burghers.[101] Lordship was no longer without competition.

Lordship also came into conflict with the notion of adequate livelihood. In its medieval form, lordship was comprehensive and all-powerful from the perspective of positive law, even if it was not so in an ethical sense. Adequate livelihood—certainly a variable quantity—was repeatedly threatened by lordship, for example, when lordship interfered in the forests and commons, when it exercised its seigneurial rights over people and deprived the peasant of his inheritance or prevented his freedom of movement. An adequate livelihood could be secured only by negating or at least restricting these rights and titles. Behind this stood the value of *freedom*, which could be realized through the reformation. The fact that personal freedom was justified with reference to Christ's redemptive death—a theologically questionable justification—merely underscores the important place freedom held in society's hierarchy of values. And we are talking not only of peasant society, since it certainly cannot be said that a state of general freedom prevailed in the cities, as any city law of a territorial city will show. Participation and freedom gave rise to the notion of political maturity. This idea of maturity is highly compatible with the reformation's theological concept of the priesthood of all believers, or, in negative terms, with the rejection of the established church's claim that it alone could mediate salvation and interpret the Scriptures.

My attempt to relate the norms and values of the common people to central theological categories of reformation thought undoubtedly requires a broader empirical underpinning. But it suffices to show that this is the ideal path to understanding the history of how the reformation was received within society. We can support this contention further by looking at the issue from an entirely different perspective.

Keith Thomas has said that the peasant did not employ any magical practices when reaping grain or milking cows, but he did do so when the health of his animals was at stake. Thomas argues that magic became superfluous with a growing understanding of the interconnections and mechanisms of common, daily occurrences.[102] Such understanding was naturally extended even further where burghers and peasants gained an insight into the political machinery as a whole. At the territorial diet one could hear that the local wine could no longer be sold because it had such dubious additives that it killed off those who drank it; this information might have helped to explain an earlier, mysterious death in one's own family. A famine turned out to be entirely homegrown when the burgher from Hall discovered in the Innsbruck council of Maximilian that the last, good harvest had been sold to Venetian buyers, down to the last bushel. Under such circumstances it is understandable that scholars have observed that in the fifteenth century the laity no longer believed in legends the way it had in earlier times[103] or that miracles came under pressure to prove their effectiveness and needed notarization in order to be accepted.[104] None of this is intended to cast doubt on the strongly developed popular piety of the pre-reformation period, although at the same time the role of the magical in dealing with daily life must not be overestimated. Analyses of pre-reformation visitation records have shown that religiosity does seem for the most part to have moved within the framework of the church and that it drifted into theologically and ecclesiastically unclear territory only in certain specific areas, as for example in the worship of weather saints.[105] The growing cross and Christ worship in Germany, as in Europe in general,[106] indicates that the common people were drawing closer to the core of Christianity. If the frequently quoted description of the religious situation in the imperial city of Biberach on the eve of the reformation[107] is in fact representative of southern Germany, which the scholarly literature apparently assumes is the case,[108] then Catholic piety, at least in the pre-reformation era, was not substantially different from that in the pre-conciliar period of Vatican II.[109] This should caution us against overemphasizing theologically dubious, magical, and pagan practices prior to the reformation. Had such practices been indispensable for coping with life, the reception process of the reformation would defy any sensible explanation. The attempt to argue that anxiety and fear drove people to the reformation fails because of a lack of empirical evidence and because the existing interpretative models are not very plausible.[110] In contrast, the observation that the laity exerted an increasing influence on late medieval religion as a whole has explanatory value.[111] What we are dealing with, to use the words of W. A. Christian, is "the paganization of Christianity," in the sense of a Christianization of the countryside through the endowing of chapels, pilgrimages, and miracle worship.[112] In southern Germany this found expression and amplification in the efforts on the part of the communities to acquire the right of electing their pastors. Natalie Z. Davis may have had these and similar phenomena in mind when she said of the common people that they "were innovative in dealing with the holy."[113]

The religious life of the common people in Central Europe took place within the church and at the periphery of the church, but hardly outside of the church. This is *one* precondition for the fact that the reformers were able from the start to have any resonance with the people. The *other*, more important precondition, and at the same time the innovative accomplishment of the common people in the early sixteenth century, is that they "introduced" the reformation by digesting the theological appeal of the reformers through the burgher-peasant social organization of the community. Community means—to repeat it for the last time—that in principle every member of the community is responsible for the political order. This principle found expression in the institution of the communal assembly, which decided on such far-reaching issues as renewal of the town law or village by-laws, and assigned the communal offices by means of election. The communalization of the church, in its dual manifestation of far-reaching decisions about the profession of the faith and the election of the pastor by the communal assembly, brought this late medieval development to its logical completion (see Fig. 4).

The way in which the reformation message was absorbed and adapted presupposes that this appeal was highly congenial to communalism. This raises the question of whether reformation theology is even conceivable without the preceding communalism. Rhetorically phrased: Was there a compelling theological reason why the reformers chose to translate *ecclesia* not as "church" but as "community"? Was there a compelling theological reason why they denied the church's mediation of grace, and instead referred the independent and mature Christian directly to his merciful God?

Such questions nourish the suspicion that communalism was the vehicle which the progressive theologians of the sixteenth century used—unconsciously, of course—in order to gain a listening. What made the reformation so threatening was the fact that the theologians were playing dangerously with the social movement of communalism, and this compelled the princes to take a stand against the communal reformation.

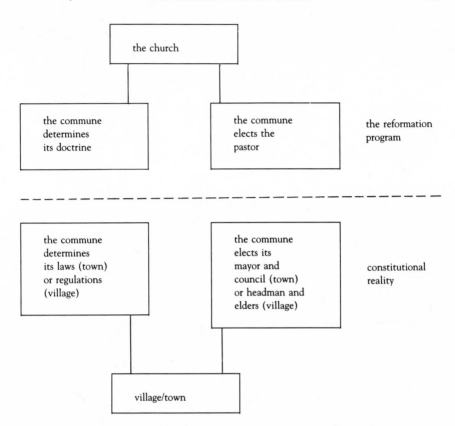

FIGURE 4 IDEOLOGY AND REALITY IN THE COMMUNAL REFORMATION

Notes

1. In earlier writings I have already discussed the following historical facts and the main lines of interpretation based on them. Here I shall limit myself to modifications dictated by the specific question we are examining. In the cursory remarks on the village I am following the main outlines of my essay, "Les communautés villageoises en Allemagne," *Flaran* 4 (1982): 130–142. For the urban area I draw on Peter Blickle and Renate Blickle, eds., *Schwaben von 1268 bis 1803*, Dokumente zur Geschichte von Staat und Gesellschaft in Bayern, part II, vol. 4 (Munich, 1979), 115–119.

2. The question about the origins of the village commune has led to sharp scholarly controversies in Germany. The emergence of the village commune from the manor has been advocated by Alphons Dopsch, *Herrschaft und Bauer in der deutschen Kaiserzeit* (Jena, 1939), esp. 107ff. Franz Steinbach, "Ursprung und Wesen der

Landgemeinde nach rheinischen Quellen," in Theodor Mayer, ed., *Die Anfänge der Landgemeinde und ihr Wesen*, Vorträge und Forschungen, vol. 7 (Constance, 1964), 245–288, esp. 205, sees the village commune as a subdivision of larger counties (*Gerichtsverbände*) of the early and High Middle Ages. Finally, the *Vogtei* (bailiwick) has been put forth as the starting point for the formation of the village commune by Karl Siegfried Bader, *Dorfgenossenschaft*, 2d ed. (Weimar, 1962), 88, 91, 101; complemented for the purposes of our discussion by his "Entstehung und Bedeutung der oberdeutschen Dorfgemeinde," *Zeitschrift für württembergische Landesgeschichte* 1 (1937). The most recent, much more far-reaching study for the Swiss region, which can probably claim wider applicability, is that of Rogier Sablonier, "Das Dorf im Übergang vom Hoch- zum Spätmittelalter. Untersuchungen zum Wandel ländlicher Gemeinschaftsformen im ostschweizerischen Raum," in Lutz Fenske, Werner Rösener, and Thomas Zotz, eds., *Institutionen, Kultur und Gesellschaft im Mittelalter. Festschrift für Josef Fleckenstein* (Sigmaringen, 1984), 727–745.

3. Worked out especially in the studies of Karl Bosl. A summary overview in Karl Bosl, "Staat, Gesellschaft, Wirtschaft im deutschen Mittelalter," in Bruno Gebhardt, ed., *Handbuch der deutschen Geschichte*, vol. 1, 9th ed. (Stuttgart, 1970), 807–814. Bosl has stressed the origins in the manorial system even more strongly in "Gesellschaftsprozeß und Gesellschaftssrukturen im Mittelalter," in Karl Bosl and Eberhard Weis, *Die Gesellschaft in Deutschland*, vol. 1: *Von der fränkischen Zeit bis 1848* (Munich, 1976), 79ff.

4. The last comprehensive account by Friedrich Lütge, *Geschichte der deutschen Agrarverfassung vom frühen Mittelalter bis zum 19. Jahrhundert*, Deutsche Agrargeschichte, vol. 3, 2d ed. (Stuttgart, 1967), esp. 50–56, 83–94. See now Ludolf Kuchenbuch, *Bäuerliche Gesellschaft und Klosterherrschaft im 9. Jahrhundert. Studien zur Sozialstruktur der Familia der Abtei Prüm*, Beihefte der Vierteljahrschrift für Sozial- und Wirtschaftsgeschichte, vol. 66 (Wiesbaden, 1978).

5. Reinhard Wenskus, Herbert Jankuhn, and Klaus Grinda, eds., *Wort und Begriff "Bauer,"* Abhandlungen der Akademie der Wissenschaften in Göttingen., Phil.-hist. Klasse, 3d ser., vol. 89 (Göttingen, 1975); supplemented by Werner Conze, "Bauer, Bauernstand, Bauerntum," in Otto Brunner, Werner Conze, Reinhold Koselleck, eds., *Geschichtliche Grundbegriffe. Historisches Lexikon*, vol. 1 (Stuttgart, 1972), 408ff.

6. The recent debate has been critically reviewed (and given a different accent) by Otto Gerhard Oexle, "Die funktionale Dreiteilung der 'Gesellschaft' bei Adalbert von Laon," *Frühmittelalterliche Studien* 12 (1978): 1–54, esp. 50.

7. Handbook summary in Heinrich Mitteis and Heinz Lieberich, *Deutsche Rechtsgeschichte*, 16th ed. (Munich, 1981), 169.

8. From the perspective of constitutional law see Lütge, *Geschichte der deutschen Agrarverfassung*, 119–158; from the economic perspective see Wilhelm Abel, *Geschichte der deutschen Landwirtschaft vom frühen Mittelalter bis zum 19. Jahrhundert*, Deutsche Agrargeschichte, vol. 2, 2d ed. (Stuttgart, 1967), 165ff., 210ff.

9. For a larger overview see the old but still valuable work of Karl O. Müller, *Die oberschwäbischen Reichsstädte* (Stuttgart, 1912). For similarities with and differences to adjoining Switzerland, cf. Hans Conrad Peyer, "Schweizer Städte des Spätmittelalters im Vergleich mit den Städten der Nachbarländer," in Hans Conrad Peyer, *Könige, Stadt und Kapital. Aufsätze zur Wirtschafts- und Sozialgeschichte des Mittelalters* (Zurich, 1982), 262–270.

10. Ewald Liedl, *Gerichtsverfassung und Zivilprozeß in der Freien Reichstadt Augsburg*, Abhandlungen zur Geschichte der Stadt Augsburg, vol. 12 (Augsburg, 1958), with the quote at 20.

11. Johann Christian Lünig, *Das Teutsche Reichs-Archiv*, 24 volumes (Leipzig, 1710–1722), here vol. 13: 99f.

12. See the dates in *Historischer Atlas von Bayern*, Teil Schwaben, Heft 4: *Memmingen* (Munich, 1967), 49–54.

13. Bayerisches Hauptstaatsarchiv, Abteilung I, Reichsstadt Memmingen, Literalien 8, fol. 24.

14. A later real type of "Eigenverfassung," which was in the process of dissolution but can still be reconstructed, is described by Renate Blickle, "'Spenn und Irrung' im 'Eigen' Rottenbuch," in Peter Blickle, ed., *Aufruhr und Empörung? Studien zum bäuerlichen Widerstand im Alten Reich* (Munich, 1980), 69–145. With some methodological reservations see also the stimulating monograph by Hanna Rabe, *Das Problem Leibeigenschaft*, Beihefte der Vierteljahrschrift für Sozial- und Wirtschaftsgeschichte, vol. 64 (Wiesbaden, 1977).

15. Of fundamental importance is Bader, *Dorfgenossenschaft*, 292–319, 367ff. Indispensable for a regional differentiation is Theodor Mayer, ed., *Die Anfänge der Landgemeinde und ihr Wesen*, 2 vols., Vorträge und Forschungen, vols. 7–8 (Constance, 1964).

16. Gerhard Heitz and Günter Vogler, "Agrarfrage, bäuerlicher Klassenkampf und bürgerliche Revolution in der Übergangsphase vom Feudalismus zum Kapitalismus," *Zeitschrift für Geschichtswissenschaft* 28 (1980): 1060–1078. Hartmut Harnisch, "Landsgemeinde, feudalherrlicher bäuerlicher Klassenkampf und Agrarverfassung im Spätfeudalismus," *Zeitschrift für Geschichtswissenschaft* 26 (1978): 887–897.

17. Ignaz von Zingerle and Jospeh Egger, eds., *Die Tirolischen Weistümer. Part 4: Burggrafenamt und Etschland*, Österreichische Weistümer, vol. 5 (Vienna, 1888), 451. Additional, similar examples are scattered throughout this volume.

18. Paul Gehring, ed., *Nördliches Oberschwaben*, Württembergische Ländliche Rechtsquellen, vol. 3 (Stuttgart, 1941), 97–100.

19. Walter Müller, ed., *Die Rechtsquellen des Kantons St. Gallen*, part 1: *Die Rechtsquellen der Abtei St. Gallen*, 2d series, vol. 1: *Die allgemeinen Rechtsquellen der alten Landschaft*, Sammlung Schweizerischer Rechtsquellen, vol. 14 (Aarau, 1974), 271.

20. In contrast to the administrative organs of the village, the village court has been little studied. The *Weistümer* of the fourteenth through the sixteenth centuries contain relatively few provisions about court procedure. Only at the end of the sixteenth century with the increasing reception of Roman law were village court procedures also fixed more precisely; but inferences from this period back to the late Middle Ages are hardly permissible. Since the jurisdiction of the village court was often not defined, it is difficult to uncover the seigneurial and communal roots of the village court.

21. Zingerle and Egger, *Die Tirolischen Weistümer*, vol. 4: 163.

22. Andrea Schorta, ed., *Die Rechtsquellen des Kantons Graubünden*, part 1: *Der Gotteshausbund*, vol. 2: *Unterengadin*, Sammlung Schweizerischer Rechtsquellen, vol. 15 (Aarau, 1981), 600–618, with the quote at 618.

23. Nikolaus Grass and Karl Finsterwalder, eds., *Tirolische Weistümer*, vol. 5, part 1 (Innsbruck, 1966), 339.

24. Robert Hoppeler, ed., *Die Rechtsquellen des Kantons Zürich*, part 1: *Öffnungen und Hofrechte*, 2 vols., Sammlung Schweizerischer Rechtsquellen, vol. 1 (Aarau, 1910–1915), vol. 1: 212.

25. Ibid., vol. 2: 50.

26. Ibid., vol. 1: 204.

27. Ibid., 359.

28. Gehring, *Nördliches Oberschwaben*, 78.

29. For this sketch I base myself on the preliminary studies by P. Blickle and R. Blickle, *Schwaben*, 122–127. A few statements and formulations, which would not gain in precision or clarity by being rewritten, have been taken over verbatim from that

work. For a comprehensive overview of the development in Germany as a whole see E. Maschke, "Deutsche Städte am Ausgang des Mittelalters," in Wilhelm Rausch, ed., *Die Stadt am Ausgang des Mittelalters*, Beiträge zur Geschichte der Städte Mitteleuropas, vol. 3 (Linz, 1974), 1–44.

30. A larger survey that is still useful is Peter Eitel, *Die oberschwäbischen Reichstädte im Zeitalter der Zunftherrschaft. Untersuchungen zu ihrer politischen und sozialen Struktur unter besonderer Berücksichtigung der Städte Lindau, Memmingen, Ravensburg und Überlingen*, vol. Schriften zur südwestdeutschen Landeskunde, vol. 8 (Stuttgart, 1970), esp. 18–37. For the European context see Antony Black, *Guilds and Civil Society in European Political Thought from the Twelfth Century to the Present* (London, 1984), esp. 66–75.

31. Eberhard Naujoks, "Obrigkeit und Zunftverfassung in den süddeutschen Reichsstädten," *Zeitschrift für württembergische Landesgeschichte* 33 (1974): 61ff.

32. Especially Bader, *Dorfgenossenschaft*.

33. Irmtraut Eder, *Die saarländischen Weistümer. Dokumente der Territorialpolitik*, Veröffentlichungen der Kommission für saarländische Landesgeschichte und Volksforschung, vol. 8 (Saarbrücken, 1978), with the quote at 125. See further, Rudolf Hinsberger, *Die Weistümer des Klosters St. Matthias/Trier. Studien zur Entwicklung des ländlichen Rechts im frühmodernen Territorialstaat* (Stuttgart and New York, 1989).

34. Herbert Reyer, *Die Dorfgemeinde im nördlichen Hessen. Untersuchungen zur hessischen Dorfverfassung im Spätmittelalter und in der frühen Neuzeit*, Schriften des Hessischen Landesamtes für geschichtliche Landeskunde, vol. 38 (Marburg, 1983).

35. See Karlheinz Blaschke, "Grundzüge und Probleme einer sächsichen Agrarverfassungsgeschichte," *Zeitschrift der Savigny-Stiftung für Rechtsgeschichte, germanistische Abteilung* 82 (1965): 223–287; Herbert Helbig, *Gesellschaft und Wirtschaft der Mark Brandenburg im Mittelalter*, Veröffentlichungen der Historischen Kommission zu Berlin, vol. 41 (Berlin and New York, 1973), 11ff., 41ff.

36. Roland Mousnier, *Les institutions de la France sous la monarchie absolute*, vol. 1 (Paris, 1974), 428.

37. C. S. L. Davies, "Die bäuerliche Gemeinde in England (1400–1800)," in Winfried Schulze, *Aufstände, Revolten, Prozesse. Beiträge zu bäuerlichen Widerstandsbewegungen im frühneuzeitlichen Europa*, Geschichte und Gesellschaft. Bochumer Historische Studien, vol. 27 (Stuttgart, 1983), 41–59, with the quote at 52.

38. See the basic conception of Black, *Guilds and Civil Society*.

39. In the assessment of Dietrich Kurze, *Pfarrerwahlen im Mittelalter. Ein Beitrag zur Geschichte der Gemeinde und des Niederkirchenwesens*, Forschungen zur kirchlichen Rechtsgeschichte, vol. 6 (Cologne and Graz, 1966), 308.

40. Bader, *Dorfgenossenschaft*, 198, 200.

41. Kurze, *Pfarrerwahlen*, 315. The observations apply to the late Middle Ages.

42. Emphasized in particular by Bader, *Dorfgenossenschaft*, 210.

43. Zingerle and Egger, *Die Tirolischen Weistümer*, vol. 4: 314.

44. Examples in Kurze, *Pfarrerwahlen*, 273, 302, and more, as well as in Bader, *Dorfgenossenschaft*, 207–211.

45. How complex the situation could be in specific cases, without going into great detail, is attested by the example of the community of Baltringen, which, as is generally known, attained some fame in the Peasants' War. See on this the divergent interpretations of Kurze, *Pfarrerwahlen*, 280, and Hermann Tüchle, "Kirchliche Verhältnisse im Laupheimer Raum," in *Laupheim 778–1978* (Stuttgart, 1979), 81.

46. Zingerle and Egger, *Die Tirolischen Weistümer*, vol. 4: 251.

47. See the examples in Bader, *Dorfgenossenschaft*, 202ff.; Kurze, *Pfarrerwahlen*, passim.

48. Kurze, *Pfarrerwahlen*, 323.

49. The full quote is from Kurze, *Pfafferwahlen*, 280.
50. Ibid., 310.
51. Ibid., 319.
52. The necessary details are in Kurze, *Pfafferwahlen*, with a summary at 323; and Bader, *Dorfgenossenschaft*, 198f.
53. Peter Blickle, *Landschaften, Landschaften im Alten Reich. Die staatliche Funktion des gemeinen Mannes in Oberdeutschland* (Munich, 1973), 314.
54. Kurze, *Pfarrerwahlen*, 315.
55. Ibid., 340.
56. Ibid., 489f.
57. Bader, *Dorfgenossenschaft*, 183.
58. William A. Christian, Jr., *Local Religion in Sixteenth-Century Spain* (Princeton, 1981), 71.
59. For Spain, convincingly, Christian, *Local Religion* and *Apparitions in Late Medieval and Renaissance Spain* (Princeton, 1981), 12ff., 104ff. For England, although with a claim to wider applicability, see Keith Thomas, *Religion and the Decline of Magic* (New York, 1971), 28. For Switzerland, see Sablonier, "Dorf im Übergang," 736, who has recently written, in my view very appropriately, of a "villagization of the church."
60. Ernst Walder, "Das torechte Leben von 1477 in der bernischen Politik 1477 bis 1481," *Berner Zeitschrift für Geschichte und Heimatkunde* 45 (1983): 74–134, with the quotes at 113ff.
61. Ernst Walder, "Zu den Bestimmungen des Stanser Verkommnisses von 1481 über verbotene Versammlungen und Zusammenschlüsse in der Eidgenossenschaft," in *Gesellschaft und Gesellschaften. Festschrift zum 65. Geburtstag von Ulrich im Hof*, ed. Nicolai Bernhard and Quirinus Reichen (Bern, 1982), 80–94, with the quotes at 92f.
62. Marc Bloch, *Caractère originaux de l'histoire rurale française*, vol. 1 (Paris, 1952), 175.
63. In what follows I have merely summarized older works of my assistants and my own studies. With the exception of quotes, I have dispensed with individual references. See P. Blickle, P. Bierbrauer, R. Blickle, and C. Ulbrich, *Aufruhr und Empörung? Studien zum bäuerlichen Widerstand im Alten Reich* (Munich, 1980); Peter Blickle, "Bäuerliche Erhebungen im spätmittelalterlichen Reich," *Zeitschrift für Agrargeschichte und Agrarsoziologie* 27 (1979): 208–231. See also the essays dealing with Austria, Switzerland, and southern Germany in Schulze, *Aufstände*.
64. Albert Ilien und Utz Jeggle, *Leben auf dem Dorf. Zur Sozialgeschichte des Dorfes und Sozialpsychologie seiner Bewohner* (Opladen, 1978), supplemented for western Europe by K. Thomas, *Religion and the Decline of Magic*, 527.
65. Basic reference is to the works of Karl Siegfried Bader. Bader is the leading expert on the late medieval village, and he by no means places the "community of conflict" (*Konfliktgemeinschaft*) into the foreground.
66. The path-breaking work in this respect is Werner Troßbach, "Bauernbewegungen im Wetterau-Vogelsberg-Gebiet 1648–1806: Soziale Bewegung und politische Erfahrung," Ph.D. dissertation, Bochum, 1983; and see Troßbach, "Bauernbewegungen in deutschen Kleinterritorien zwischen 1648 and 1789," in Schulze, *Aufstände*, 233–260, esp. 250f.
67. See, as an example, Johannes Häne, "Der Klosterbruch zu Rorschach und die St. Galler Krieg 1489–1490," *Mitteilungen zur vaterländischen Geschichte*, hg. vom Historischen Verein des Kantons St. Gallen 26 (1895): 73, 86, 97.
68. On this see P. Blickle and R. Blickle, *Schwaben*, 96.
69. Renate Blickle-Littwin, "Besitz und Amt," *Zeitschrift für bayerische Landesgeschichte* 40 (1977): 278–290.

70. David W. Sabean, *Landbesitz und Gesellschaft am Vorabend des Bauernkriegs. Eine Studie der sozialen Verhältnisse im südlichen Oberschwaben in den Jahren vor 1525*, Quellen und Forschungen zur Agrargeschichte 26 (Stuttgart, 1972). Sabean has generalized his approach in "The Communal Bias of Pre-1800 Peasant Uprisings in Western Europe," *Comparative Politics* (April, 1976): 355–364.

71. Henry J. Cohn, review in *English Historical Review* 92 (1977): 855–858.

72. This problem and its attendant implications has been treated by Peter Bierbrauer, "Freiheitsvorstellungen in der ländlichen Gesellschaft," Ph.D. dissertation, Saarbrücken, 1984.

73. Robert von Keller, *Freiheitsgarantien für Personen und Eigentum im Mittelalter* (Heidelberg, 1933); and see also Konrad Beyerle's preface (7) with references.

74. Hans Georg Wirz, ed., *Das Weiße Buch von Sarnen*, Quellenwerk zur Entstehung der Schweizerischen Eidgenossenschaft, part III, vol. 1 (Aarau, 1947), 31.

75. Müller, *Rechtsquellen St. Gallen*, 259.

76. Ibid., 260.

77. Häne, "Klosterbruch zu Rorschach," 83f. (both quotes).

78. Müller, *Rechtsquellen St. Gallen*, 259ff., 263ff.; Franz, *Quellen*, 28–36; Werner Näf, ed., *Herrschaftsverträge des Spätmittelalters* (Frankfurt a. M., 1951), 71–77.

79. The references are in *Monumenta Boica*, vol. 33b (reprinted ed., 1964), 205ff.; Claudia Ulbrich, *Leibherrschaft am Oberrhein im Spätmittelalter*, Veröffentlichungen des Max-Planck-Instituts für Geschichte, vol. 58 (Göttingen, 1979), 59–95; Franz, *Quellen*, 9–12, 28–36.

80. "Der Kemptner Leibeigenschaftsrodel," *Zeitschrift für bayerische Landesgeschichte* 42 (1979): 591.

81. Hans Patze, ed. *Die Grundherrschaft im späten Mittelalter*, Vorträge und Forschungen, vols. 26–27 (Sigmaringen, 1983), here at vol. 2: 341 (summary by A. Haverkamp).

82. Hermann Wopfner, *Beiträge zur Geschichte der freien bäuerlichen Erbleihe Deutschtirols im Mittelalter*, Untersuchungen zur Deutschen Staats- und Rechtsgeschichte, vol. 67 (Breslau, 1916); Peter Blickle, "Grundherrschaft und Agrarverfassung," in Patze, *Grundherrschaft im späten Mittelalter*, vol. 1: 241–261.

83. Thomas Aquinas, *Summa theologica* II, 66, 2.

84. Günther Franz, ed., *Thomas Müntzer. Schriften und Briefe. Kritische Gesamtausgabe*, Quellen und Forschungen zur Reformationsgeschichte, vol. 33 (Gütersloh, 1968), 329.

85. For the critical passage in Utopia, see E. Wurtz, J. H. Hexter, eds., *The Complete Works of St. Thomas More*, vol. 4, 4th ed. (New Haven and London, 1979), 102, lines 20–26. My reflections on the problem area of "Eigenschaft–Eigentum" are based for the most part on the work of Renate Blickle, "Agrarische Konflikte und Eigentumsordnung in Altbayern 1400–1800," in Schulze, *Aufstände*, 166–187, plus additional material on Swabia.

86. Heinrich Koller, ed., *Reformation Kaiser Sigmunds*, Monumenta Germaniae Historica, Staatsschriften des späteren Mittelalters, vol. 6 (Stuttgart, 1964), 276, lines 13–15, manuscript version N.

87. Quoted by Walter Müller, "Wurzeln und Bedeutung des grundsätzlichen Widerstandes gegen die Leibeigenschaft im Bauernkrieg 1525," *Schriften des Vereins für Geschichte des Bodensees und seiner Umgebung* 93 (1975): 25.

88. Renate Blickle, "Agrarische Konflikte und Eigentumsordnung in Altbayern 1400–1800," in Schulze, *Aufstände*, 176.

89. I exclude questions of taxation and defense, which would illuminate the same thing, merely from a different perspective. When individual references are not given, they can be found in my *Landschaften* by means of the indices.

90. Dionys Imesch, ed., *Die Walliser Landratsabschiede*, vol. 1 (Brig, 1916): 378ff.
91. Müller, *Rechtsquellen St. Gallen*, 181f.
92. Hauptstaatsarchiv Stuttgart, B 486 document 154.
93. Franz, *Quellen Bauernkrieg*, 28.
94. See on this the contributions by Otto Brunner, *Neue Wege der Verfassung- und Sozialgeschichte*, 2d ed. (Göttingen, 1968).
95. For peasant society see the still valuable and important works of Aleksander Vasilevich Chayanov, "Zur Frage einer Theorie der nichtkapitalistischen Wirtschaftssysteme," *Archiv für Sozialwissenschaft und Sozialpolitik* 59 (1924): 577–613, and more broadly Robert Redfield, *The Little Community*, 10th ed. (Chicago, 1973). For burgher society see the stimulating work of Black, *Guilds and Civil Society*, though he largely misses the connections between city and land.
96. Peter Laslett, "Familie und Industrialisierung: eine 'starke Theorie,'" in Werner Conze, ed., *Sozialgeschichte der Familie in der Neuzeit Europas*, Industrielle Welt, vol. 21 (Stuttgart, 1976), 13–31, with the quote at 13.
97. Michael Mitterauer and Reinhard Sieder, *Vom Patriarchat zur Partnerschaft. Zum Strukturwandel der Familie* (Munich, 1977), 146.
98. Sabean, *Landbesitz und Gesellschaft*, 89; Saarbrücker Arbeitsgruppe, "Die spätmittelalterliche Leibeigenschaft in Oberschwaben," *Zeitschrift für Agrargeschichte und Agrarsoziologie* 22 (1974): 29.
99. See Otto Brunner, *Land und Herrschaft. Grundfragen der territorialen Verfassungsgeschichte Österreichs im Mittelalter*, 6th ed. (Vienna, 1970). Brunner, who is concerned primarily with contemporary concepts, does bring in the *bonum commune*. The instances of attested usage are given by Adolf Diehl, "Gemeiner Nutzen im Mittelalter. Nach süddeutschen Quellen," *Zeitschrift für württembergische Landesgeschichte* 1 (1937): 297–300; Johannes W. Pichler, *Necessitas, ein Element des mittelalterlichen und neuzeitlichen Rechts* (Berlin, 1983), esp. 58, 64.
100. Hans Maier, *Die ältere deutsche Staats- u. Verwaltungslehre*, 2d. ed. (Munich, 1980), 159–163. Some very scattered references for the late fifteenth century in Diehl, "Gemeiner Nutzen," 311.
101. What I describe as participation in my argument is largely interchangeable with Löwenthal's "principle of institutional pluralism." See Richard Löwenthal, "Kontinuität und Diskontinuität: Zur Grundproblematik des Symposiums," in Karl Möckl and Karl Bosl, eds., *Der moderne Parlamentarismus und seine Grundlagen in der ständischen Repräsentation* (Berlin, 1977), 341–356, esp. 346f.
102. Thomas, *Religion and the Decline of Magic*, 648.
103. Werner Williams-Krapp, "Laienbildung und volkssprachliche Hagiographie im späten Mittelalter," in Ludger Grenzmann and Karl Stackmann, eds., *Literatur und Laienbildung im Spätmittelalter und in der Reformationszeit* (Stuttgart, 1984), 697–709.
104. Christian, *Local Religion*, 103.
105. Peter Thaddäus Lang, "Würfel, Wein und Wettersegen—Klerus und Gläubige im Bistum Eichstätt am Vorabend der Reformation," in Volker Press and Dieter Stievermann, eds., *Martin Luther. Probleme seiner Zeit* (Stuttgart, 1985), 219–243, esp. 235, on the veneration of the weather patrons.
106. Christian, *Local Religion*, 185. See in general Josef Lortz, "Zur Problematik der kirchlichen Mißstände im Spätmittelalter," *Trierer Theologische Zeitschrift* 58 (1949): 1–26, 212–227, 257–279, 347–357.
107. A. Schilling, ed., "Die religiösen und kirchlichen Zustände der ehemaligen Reichsstadt Biberach unmittelbar vor Einführung der Reformation. Geschildert von einem Zeitgenossen," *Freiburger Diöcesan-Archiv* 19 (1887): 1–191.
108. The source is, for example, the basis of the chapter "Kirchliches Leben und

Frömmigkeit" in Martin Brecht and Hermann Ehmer, *Südwestdeutsche Reformationsgeschichte. Zur Einführung der Reformation im Herzogtum Württemberg* (Stuttgart, 1984), 40–47; Robert W. Scribner, "Ritual and Popular Religion in Catholic Germany at the Time of the Reformation," *Journal of Ecclesiastical History* 35 (1984): 47–77.

109. This conclusion is based on personal experiences in Biberach in the years 1945–1950.

110. See Lawrence G. Duggan, "Fear and Confession on the Eve of the Reformation," *Archiv für Reformationsgeschichte* 75 (1984): 153–175.

111. Donald Weinstein and Rudolph M. Bell, *Saints and Society. The Two Worlds of Western Christendom, 1000–1700* (Chicago and London, 1982), 167ff.; Thomas, *Religion and the Decline of Magic*, 28; Christian, *Local Religion*, 181.

112. Christian, *Local Religion*, 181.

113. Natalie Zemon Davis, "Some Tasks and Themes in the Study of Popular Religion," in Charles Trinkhaus and Heiko A. Oberman, eds., *The Pursuit of Holiness in Late Medieval and Renaissance Religion. Papers from the University of Michigan Conference*, Studies in Medieval and Reformation Thought, vol. 10 (Leiden, 1974), 309.

Conclusion: The Reformation of the Princes versus the Communal Reformation

Communalism as a way of life shows a marked affinity to republicanism as a form of government. Without a high level of communal autonomy, the northern parts of the Burgundian dominions would hardly have thought of constituting themselves as the United Netherlands. Without the developed communal rights of the villages and valleys, the prince-bishoprics of Chur and Sitten/Sion would hardly have become the republics of Graubünden and Wallis/Valais, to say nothing of the Swiss Confederacy. There was good reason why "to turn Swiss" and "to set up a confederacy" became universally understood code phrases for political ways of life alternative to the princely and monarchical forms of rule characteristic of the Middle Ages. Martin Luther already called these European anomalies "democracies," noting that "*Ubi plures regunt*, as in Switzerland," one was dealing with a *democratia*. And it was probably not exactly an expression of sympathy when in the postscript he defined *democratia* more precisely as the place "where rules the common man," whom Luther elsewhere called "Mr. Everybody."[1] When this common man perceived and appropriated the ideas of the reformation through his integration into a communal association, communalism received an ideological, a theologically rooted justification. This greatly heightened the threat to the old order, as always happens when amorphous mass movements turn into conscious class movements. The critical mass was reached around 1525, and thereafter the communal reformation turned into the reformation of the princes.

Many scholarly assessments support the insight, which is hardly any longer contestable although still contested, that the year 1525 also saw a turning point in the reformation. "As a movement the reformation experienced a decisive blow after the events of 1525," as Ernst W. Zeeden has noted; "it was broken and lost much of its original vigor."[2] Bernd Moeller speaks of a "turning point," noting that, on the one hand, we can observe in part a "sobering, a clarification, as well as disappointment" and, on the other hand, that "within Luther's sphere of influence, . . . the tendency towards the institutionalization of the church with the help of the state" prevailed.[3] Heinrich Lutz sums up the "situation after 1525" by pointing out that Luther and his supporters turned toward the princes. "The place of the original conception, that the renewal of the church should occur, as much as possible out of the inherent strength of the communities" (Karl Holl), was now replaced step by step by an elaborate system of official territorial churches (obrigkeitliche Landeskirchen).[4] As the Luther expert Marc Lienhard put it, "the time of the church constitutions [Kirchenordnungen] had [now] come, and also the time to call back those preachers who were considered too radical."[5] More specialized studies corroborate these general judgments. "The defeat of the peasants also put an end to the reformation in the countryside," and "the decision was thus made on the political future of the reformation in the triangle between Alsace, Switzerland, and southern Germany."[6] In this way the "principle of the communal church, which would have corresponded to confessionalization and the more personal notion of Christianity," fell by the wayside.[7]

Rainer Wohlfeil not only notes the fact of a turning point in the course of the reformation, he also offers an explanation. As he sees it, the "phase of an evangelical reformation from the top or guided from the top," which set in after the defeat of the peasants, was motivated by "fear of social upheavals."[8] After this time we can clearly observe efforts by the imperial estates "to disconnect any socially transforming implications from the evangelical reformation, and to regard and implement the reformation as a policy of the authorities."[9] Although the "repudiation of the 'common man's' demand for a voice and for participation" did not mean that "his participation in the evangelical movement disappeared entirely . . . , in the long run it ceased to be a historical force."[10] Future work will have to follow up on this critical point identified by Wohlfeil. In fact, the dialectical change from the communal reformation to the princes' reformation can be substantiated with further arguments, if we return once again to the late medieval developments from communalism to republicanism, and the reaction of the authorities, clergymen, practitioners, and theoreticians to these changes.

Contemporaries of the reformation, along with their fathers and grandfathers, had an unusual experience, one unknown to earlier generations, of armed resistance of the common people to their lords. The revolts in the large territories such as Salzburg, Inner Austria, and Württemberg, in the majority of the southern German monastic lordships, and in the city-states of Zurich and Bern attest that this resistance was a mass phenomenon. The Bundschuh in the upper Rhine Valley uprisings revealed the threat this mass movement posed to the traditional princely, aristocratic, and ecclesiastical lordship, since the peasants and burghers found in the notion of "godly law" an aggressive formula for fundamental social and political changes, which could question the entire existing legal and political order. Preventing peasant resistance, or at least containing it, had to become a life-and-death question for the political system of the empire.

The imperial Public Peace (*Reichslandfriede*) of 1495 does not seem to have sufficiently grasped this problem, judging from its statutes. We might even ask whether the problem had even penetrated into the general awareness of the imperial estates, which is doubtful in view of the fact that the unrest was regionally limited to the southern German region. In the two central regulations of 1495—"from the time of this announcement no one, regardless of what honor, estate, or circumstance he may be, shall befeud, wage war on, rob, capture, attack, or besiege anyone else," and "all open feuds and violent defense throughout the entire empire are abrogated and abolished"—the imperial estates were apparently thinking only of the feud and thus exclusively of the nobility.[11] The implementing statutes for the imperial peace, which were passed by subsequent imperial diets into the 1520s, confirm the discussion's movement along the course marked out in 1495.[12] Preventive or restraining measures against unrest therefore had to be taken initially at local or regional levels.

The first known example of the criminalization of independent, unlawful action against the authorities is found in the Compact of Stans from the year 1481, a document we have already touched on several times. In it, the members of the Swiss Confederacy pledged mutual assistance in case of "arbitrary violence" and "revolt."[13] The lively diplomatic activities that preceded the agreement throughout the confederacy probably found an echo in neighboring southern Germany, even though that has so far not been corroborated in the sources. But the pressure to put an end to violent acts against the authorities did not have to come from outside. Ominous conflicts began to loom with the Bundschuh rising along the upper Rhine.

It is surely no coincidence that the first, broader territorial constitution containing a "revolt statute" comes from Baden around 1495.[14] It commands that "our people, upon their promise and on pain of severe punishment to life and property, shall not jointly enter into or form any alliance, association, or union which in any way is or will be directed against us, our heirs, or our people."[15] It seems natural to make a connection between this unique early document from the empire and the Bundschuh in 1493 on the upper Rhine, even though the Bundschuh did not affect the margraviate of Baden directly.[16] This conspiracy did, however, prompt all the rulers on the upper Rhine to take feverish preventive measures.[17]

What the Compact of Stans and the territorial constitution from Baden lack, namely a detailing of punishments, came in an imperial decree of 1502. The concrete background to this document was the Untergrombach Bundschuh in 1502. In order to take measures against the rebels, the ecclesiastical and secular princes of the upper Rhine, under the leadership of the prince elector Philipp of the Palatinate, had decided to take joint action and had procured a corresponding decree from Emperor Maximilian. It informed all imperial estates that

> . . . many inhabitants of the Holy Empire, together with their supporters,
> . . . are rising up and . . . are seducing the common people into forming a
> band, conspiracy, and union, and to oppose the magistrates, all authority, the

clergy, Christian order, with the intention that the subjects of the princes, lords, and cities . . . shall help them in shaking off their subject status.

The decree concludes from this that

. . . such a thing can give rise to an eradication of all peace, all order, a destruction of the common weal and the clergy, of all godly, human, ecclesiastical and secular rights, all authority and government of the princes, the nobility, the cities, and others.[18]

Maximilian promulgated a penal code valid for the entire empire. As the decree makes quite clear, the Bundschuh, and only the Bundschuh—and not resistance as such—was criminalized through a precise definition of punishments: death for the Bundschuh's members, particularly for its leaders and instigators, and punishment of others at the lords' discretion for failure to inform on the movement.

Difficulties seem to have arisen from the need to define clearly the Bundschuh's criminal offense. The decree provides not precise definitions but only a summary of transgressions. Three "crimes" are highlighted: the overthrow of the existing political order, conspiracy, and the breaking of oaths to rulers. What makes this list important is that it reveals some uncertainties in dealing with the problem.[19]

Another decisive step along the chosen path of repression was taken by the duchy of Württemberg following the uprising of the "Poor Conrad" in 1514. The Agreement of Tübingen contains something that is often ignored or overlooked in the scholarly discussion, namely a "revolt statute," which takes up about a third of the entire text. It provides that

If it should happen henceforth that anyone, whoever he may be, should make or undertake an uprising and revolt against the lordship, against the lord prince's council, officers [amptleut], servants, prelates, clergy, burgomasters, courts, councils, or otherwise against the notables [erberkait] in order to oppress them . . . he shall forfeit his life and limb, and upon him shall be imposed and carried out his deserved punishment, that is with quartering, breaking on the wheel, beheading, hanging, chopping off of the hands, and so forth.[20]

The other punitive measures are those established by Maximilian's decree of 1502. In 1502 resistance was criminalized because it overthrew the political order. By 1514 the Agreement of Tübingen criminalized resistance as a revolt against lordship, whether or not it threatened political order. Yet, the "Poor Conrad" in Württemberg did not pursue the Bundschuh's radical program, for it did not intend to overthrow the political order. Rather, the Württemberg burghers and peasants aimed only to gain an appropriate representation in the Württemberg diets, since at this time passive suffrage was completely, and active suffrage overwhelmingly restricted to the leading notables of the cities. The territorial princes and estates must have been aware of this. Nevertheless, the official side conveyed an entirely different picture to the outside world. In their printed justification to all the imperial estates, the duke and territorial estates tried to present the "Poor Conrad" as a Bundschuh, referring to that end to the "godly law" allegedly demanded by the Württemberg peasants.[21] The propaganda seems to have worked, for a territorial diet of Breisgau and Sundgau in Nearer Austria explicitly labeled the "Poor Conrad" a "Bundschuh,"[22] and in the imperial knights' gravamina from 1523, any revolt was defined as "a Bundschuh or poor Conrad."[23]

Another notable thing about the revolt statute in the Agreement of Tübingen is that it was inserted in its entirety into the letter of justification sent to the imperial estates by the duke and the regional estates, and was also taken over into the Württemberg territorial constitution from 1515, and into the loyalty oath of the subjects.[24]

The Bundschuh rising and the Poor Conrad, together with the authorities' countermeasures and propaganda, apparently caused revolt to be rated as an extremely dangerous problem. This is clearly revealed in Charles V's electoral capitulation of 1519, in which the electors placed the emperor under obligation "to put an end to all improper, hateful alliances, unions, and associations of subjects, the nobility, and the common people, as well as uprisings, revolts, and wanton violence against the prince electors, princes, and others."[25] The nobility referred to, the knights, immediately protested against being associated with the disobedience of common subjects. The knights assured their betters that they would be found on the side of the imperial princes "should there be a Bundschuh or Poor Conrad uprising." This was in 1523. What imperial decrees, princely propaganda, territorial constitutions, and the electoral capitulation of 1519 all sought to prevent, did occur two years after the knights' assurance—the Revolution of 1525.

The Peasants' War for the first time put resistance on the agenda of the imperial diet. The recess (*Abschied*) of the imperial diet of Augsburg in 1525 stated that

> . . . in the meantime all prince electors, princes, and estates, in their principalities, lordships, and territories, shall, with good military preparedness, be most vigilant and watchful whether any uprising, revolt, or disobedience from the subjects against the authorities are about to arise and happen. This shall be done in order that they may put up strong resistance and take defensive measures at the very outset before the disobedient subjects increase in number and gather together, and also that they may in other ways adhere to and support the emperor's and the empire's peace.[26]

In this way the combined transgressions of "uprising, revolt, and disobedience" became an offense against the imperial peace by being defined as disobedience against the authorities. This passage, which was still phrased in rather general terms, was elaborated upon at the imperial diet of Speyer in 1526. Following the emperor's instructions, the imperial estates dealt at great length with the events of 1525.[27] In their recess they applied the penal clauses of the imperial peace to the rebels, placing such folk under imperial ban, "such that their body and property are outside the law, and no one who lays hands on them can be accused of a felony or held responsible."

The laws enacted by the princes and the empire in 1481–1502 and 1525–1526 to prevent acts of resistance deserve a closer look from two different perspectives. First, within a single generation the offense of high treason was created. Second, the increase in high treason was interpreted as a result of the reformation.

As a mass phenomenon, "uprising and revolt," as contemporaries described it, characterized in particular the early sixteenth century. It was apparently inconceivable to a society dominated by the nobility that subjects were thinking of armed resistance—at least the lack of attention to the issue in the imperial peace of Worms indicates as much. In contrast to the prohibition against the feud, which was intended to protect persons, the prohibition against high treason sought to protect institutions and constitutions. The newly created norms of criminal law protected not the prince or the lord, but authority as such, the state. According to modern German, Austrian, and Swiss law, deliberate attacks against the internal existence and the constitutional order of the state are considered high treason. The example of the Poor Conrad shows us the strategic achievement of the empire and the imperial princes, when they subsumed passive resistance, even though it intended no constitutional changes, under the offense of high treason. This made resistance much more difficult, if not impossible, for any grievance which was voiced with sufficient vigor to be heard could fall under suspicion of high treason. It is no surprise that no other peasant unrest occurred during the sixteenth century after 1525, with one exception in Austria. It seems much more surprising that the peasantry once again developed enough vigor during the seventeenth and eighteenth centuries to become, by its acts of resistance, an important factor of modernization, as the most recent scholarship has shown.[28]

Of momentous importance for the reformation was the association of high treason with the evangelical movement. Grounds for a charge of high treason could most easily be established where subjects programmatically tried to put into practice new legal principles. This is why the duke of Württemberg made the false, or at least dubious, allegation that the Poor Conrad movement derived its legitimacy from the notion of godly law and that its aim was to put it into practice. Where the new legal principle did emerge openly was in the godly law of the Peasants' War. This was justification enough for Charles V to claim, in his summons to the diet of Speyer in 1526, that "the discord . . . in regard to matters of the holy Christian faith and religion" was "not the least cause . . . of the recent uprising of the common man,"[29] and the Bern chronicler Anshelm confirms that this was a widespread perception in the empire,

. . . as the peasants and their followers have undertaken to liberate the gospel and themselves through revolt, their undertaking has been defeated by revolt, in that the evangelical doctrine and preaching, under the name of

Luther and Zwingli and the Baptists, has been denounced as "evanhellish"[30] and rebellious.[31]

• Never again in German history would subjects justify their demands by invoking godly law.

The reformers themselves made sure of that. Just as the lords interpreted resistance as high treason against the state, the reformers—without exception—interpreted it as treason against the gospel.[32] Not one failed to take a stance against the common man in 1525: Martin Luther, Philipp Melanchthon, Johannes Brenz, Urbanus Rhegius, Johannes Lachmann, Johannes Eberlin von Günzburg, Johann Agricola, Wolfgang Capito, Matthias Zell, Martin Bucer, and Huldrych Zwingli. Once more the common people with their common sense had been told in no uncertain terms that the gospel could not be invoked for the social and political order; in other words, the gospel was basically not relevant for concrete actions. As theologians the reformers did not stoop to joining the laity when it came to interpreting the gospel—theologians have never done that. As intellectuals the reformers did not stoop to the political aspirations of the rabble—intellectuals have rarely done that. In this respect the behavior of the reformers was very conventional. However, there is good reason to think that the reformation would not have made it beyond the monastic walls and the university lecture halls had its theology and ethics not been so highly compatible with the concrete reality of communalism. How else can one explain that the reformation as a social movement was, in the first instance, not a movement of princes, the nobility, bishops, and prelates, but one of peasants and burghers, more specifically of communities? This could lead one to ask to what extent reformation theology was in fact indebted to the personal religious anxieties of the reformers; this, of course, would be a book in itself. But we must definitely give some thought to the question of what actually became of the axioms of reformation theology, communal Christendom, and the pure gospel.

The growing awareness by the authorities about the threat to the social order was accompanied by the growing misgivings among the reformers about leaving the responsibility for the reformation to the laity. Luther felt that way after the unrest in Wittenberg in 1521, Zwingli after the unrest in Zurich in 1523. The reformers forbade the common people to call for the salvation of the world by referring to the gospel. In 1525, at the latest, all were agreed on this point, even though it was originally not so clear that they would be; suffice it to mention Zwingli's writings from 1523.

Despite an overall agreement, uncertainties and divergences did of course exist when it came to the details. In the south of the empire the reformers were far more upset than in the north, and for good reason, since they had, after all, come out much more clearly in support of the notion that the gospel was relevant for the here and now. The secular priests of Zurich had rendered their opinion to the council by saying "that we shall release our serfs from such servility," on the grounds that "as children of God" they should all "live together in brotherly manner." But this decision was not in any way based on the fact that Zwingli had accepted the argument of the Zurich peasants that serfdom was "directly counter to God's will and to his infallible word."[33] The gospel did not provide any concrete instructions for action, Brenz declared, but it did lay out a framework within which one was to move. "God the highest Lord does not care whether the lords alone or the subjects alone own the woods . . . , what he does care about is that the lords help the subjects in the interest of the common weal."[34] This is a formulation that Rhegius might also have used.[35] As Zwingli, Brenz, and Rhegius saw it, the balancing of the interests of lords and subjects should be accomplished in the spirit of brotherly love, the meaning of which was defined by the gospel. In southern Germany, the common people were seen "from the perspective of the social situation, and the theological aspect was limited to preventing the improper use of the gospel."[36]

How very different Luther and his closer circle—Melanchthon, Agricola, Poliander, in part also Lachmann. For these men the year 1525 took on eschatological, even apocalyptic features. Even theologians tell us that this was the least difficult way out.[37] Melanchthon put it even more bluntly than Luther, saying that what the gospel demanded was the preservation of the political status quo; anyone who used the gospel to justify demands, however legitimate, was of the devil.[38] Here we encounter again Luther's argument of the false prophets, which then also had clear consequences in Melanchthon's reasoning. "That the churches everywhere have the right of electing and appointing pastors" holds true only where "a godfearing authority wishes to have the gospel preached," and with the qualification that "in such elections a prince [must] also be present . . . , so that nothing rebellious is preached or undertaken."[39] The community's decision on the true doctrine was thus suspended, and the election of the pastors had become a meaningless act of consent. Theoretically the point had now been reached where in practical terms church visitations and church constitutions could begin. Melanchthon told a German prince elector, the Count Palatine of the Rhine, that "it is necessary for such a wild and uncouth people as the Germans to have less freedom than they now have."[40] The princes were undoubtedly of the same opinion. In their positions, Melanchthon and other friends of Luther are little more than mediocre copyists of the Wittenberg reformer, but they did help to ensure that Luther prevailed in the empire, with consequences for the Central European region that are difficult to calculate. Even from a European perspective the suppression of the peasants, burghers, and miners presents itself "as a bleak paraphrase of the entire reformation."[41] The "revolt statutes" which the princes promulgated before, during, and after 1525, and which were worked into the territorial constitutions and inserted into oaths of loyalty, are in a sense the political orchestration of themes sounded by the theologians. To put it in general terms, the communities were everywhere at the very least placed under the tutelage of the authorities. In the wider setting of these events we can see the roots for the emergence of a new, although not necessarily better, age;[42] at least this is a view that is by no means unfamiliar even outside of Central Europe. In the late summer of 1525 the authorities and the reformers had weathered the worst, and communalism was in decline.

In view of the late medieval development of communalism, it was natural that the peasants and burghers searched for an ideology that was capable of securing the principles of communal life—hard work, social equality, and political independence—within a world that still bore a strongly aristocratic imprint. To that end they took hold of the "pure gospel" of the reformation. Eventually Luther forbade them to do so. But what was Luther himself doing when he declared: "Secular empires cannot exist where there is not inequality in respect to persons, that some are free, some in bondage, some lords, some subjects"?[43] He was calling on Scripture!

There is a splendidly vivid document in which the interests of the authorities and the reformers found a formulation that pointed to the future: the "Instruction on the preaching of the gospel" by the Margraves Casimir and George of Brandenburg (August 1525).[44]

After the recent uprisings and unrests, which for the most part were caused by ignorant and unskilled preachers and preaching, it is . . . the belief and command of my gracious lords . . . that the holy gospel and the Word of God of the New and Old Testament be preached purely and clearly in their principality, lands, and territories.

And what does "pure gospel" now mean? It would be a misunderstanding to assume "that the faith in God and Jesus Christ alone . . . is sufficient for attaining eternal salvation." Good works were indispensable for salvation, "since where these good works do not follow, there also is no true, proper, loving, saving faith." It was furthermore impressed upon the clergy what Christian freedom was. Christian freedom meant "keeping God's commandments and doing good works with a free, willing heart and with pleasure . . . and being obedient to authority."

Notes

1. The references in Hans Maier, "Demokratie," in Joachim Ritter, ed., Historisches Wörterbuch der Philosophie, 2 vols. (Basel, 1972), 53.
2. Ernst Walter Zeeden, "Deutschland von der Mitte des 15. Jahrhunderts bis zum Westfälischen Frieden (1648)," in Theodor Schieder, ed., Handbuch der europäischen Geschichte, vol. 3 (Stuttgart, 1971): 445–580, with the quote at 519.
3. Bernd Moeller, Reichsstadt und Reformation, Schriften des Vereins für Reformationsgeschichte, no. 180 (Gütersloh, 1962), 101.
4. Heinrich Lutz, Reformation und Gegenreformation, Oldenbourg Grundriß der Geschichte, vol. 10 (Munich, 1979), 37.
5. Marc Lienhard, Martin Luther. Un temps, une vie, un message (Paris and Geneva, 1983), 427.
6. Hans-Jürgen Goertz, "Aufstand gegen den Priester. Antiklerikalismus und reformatorische Bewegungen," in Peter Blickle, ed., Bauer, Reich und Reformation. Festschrift

für Günther Franz zum 80. Geburtstag (Stuttgart, 1982), 208; Heiko A. Oberman in Lewis W. Spitz, ed., *Humanismus und Reformation als Kulturelle Kräfte in der deutschen Geschichte*, Veröffentlichungen der Historischen Kommission zu Berlin, vol. 51 (Berlin, 1981), 183.

7. Winfried Becker, *Reformation und Revolution*, Katholisches Leben und Kirchenreform im Zeitalter der Glaubensspaltung, vol. 34 (Münster, 1974), 40.

8. Rainer Wohlfeil, *Einführung in die Geschichte der deutschen Reformation* (Munich, 1982), 27f.; idem, "Das Schicksal der Reformation vor und nach dem Augsburger Reichstag," in Bernhard Lohse and Otto Hermann Pesch, eds., *Das 'Augsburger Bekenntnis' von 1530 damals und heute* (Munich and Mainz, 1980), 85.

9. Wohlfeil, *Einführung*, 28.

10. Wohlfeil, "Schicksal," 85. This can also be seen as a response to the contrary view of Franz Lau, "Reformation als spontane Volksbewegung." My own position is stated in *Die Revolution von 1525*, 2d ed. (Munich, 1981), 274–278. Other counterarguments to Lau's thesis can be found in the latest studies by Gerald Strauss, who shows how little Lutheran indoctrination about the state penetrated common people, and who links their reservedness to the events of 1525. Gerald Strauss, *Luther's House of Learning. Indoctrination of the Young in the German Reformation* (Baltimore, 1978), 301ff.

11. Quoted after Heinz Angermeier, ed., *Deutsche Reichstagsakten unter Maximilian I.*, vol. 5: *Reichstag von Worms 1495*, Deutsche Reichstagsakten, Mittlere Reihe, no. 5, vol. 1, part 1 (Göttingen, 1981), 363f.

12. Johann Jakob Schmauss, ed., *Neuere und vollständigere Sammlung der Reichs-Abschiede* (Frankfurt am Main, 1747), 30f. (1497), 39–42 (1498), 63–66 (1500), 102 (1505), 133 (1510), 136f. (1512), 194–203 (1521), 229f. (1522).

13. Ernst Walder, "Das torechte Leben von 1477 in der bernischen Politik 1477 bis 1481," *Berner Zeitschrift für Geschichte und Heimatkunde* 45 (1983): 74–134, with the quotes at 113ff.

14. The dating itself is uncertain. The arguments for 1495 in Gustaf Klemens Schmelzeisen, ed., *Polizei- und Landesordnungen*, Halbband 1: *Reich und Territorien*, Quellen zur Neueren Privatrechtsgeschichte Deutschlands, vol. 2 (Münster, 1968), 34.

15. The text according to Rudolf Carlebach, *Badische Rechtsgeschichte*, vol. 1 (Heidelberg, 1906), 109.

16. Alfred Rosenkranz, *Der Bundschuh. Die Erhebung des südwestdeutschen Bauernstandes in den Jahren 1493–1517*, 2 vols. (Heidelberg, 1927), vol. 1: 9–136.

17. We must single out especially the alliance of the "lower Rhine" (*Niedere Vereinigung*, the counterpart to the "upper alliance" of the Swiss confederacy), which the estates of the upper Rhine renewed on 12 August 1493, on the occasion of the Sélestat Bundschuh. See ibid., 221.

18. Ibid., 110.

19. Ibid., 230ff.

20. The text is readily accessible in Werner Näf, ed., *Herrschaftsverträge des Spätmittelalters*, Quellen zur neueren Geschichte, herausgegeben vom Historischen Institut der Universität Bern, vol. 17, 2d ed. (Frankfurt a. M., 1975), 71–77, with the quote at 74.

21. "Wahrhafftig vnderrichtung der vffrurn vnnd handlungen sich im furstenthum Wirtemperg begeben," Tübingen 1514. Additional evidence for the effort on the part of the authorities to present the "Poor Conrad" to the empire as a Bundschuh in Wilhelm Ohr, "Die Entstehung des Bauernaufruhrs vom armen Konrad 1514," *Württembergisches Vierteljahrsheft für Landesgeschichte*, new ser. 22 (1913): 1–50, esp. 46; Heinrich Öhler, "Der Aufstand des Armen Konard im Jahre 1514," 38 (1932): 467–482, esp. 474f.

Conclusion 203

22. Archives départementales du Haut-Rhin Colmar, C7, fol. 161. The estates were aware, we read here, "that the subjects and residents of the duchy of Württemberg recently [engaged in] an uprising, tumult, and unlawful undertaking called the Bundschuh." (The reference was kindly passed on by Dr. Claudia Ulbrich, Wiebelskirchen.)

23. Hanns Hubert Hofmann, ed., *Quellen zum Verfassungsorganismus des heiligen römischen Reiches deutscher Nation 1495–1815*, Ausgewählte Quellen zur deutschen Geschichte, vol. 13 (Darmstadt, 1976), 71.

24. Printed in A. L. Reyscher, ed., *Sammlung der württembergischen Gesetze*, vol. 12 (Stuttgart, 1841): 26f.

25. August Kluckhohn, ed., *Deutsche Reichstagsakten unter Kaiser Karl V*, vol. 1, Deutsche Reichstagsakten jüngere Reihe, no. 1 (Gotha, 1893), 868. For a background to this document see 770, 822.

26. Schmauss, *Reichs-Abschiede*, 271.

27. Ibid., 274 (para. 5). In recent years the treatment of the Peasant War at the diet of 1526 has been widely examined, so that I can refer for the details of my argumentation to this literature (even though it pursued different problems). The discussion began with G. Vogler, "Der deutsche Bauernkrieg und die Verhandlungen des Reichstags zu Speyer 1526," in R. Vierhaus, ed., *Herrschaftsverträge, Wahlkapitulationen, Fundamentalgesetze*, Veröffentlichungen des Max-Planck-Instituts für Geschichte 56 (Göttingen, 1977), 173–191, and ends with Helmut Gabel and Winfried Schulze, "Folgen und Wirkungen," in Horst Buszello et al., eds., *Der deutsche Bauernkrieg* (Stuttgart, 1984), 322–349, esp. 335–340, who survey and assess the literature that appeared in the intervening years.

28. Jerome Blum, *The End of the Old Order in Rural Europe* (Princeton, 1978), 332–353. Winfried Schulze, *Bäuerlicher Widerstand und feudale Herrschaft in der frühen Neuzeit*, Neuzeit im Aufbau, vol. 6 (Stuttgart-Bad Canstatt, 1980), esp. 128–142.

29. Schmauss, *Reichs-Abschiede*, 273.

30. *Evanhellisch*, a play on *evangelisch* = evangelical.

31. Günther Franz, ed., *Quellen zur Geschichte des Bauernkrieges*, Ausgewählte Quellen zur deutschen Geschichte der Neuzeit. Freiherr vom Stein-Gedächtnisausgabe, vol. 2 (Darmstadt, 1963), 582.

32. Hubert Kirchner, "Der deutsche Bauernkrieg im Urteil der Freunde und Schüler Luthers," unpublished Habilitationsschrift, Greifswald, 1969, 300. This work is fundamental for the arguments that follow. See also Justus Maurer, *Prediger im Bauernkrieg*, Calwer Theologische Monographien, vol. 5 (Stuttgart, 1979), esp. 263–275. I did not deal more closely with the essay of Robert Kolb, "The Theologians and the Peasants: Conservative Evangelical Reaction to the German Peasant Revolt," *Archiv für Reformationsgeschichte* 49 (1978): 103–131, which adds little to the work of Kirchner (which Kolb did not use).

33. The references, together with a clear correction of hitherto positive interpretations of Zwingli's position, in Walter Müller, "Wurzeln und Bedeutung des grundsätzlichen Widerstandes gegen die Leibeigenschaft im Bauernkrieg 1525," *Schriften des Vereins für Geschichte des Bodensees und seiner Umgebung* 93 (1975): 21f., with the quotes at 15 and 21.

34. Quoted by Kirchner, "Freunde Luthers," 93.

35. See ibid., 154.

36. Ibid., 307.

37. Thus the explicit interpretation of Kirchner, "Freunde Luthers," 84, with which we can basically agree after our own analysis of Luther's Peasant War writings.

38. The references in Franz, *Quellen*, 185, 187.

39. Ibid., 182.

40. The references from Franz, *Quellen*, 185.
41. Helmut Diwald, *Anspruch auf Mündigkeit. Europa um 1400–1555*, Propyläen Geschichte Europas, vol. 1 (Berlin, 1975), 342. See Ferdinand Seibt, *Revolutionen in Europa. Ursprung und Wege innerer Gewalt. Strukturen, Elemente, Exempel* (Munich, 1984), 243.
42. See Donald Weinstein and Rudolph M. Bell, *Saints and Society. The Two Worlds of Western Christendom, 1000–1700* (Chicago and London, 1982), 12. This was also the argument of the older ethnology, for example, Will-Erich Peuckert, *Deutscher Volksglaube des Spätmittelalters* (Stuttgart, 1942; reprint, Hildesheim and New York, 1978), 7–12.
43. WA 18, 327, lines 6–8. On the interpretation see Kirchner, "Freunde Luthers," 42.
44. Franz, *Quellen*, 587–591.

Bibliography

The bibliography contains only works that are cited more than once. All other titles are listed in the footnotes with the necessary bibliographical information.

ABBREVIATIONS

WA   Luther, Martin. *Werke. Kritische Gesamtausgabe.* 60 vols. Weimar: Böhlau, 1883–1980. References include volume number.

ZW   Zwingli, Huldreich, *Sämtliche Werke.* 14 vols. Corpus Reformatorum, vols. 88–101. Berlin and Zurich: C. A. Schwetzschke, 1905–1983. References include volume number.

ZI   Pamphlet collection of the special research section Late Middle Ages and Reformation, Project Zeeden 1 (headed by Dr. H.-J. Köhler). Cited with pamphlet numbers.

SOURCES

Clemen, Otto, ed. *Flugschriften aus den ersten Jahren der Reformation.* 4 vols. Halle, 1907–1911. Reprint, Nieuwkoop: B. de Graaf, 1967.

Dürr, Emil, and Paul Roth, eds. *Aktensammlung zur Geschichte der Basler Reformation in den Jahren 1519 bis Anfang 1534.* 6 vols. Basel: Verlag der Historischen und Antiquarischen Gesellschaft, 1921–1950.

Egli, Emil, ed. *Aktensammlung zur Geschichte der Zürcher Reformation in den Jahren 1519–1533.* Zurich: Meyer & Zeller, 1879. Reprinted, Aalen: Scientia, 1973.

Enders, Ludwig, ed. *Johannes Eberlin von Günzburg, Sämtliche Schriften.* 3 vols. in 2. Flugschriften aus der Reformationszeit, vols. 11, 15, 18. Halle: Max Niemeyer, 1896–1902.

Franz, Günther, ed. *Der deutsche Bauernkrieg, Aktenband.* 2d ed. Darmstadt: Wissenschaftliche Buchgesellschaft, 1968.

———, ed. *Quellen zur Geschichte des Bauernkrieges.* Ausgewählte Quellen zur deutschen Geschichte der Neuzeit. Freiherr vom Stein-Gedächtnisausgabe, vol. 2. Darmstadt: Wissenschaftliche Buchgesellschaft, 1963.

Fuchs, Walther Peter, and Günther Franz, eds. *Akten zur Geschichte des Bauernkrieges in Mitteldeutschland.* 2 vols. Jena: Frommann, 1942. Reprinted, Aalen: Scientia, 1964.

Gehring, Paul, ed. *Nördliches Oberschwaben.* Württembergische Ländliche Rechtsquellen, vol. 3. Stuttgart: W. Kohlhammer, 1941.

Hoppeler, Robert, ed. *Die Rechtsquellen des Kantons Zürich.* Part 1: *Offnungen und Hofrechte.* 2 vols. Sammlung Schweizerischer Rechtsquellen, vol. 1. Aarau: Sauerländer, 1910–1915.

Jecklin, Constanz, ed. *Urkunden zur Verfassungsgeschichte Graubündens.* Beilage zu Jahresberichte der historisch-antiquarischen Gesellschaft von Graubünden, 3 issues (with consecutive pagination). Chur: Hitz, 1883–1886.

Leist, Friedrich, ed. *Quellen-Beiträge zur Geschichte des Bauern-Aufruhrs in Salzburg 1525 und 1526.* Salzburg: Kerber, 1888.

Merx, Otto, and Günther Franz, ed. *Akten zur Geschichte des Bauernkriegs in Mitteldeutschland.* 1 vol. in 2. Leipzig: Teubner, 1923–1924. Reprinted, Aalen: Scientia, 1964.

Müller, Walter, ed. *Die Rechtsquellen des Kantons St. Gallen.* Part 1: *Die Rechtsquellen* der Abtei St. Gallen, 2d series, vol. 1: *Die allgemeinen Rechtsquellen der alten Landschaft*. Sammlung Schweizerischer Rechtsquellen, vol. 14. Aarau: Sauerländer, 1974.

Muralt, Leonhard von, and Walter Schmid, eds. *Quellen zur Geschichte der Täufer in der Schweiz*. Zurich: Hirzel, 1952.

Rosenkranz, Albert, ed. *Der Bundschuh. Die Erhebung des südwestdeutschen Bauernstandes in den Jahren 1493–1517*. Vol. 2: *Quellen*. Heidelberg: Carl Winter, 1927.

Schade, Oskar, ed. *Satiren und Pasquille aus der Reformationszeit*. 3 vols. Hannover: C. Rumpeler, 1863.

Schmauss, Johann Jakob, ed. *Neue und vollständige Sammlung der Reichs-Abschiede, Welche von den Zeiten Kayser Konrads des II. bis jetzo auf den Teutschen Reichs-Tagen abgefasst worden*. 2 vols. Frankfurt am Main: E. A. Koch, 1747.

Steck, Rudolf, and Gustav Tobler, eds. *Aktensammlung zur Geschichte der Berner Reformation 1521–1532*. Vol. 1. Bern: K. J. Wyss Erben, 1923.

Strickler, Johannes, ed. *Actensammlung zur Schweizerischen Reformationsgeschichte in den Jahren 1521–1532 im Anschluss an die gleichzeitigen eidgenössischen Abschiede*. Vol. 1: *1521–1528*. Zurich: Meyer & Zeller Reprint. Zurich: Theologische Buchhandlung, 1989.

————, ed. *Amtliche Sammlung der älteren eidgenössischen Abschiede*. Vol. 4,1a. Lucerne, 1876.

Struck, Wolf-Heino, ed. *Der Bauernkrieg am Mittelrhein und in Hessen. Darstellung und Quellen*. Veröffentlichungen der Historischen Kommission für Nassau, vol. 21. Wiesbaden: Selbstverlag der Historischen Kommission für Nassau, 1975.

Stupperich, Robert, ed. *Martin Bucers Deutsche Schriften*. Vol. 1: *Frühschriften 1520–1524*. Martini Buceri opera omnia, Series I. Gütersloh: Gerd Mohn; Paris: Presses Universitaires de France, 1960.

Vischer, Wilhelm, and Alfred Stern, eds. *Basler Chroniken*. Vol. 1. Leipzig, 1872.

Vogt, Wilhelm, ed. "Die Correspondenz des schwäbischen Bundeshauptmannes Ulrich Artzt von Augsburg aus den Jahren 1524–1527. Ein Beitrag zur Geschichte des Schwäbischen Bundes und des Bauernkrieges." *Zeitschrift des Historischen Vereins für Schwaben und Neuburg* 6 (1879): 281–404; 7 (1880): 233–380; 9 (1882): 1–62; 10 (1883): 1–298.

Wopfner, Hermann, ed. *Quellen zur Geschichte des Bauernkrieges in Deutschtirol 1525*. Acta Tirolensia, vol. 3. Innsbruck: Wagner, 1908. Reprinted, Aalen: Scientia, 1973.

Zingerle, Ignaz von, and Joseph Egger, eds. *Die Tirolischen Weistümer*. Part 4: *Burggrafenamt und Etschland*. Österreichische Weistümer, vol. 5. Vienna: Braumüller, 1888.

SECONDARY WORKS

Althaus, Paul. "Luthers Haltung im Bauernkrieg. Ein Beitrag zur lutherischen Sozialethik." In Paul Althaus, *Evangelium und Leben*, 144–190. Gütersloh: Gerd Mohn, 1927. Quotes are taken from the reprint, Basel, 1953.

Arnold, Klaus. "Damit der am man vnnd gemainer nutz iren furgang haben . . . Zum deutschen 'Bauernkrieg' als politischer Bewegung: Wendel Hiplers und Friedrich Weygandts Pläne einer 'Reformation' des Reiches." *Zeitschrift für Historische Forschung* 9 (1982): 257–313.

————. "Die Stadt Kitzingen im Bauernkrieg." *Mainfränkisches Jahrbuch für Geschichte und Kunst* 287 (1975): 11–50.

Bader, Karl Siegfried. *Ausgewählte Schriften zur Rechts- und Landesgeschichte*. 3 vols. Sigmaringen: Jan Thorbecke, 1983–1984.

————. *Dorfgenossenschaft und Dorfgemeinde. Studien zur Rechtsgeschichte des mittelalterlichen Dorfes*, vol. 2. 2d ed. Weimar: H. Böhlaus Nachfolger, 1962.

Bátori, Ingrid, ed. *Städtische Gesellschaft und Reformation. Kleine Schriften 2.* Spätmittelalter und Frühe Neuzeit. Tübinger Beiträge zur Geschichtsforschung, vol. 12. Stuttgart: Klett-Cotta, 1980.

Becker, Winfried. *Reformation und Revolution. Katholisches Leben und Kirchenreform im Zeitalter der Glaubensspaltung,* vol. 34. Münster: Aschendorff, 1974.

Bierbrauer, Peter. "Das Göttliche Recht und die naturrechtliche Tradition." In Peter Blickle, ed., *Bauer, Reich und Reformation. Festschrift für Günther Franz zum 80. Geburtstag,* 21–34. Stuttgart: Eugen Ulmer, 1982.

Black, Antony. *Guilds and Civil Society in European Political Thought from the Twelfth Century to the Present.* London: Methuen, 1984.

Blickle, Peter. "Bäuerliche Rebellionen im Fürststift St. Gallen." In Peter Blickle., ed., *Aufruhr und Empörung? Studien zum bäuerlichen Widerstand im Alten Reich,* 215–295. Munich: R. Oldenbourg, 1980.

———. *Deutsche Untertanen. Ein Widerspruch.* Munich: C. H. Beck, 1981.

———. *Landschaften im Alten Reich. Die staatliche Funktion des gemeinen Mannes in Oberdeutschland.* Munich: R. Oldenbourg, 1973.

———. "Nochmals zur Entstehung der Zwölf Artikel." In Peter Blickle, ed., *Bauer, Reich und Reformation. Festschrift für Günther Franz zum 80. Geburtstag,* 286–308. Suttgart: Eugen Ulmer, 1982.

———. *Die Reformation im Reich.* Uni-Taschenbücher, vol. 1181. Stuttgart: Eugen Ulmer, 1982.

———. *Die Revolution von 1525.* Munich: R. Oldenbourg, 1975. 2d ed., 1981.

Blickle, Peter, Andreas Lindt, and Alfred Schindler, eds., *Zwingli und Europa. Referate und Protokoll des Internationalen Kongresses aus Anlaß des 500. Geburtstages von Huldrych Zwingli vom 26. bis 30. März 1984.* Zurich: Vandenhoeck & Ruprecht, 1985.

Blickle, Peter, and Renate Blickle. *Schwaben von 1268 bis 1803.* Dokumente zur Geschichte von Staat und Gesellschaft in Bayern, part II, vol. 4. Munich: C. H. Beck, 1979.

Böckmann, Paul. "Der gemeine Mann in den Flugschriften der Reformation." *Deutsche Vierteljahreschrift für Literaturwissenschaft und Geistesgeschichte* 22 (1944): 186–230.

Brady, Thomas A., Jr. *Ruling Class, Regime and Reformation in Strasbourg, 1520–1555.* Studies in Medieval and Reformation Thought, vol. 22. Leiden: E. J. Brill, 1978.

———. *Turning Swiss: Cities and Empires, 1450–1550.* Cambridge Studies in Early Modern History. Cambridge and New York: Cambridge University Press, 1985.

Brendler, Gerhard. *Martin Luther. Theologie und Revolution.* Berlin: Akademie-Verlag, 1983.

Bücking, Jürgen. *Michael Gaismair: Reformer-Sozialrebell-Revolutionär. Seine Rolle im Tiroler 'Bauernkrieg' (1525/32).* Spätmittelalter und Frühe Neuzeit. Tübinger Beiträge zur Geschichtsforschung, vol. 5. Stuttgart: Klett-Cotta, 1978.

Burke, Peter. *Popular Culture in Early Modern Europe.* New York: Harper & Row, 1978.

Christian, William A., Jr. *Local Religion in Sixteenth-Century Spain.* Princeton: Princeton University Press, 1981.

Claus, Helmut. *Der deutsche Bauernkrieg im Druckschaffen der Jahre 1524–1526. Verzeichnis der Flugschriften und Dichtungen.* Veröffentlichungen der Forschungsbibliothek Gotha, vol. 16. Gotha: Method. Zentrum für wissenschaftliche Bibliotheken, 1975.

Cole, Richard G. "The Reformation Pamphlet and Communication Processes." In Hans-Joachim Köhler, ed., *Flugschriften als Massenmedium der Reformationszeit. Beiträge zum Tübinger Symposion 1980,* Spätmittelalter und Frühe Neuzeit. Tübinger Beiträge zur Geschichtsforschung, vol. 13, 139–161. Stuttgart: Klett-Cotta, 1981.

Conrad, Franziska, *Reformation in der bäuerlichen Gesellschaft. Zur Rezeption reformatorischer Theologie im Elsaß.* Veröffentlichungen des Instituts für Europäische Geschichte Mainz, vol. 116. Stuttgart: Franz Steiner, 1984.

Davis, Natalie Z. "Some Tasks and Themes in the Study of Popular Religion." In Charles

Trinkhaus and Heiko A. Oberman, eds., *The Pursuit of Holiness in Late Medieval and Renaissance Religion. Papers from the University of Michigan Conference*, Studies in Medieval and Reformation Thought, vol. 10, 307–336. Leidan: E. J. Brill, 1974.

Demandt, Dieter. "Konflikte um die geistlichen Standesprivilegien im spätmittelalterlichen Colmar," in Ingrid Bátori, ed., *Städtische Gesellschaft und Reformation. Kleine Schriften 2*, Spätmittelalter und Frühe Nezeit. Tübinger Beiträge zur Geschichtsforschung, vol. 12, 136–154. Stuttgart: Klett-Cotta, 1980.

Dickens, Arthur G. *The German Nation and Martin Luther*. New York: Harper & Row, 1974.

Diehl, Adolf. "Gemeiner Nutzen im Mittelalter. Nach süddeutschen Quellen." *Zeitschrift für württembergische Landesgeschichte* 1 (1937): 296–315.

Dörrer, Fridolin, ed. *Die Bauernkriege und Michael Gaismair*. Veröffentlichungen des Tiroler Landesarchivs, vol. 2. Innsbruck: Tiroler Landesarchiv, 1982.

Dülmen, Richard van. *Reformation als Revolution. Soziale Bewegung und religiöser Radikalismus in der deutschen Reformation*. Munich: Deutscher Taschenbuch Verlag, 1977.

Edwards, Mark U., Jr. *Luther and the False Brethren*. Stanford: Stanford University Press, 1975.

Egli, Gottfried. "Die Reformation im Toggenburg." Dissertation, Zurich, 1955.

Ehrbrecht, Wilfried. "Köln—Osnabrück—Stralsund. Rat und Bürgerschaft hansischer Städte zwischen religiöser Erneuerung und Bauernkrieg." In Franz Petri, ed., *Kirche und gesellschaftlicher Wandel in deutschen und niederländischen Städten der werdenden Neuzeit*, Städteforschung, vol. A 10, 23–63. Cologne and Vienna: Böhlau, 1980.

Eitel, Peter. *Die oberschwäbischen Reichsstädte im Zeitalter der Zunftherrschaft. Untersuchungen zu ihrer politischen und sozialen Struktur unter besonderer Berücksichtigung der Städte Lindau, Memmingen, Ravensburg und Überlingen*. Schriften zur südwestdeutschen Landeskunde, vol. 8. Stuttgart: Müller & Gräff, 1970.

Farner, Alfred. *Die Lehre von Kirche und Staat bei Zwingli*. Tübingen: J. C. B. Mohr (Paul Siebeck), 1930.

Franz, Günther. *Der deutsche Bauernkrieg*. 11th ed. Darmstadt: Wissenschaftliche Buchgesellschaft, 1977.

Goertz, Hans-Jürgen. "Aufstand gegen den Priester. Antiklerikalismus und reformatorische Bewegungen." In Peter Blickle, ed., *Bauer, Reich und Reformation. Festschrift für Günther Franz zum 80. Geburtstag*, 182–209. Stuttgart: Eugen Ulmer, 1982.

————. *Die Täufer. Geschichte und Deutung*. Munich: C. H. Beck, 1980.

————, ed. *Umstrittenes Täufertum, 1525–1975. Neue Forschungen*. Göttingen: Vandenhoeck & Ruprecht, 1975.

Grenzmann, Ludger, and Karl Stackmann, eds. *Literatur und Laienbildung im Spätmittelalter und in der Reformationszeit. Symposion Wolfenbüttel 1981*. Stuttgart: J. B. Metzler, 1984.

Greyerz, Kaspar von. "Religion und Gesellschaft in der frühen Neuzeit. (Einführung in Methoden und Ergebnisse der sozialgeschichtlichen Religionsforschung)." *Schweizerische Gesellschaft für Wirtschafts- und Sozialgeschichte* 3 (1984): 13–36.

Guggisberg, Hans R., and Hans Füglister. "Die Basler Weberzunft als Trägerin der reformatorischen Propaganda." In Bernd Moeller, ed., *Stadt und Kirche im 16. Jahrhundert*, Schriften des Vereins für Reformationsgeschichte, no. 190, 48–56. Gütersloh: Gerd Mohn, 1978.

Häne, Johannes. "Der Klosterbruch zu Rorschach und der St. Galler Krieg 1489–1490." *Mitteilungen zur vaterländischen Geschichte*, hg. vom Historischen Verein des Kantons St. Gallen 26 (1895): 1–272.

Hippel, Wolfgang von. *Die Bauernbefreiung im Königreich Württemberg*. Vol. 1. Forschungen zur deutschen Sozialgeschichte, vol. I,1. Boppard am Rhein: Harald Boldt, 1977.

Jahns, Sigrid. *Frankfurt, Reformation und Schmalkaldischer Bund. Die Reformations-, Reichs- und Bündnispolitik der Reichsstadt Frankfurt am Main 1525–1536.* Studien zur Frankfurter Geschichte, vol. 9. Frankfurt am Main: Kramer, 1976.

Jezler, Peter, Elke Jezler, and Christine Göttler. "Warum ein Bilderstreit? Der Kampf gegen die 'Götzen' in Zürich als Beispiel." *Unsere Kunstdenkmäler* 35 (1984): 276–296.

Kaser, Kurt. *Politische und soziale Bewegungen im deutschen Bürgertum zu Beginn des 16. Jahrhunderts mit besonderer Rücksicht auf den Speyerer Aufstand im Jahre 1512.* Stuttgart: W. Kohlhammer, 1899.

Kießling, Rolf. *Bürgerliche Gesellschaft und Kirche in Augsburg im Spätmittelalter. Ein Beitrag zur Strukturanalyse der oberdeutschen Reichsstadt.* Abhandlungen zur Geschichte der Stadt Augsburg, vol. 19. Augsburg: Mühlberger, 1971.

Kirchner, Hubert. "Der deutsche Bauernkrieg im Urteil der Freunde und Schüler Luthers." Unpublished Habilitationsschrift. Greifswald, 1969.

Köhler, Hans-Joachim. "Erste Schritte zu einem Meinungsprofil der frühen Reformationszeit." In Volker Press and Dieter Stievermann, eds., *Martin Luther. Probleme seiner Zeit,* 244–281. Stuttgart: Klett-Cotta, 1985.

———. ed. *Flugschriften als Massenmedium der Reformationszeit. Beiträge zum Tübinger Symposion 1980.* Spätmittelalter und Frühe Neuzeit. Tübinger Beiträge zur Geschichtsforschung, vol. 13. Stuttgart: Klett-Cotta, 1981.

Kurze, Dietrich. *Pfarrerwahlen im Mittelalter. Ein Beitrag zur Geschichte der Gemeinde und des Niederkirchenwesens.* Forschungen zur kirchlichen Rechtsgeschichte, vol. 6. Cologne and Graz: Böhlau, 1966.

Lang, Peter Thaddäus. "Würfel, Wein und Wettersegen—Klerus und Gläubige im Bistum Eichstätt am Vorabend der Reformation." In Volker Press and Dieter Stievermann, eds., *Martin Luther. Probleme seiner Zeit,* 219–243. Stuttgart: Klett-Cotta, 1985.

Lau, Franz. "Der Bauernkrieg und das angebliche Ende der lutherischen Reformation als spontaner Volksbewegung." *Luther-Jahrbuch* 26 (1959): 109–134. Reprinted in Walther Hubatsch, ed., *Wirkungen der deutschen Reformation bis 1555,* Wege der Forschung, vol. 203, 69–100. Darmstadt: Wissenschaftliche Buchgesellschaft, 1967.

Lehmann, Hartmut. "Luther und der Bauernkrieg." *Geschichte in Wissenschaft und Unterricht* 20 (1969): 129–139.

Lienhard, Marc. *Martin Luther. Un temps, une vie, un message.* Paris and Geneva: Labor et Fides, 1983.

———. "Mentalité populaire, gens d'église et mouvement évangélique à Strasbourg en 1522–1523: Le pamphlet 'Ein brüderlich warnung an meister Mathis . . .' de Steffan von Büllheym." In *Horizons européens de la réforme en Alsace. Mélange offerts à Jean Rott,* 37–62. Strasbourg: Librairie Istra, 1980.

Locher, Gottfried W. "Grundzüge der Theologie Huldrych Zwinglis im Vergleich mit derjenigen Martin Luthers und Johannes Calvins," in Gottfried W. Locher, *Huldrych Zwingli in neuer Sicht. Zehn Beiträge zur Theologie des Zürcher Reformators,* 173–274. Zurich and Stuttgart: Zwingli-Verlag, 1969.

———. *Die Zwinglische Reformation im Rahmen der europäischen Kirchengeschichte.* Göttingen and Zurich: Vandenhoeck & Ruprecht, 1979.

Loosz-Corswarem, Clemens von. "Die Kölner Artikelserie von 1525. Hintergründe und Verlauf des Aufruhrs von 1525 in Köln." In Franz Petri, ed., *Kirche und gesellschaftlicher Wandel in deutschen und niederländischen Städten der werdenden Neuzeit,* 65–153. Städteforschung, vol. A 10. Cologne and Vienna: Böhlau, 1980.

Lutz, Robert H. *Wer war der gemeine Mann? Der dritte Stand in der Krise des Spätmittelalters.* Munich: R. Oldenbourg, 1979.

Maier, Hans. *Die ältere deutsche Staats- u. Verwaltungslehre.* 2d. ed. Munich: C. H. Beck, 1980.

Maurer, Hans-Martin. "Der Bauernkrieg als Massenerhebung. Dynamik einer revolutionären Bewegung." In *Bausteine zur geschichtlichen Landeskunde von Baden-Württemberg*, ed. Günther Haselier, 255–295. Stuttgart: W. Kohlhammer, 1979.

Maurer, Justus. *Prediger im Bauernkrieg*. Calwer Theologische Monographien, vol. 5. Stuttgart: Calwer Verlag, 1979.

Moeller, Bernd. *Deutschland im Zeitalter der Reformation*. Deutsche Geschichte, vol. 4. Göttingen: Vandenhoeck & Ruprecht, 1977.

———. "Kleriker als Bürger," in *Festschrift für Hermann Heimpel zum 70. Geburtstag*, Veröffentlichungen des Max-Planck-Instituts für Geschichte, vol. 36, 2, 195–224. Göttingen: Vandenhoeck & Ruprecht, 1972.

———. "Luther und die Städte." In Bernd Moeller, *Aus der Lutherforschung. Drei Vorträge*, edited by the Gemeinsame Kommission der Rheinisch-Westfälischen Akademie der Wissenschaften and the Gerda-Henkel-Stiftung, 9–26. Cologne and Opladen: Westdeutscher Verlag, 1983.

———. *Reichsstadt und Reformation*. Schriften des Vereins für Reformationsgeschichte, no. 180. Gütersloh: Gerd Mohn, 1962.

———. "Stadt und Buch." In Wolfgang J. Mommsen, ed., *Stadtbürgertum und Adel in der Reformation*, Veröffentlichungen des Deutschen Historischen Instituts London, vol. 5. Stuttgart: Klett-Cotta, 1979.

———. ed. *Stadt und Kirche im 16. Jahrhundert*. Schriften des Vereins für Reformationsgeschichte, no. 190. Gütersloh: Gerd Mohn, 1978.

———. "Zwinglis Disputationen. Studien zu den Anfängen der Kirchenbildung und des Synodalwesens im Protestantismus." 2 parts. *Zeitschrift der Savigny-Stiftung für Rechtsgeschichte, Kanonistische Abteilung* 56 (1970): 272–324; 60 (1974): 213–364.

Mörke, Olaf. *Rat und Bürger in der Reformation. Soziale Gruppen und kirchlicher Wandel in den welfischen Hansestädten Lüneburg, Braunschweig und Göttingen*. Veröffentlichungen des Instituts für historische Landesforschung der Universität Göttingen, vol. 19. Hildesheim: August Lax, 1983.

Mommsen, Wolfgang J., ed. *Stadtbürgertum und Adel in der Reformation. Studien zur Sozialgeschichte der Reformation in England und Deutschland*. Veröffentlichungen des Deutschen Historischen Instituts London, vol. 9. Stuttgart: Klett-Cotta, 1979.

Müller, Walter. "Wurzeln und Bedeutung des grundsätzlichen Widerstandes gegen die Leibeigenschaft im Bauernkrieg 1525." *Schriften des Vereins für Geschichte des Bodensees und seiner Umgebung* 93 (1975): 1–41.

Muralt, Leonhard von. "Renaissance und Reformation," in *Handbuch der Schweizer Geschichte*, vol. 1: 1–41. Zurich: Verlag Berichthaus, 1972.

———. "Stadtgemeinde und Reformation in der Schweiz." *Zeitschrift für Schweizerische Geschichte* 10 (1930): 349–570.

Obelkevich, James, ed. *Religion and the People, 800–1700*. Chapel Hill: University of North Carolina Press, 1979.

Oberman, Heiko A. *Werden und Wertung der Reformation. Vom Wegestreit zum Glaubenskampf*. Tübingen: J. C. B. Mohr [Paul Siebeck], 1977.

Ozment, Steven E. *The Reformation in the Cities. The Appeal of Protestantism to Sixteenth-Century Germany and Switzerland*. New Haven and London: Yale University Press, 1975.

Peuckert, Will-Erich. *Deutscher Volksglaube des Spätmittelalters*. Stuttgart: Spemann, 1942. Reprinted, Hildesheim and New York: Georg Olms, 1978.

Pfeiffer, Gerhard. "Das Verhältnis von politischer und kirchlicher Gemeinde in den deutschen Reichsstädten." In Walther Peter Fuchs, ed., *Staat und Kirche im Wandel der Jahrhunderte*, 79–99. Stuttgart: W. Kohlhammer, 1966.

Postel, Rainer, "Bürgerausschüsse und Reformation in Hamburg." In Wilfried Ehbrecht, ed., *Städtische Führungsgruppen und Gemeinde in der werdenden Neuzeit*, Städteforschung, vol. A 9. 369–383. Cologne and Vienna: Böhlau, 1980.

Rammstedt, Otthein. "Stadtunruhen 1525." In Hans-Ulrich Wehler, ed., *Der Deutsche Bauernkrieg 1524–1526*, Geschichte und Gesellschaft, Sonderheft 1, 239–276. Göttingen: Vandenhoeck & Ruprecht, 1975.

Rapp, Francis. *Réformes et Réformation à Strasbourg. Eglise et société dans le diocèse de Strasbourg (1450–1525)*. Collection de l'Institut des Hautes Etudes Alsaciennes 23. Paris: Éditions Ophrys, 1974.

Rogge, Joachim. *Der Beitrag des Predigers Jakob Strauss zur frühen Reformationsgeschichte*. Theologische Arbeiten, vol. 6. Berlin: Evangelische Verlagsanstalt, 1957.

Rosenkranz, Albert. *Der Bundschuh. Die Erhebungen des südwestdeutschen Bauernstandes in den Jahren 1493–1517*. Vol. 1: *Darstellung*. Heidelberg: Carl Winter, 1927.

Rublack, Hans-Christoph. *Eine bürgerliche Reformation: Nördlingen*. Quellen und Forschungen zur Reformationsgeschichte, vol. 51. Gütersloh: Gerd Mohn, 1982.

———. "Forschungsbericht Stadt und Reformation." In Bernd Moeller, ed., *Stadt und Kirche im 16. Jahrhundert*. Schriften des Vereins für Reformationsgeschichte, no. 190, 9–26. Gütersloh: Gerd Mohn, 1978.

———. *Gescheiterte Reformation. Frühreformatorische und protestantische Bewegungen in süd- und westdeutschen geistlichen Residenzen*. Spätmittelalter und Frühe Neuzeit. Tübinger Beiträge zur Geschichtsforschung, vol. 4. Stuttgart: Klett-Cotta, 1978.

———. "Die Reformation in Kitzingen." In Dieter Demandt and Hans-Christoph Rublack, *Stadt und Kirche In Kitzingen. Darstellung und Quellen zu Spätmittelalter und Reformation*, Spätmittelalter und Frühe Neuzeit. Tübinger Beiträge zur Geschichtsforschung, vol. 10, 34–96, 101–321. Stuttgart: Klett-Cotta, 1978.

Sablonier, Roger. "Das Dorf im Übergang vom Hoch- zum Spätmittelalter. Untersuchungen zum Wandel ländlicher Gemeinschaftsformen im ostschweizerischen Raum." In Lutz Fenske, Werner Rösener, and Thomas Zotz, eds., *Institutionen, Kultur und Gesellschaft im Mittelalter. Festschrift für Josef Fleckenstein*, 727–745. Sigmaringen: Jan Thorbecke, 1984.

Schildhauer, Johannes. *Soziale, politische und religiöse Auseinandersetzungen in den Hansestädten Stralsund, Rostock und Wismar im ersten Drittel des 16. Jahrhunderts*. Abhandlungen zur Handels- und Sozialgeschichte, vol. 2. Weimar: Böhlau, 1959.

Schilling, Heinz. "Aufstandsbewegungen in der stadtbürgerlichen Gesellschaft des Alten Reiches. Die Vorgeschichte des Münsteraner Täuferreichs, 1525–1534." In Hans-Ulrich Wehler, ed., *Der Deutsche Bauernkrieg 1524–1526*, Geschichte und Gesellschaft, Sonderheft 1, 293–238. Göttingen: Vandenhoeck & Ruprecht, 1975.

———. *Konfessionskonflikt und Staatsbildung. Eine Fallstudie über das Verhältnis von religiösem und sozialem Wandel in der Frühneuzeit am Beispiel der Grafschaft Lippe*. Quellen und Forschungen zur Reformationsgeschichte, 48. Gütersloh: Gerd Mohn, 1982.

Schmidt, Heinrich R. *Reichsstädte, Reich und Reformation. Korporative Religionspolitik 1521–1529/30*. Veröffentlichungen des Instituts für Europäische Geschichte Mainz, vol. 122. Wiesbaden: Franz Steiner, 1986.

Schultze, Alfred. *Stadtgemeinde und Reformation*. Recht und Staat in Geschichte und Gegenwart, no. 11. Tübingen: J. C. B. Mohr (Paul Siebeck), 1918.

Schulze, Winfried, ed. *Aufstände, Revolten, Prozesse. Beiträge zu bäuerlichen Widerstandsbewegungen im frühneuzeitlichen Europa*. Geschichte und Gesellschaft. Bochumer Historische Studien, vol. 27. Stuttgart: Klett-Cotta, 1983.

Scribner, Robert W. "Civic Unity and the Reformation in Erfurt." *Past and Present* 66 (1975): 29–66.

———. "Flugblatt und Analphabetentum. Wie kam der gemeine Mann zu reformatorischen Ideen?" In Hans-Joachim Köhler, ed., *Flugschriften als Massenmedium der Reformationszeit. Beiträge zum Tübinger Symposion 1980*, Spätmittelalter und Frühe Neuzeit. Tübinger Beiträge zur Geschichtsforschung, vol. 13, 65–76. Stuttgart: Klett-Cotta, 1981.

———. *For the Sake of Simple Folk. Popular Propaganda for the German Reformation.* Cambridge Studies in Oral and Literate Culture, vol. 2. Cambridge: Cambridge University Press, 1981.

Seebass, Gottfried. "Stadt und Kirche in Nürnberg im Zeitalter der Reformation." In Bernd Moeller, ed., *Stadt und Kirche im 16. Jahrhundert*, Schriften des Vereins für Reformationsgeschichte, no. 190, 66–86. Gütersloh: Gerd Mohn, 1978.

Spitz, Lewis, ed. *Humanismus und Reformation als Kulturelle Kräfte in der deutschen Geschichte.* Veröffentlichungen der Historischen Kommission zu Berlin, vol. 51. Berlin and New York: W. de Gruyter, 1981.

Stratenwerth, Heide. *Die Reformation in der Stadt Osnabrück.* Veröffentlichungen des Instituts für Europäische Geschichte Mainz, vol. 61. Wiesbaden: Franz Steiner, 1971.

Thomas, Keith. *Religion and the Decline of Magic.* New York: Scribner, 1971.

Vasella, Oskar. "Bauernkrieg und Reformation in Graubünden 1525–1526." *Zeitschrift für Schweizerische Geschichte* 20 (1940): 1–65.

———. "Die Entstehung der bündnerischen Bauernartikel vom 25. June 1526." *Zeitschrift für Schweizerische Geschichte* 21 (1941): 58–78.

Vogler, Günther. "Ein Vorspiel des deutschen Bauernkrieges im Nürnberger Landgebiet 1524." In Gerhard Heitz et al., eds., *Der Bauer im Klassenkampf. Studien zur Geschichte des deutschen Bauernkrieges und der bäuerlichen Klassenkämpfe im Spätfeudalismus*, 49–81. Berlin: Akademie-Verlag, 1975.

———. *Nürnberg 1524/25. Studien zur Geschichte der reformatorischen und sozialen Bewegung in der Reichstadt.* Berlin: Deutscher Verlag der Wissenshaften, 1982.

Wackernagel, Rudolf. *Geschichte der Stadt Basel.* Vol. 3. Basel: Helbing & Lichtenhahn, 1924.

Walder, Ernst. "Reformation und moderner Staat." *Archiv des Historischen Vereins des Kantons Bern* 64/65 (1980/81): 445–583.

Walder, Ernst. "Das torechte Leben von 1477 in der bernischen Politik 1477 bis 1481," *Berner Zeitschrift für Geschichte und Heimatkunde* 45 (1983): 74–134.

Weinstein, Donald, and Rudolph M. Bell. *Saints and Society. The Two Worlds of Western Christendom, 1000–1700.* Chicago and London: University of Chicago Press, 1982.

Wohlfeil, Rainer. *Einführung in die Geschichte der deutschen Reformation.* Munich: C. H. Beck, 1982.

———. "Das Schicksal der Reformation vor und nach dem Augsburger Reichstag." In Bernhard Lohse and Otto Hermann Pesch, eds., *Das 'Augsburger Bekenntnis' von 1530 damals und heute*, 79–98. Munich: Kaiser, 1980.

Zimmermann, Gunter. *Die Antwort der Reformatoren auf die Zehntenfrage. Eine Analyse des Zusammenhanges von Reformation und Bauernkrieg.* Europäische Hochschulschriften, ser. III, vol. 164. Frankfurt am Main and Bern: Peter Lang, 1982.

Index

"Admonition to Peace in Response to
the 'Twelve Articles' of the Peasants
in Swabia" (Luther), 123, 140–44
"Admonition to Peace in Response to
the 'Twelve Articles' of the Peasants
in Swabia, Also Against the Robbing
and Murdering Hordes of the Other
Peasants" (Luther), 144
"Against the Robbing and Murdering
Hordes of the Peasants" (Luther),
142–43, 144
Agreement of Tübingen, 196–97
Agricola, Johann, 199, 200
Alber, Matthäus (preacher of
Reutingen), 75
Albrecht I (king of Germany), 173
Allgäu: godly justice in, 137–39;
opposition to serfdom in, 137–38;
peasants' reformation, 13, 20, 22–23,
25, 26, 27, 44
Allgäu Band, 22–23
Alsace: evangelical movement in, 101;
late medieval changes in, 164;
peasants' reformation in, 13, 14, 102;
peasant theology in, 12; political order
in, 50; preaching ordinance in, 74–75,
83; tithe in, 42; urban reformation in,
102
Althaus, Paul, 144
Altruism, 29, 124
Amorbach Articles, 31, 32
Anabaptist movement, 3, 51, 104–6,
114, 125, 126
Andlau, Peter von, 154
Anshelm, Valerius (chronicler of Bern),
198
Anticlericalism. See Common man,
opposition to clergy
Appenzell: in Swiss Confederation,
171–72; war in (15th century), 169
Arnoldi of Usingen, 65
Assault on the clergy (Pfaffensturm), 64
Augsburg: late medieval changes in,
157–58, 163; role of guilds in, 163
Austria, duchy of: political order in, 51

Baden, margraviate of: defeat of peasants
in, 107; territorial constitution for,
195
Bader, Karl Siegfried, 163, 164, 167
Baltringen Band, 23, 26, 44
Baltringen region, peasants' reformation
in, 13, 20, 26, 43, 44
Bamberg, urban reformation in, 102
Basel: peasants' reformation in, 31; role
of guilds in, 71–73, 85; urban
reformation in, 69–73, 83, 102
Becker, Winfried, 46
Beggell, Jakob, 138
Bern, peasants' reformation in, 31,
51–52, 53
Bern Disputation, 51, 52
Bertschi, Max, 70
Beyerle, Konrad, 171
Billiter, Nikolaus, 17
Black Band, 30
Black Forest: peasants' reformation in,
13, 33, 47; Peasants' War in, 72;
political order in, 50
Bloch, Marc, 169
Böckmann, Paul, 132
Bopfingen, defeat of peasants in, 107
Botho of Stolberg (count), 75
Brady, Thomas A., Jr., 82, 83
Brandenburg: communal representation
in, 177; peasants' reformation in, 13,
14
Breisgau: peasants' reformation in, 33;
Peasants' War in, 72
Brenz, Johannes, 124, 199, 200
Bucer, Martin: and doctrine of
justification, 113; opposition to
common man, 199; pamphlets by,
128, 129, 130; and people's
reformation, 3; and role of community
in church, 124–25
Burghers' reformation. See Reformation,
urban

Capito, Wolfgang, 199
Casimir of Brandenburg–Ansbach

(margrave), 15, 67, 68, 201
Catholic Forest Cantons, 51
Charles V (Holy Roman emperor), 197,
198
Christian, William A., Jr., 184
Christian humanists, 113–14
Christian Unions, 13, 14, 20–21, 24,
26, 47, 50, 102
Chur, bishopric of. *See* Graubünden,
canton of
Church constitutions (*Kirchenordnungen*),
82, 194
Church wardens (*Kirchenpfleger*), 165
Clandestine preachers (*Winkelprediger*),
127
Clergy: dispute over support of, 14–15,
18; forgery by, 45, 61n.182;
identifying nonevangelical, 127;
immunity of, 79; and Luther's
priesthood of all believers, 122, 123;
obligations of citizenship on, 77,
79–81, 102; opposition to, 16, 17–18;
pluralism among, 38
Colmar, evangelical movement in, 87
Cologne, archbishopric of: peasants'
reformation in, 13
Common man: definition of, 4–5, 102;
opposition to, 199; opposition to
clergy, 16, 17–18, 21–22, 64–65, 77.
See also People (*das Volk*)
Common weal, 47, 48, 133, 181–82
Communalization: administration and
justice, 159–64; and adoption of
reformation ideas, 178–84; of the
church, 164–68; definition of, 154–55;
and dissolution of high medieval
structures, 155–59; and outside
authority, 168–76; and representation,
176–78
Communal reformation, 100–101, 104–8,
115
Communication: acting, 115; literary,
115–20, 132; oral, 115; and
popularizing of reformation, 126–32;
visual, 115
Community (*Gemeinde*): authority over
clergy, 14–16, 19, 20–26, 27, 28, 30,
31–32, 33, 34–39, 75, 123, 165; as
basis of political order, 49–50, 184;
and church, 111–112, 153; and
development of administrative
structures, 159–64; as idea in theology

of Luther, 120–23; and people's
reformation, 3, 84–86, 99–101;
pre-Reformation form of, 79;
relationship to outside world, 168–76;
role in communal reformation,
100–101; theological justification for
control by, 40–46, 99; as unifying
idea, 6, 111
Compact of Stans, 168, 195
"Complaint and Answer of Lutheran and
Popish Priests" (a Lutheran pastor),
128
Confederacy of Uri, Schwyz, and
Nidwalden, 153
Conrad, Franziska, 119
Consultations of the districts
(*Ämterbefragungen*), 101
"Conversation booklet New Karsthans"
(Bucer), 128–29
Culsaner, Johann, 65

Davis, Natalie Z., 184
Dickens, Arthur G., 2, 63
Diebold, Kunz, 47
Ditmarsh, 153, 166

Eberlin von Günzburg, Johannes, 128,
129–30, 199
Ecclesiastical courts, 35, 36, 39–40
"Eighteen Conclusions Concerning a
Wholly Christian Life, Wherein it
Consists" (Hubmaier), 125
Engadin, development of administrative
structures in, 160
English Peasants' War (1381), 169
Equality, and people's reformation, 3
Erasmus of Rotterdam, 69, 175
Erfurt: Peasants' War in, 65; urban
reformation in, 64–67, 69, 83, 102
Erfurt Articles, 66
Ethical principles, for social and political
order, 46–49, 99, 100
Evangelical movement, 63, 65, 67, 68,
70, 75–77, 82, 85, 86–88, 101, 106
Fig. 2, 194
"Exposition and Basis of the
Conclusions" (Zwingli), 132–33, 136

Farner, Alfred, 126
Febvre, Lucien, 116
Federal Ordinance (*Bundesordnung*), 13,
14, 26, 33, 36, 42, 44, 139

Feine, Hans Erich, 164
Ferdinand (archduke of Austria), 27, 43, 44, 75
Feudalism. *See* Manorial system (*Villikationssystem*); Serfdom
Franconia: Anabaptist movement in, 105; decisions on theological disputes in, 43; defeat of peasants in, 104; late medieval changes in, 164; peasants' reformation in, 13, 14, 15–16, 31, 32, 33, 38, 102; Peasants' War in, 68; political order in, 51; tithe in, 42; urban reformation in, 102
Frankfurt, appointment of clergy in, 84
Franz, Günter, 107
Freiburg im Breisgau, peasants' reformation in, 13

Gaisberg, Franz, 36
Gaismair, Michael, 3, 13, 26, 56n.66
Gebhard (pastor of Gantersheim), 37
George of Brandenburg (margrave), 201
Gerber, Erasmus, 13
Glarus, peasants' reformation in, 52, 53
Göldi, Heinrich, 16
Good administration (*gute Polizei*), 81
Gospel, 73–74, 98–99, 100, 103, 105, 111, 126, 127, 133–34, 137, 142, 153, 199–201
Graubünden, canton of: election of pastors in, 166; peasants' reformation in, 13, 33–36, 52, 53
Gray League (*Grauer Bund*), 34
Guild democracy (*Zunftdemokratie*), 162
Guilds, 71–73, 85, 102, 162–63

Habsburgs, and peasants' reformation, 13, 75
Hainzelmännin von Bachen, Nesa, 138
Hamburg: disputation of, 86; reformation committee in, 85; urban reformation in, 108
Heilbronn: defeat of peasants in, 107; role of guilds in, 102; urban reformation in, 108
Hesse: communal representation in, 177; peasants' reformation in, 14
Hessia, late medieval changes in, 163
Hipler, Wendel, 32
Holl, Karl, 194
Holy Roman Empire, impact of reformation on, 107

Hottinger, Jakob, 17
Household establishment, rule of, 179–80
Hubmaier, Balthasar, 3, 125

Ilanz Articles, 34
Ilanz Manifestos (*Artikelbriefe*), 33, 34, 35–36
"Inexpensive" church, 36, 38–39, 79

Johann (duke of Saxony), 30
John Frederick (duke of Saxony), 124
Justification, doctrine of, 98, 112–15

"Karsthans" (Vadian), 128–29
Kaser, Kurt, 82
Kaufbeuren: defeat of peasants in, 107; evangelical preaching in, 138; role of guilds in, 163
Keller, Robert von, 171
Kempten, grievance list from, 170, 174
Kern, Ulrich, 15
Kessler, Johann, 44
Kettenbach, Heinrich von, 123–24
Kett's Rebellion (1450), 169
Kitzingen, urban reformation in, 67–69, 102
Klettgau: godly justice in, 139; peasants' reformation in, 13, 43, 44
Knüchel, Hans, 130–32
Köhler, Hans-Joachim, 117, 118
Kurze, Dietrich, 165, 166–67

Lachmann, Johannes, 199, 200
Lake Constance region: evangelical movement in, 76; opposition to serfdom in, 48; peasants' reformation in, 13, 20, 24, 25, 26
Lamp, Claus, 126
Land, Matthäus (archbishop), 33
Laslett, Peter, 179
Lateran Council, 79
League of God's House (*Gotteshausbund*), 34
League of the Ten Jurisdictions (*Zehngerichtebund*), 34
League on the Lake (*Bund ob dem See*), 169
Leinhard, Marc, 194
Lordship, 173–76, 182. *See also* Nobility
Lorenz, Dr. (parish priest in Zurich), 16–17
Lorraine, duchy of: peasants' reformation

in, 14; political order in, 51
Lotzer, Sebastian, 13
Luther, Martin: compared to Müntzer, 114–15; compared to Zwingli, 113–14, 125–26, 133, 134, 135, 136, 137; and concept of community, 120–23; continuing popularity of, 107; and definition of reformation, 2, 63; and *democratia*, 193; and doctrine of justification, 112, 113, 114; doctrine on redemption, 5; and obedience to God, 134; opposition to, 105; opposition to common man, 199, 200; opposition to peasants and Peasants' War, 12, 137, 140–45, 193–94; opposition to Zwingli and Müntzer, 132, 133–36, 137, 144, 145; publications by, 116–17, 118, 120, 129; reaction to society, 137; reform theologies deviating from, 1, 123–26; rejected by Anabaptists and spiritualists, 105; and role of preacher in community, 132; and secular empires, 201; supporters of, 64, 66, 70, 145; view of the Eucharist, 42
Lutz, Heinrich, 194
Lutzenberger, Jakob, 138

Macek, Josef, 3
Mainz, archbishopric of: evangelical movement in, 87; peasants' reformation in, 13, 14, 32; preaching ordinance in, 75; tithe in, 41; urban reformation in, 64–67
Manorial system (*Villikationssystem*): description of, 155; dissolution of, 155–59
Marburg Disputation, 126
Maximilian I (Holy Roman emperor), 1, 160, 183, 195–96
Melanchthon, Philipp, 181, 199, 200
Memmingen: defeat of peasants in, 107; disputation of, 86; evangelical movement in, 87, 101; late medieval changes in, 158; peasants' reformation in, 47; political order in, 51; reformation committee in, 85; role of guilds in, 163; tithe in, 42; urban reformation in, 108
Meran Articles (of the Tyrol), 28–29, 33, 36
Military Ordinance, 14

Moeller, Bernd: and community, 87–88; and people's reformation, 82; and relationship between urban and rural culture in Germany, 5; role of book production in reformation, 116, 117; and urban reformation, 3, 63; and year 1525 as a turning point, 193
More, Thomas, 175
Mühlhausen, defeat of peasants in, 107
Müntzer, Thomas: and Anabaptist movement, 105; death of, 145; and doctrine of justification, 114–15; opposition to, 132, 144, 145; opposition to private property, 175; and people's reformation, 3, 13
Mystical spirit-theologians, 113, 114–15

Nobility: disinterest in urban reformation, 11; response to peasants' reformation, 13–14, 53. *See also* Reformation, princes'
Nordhausen: civic obligation of clergy in, 80; defeat of peasants in, 107
Nördlingen, patronage in, 78
Nuremberg: evangelical movement in, 76, 77, 101; patronage in, 78; political order in, 51; urban reformation in, 102

Obelkevich, James, 5
Oberman, Heiko A., 3
Ochsenhausen, lifting of ban on free travel by serfs, 173
Odenwald, peasants' reformation in, 13
Oecolampadius, Johannes, 70, 113
"On Godly and Human Justice" (Zwingli), 132, 133–36
"On the Appointment of the Ministers of the Church" (Luther), 122
"On the Preachership" (Zwingli), 125
Ozment, Steven, 63, 82

Palatinate, peasants' reformation in, 13, 14
Patronage, 78, 99
Peasants: definition of, 4–5, 11; revolts by, 169. *See also* Common man; Peasants' War (1525); Reformation, peasants'
Peasants' reformation, 4, 11–14, 32–33, 40–53 passim, 98–108 passim
Peasants' War (1525): and Anabaptist movement, 105; description of, 12–14;

documentation of, 12; impact on reformation, 104; Luther's opposition to, 12, 137, 140–45, 193–94; as offense against imperial peace, 197; and people's reformation, 3; and urban reformation, 65
Pellican, Conrad, 70
People (*das Volk*), 5
People's reformation, 3–4, 82–84
Perginer, Diepold, 68
Pfaffenweiber (priests' women), 79
Philipp of the Palatinate (prince elector), 195
"Pleasant dialogue and conversation between a priest and a village mayor, A" (Bucer), 128
Poliander, Johann, 200
Poor Conrad uprising, 169, 196, 197, 198
Poverty, and Christian charity, 28–29, 30
Preacherships, 78–79
Princely reformation, 2
Princes' reformation, 2–3, 11, 69, 104, 193
Printing press, impact of, 13, 116–17
Privy councils, 163
Public Peace (*Reichslandfreide*), 195

Rammstedt, Otthein, 84
Reformation: communal, 100–101, 104–8, 115; dissemination of ideas about, 115–19; peasants', 4, 11–14, 32–33, 40–53 passim, 98–108 passim; people's, 3–4, 82–84; popularization of, 126–32; princely, 2; princes', 2–3, 11, 69, 104, 193; storm years (*Sturmjahre*) of, 1–2; urban, 2–3, 4, 11, 63–64, 73–88 passim, 98–108 passim; wild growth (*Wildwuchs*) of, 1–2
Reformation Decree (*Reformationsordnung*), 73
Religious Disputation of Ilanz, 35, 43
Representation, for communities, 176–78
Rettenberg, Tigen, 22, 24
Reublin, Wilhelm, 70
Rhegius, Urbanus, 199, 200
Ritter, Gerhard, 144
Rorschacher Klosterbruch (wrecking of the monastery of Rorschach), 172
Rosenberg, Hans, 3

Rosenplüt, Hans, 154
Rothenburg ob der Tauber: defeat of peasants in, 107; peasants' reformation in, 13, 43
Röubli, Wilhelm, 17
Rudolf, Johannes (abbot of Raitnau), 138

Saar-Mosel region, late medieval changes in, 163
Sabean, David, 171
St. Gall, territory of: development of administrative structures in, 160; lifting of ban on free travel by serfs, 173; peasants' reformation in, 13, 52, 160; peasants' revolt in, 45–46
Saints, veneration of, 5–6
Salzburg: defeat of peasants in, 107; ecclesiastical courts in, 39; opposition to serfdom in, 48; peasant revolt in, 169; peasants' reformation in, 13, 29–30, 38; tithe in, 42; urban reformation in, 102. *See also* Tyrol
Sam, Konrad, 75
Saxony, peasants' reformation in, 13, 14
Schaffhausen, opposition to serfdom in, 48
Schappeler, Christoph, 13, 139
Scheible, Heinz, 117
Schilling, Heinz, 82
Schindelin (pastor of Henau), 37
Schmalkaldic League, 108
Schmid, Huldrich, 22, 44
Schultze, Alfred, 63
Schwäbisch Gmünd, defeat of peasants in, 107
Schwyz: peasants' reformation in, 52; and right of communities to assemble, 168–69
Second Ilanz Manifesto (*Artikelbrief*), 33, 34, 35–36
Sélestat: defeat of peasants in, 107; disputation of, 86; patronage in, 78
Serfdom: dismantling of, 173; opposition to, 47–49, 173–74. *See also* Manorial system (*Villikationssystem*)
"Sermon addressed to all Christians about the church and its Keys and Powers, and also about the Office of the Priesthood" (Brenz), 124
"Sermon Given at Candlemas in Wittenberg by Doctor Martin Luther, 1523" (Luther), 122

"Sermon on the Christian Church, A"
(Kettenbach), 123
"Seventh Confederate" (Eberlin von
Günzburg), 129
"Short account how the village mayor
and the community of the village of
Friedhausen on Gnodenberg have
jointly chosen and elected a juror of
their village . . ." (Pamphilius
Gengenbach), 130–32
Sickingen, Franz von, 11, 129
Sigismund (king), 157
Sigmund (archduke of Austria), 1
Smirin, M. M., 3, 4
Sola fide, principle of, 112
Sola gratia, principle of, 112
Sola scriptura, principle of, 98, 112, 113,
118
Solothurn, tithe in, 42
Stäbiner, Jakob, 37
Steinmetz, Max, 3
Stenzel, Karl, 40
Stephansfeld Band, 47
Stolberg, preaching ordinance in, 74
Stralsund, evangelical movement in, 87
Strasbourg: civic obligation of clergy in,
80; ecclesiastical courts in, 40;
evangelical movement in, 77, 101;
peasants' reformation in, 47; people's
reformation in, 82, 83; political order
in, 51; role of guilds in, 85, 102;
urban reformation in, 102
Strauss, Jakob, 124, 125
Suchenwirt, Peter, 154
Sundgau: peasants' reformation in, 33;
Peasants' War in, 72
Swabian League, 169
Swiss Confederation: Anabaptist
movement in, 105, 126; ecclesiastical
emancipation in, 164–65; election of
pastors in, 166–67; expedition of
"foolish people" (torechte Leute) in,
168; late medieval changes in, 164; as
model of communes, 103; opposition
to serfdom in, 49; pamphlets in, 117;
peasants' reformation in, 13, 14–15,
51–53, 102; Peasants' War in, 72; and
political order, 51; tithe in, 41; urban
reformation in, 69–73, 88, 102. See
also Zurich Landschaft

Tauber Valley Band, 68

Tauler, Johannes, 154
Territorial constitutions
(Landesordnungen), 50
Thalmann, Dr. Anton, 38
"That a Christian Assembly or
Congregation Has the Right and
Power to Judge All Teaching and to
Call, Appoint, and Dismiss Teachers,
Established and Proven by Scripture"
(Luther), 120, 122, 123
"That each Christian Assembly be given
a Servant and not a Lord / Conclusion
and Main Articles" (Strauss), 124
Thomas, Keith, 183
Thomas Aquinas, 154, 175, 181
Three Articles (of Lake Constance
region), 24
Three Unions, 34–35, 43
Thuringia: Anabaptist movement in,
105; defeat of peasants in, 66, 104;
evangelical movement in, 84; peasants'
reformation in, 3, 13, 14; support for
Müntzer in, 145
Tithe, dispute over use of, 14, 17, 18,
19, 20, 23, 24, 25, 26, 27, 30, 31, 32,
36–37, 38, 41–42, 72, 87
Toll, Hans, 126
"To the Christian Nobility of the
German Nation Concerning the
Reform of the Christian Estate"
(Luther), 122, 129
Trier, archbishopric of, peasants'
reformation in, 13, 14
Truchsess, Georg, 13
Twelve Articles (of Upper Swabia), 13,
20, 21, 24, 25, 26, 30, 31, 32, 42, 43,
101, 123, 139, 140, 142, 144
Twenty-four Articles of the Common
Assembly of Salzburg, 29–30, 33, 36
Tyrol: church wardens in, 165;
communal representation in, 177–78;
defeat of peasants in, 107;
development of administrative
structures in, 159, 160, 161;
ecclesiastical courts in, 39, 40;
election of pastors in, 165–66;
peasants' reformation in, 13, 26–30,
33, 43, 101

Ulm: Eberlin von Günzburg's pamphlets
for, 130; godly justice in, 139;
patronage in, 78; preaching ordinance

in, 74; urban reformation in, 108
Untergrombach Bundschuh, 195–96
Upper Swabia: defeat of peasants in, 104;
    development of administrative
    structures in, 159, 162, 164;
    evangelical movement in, 101; godly
    justice in, 139; peasants' reformation
    in, 12–13, 14, 20–26, 27, 30, 33, 38,
    48; political order in, 50; preacherships
    in, 79; tithe in, 41
Urban liberties (*Stadtfreiheiten*), 171
Urban reformation, 2–3, 4, 11, 63–64,
    73–88 passim, 98–108 passim

Vadian, Joachim (Joachim von Watt),
    129
Valais, communal representation in, 178
Vargas, Ivan, 50

Wanner, Johannes, 75, 138
Welfare, common, 29
Werdenstein, Georg von, 22
Weygandt, Friedrich, 31–32
Widmer, Johannes, 16, 20
Wissembourg: Bucer's sermons in,
    124–25; role of guilds in, 102; urban
    reformation in, 108
Wohlfeil, Rainer, 116, 194
Württemberg, duchy of: defeat of
    peasants in, 107; lifting of ban on free
    travel by serfs, 173; peasants'

reformation in, 13, 14, 33, 43; Poor
    Conrad uprising in, 169, 196, 197,
    198
Würzburg, archbishopric of: peasants'
    reformation in, 13; urban reformation
    in, 102

Zeeden, Ernst W., 193
Zell, Matthias, 199
Zurich Disputation, 19, 86, 104, 125,
    133, 163
Zurich *Landschaft*: communal reformation
    in, 104; evangelical movement in, 76,
    101; peasants' reformation in,
    16–20, 30, 51–52, 53, 132; urban
    reformation in, 86. *See also* Swiss
    Confederation
Zwingli, Huldrych: and Anabaptist
    movement, 105; concepts of gospel
    and law, 133–36; and doctrine of
    justification, 113–14; Gaismair's
    support for, 26; on godly justice and
    authority, 132–36, 137; impact of, 17,
    18, 19; influence of, 137, 138–39,
    167; opposition to, 105, 132, 133–36,
    137, 144–45; opposition to common
    man, 153, 199–200; and people's
    reformation, 3; and role of community
    in church, 125–26; view of the
    Eucharist, 42